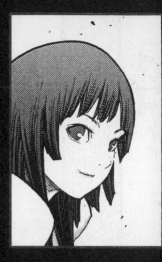

Norihiro Yagi won the 32nd Akatsuka Award for his debut work, *UNDEADMAN*, which appeared in *Monthly Shonen Jump* magazine and produced two sequels. His first serialized manga was his comedy *Angel Densetsu* (Angel Legend), which appeared in *Monthly Shonen Jump* from 1992 to 2000. His epic saga, *Claymore*, is running in *Monthly Jump Square* magazine.

In his spare time, Yagi enjoys things like the Japanese comedic duo Downtown, martial arts, games, driving, and hard rock music, but he doesn't consider these actual hobbies.

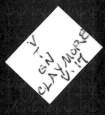

CLAYMORE VOL. 17
SHONEN JUMP ADVANCED Manga Edition

STORY AND ART BY
NORIHIRO YAGI

English Adaptation & Translation/Arashi Productions
Touch-up Art & Lettering/Sabrina Heep
Design/Courtney Utt
Editor/Leyla Aker

CLAYMORE © 2001 by Norihiro Yagi. All rights reserved. First
published in Japan in 2001 by SHUEISHA Inc., Tokyo. English
translation rights arranged by SHUEISHA Inc.

The rights of the author(s) of the work(s) in this publication
to be so identified have been asserted in accordance with the
Copyright, Designs and Patents Act 1988. A CIP catalogue record
for this book is available from the British Library.

Printed in the U.S.A.

Published by VIZ Media, LLC
P.O. Box 77010
San Francisco, CA 94107

10 9 8 7 6 5 4 3 2 1
First printing, January 2010

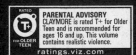

THE WORLD'S MOST
CUTTING-EDGE MANGA
SHONEN JUMP ADVANCED
www.shonenjump.com

SHONEN JUMP ADVANCED Manga Edition

Claymore

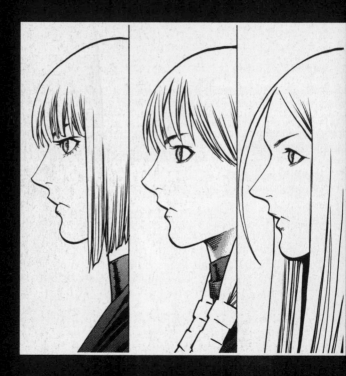

Vol. 17
The Claws of Memory

Story and Art by **Norihiro Yagi**

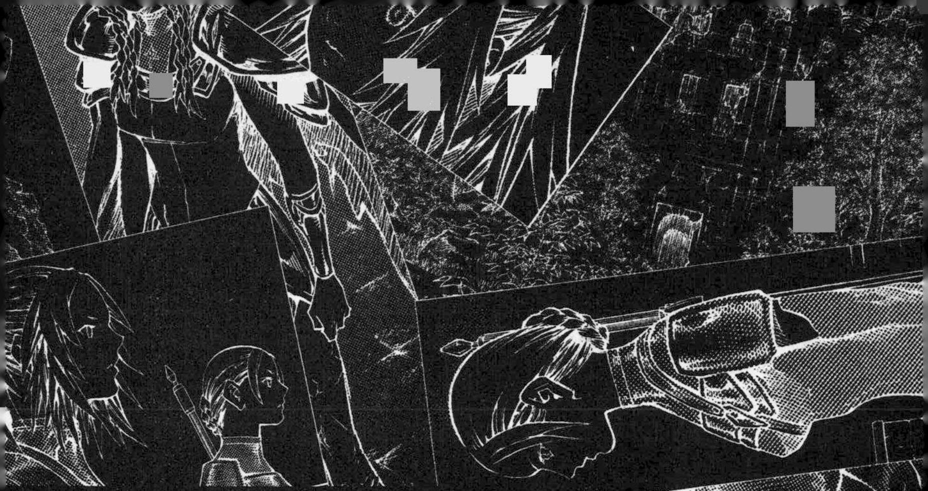

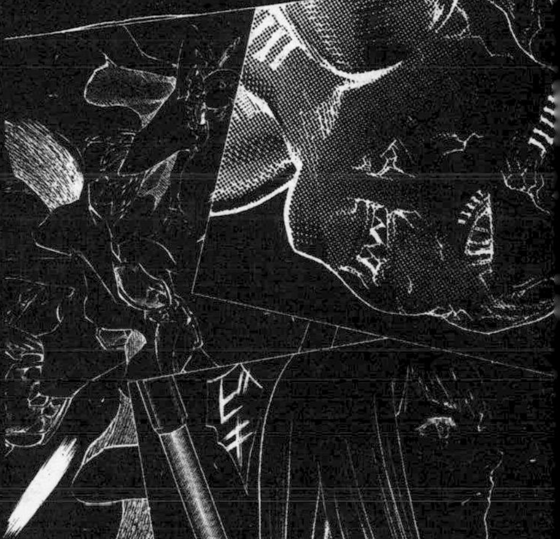

Seven years after the Battle of the North, Clare and her comrades have come to the South. They face a host of new enemies: the Abyss Feeders that defeated Isley; Alicia and Beth and Riful, who is trying to Awaken the fused form of Rafaela and Luciela.

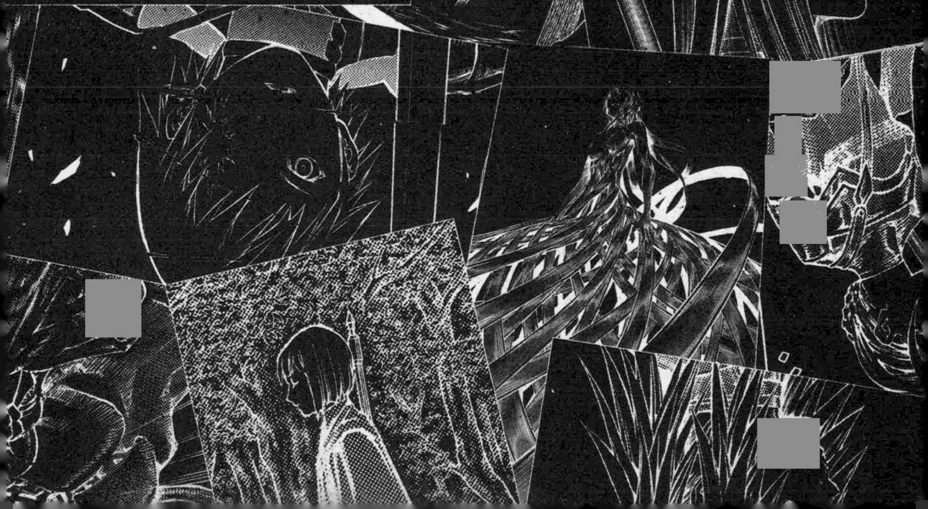

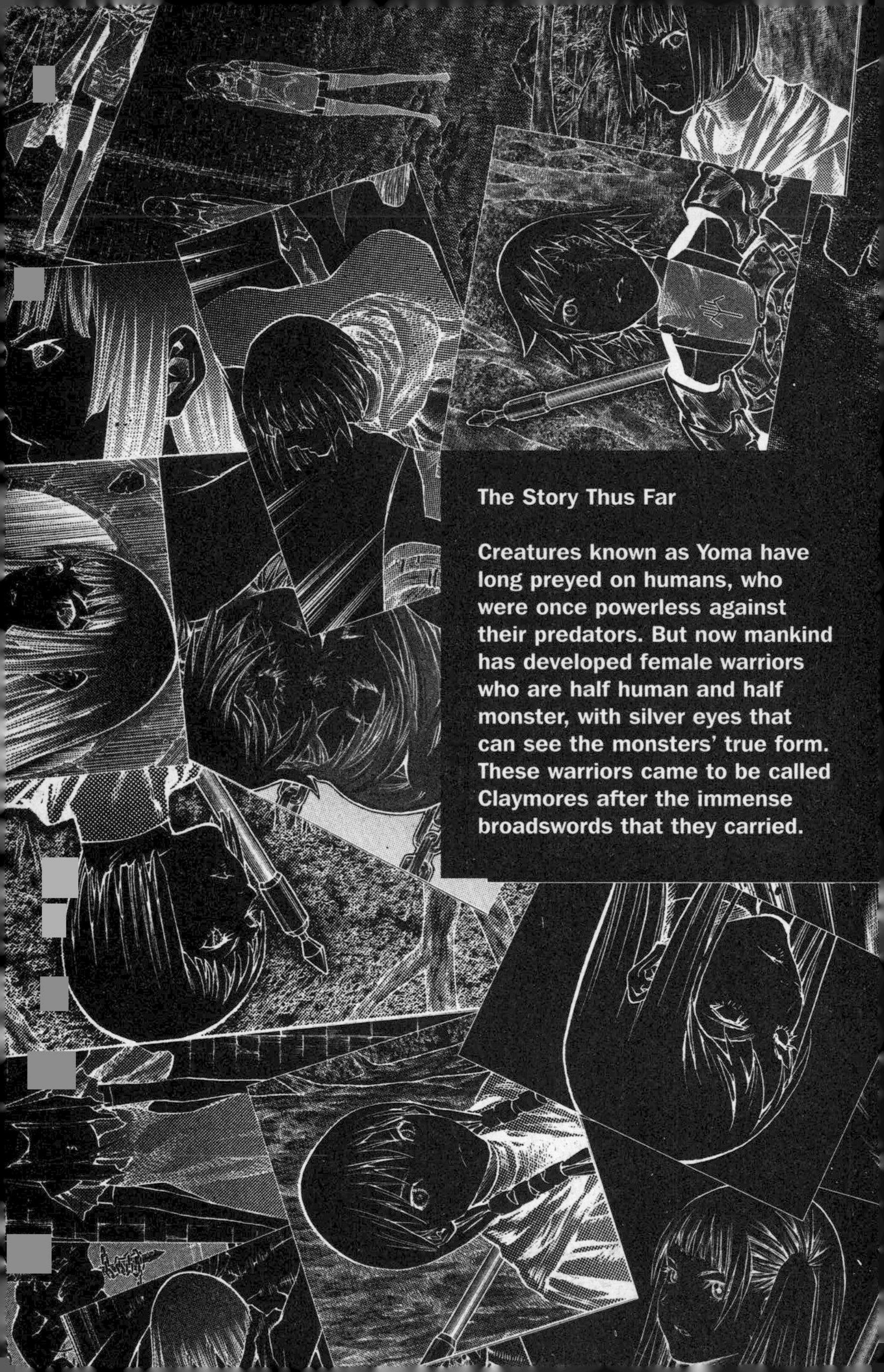

The Story Thus Far

Creatures known as Yoma have long preyed on humans, who were once powerless against their predators. But now mankind has developed female warriors who are half human and half monster, with silver eyes that can see the monsters' true form. These warriors came to be called Claymores after the immense broadswords that they carried.

Claymore
クレイモア

Vol. 17

CONTENTS

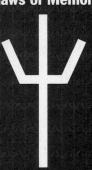

Scene 90: The Claws of Memory, Part 1

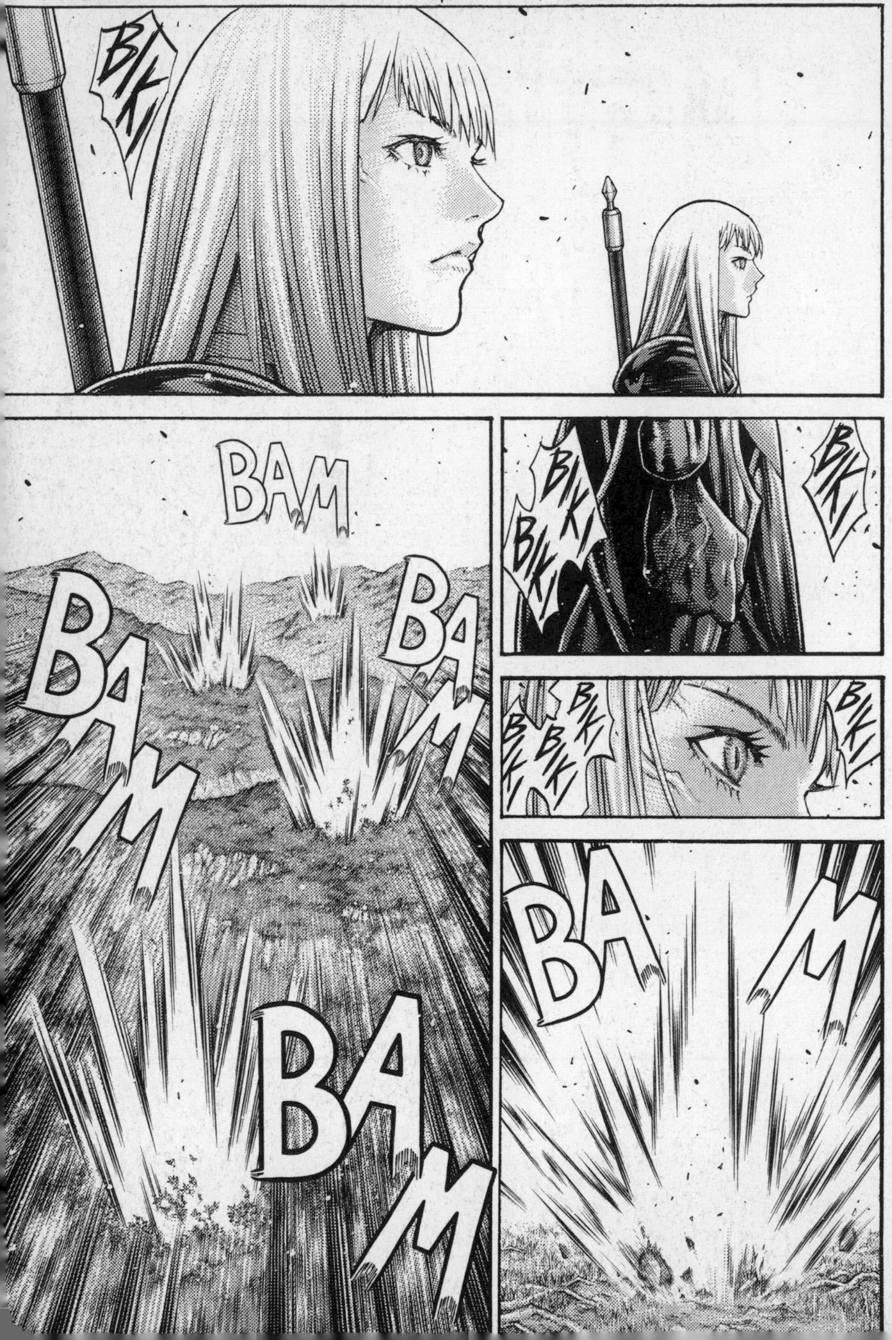
BIKI
BIKI
BIKI
BIKI
BIKI
BIKI
BIKI
BIKI
BIKI
BAM
BAM
BAM
BAM
BAM

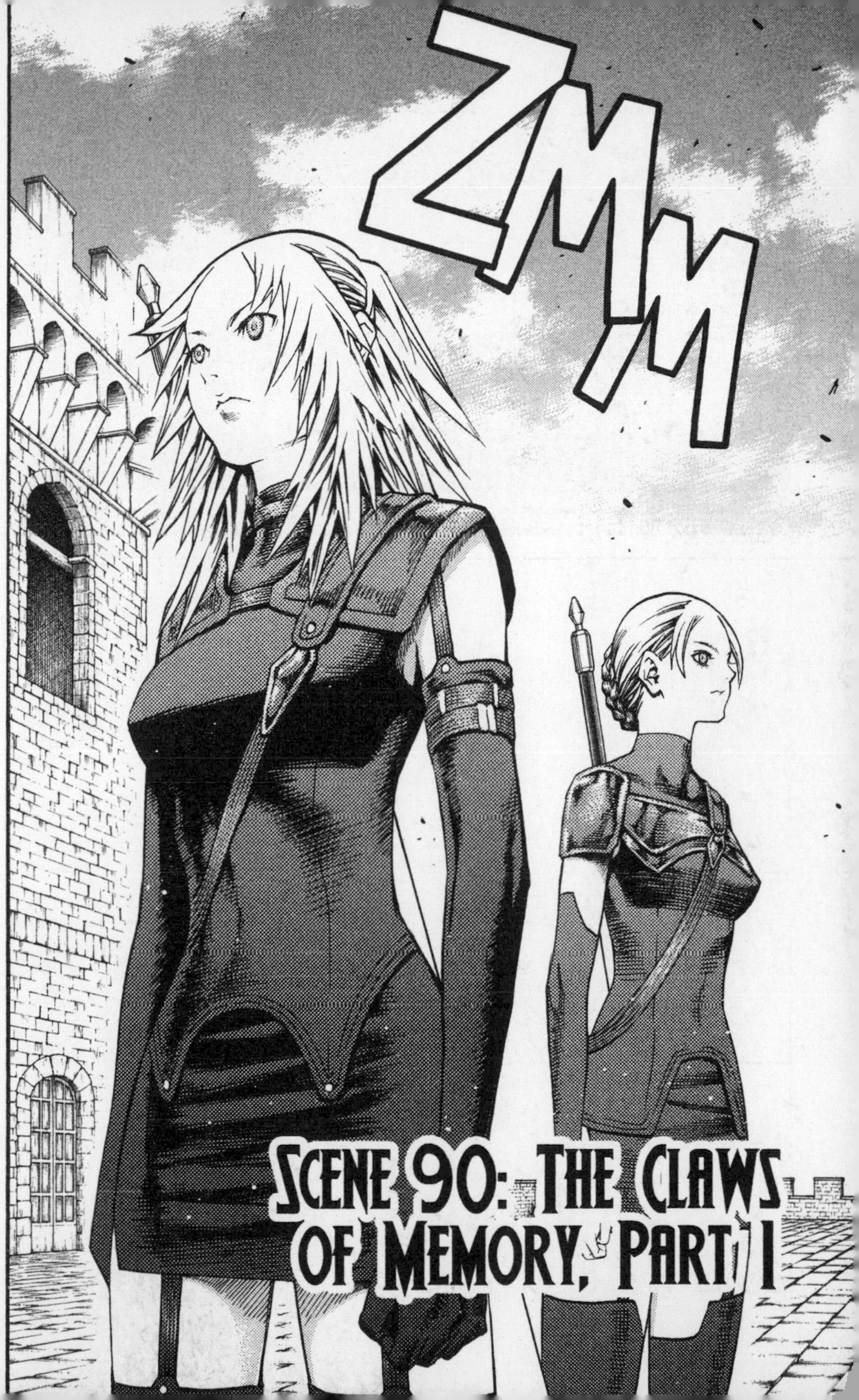
ZMMM
SCENE 90: THE CLAWS OF MEMORY, PART 1

READ THIS WAY

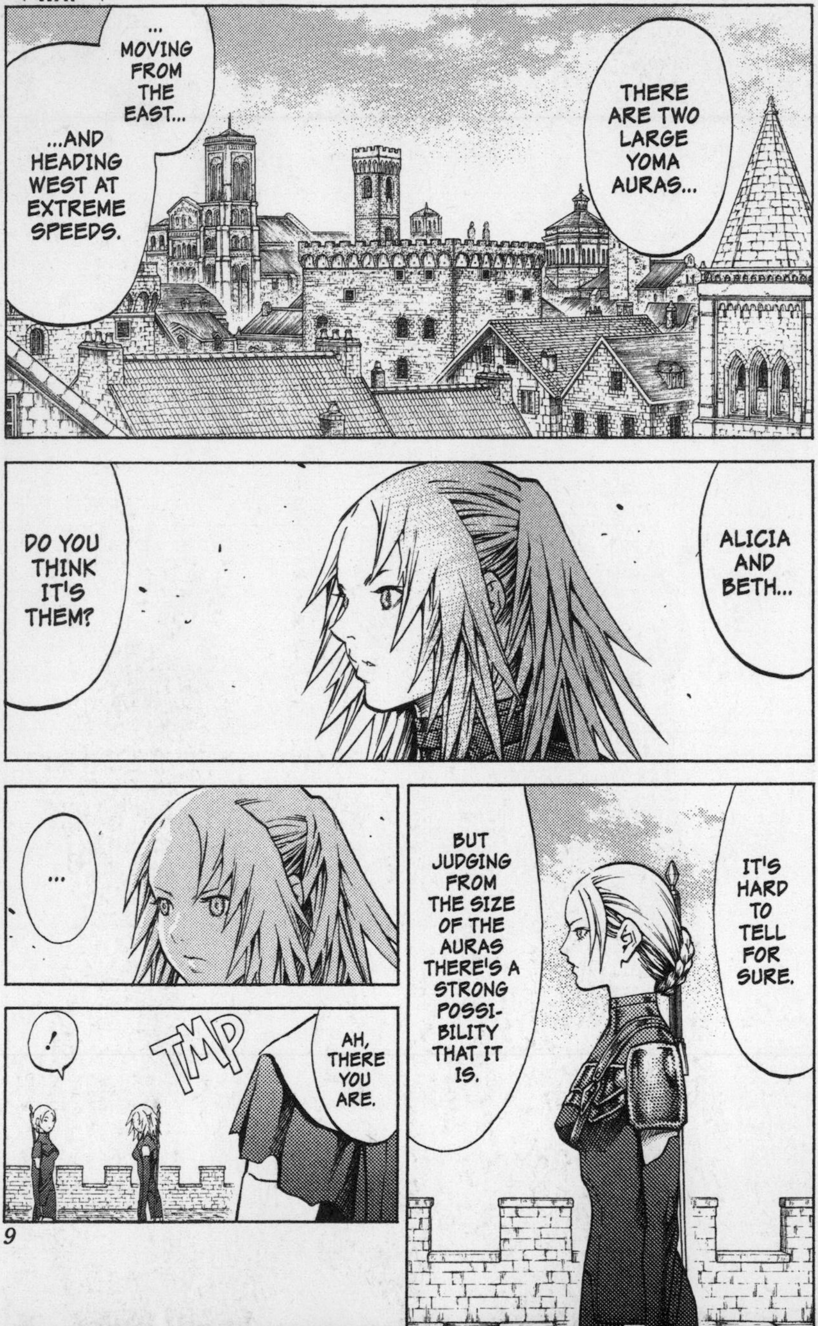
THERE ARE TWO LARGE YOMA AURAS...
... MOVING FROM THE EAST...
...AND HEADING WEST AT EXTREME SPEEDS.
ALICIA AND BETH...
DO YOU THINK IT'S THEM?
IT'S HARD TO TELL FOR SURE.
BUT JUDGING FROM THE SIZE OF THE AURAS THERE'S A STRONG POSSI-BILITY THAT IT IS.
...
AH, THERE YOU ARE.
TMP
!

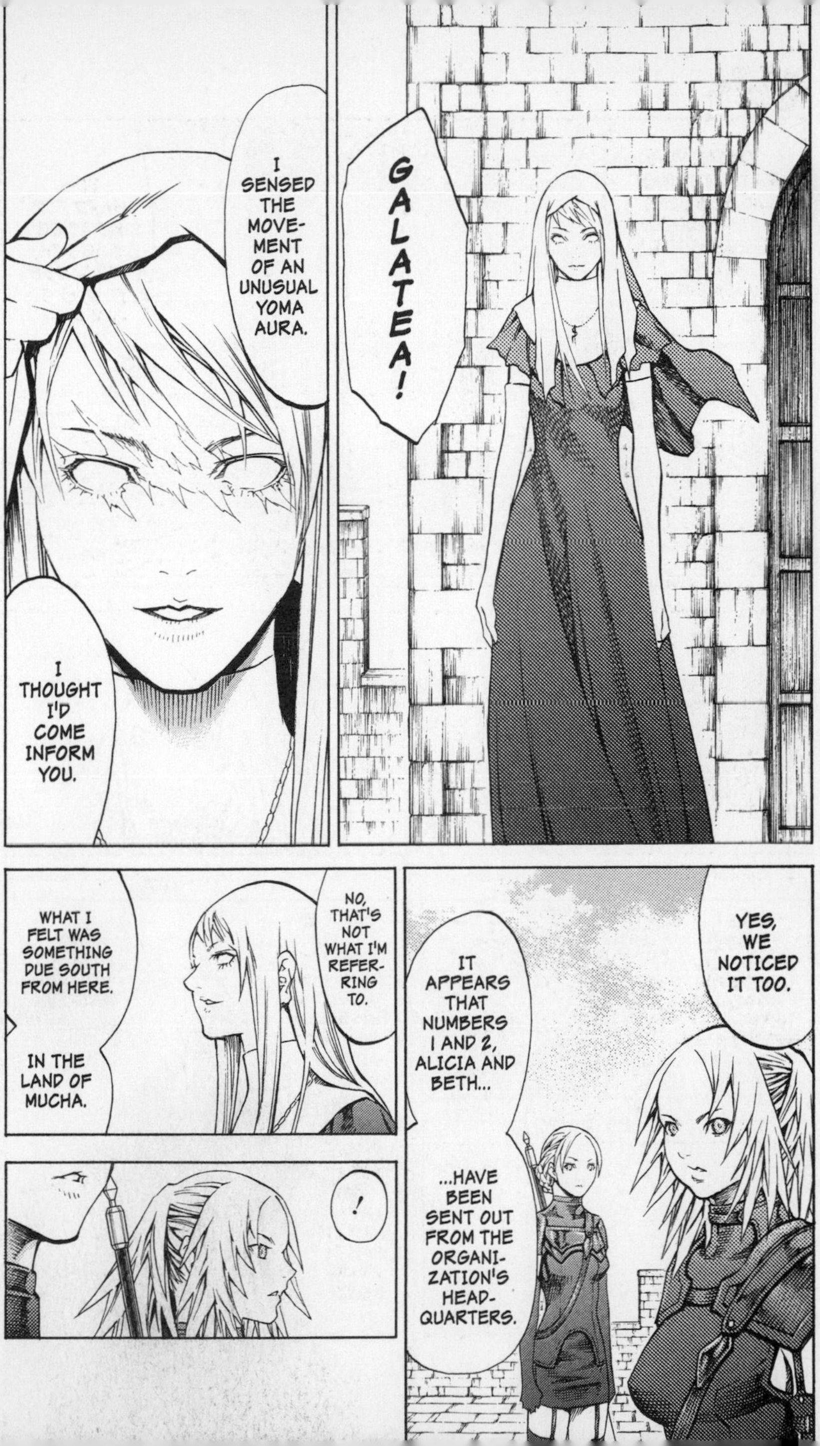
GALATEA!
I SENSED THE MOVEMENT OF AN UNUSUAL YOMA AURA.
I THOUGHT I'D COME INFORM YOU.
YES, WE NOTICED IT TOO.
IT APPEARS THAT NUMBERS 1 AND 2, ALICIA AND BETH...
...HAVE BEEN SENT OUT FROM THE ORGANIZATION'S HEADQUARTERS.
NO, THAT'S NOT WHAT I'M REFERRING TO.
WHAT I FELT WAS SOMETHING DUE SOUTH FROM HERE.
IN THE LAND OF MUCHA.
!

READ THIS WAY

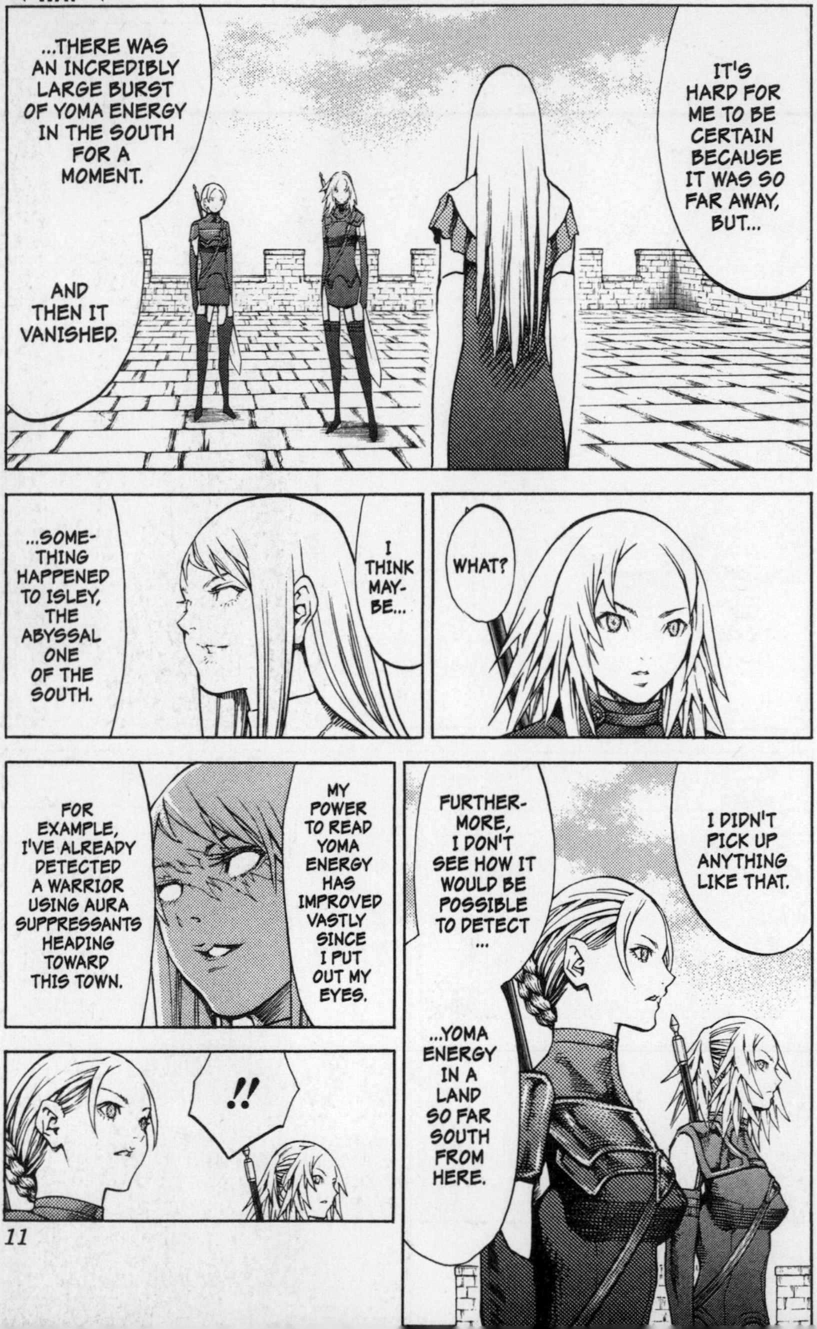
IT'S HARD FOR ME TO BE CERTAIN BECAUSE IT WAS SO FAR AWAY, BUT...
...THERE WAS AN INCREDIBLY LARGE BURST OF YOMA ENERGY IN THE SOUTH FOR A MOMENT.
AND THEN IT VANISHED.
WHAT?
I THINK MAY-BE...
...SOME-THING HAPPENED TO ISLEY, THE ABYSSAL ONE OF THE SOUTH.
I DIDN'T PICK UP ANYTHING LIKE THAT.
FURTHER-MORE, I DON'T SEE HOW IT WOULD BE POSSIBLE TO DETECT ...
...YOMA ENERGY IN A LAND SO FAR SOUTH FROM HERE.
MY POWER TO READ YOMA ENERGY HAS IMPROVED VASTLY SINCE I PUT OUT MY EYES.
FOR EXAMPLE, I'VE ALREADY DETECTED A WARRIOR USING AURA SUPPRESSANTS HEADING TOWARD THIS TOWN.
!!

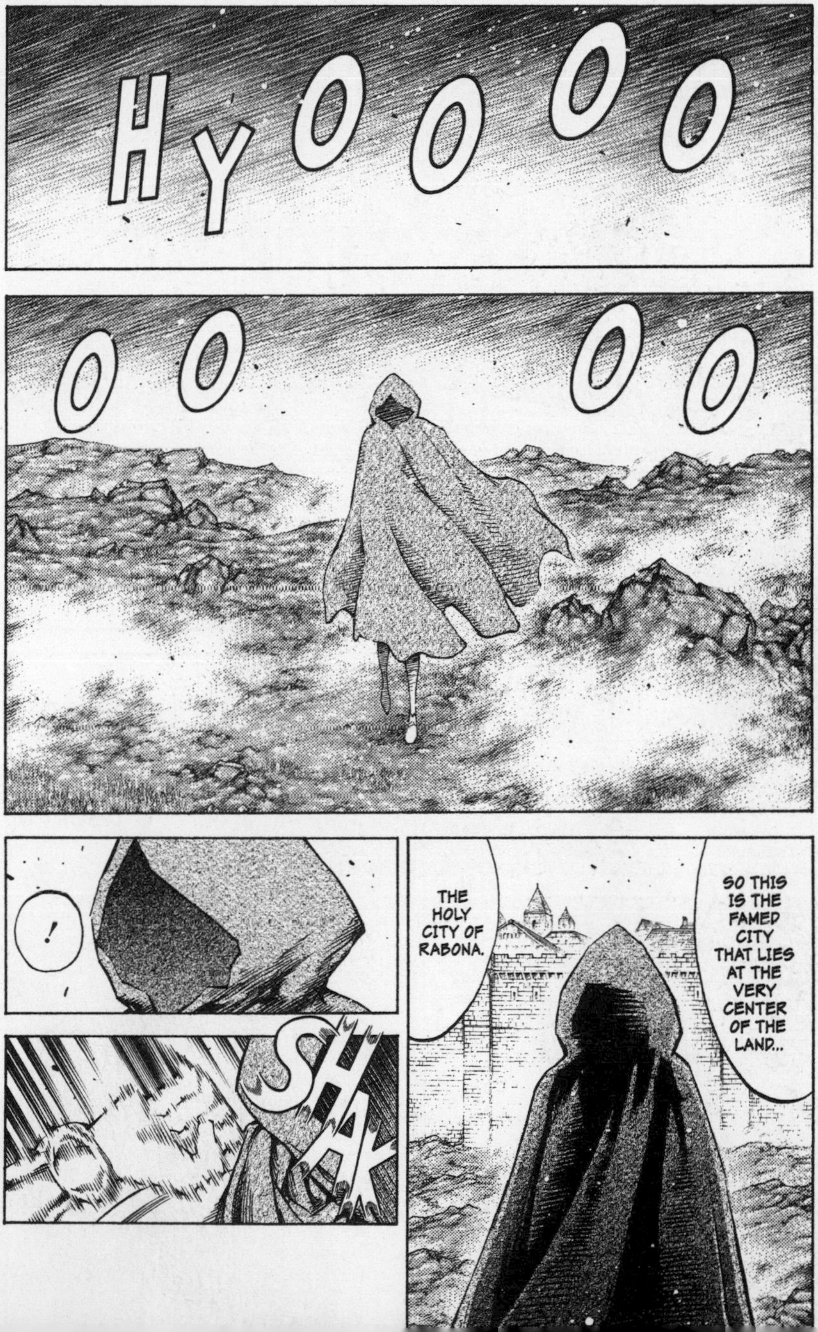
HYOOOO
OOOO
SO THIS IS THE FAMED CITY THAT LIES AT THE VERY CENTER OF THE LAND...
THE HOLY CITY OF RABONA.
!
SHAK

READ THIS WAY

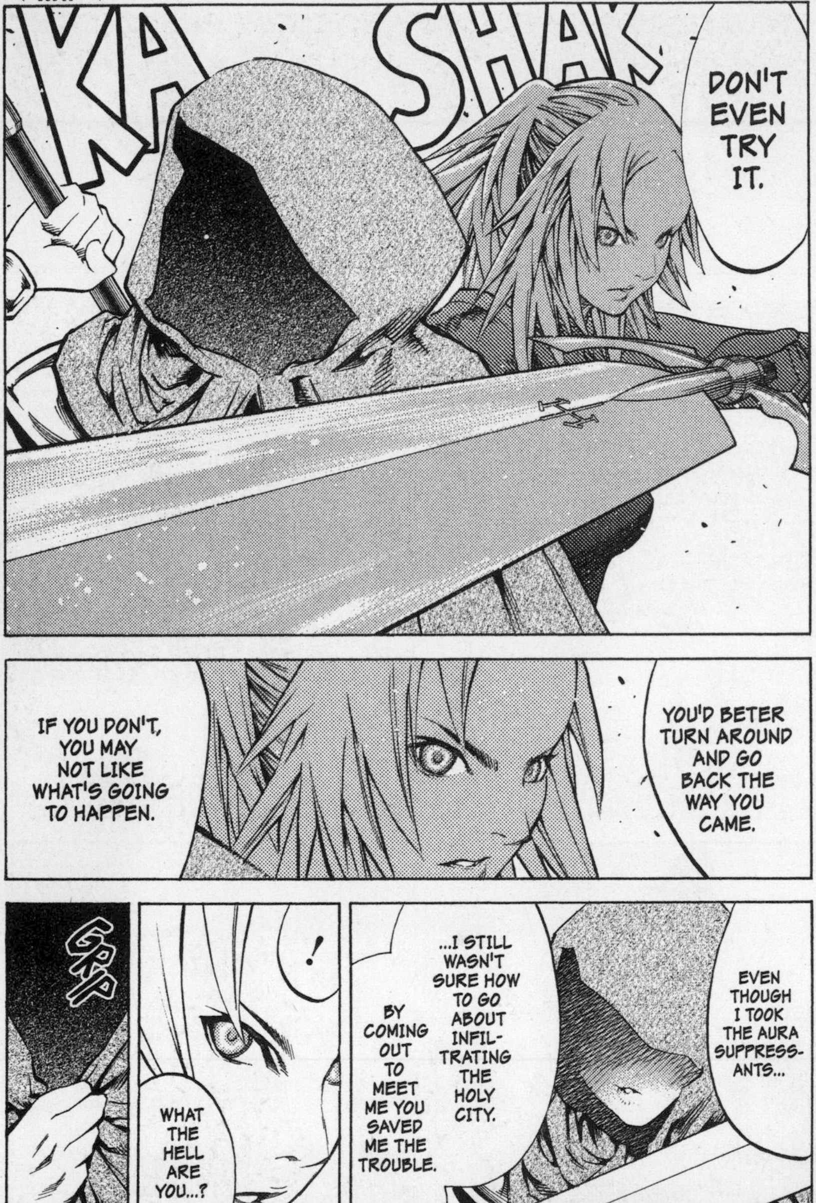
KA SHAK
DON'T EVEN TRY IT.
YOU'D BETER TURN AROUND AND GO BACK THE WAY YOU CAME.
IF YOU DON'T, YOU MAY NOT LIKE WHAT'S GOING TO HAPPEN.
EVEN THOUGH I TOOK THE AURA SUPPRESS-ANTS...
...I STILL WASN'T SURE HOW TO GO ABOUT INFIL-TRATING THE HOLY CITY.
BY COMING OUT TO MEET ME YOU SAVED ME THE TROUBLE.
!
WHAT THE HELL ARE YOU...?
GRIP

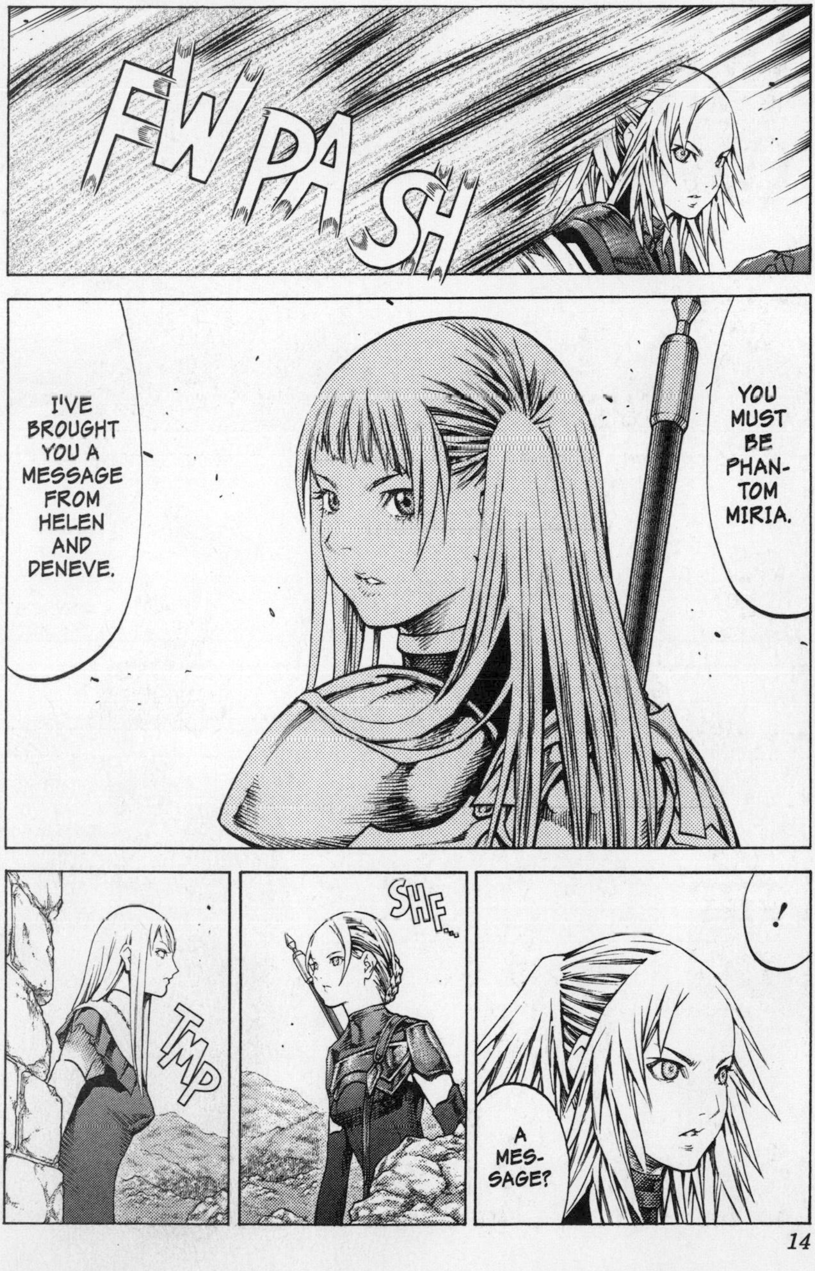
FWPASH
YOU MUST BE PHANTOM MIRIA.
I'VE BROUGHT YOU A MESSAGE FROM HELEN AND DENEVE.
!
A MES-SAGE?
SHF...
TMP

READ THIS WAY

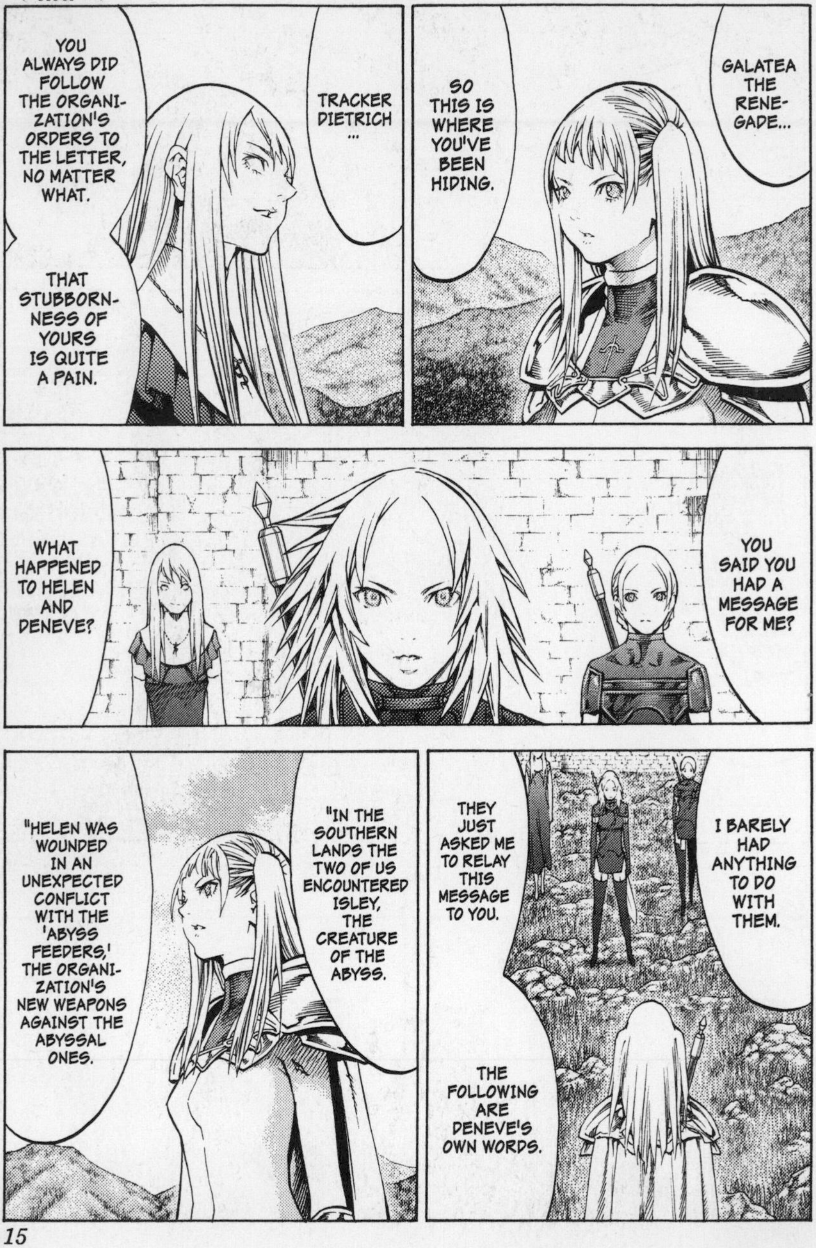
GALATEA THE RENEGADE...
SO THIS IS WHERE YOU'VE BEEN HIDING.
TRACKER DIETRICH ...
YOU ALWAYS DID FOLLOW THE ORGANIZATION'S ORDERS TO THE LETTER, NO MATTER WHAT.
THAT STUBBORNNESS OF YOURS IS QUITE A PAIN.
YOU SAID YOU HAD A MESSAGE FOR ME?
WHAT HAPPENED TO HELEN AND DENEVE?
I BARELY HAD ANYTHING TO DO WITH THEM.
THEY JUST ASKED ME TO RELAY THIS MESSAGE TO YOU.
THE FOLLOWING ARE DENEVE'S OWN WORDS.
"IN THE SOUTHERN LANDS THE TWO OF US ENCOUNTERED ISLEY, THE CREATURE OF THE ABYSS.
"HELEN WAS WOUNDED IN AN UNEXPECTED CONFLICT WITH THE 'ABYSS FEEDERS,' THE ORGANIZATION'S NEW WEAPONS AGAINST THE ABYSSAL ONES.

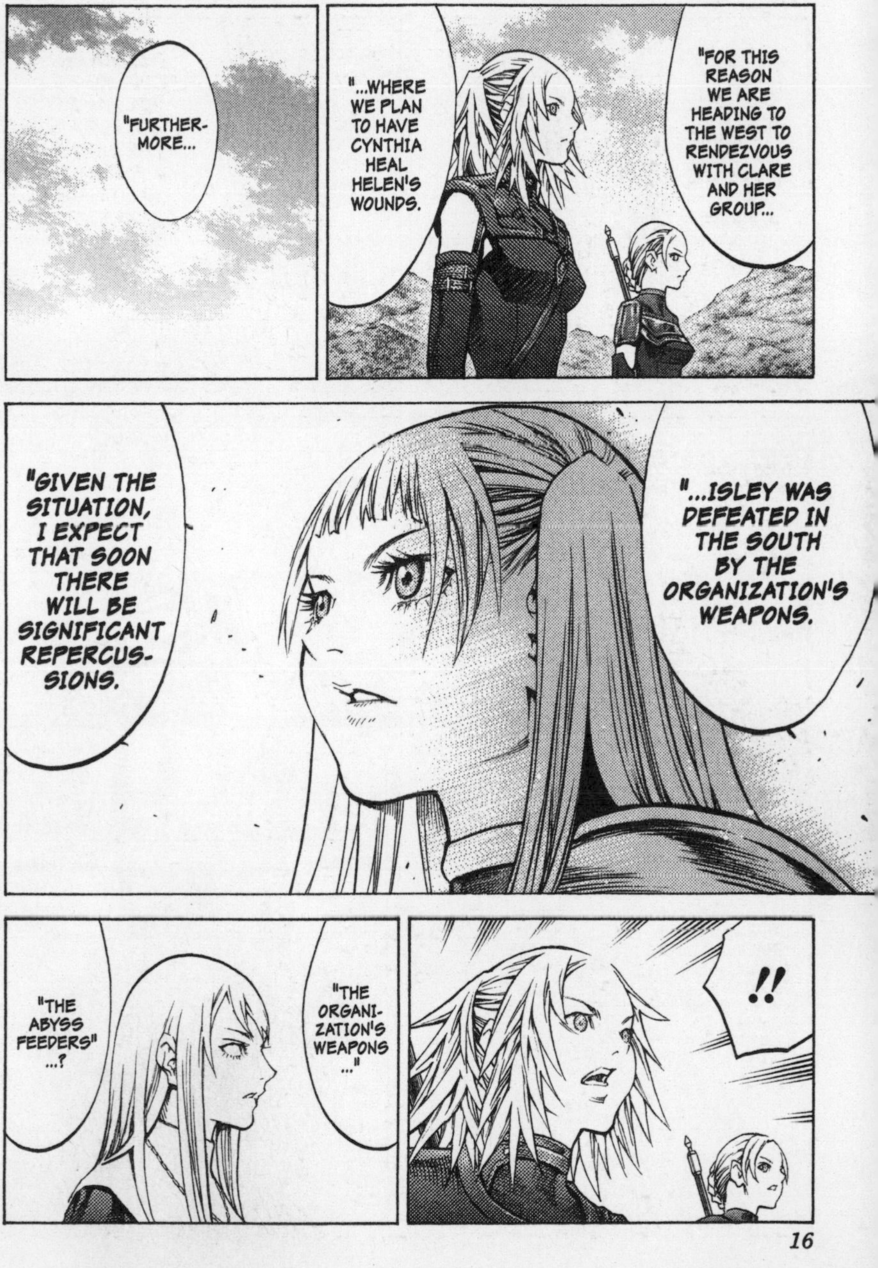
"FOR THIS REASON WE ARE HEADING TO THE WEST TO RENDEZVOUS WITH CLARE AND HER GROUP...
"...WHERE WE PLAN TO HAVE CYNTHIA HEAL HELEN'S WOUNDS.
"FURTHER-MORE...
"...ISLEY WAS DEFEATED IN THE SOUTH BY THE ORGANIZATION'S WEAPONS.
"GIVEN THE SITUATION, I EXPECT THAT SOON THERE WILL BE SIGNIFICANT REPERCUS-SIONS.
!!
"THE ORGANI-ZATION'S WEAPONS ..."
"THE ABYSS FEEDERS" ...?

READ THIS WAY

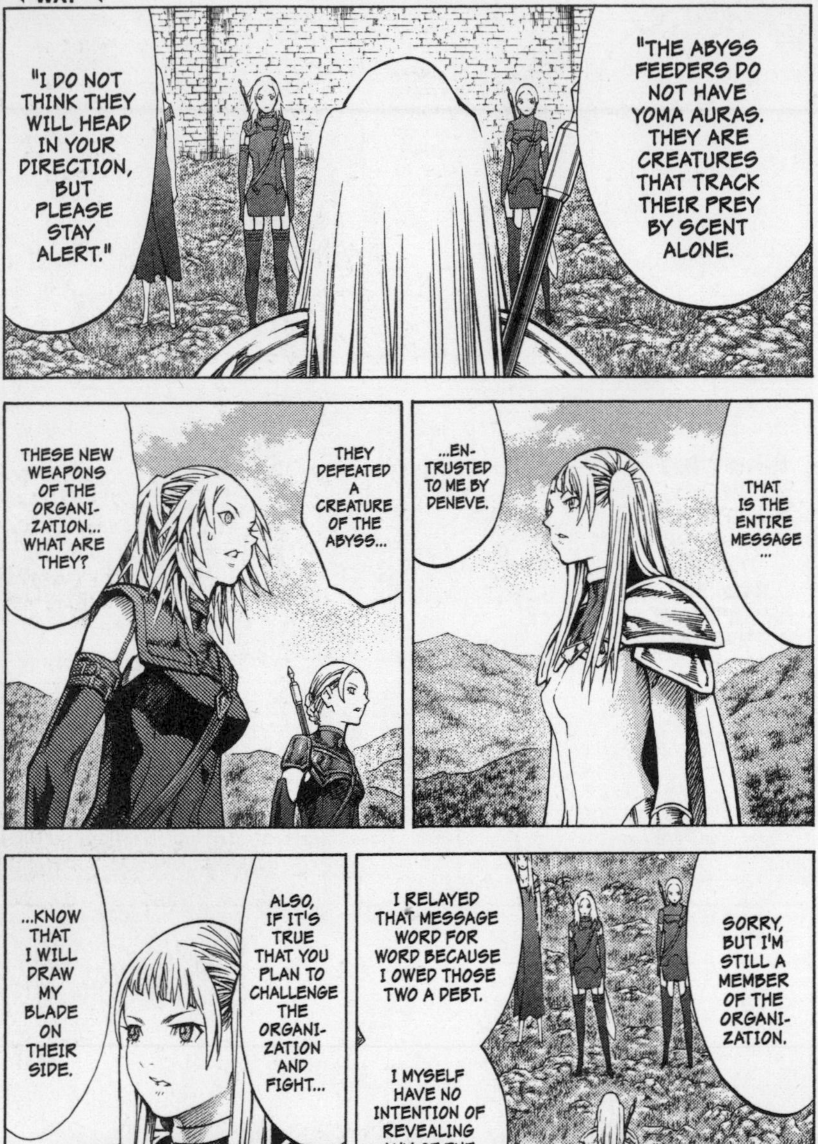
"THE ABYSS FEEDERS DO NOT HAVE YOMA AURAS. THEY ARE CREATURES THAT TRACK THEIR PREY BY SCENT ALONE.
"I DO NOT THINK THEY WILL HEAD IN YOUR DIRECTION, BUT PLEASE STAY ALERT."
THAT IS THE ENTIRE MESSAGE...
...EN-TRUSTED TO ME BY DENEVE.
THEY DEFEATED A CREATURE OF THE ABYSS...
THESE NEW WEAPONS OF THE ORGANI-ZATION... WHAT ARE THEY?
SORRY, BUT I'M STILL A MEMBER OF THE ORGANI-ZATION.
I RELAYED THAT MESSAGE WORD FOR WORD BECAUSE I OWED THOSE TWO A DEBT.
I MYSELF HAVE NO INTENTION OF REVEALING ANY OF THE ORGANIZATION'S INFORMATION.
ALSO, IF IT'S TRUE THAT YOU PLAN TO CHALLENGE THE ORGANI-ZATION AND FIGHT...
...KNOW THAT I WILL DRAW MY BLADE ON THEIR SIDE.

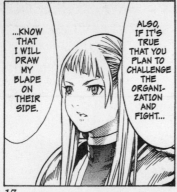

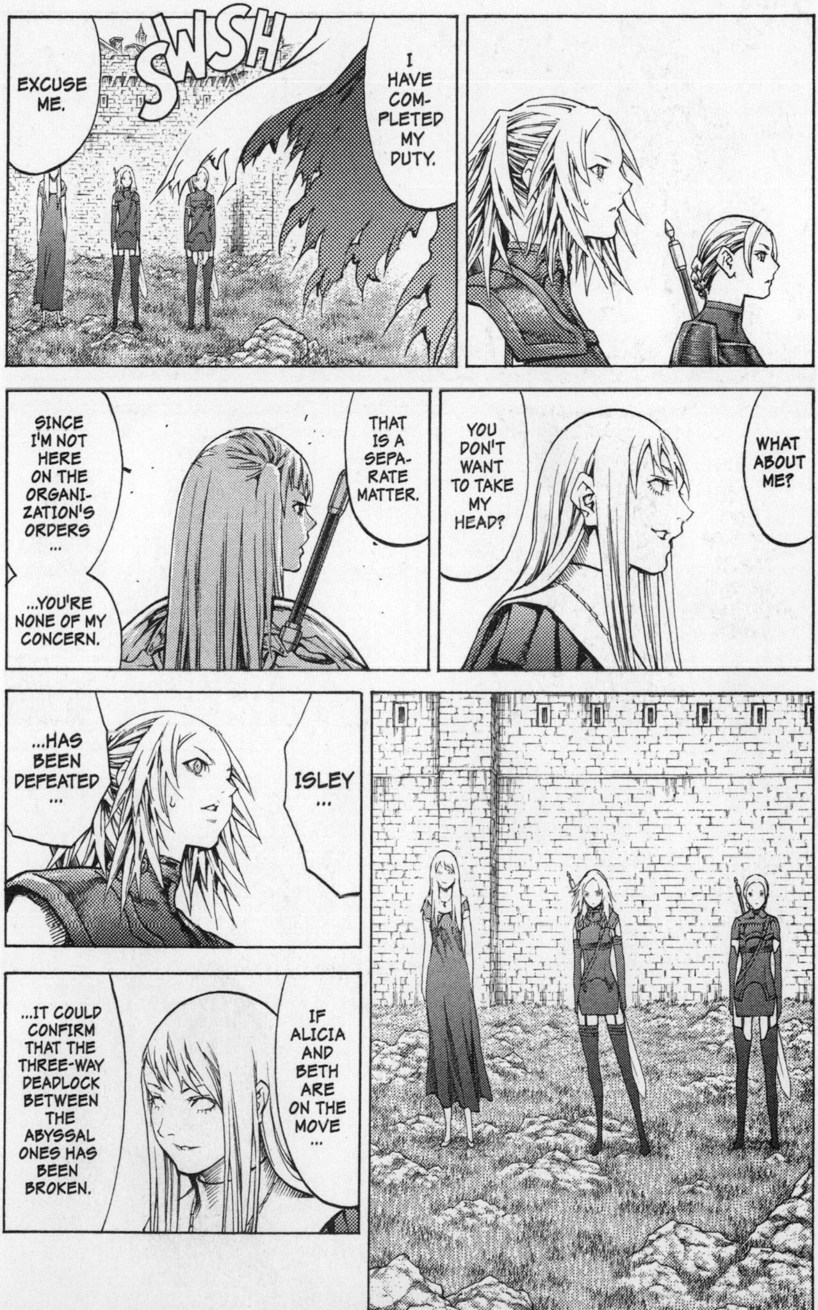
I HAVE COMPLETED MY DUTY.
SWSH
EXCUSE ME.
WHAT ABOUT ME?
YOU DON'T WANT TO TAKE MY HEAD?
THAT IS A SEPARATE MATTER.
SINCE I'M NOT HERE ON THE ORGANIZATION'S ORDERS...
...YOU'RE NONE OF MY CONCERN.
ISLEY...
...HAS BEEN DEFEATED...
IF ALICIA AND BETH ARE ON THE MOVE...
...IT COULD CONFIRM THAT THE THREE-WAY DEADLOCK BETWEEN THE ABYSSAL ONES HAS BEEN BROKEN.

READ THIS WAY

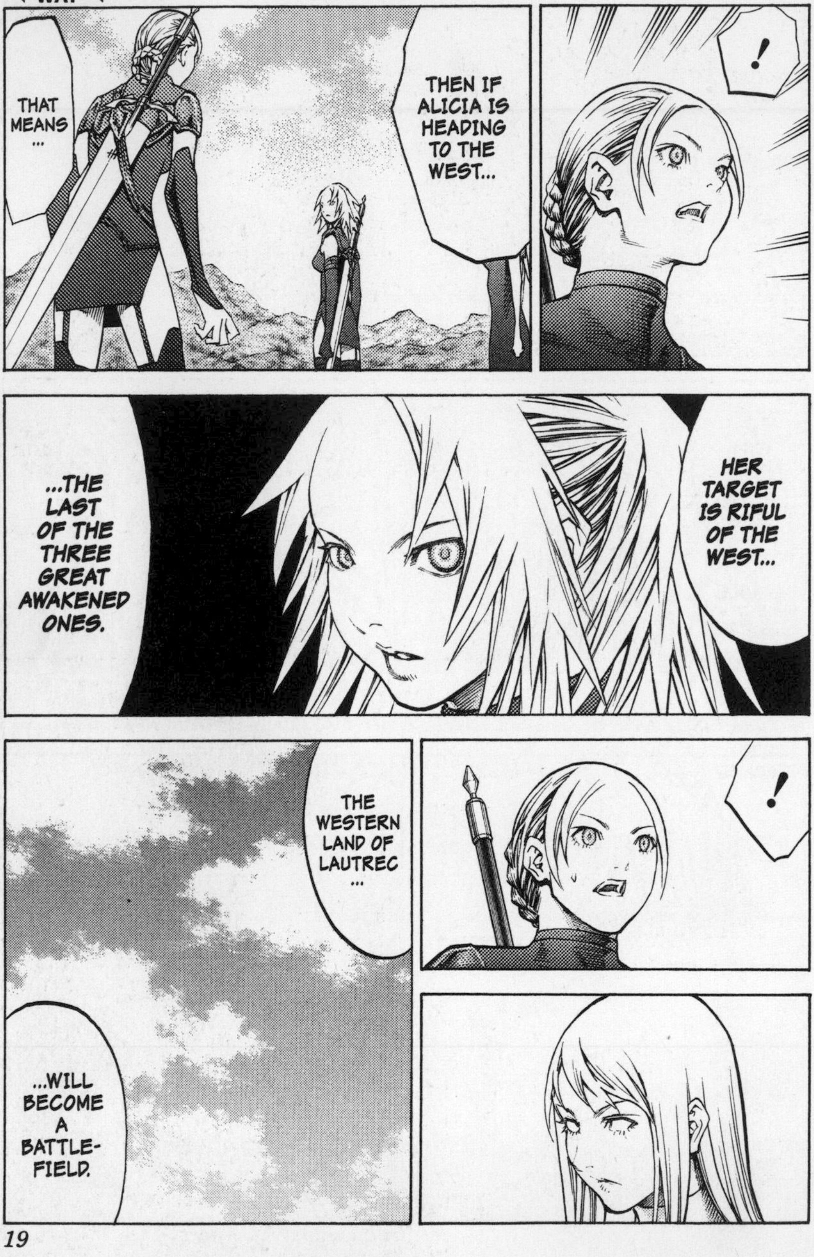
!
THEN IF ALICIA IS HEADING TO THE WEST...
THAT MEANS ...
HER TARGET IS RIFUL OF THE WEST...
...THE LAST OF THE THREE GREAT AWAKENED ONES.
!
THE WESTERN LAND OF LAUTREC ...
...WILL BECOME A BATTLE-FIELD.

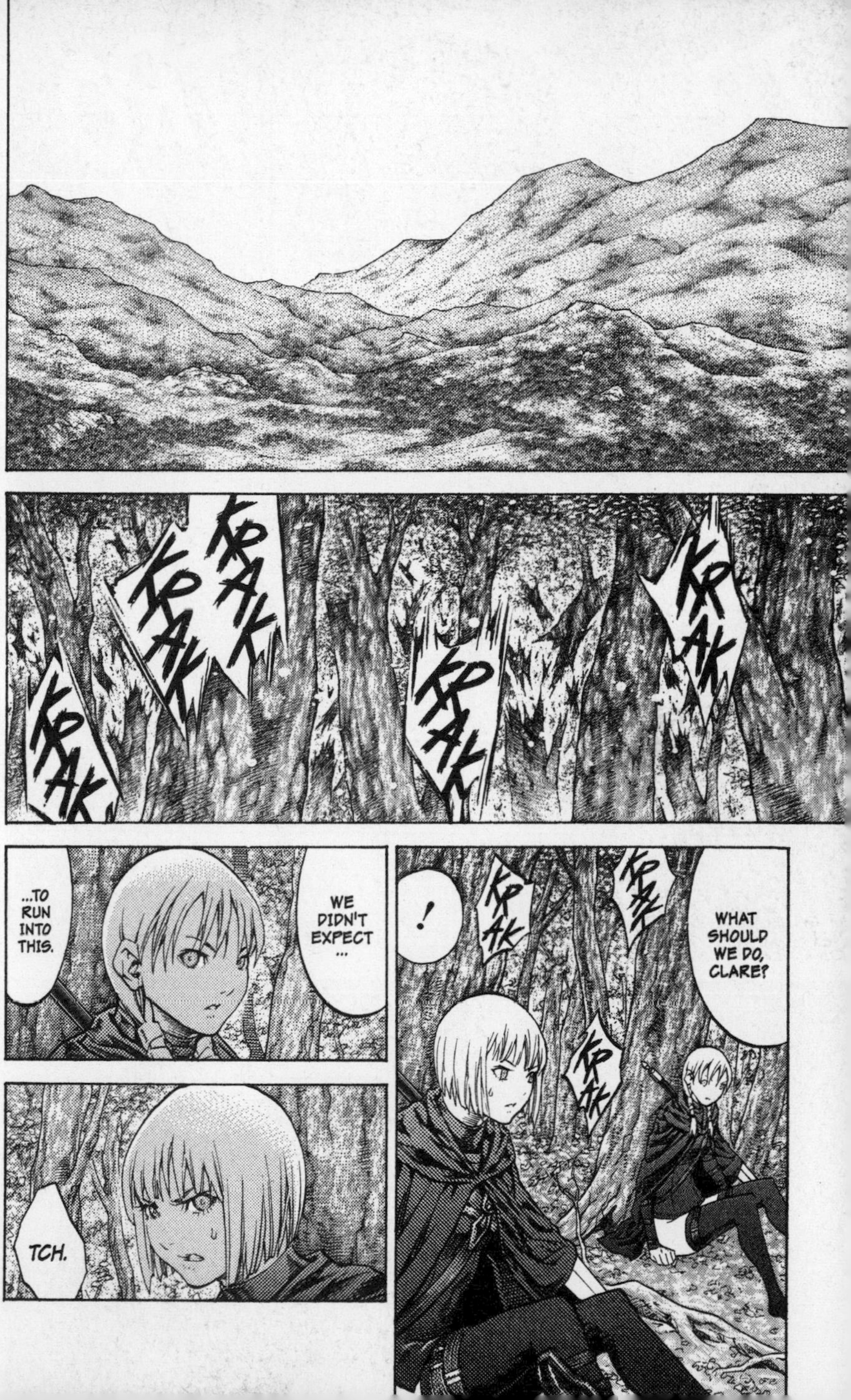
KRAK
KRAK
KRAK
KRAK
KRAK
KRAK
KRAK
WHAT SHOULD WE DO, CLARE?
!
KRAK
WE DIDN'T EXPECT ...
...TO RUN INTO THIS.
TCH.

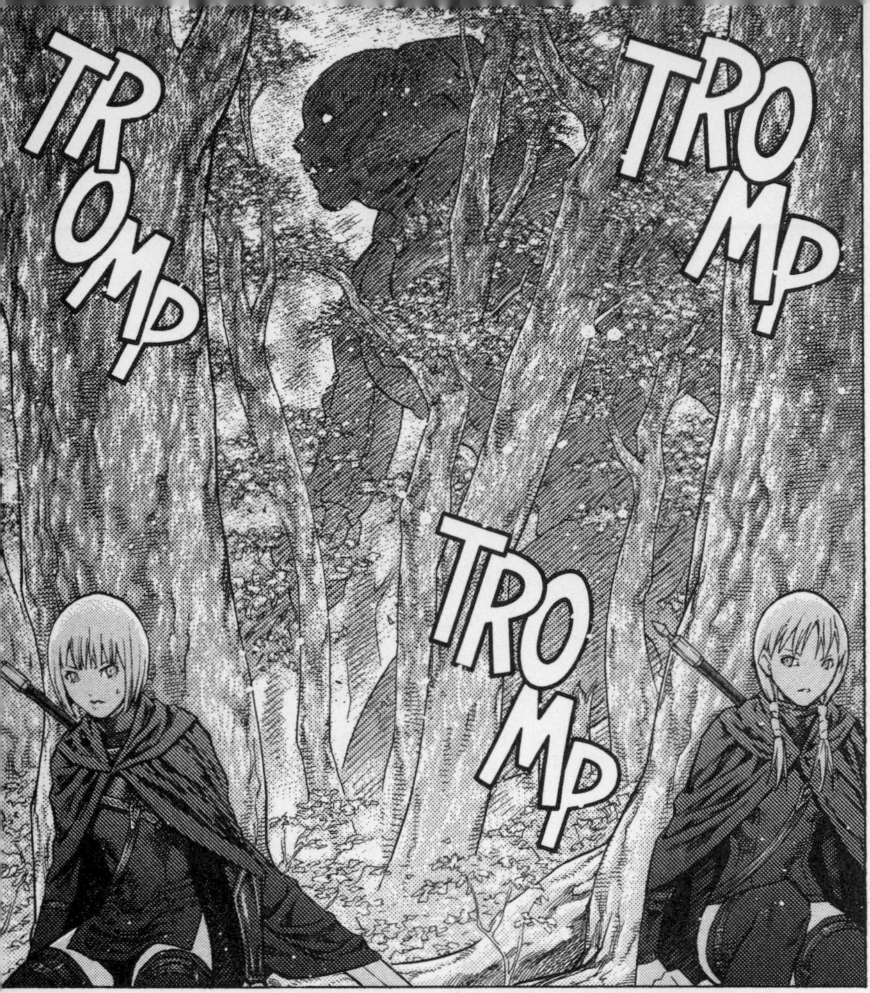
TROMP
TROMP
TROMP

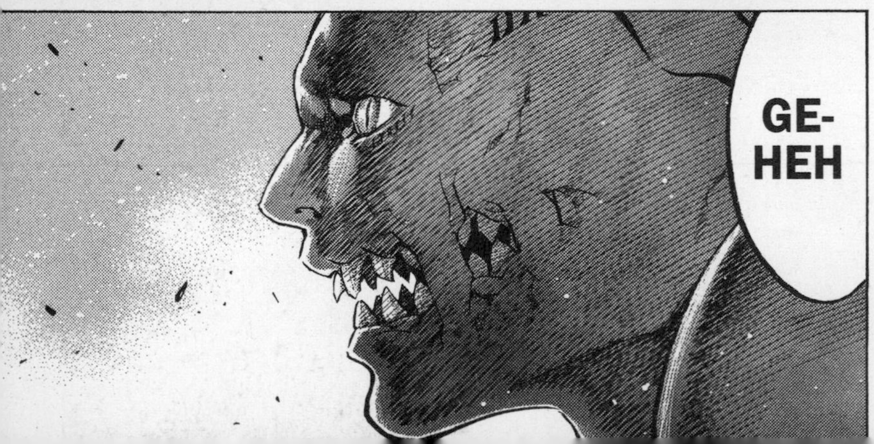
GE-
HEH

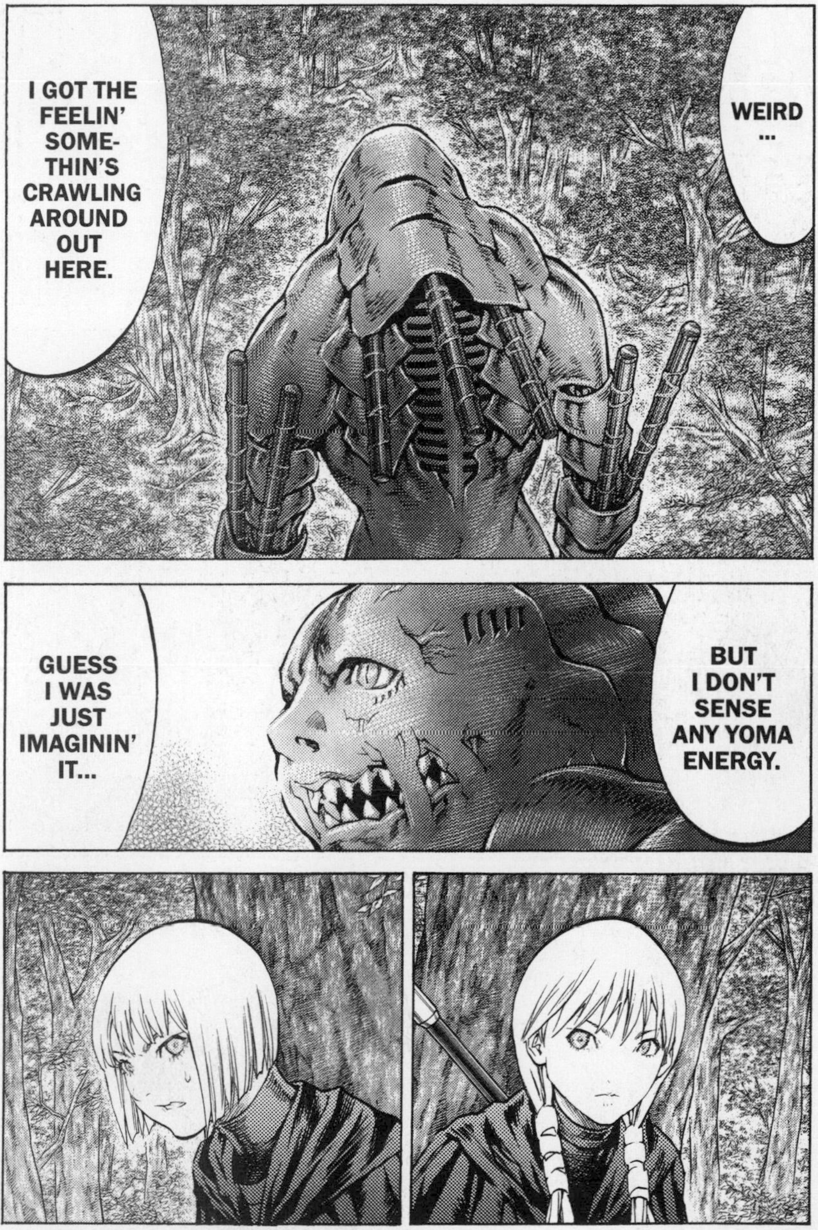
WEIRD ...
I GOT THE FEELIN' SOME-THIN'S CRAWLING AROUND OUT HERE.
BUT I DON'T SENSE ANY YOMA ENERGY.
GUESS I WAS JUST IMAGININ' IT...

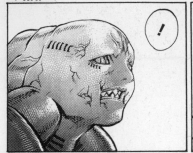

!

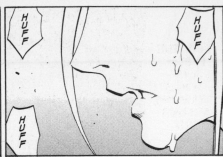

HUFF

HUFF

HUFF

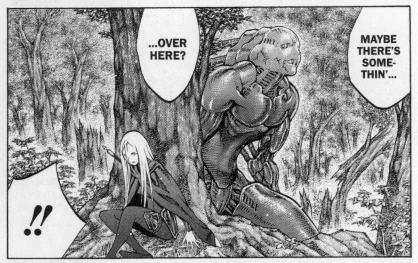

...OVER HERE?

MAYBE THERE'S SOMETHIN'...

!!

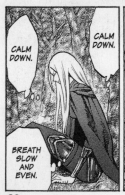

CALM DOWN.

CALM DOWN.

BREATH SLOW AND EVEN.

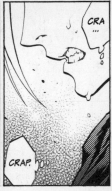

CRA...

CRAP.

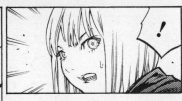

!

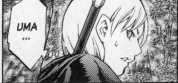

UMA...

23

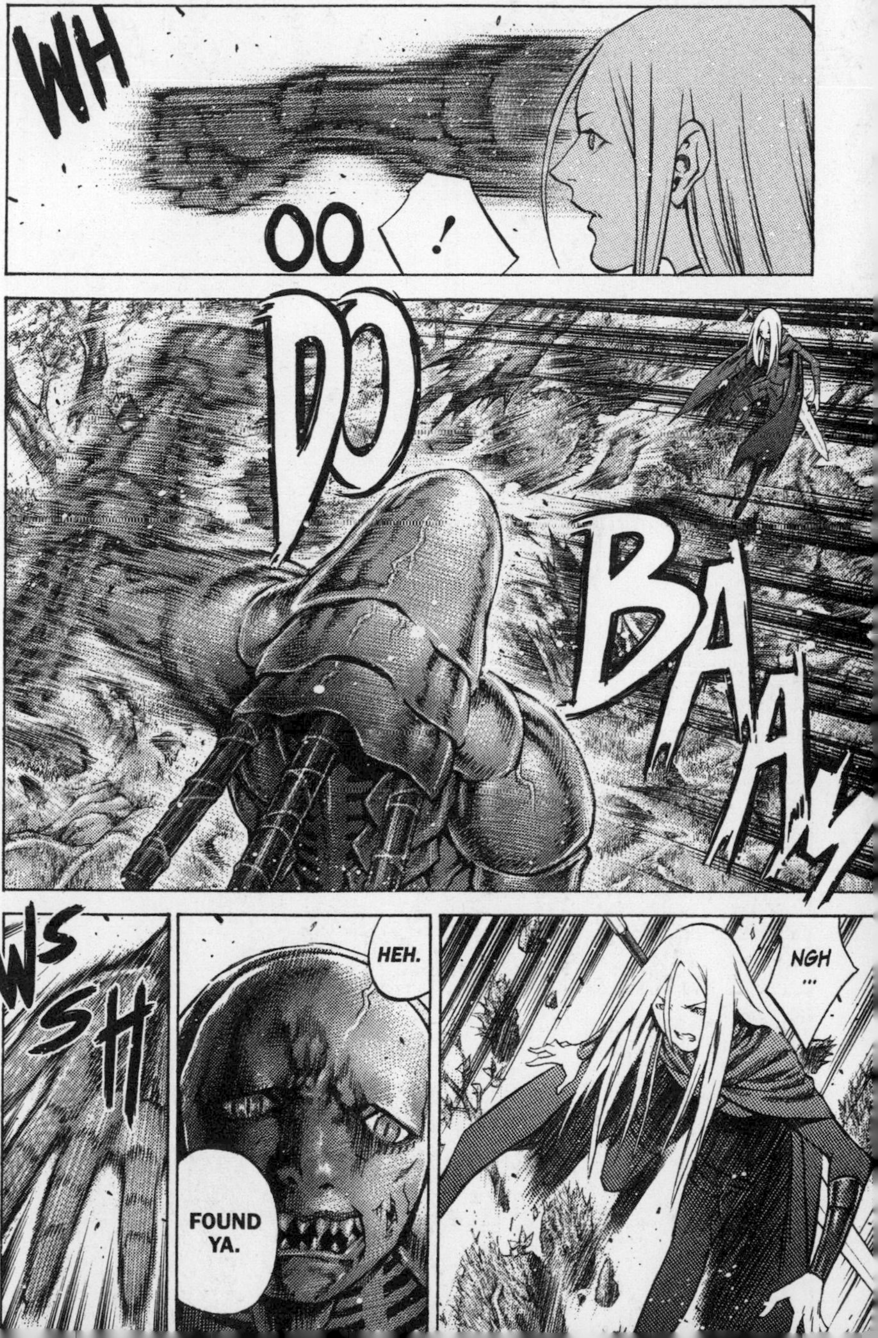
!
WH
OO
DO
BAAAM
NGH ...
HEH.
FOUND YA.
WSSH

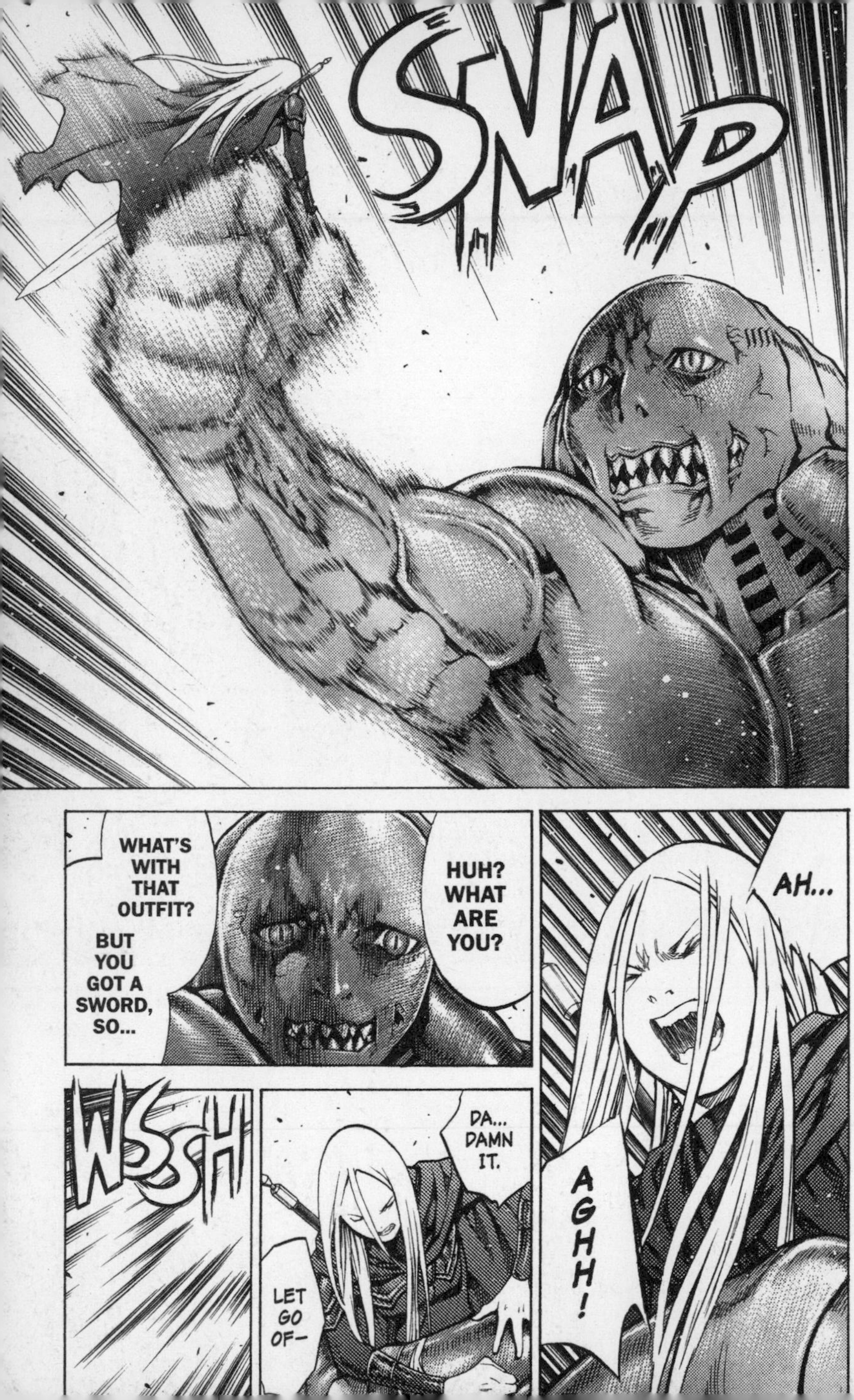
SNAP
AH...
AGHH!
HUH? WHAT ARE YOU?
WHAT'S WITH THAT OUTFIT?
BUT YOU GOT A SWORD, SO...
DA... DAMN IT.
LET GO OF—
WSSH

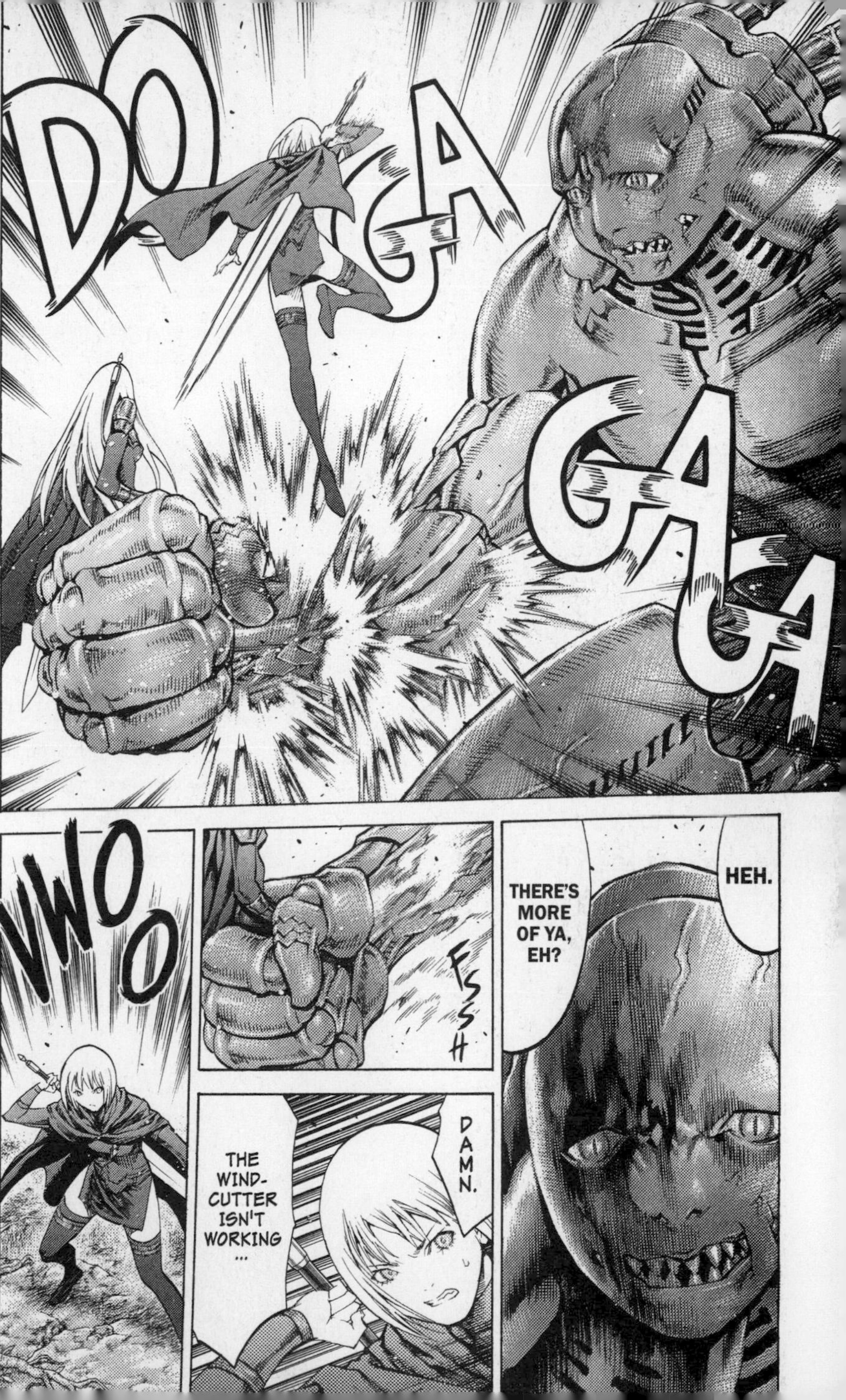
DOGA
GAGA
HEH.
THERE'S MORE OF YA, EH?
FSSH
DAMN.
THE WIND-CUTTER ISN'T WORKING...
VWOO

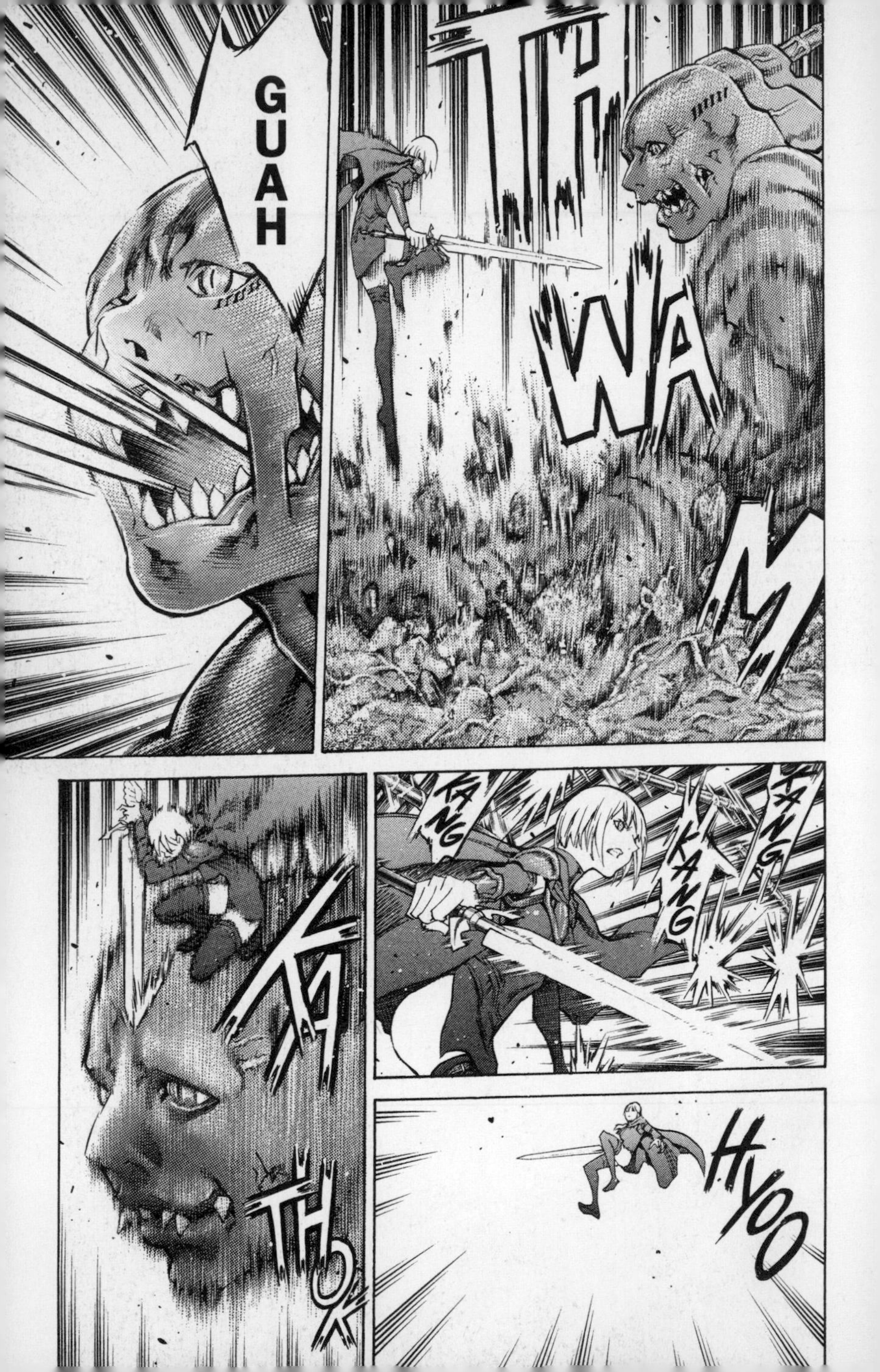
THWAM
GUAH
KANG
KANG
KANG
HYOO
THOK

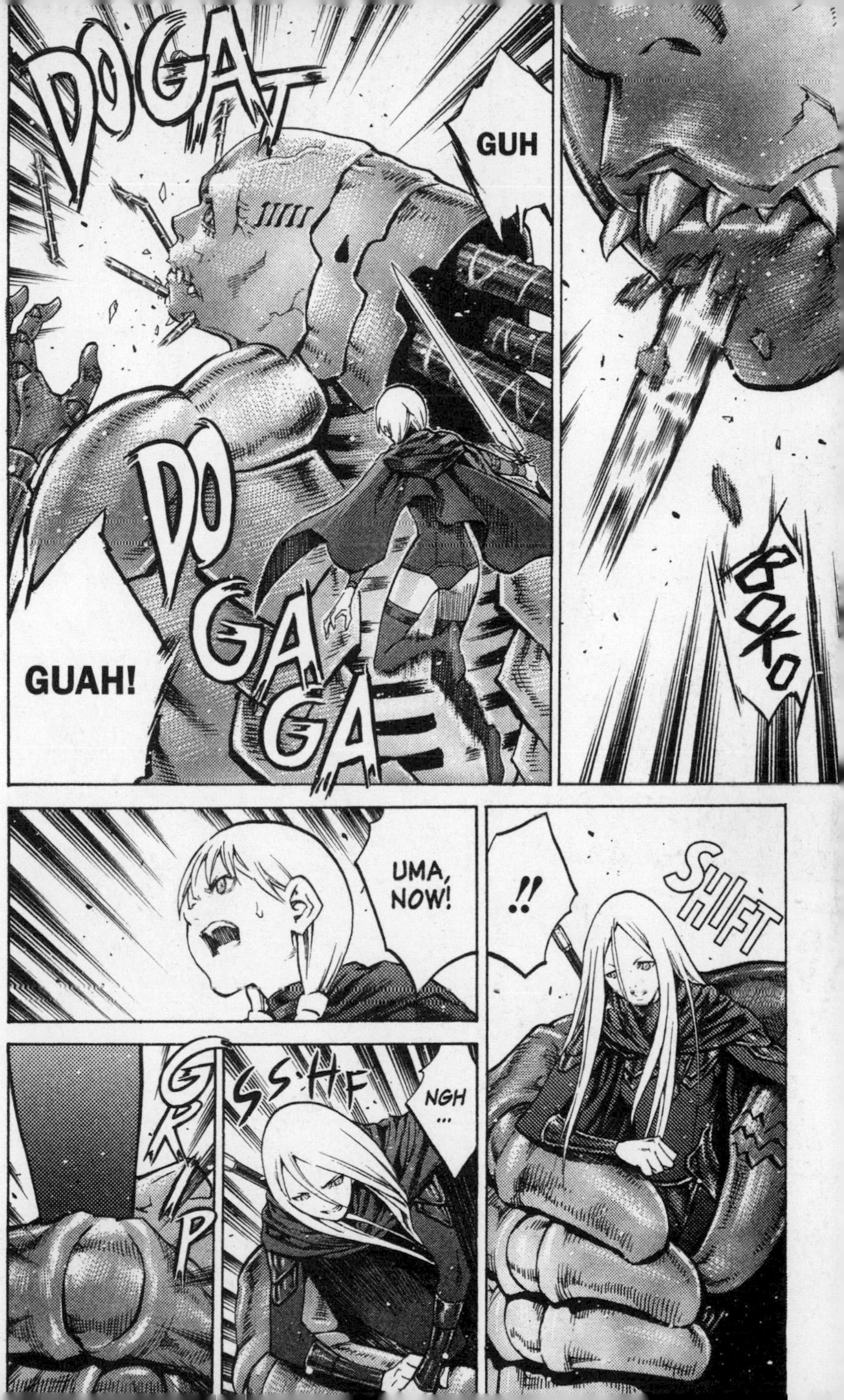
BOKO
GUH
DOGAT
DO GA GA
GUAH!
!!
SHIFT
UMA, NOW!
NGH ...
SSHF
GRIP

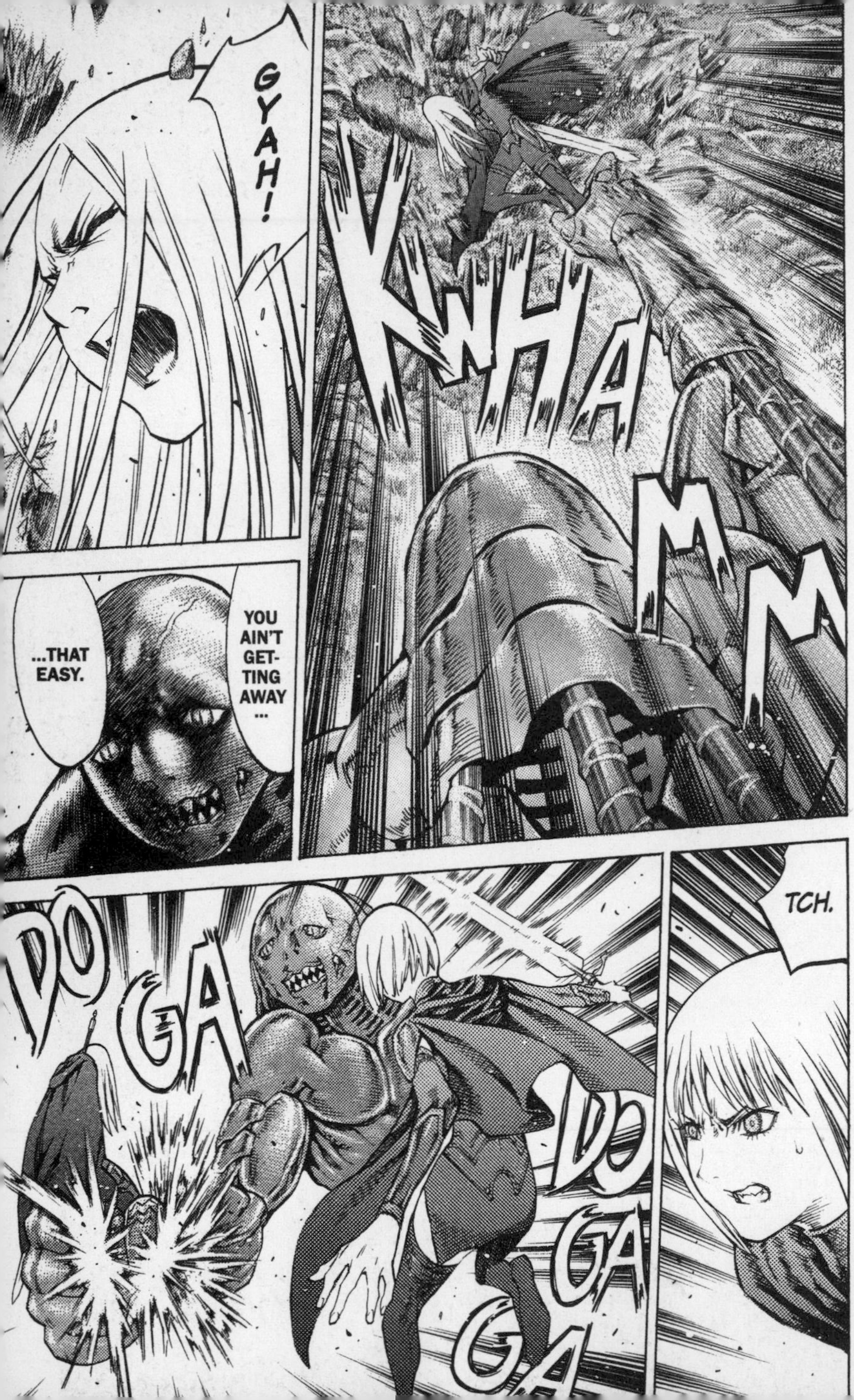
KWHAMMM
GYAH!
YOU AIN'T GET-TING AWAY ...
...THAT EASY.
TCH.
DOGAGA
DOGA

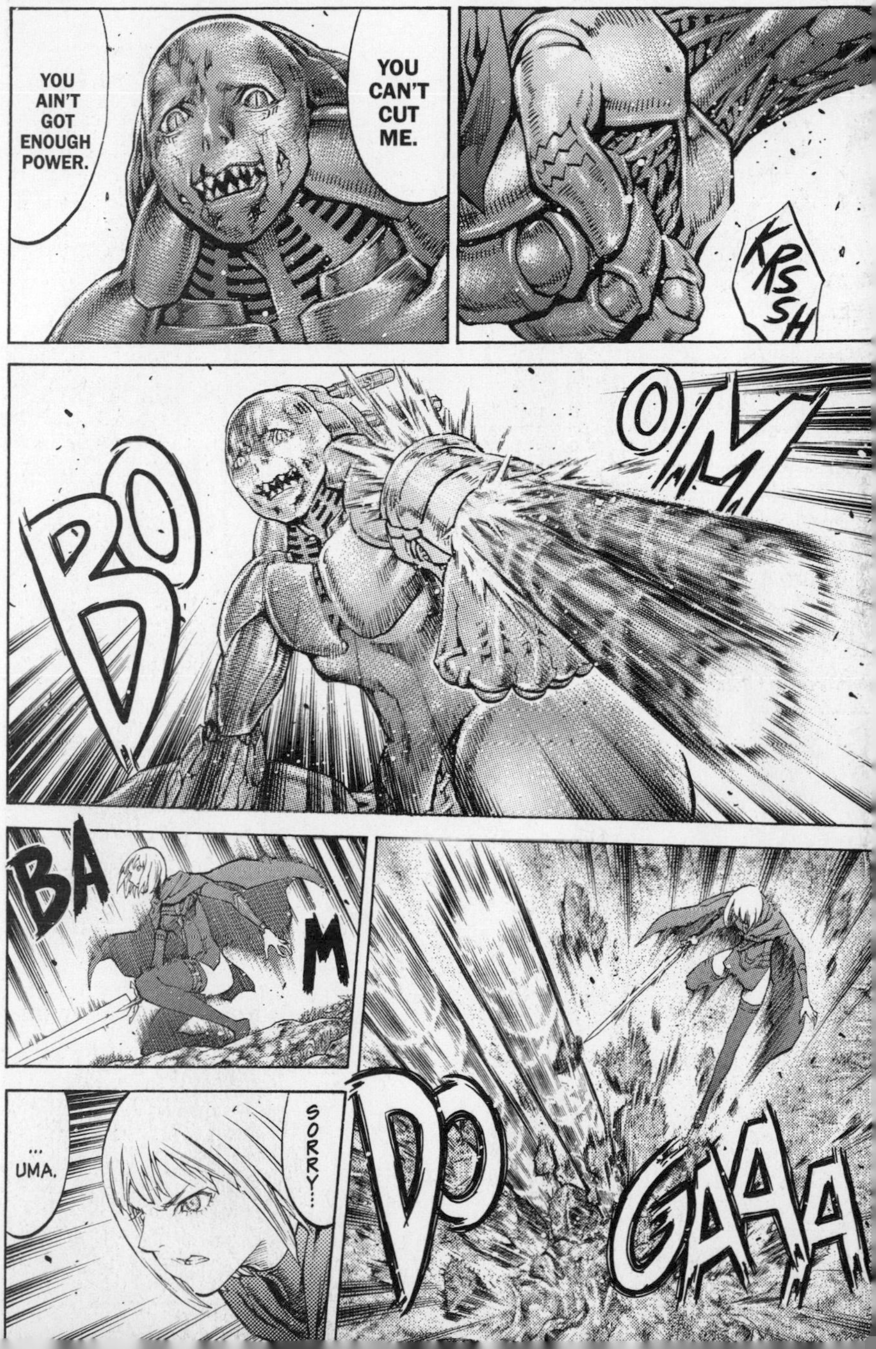
KRSH
YOU CAN'T CUT ME.
YOU AIN'T GOT ENOUGH POWER.
BOOM
DOGAAA
BAM
SORRY...
... UMA.

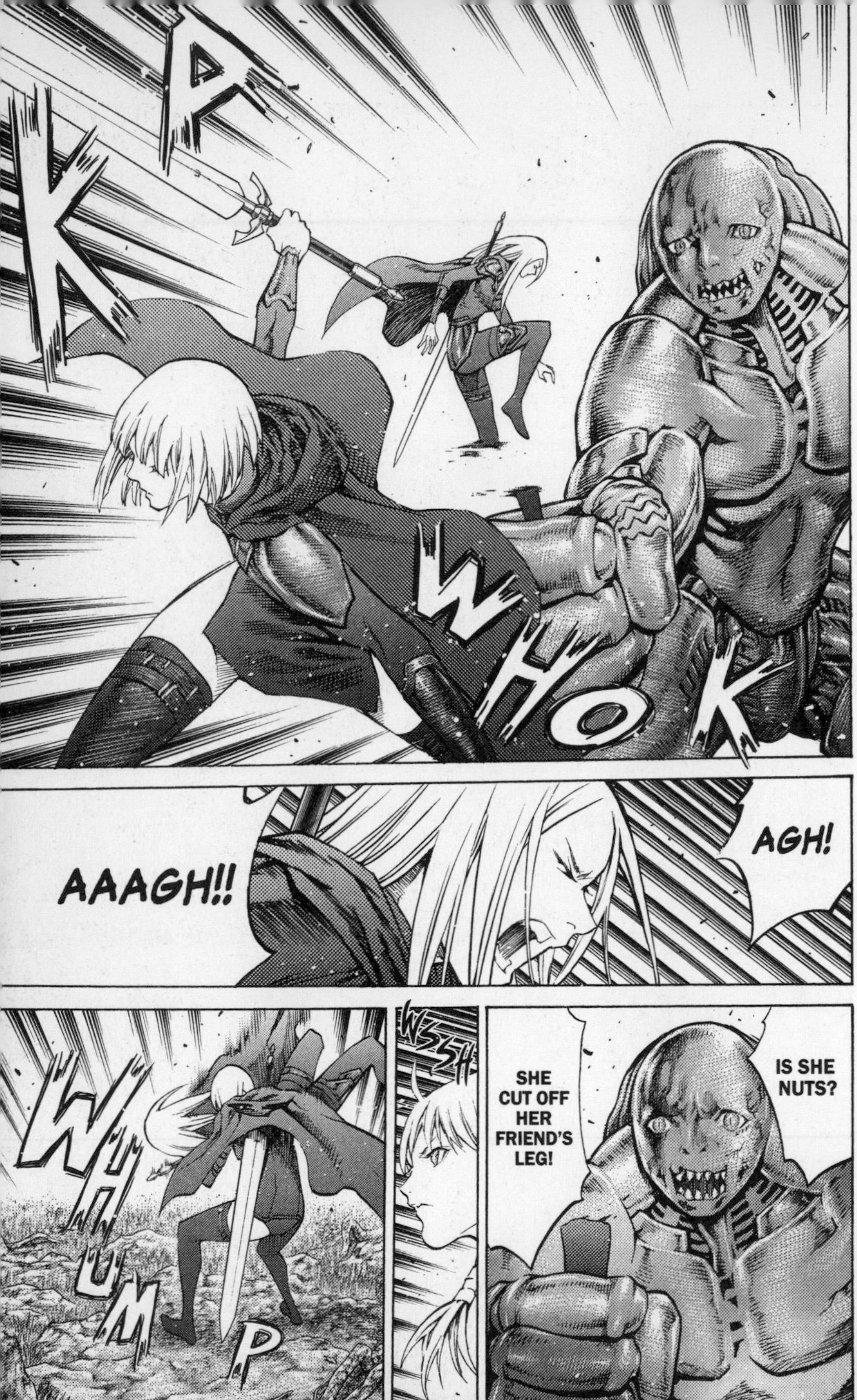
KAP
WHOK
AGH!
AAAGH!!
IS SHE NUTS?
SHE CUT OFF HER FRIEND'S LEG!
WSSH
WHUMP

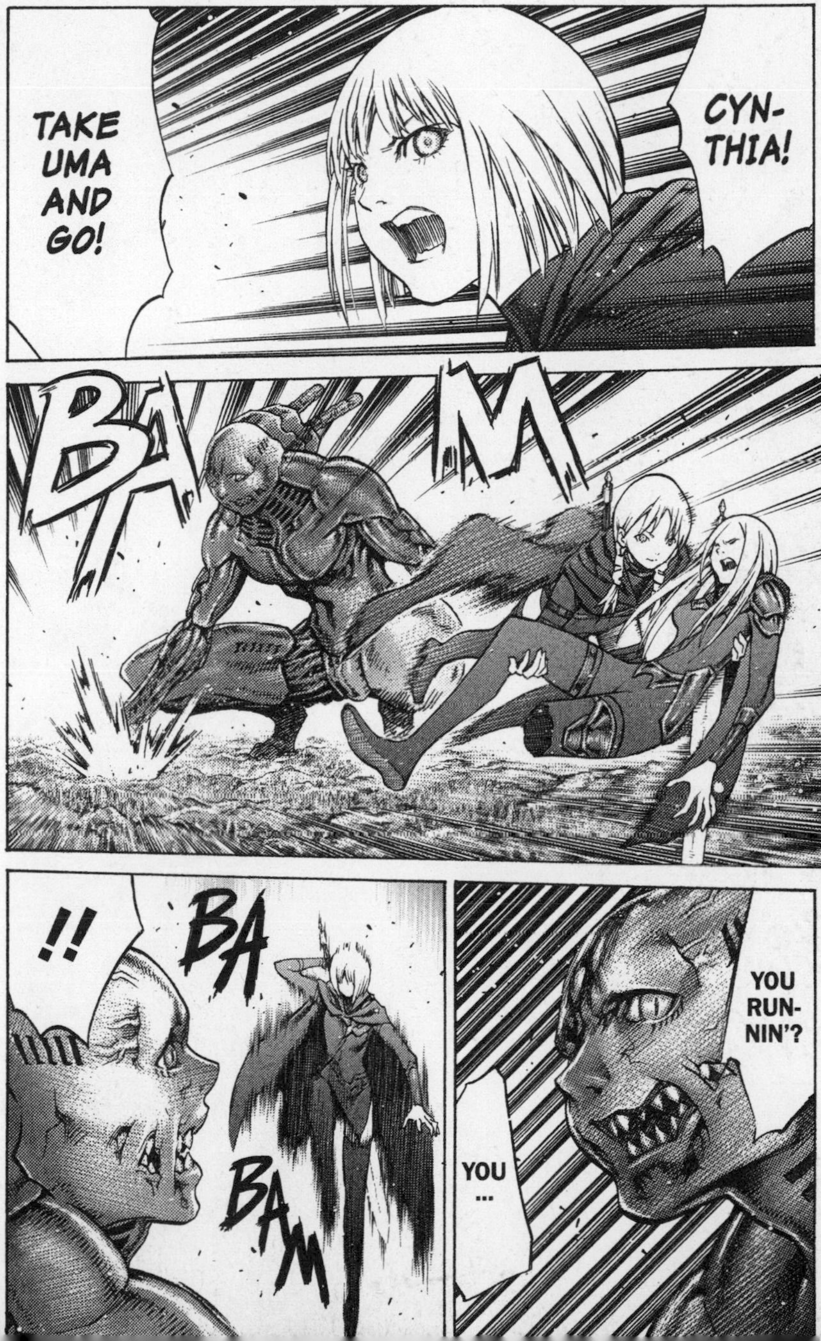
CYN-
THIA!
TAKE
UMA
AND
GO!
BAM
YOU
...
YOU
RUN-
NIN'?
!!
BA
BAM

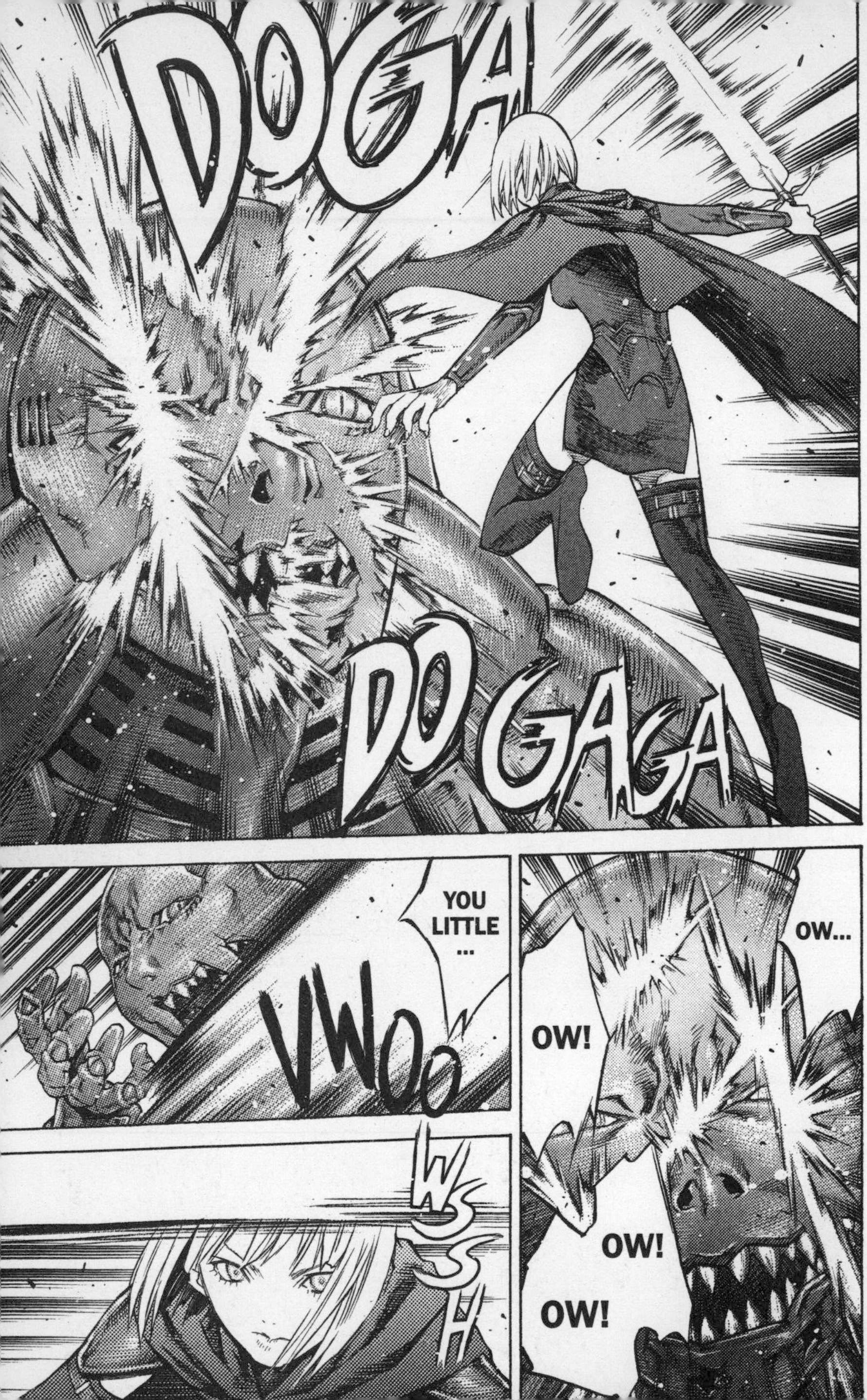
DOGA
DO GAGA
OW...
OW!
OW!
OW!
YOU LITTLE ...
VWOO
WSSH

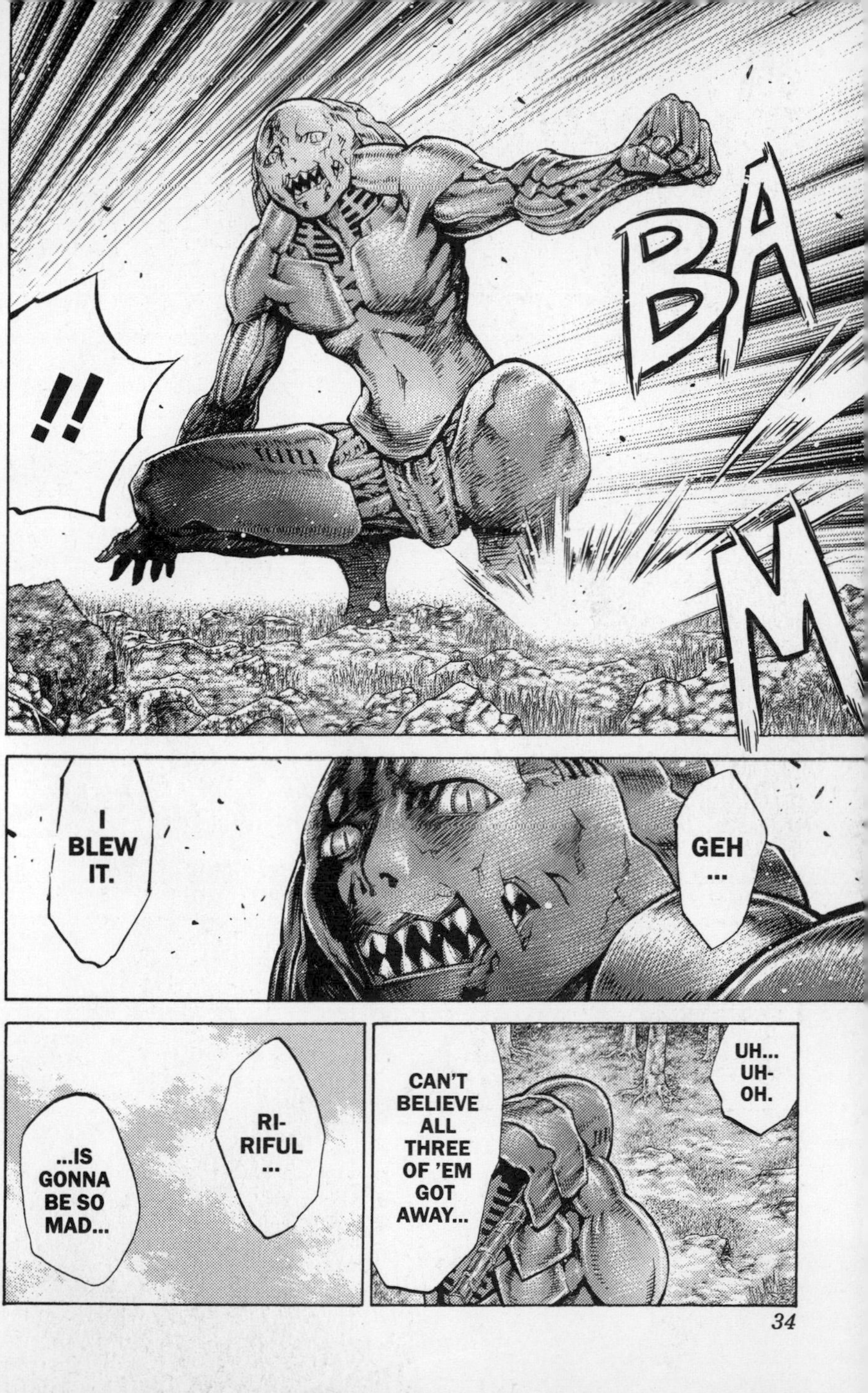
BAM
!!
GEH ...
I BLEW IT.
UH... UH-OH.
CAN'T BELIEVE ALL THREE OF 'EM GOT AWAY...
RI-RIFUL ...
...IS GONNA BE SO MAD...

READ THIS WAY

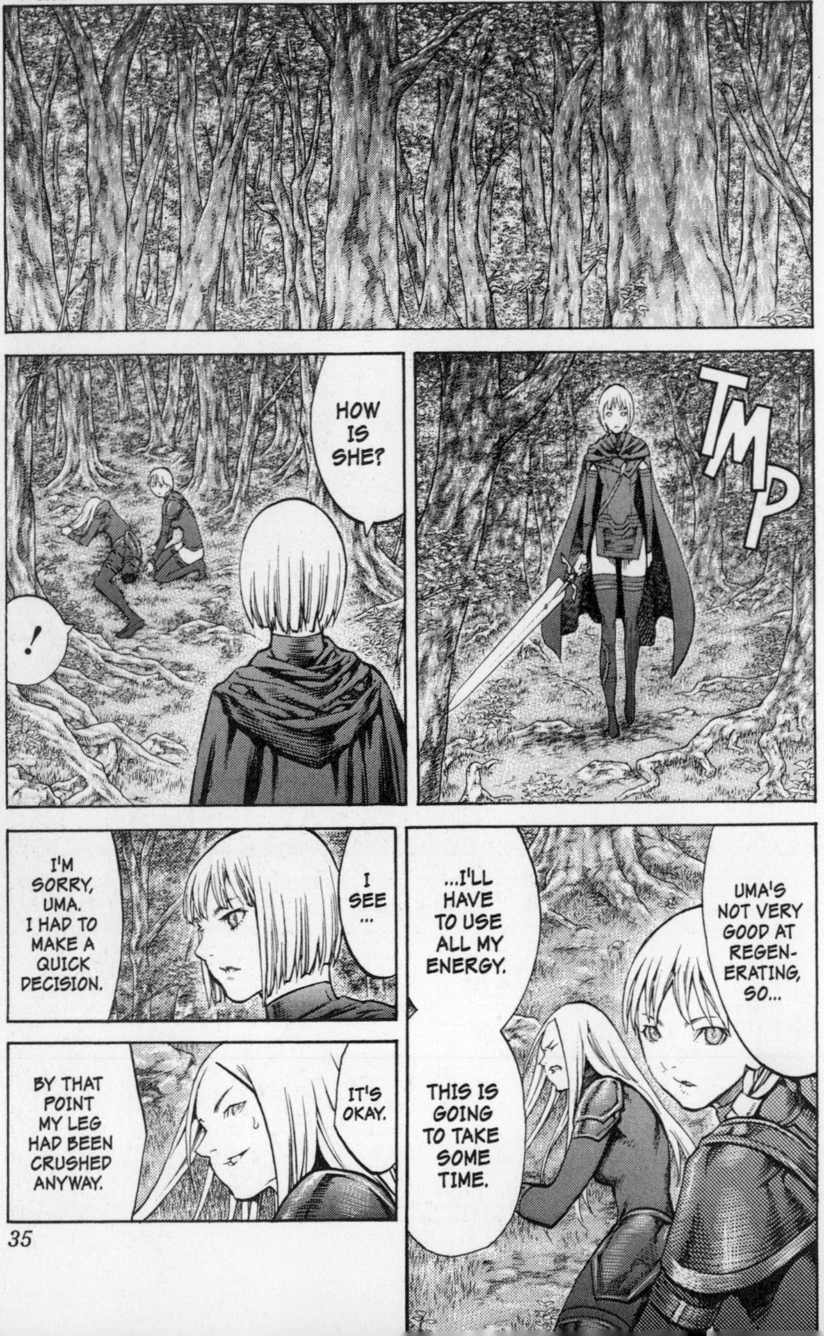

TMP
HOW IS SHE?
!
UMA'S NOT VERY GOOD AT REGEN-ERATING, SO...
...I'LL HAVE TO USE ALL MY ENERGY.
THIS IS GOING TO TAKE SOME TIME.
I SEE...
I'M SORRY, UMA. I HAD TO MAKE A QUICK DECISION.
IT'S OKAY.
BY THAT POINT MY LEG HAD BEEN CRUSHED ANYWAY.

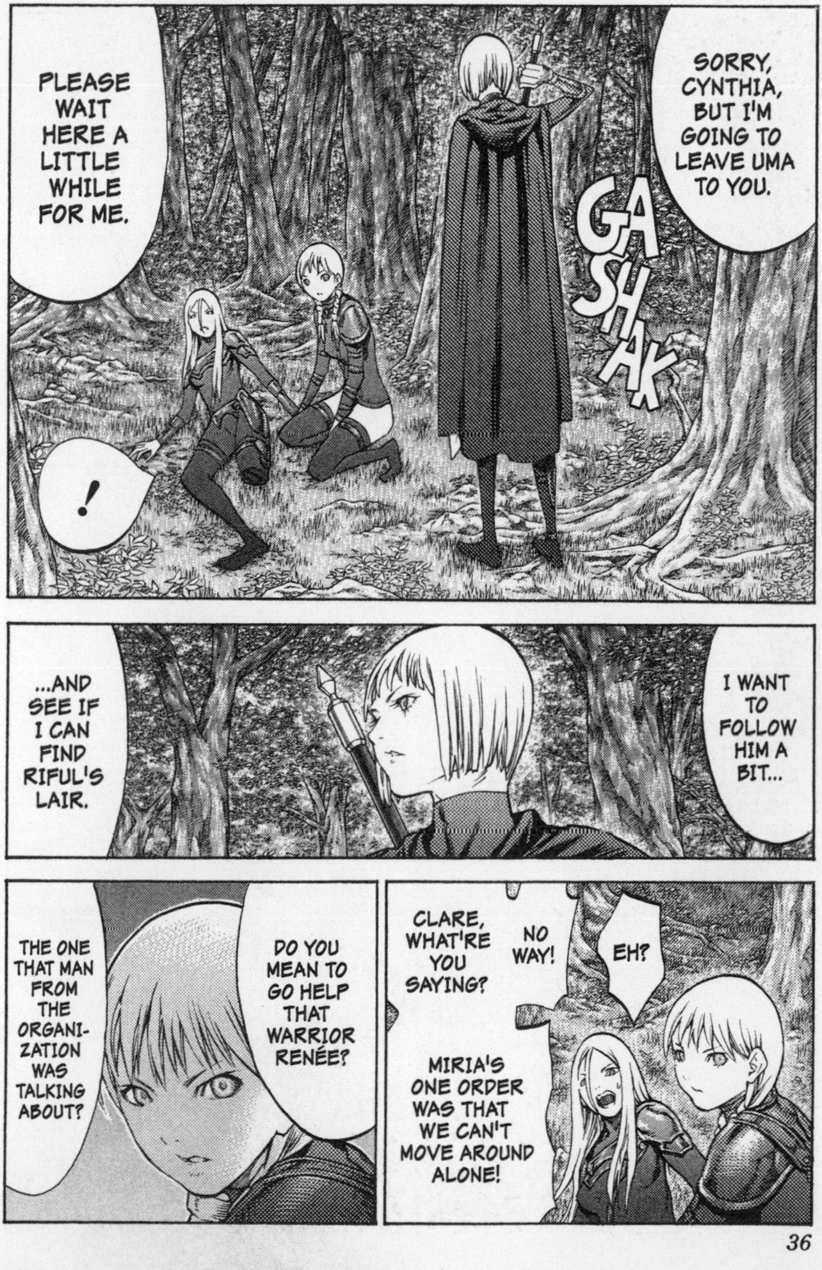
SORRY, CYNTHIA, BUT I'M GOING TO LEAVE UMA TO YOU.
GASHAK
PLEASE WAIT HERE A LITTLE WHILE FOR ME.
!
I WANT TO FOLLOW HIM A BIT...
...AND SEE IF I CAN FIND RIFUL'S LAIR.
EH?
NO WAY!
CLARE, WHAT'RE YOU SAYING?
MIRIA'S ONE ORDER WAS THAT WE CAN'T MOVE AROUND ALONE!
DO YOU MEAN TO GO HELP THAT WARRIOR RENÉE?
THE ONE THAT MAN FROM THE ORGANI-ZATION WAS TALKING ABOUT?

READ THIS WAY

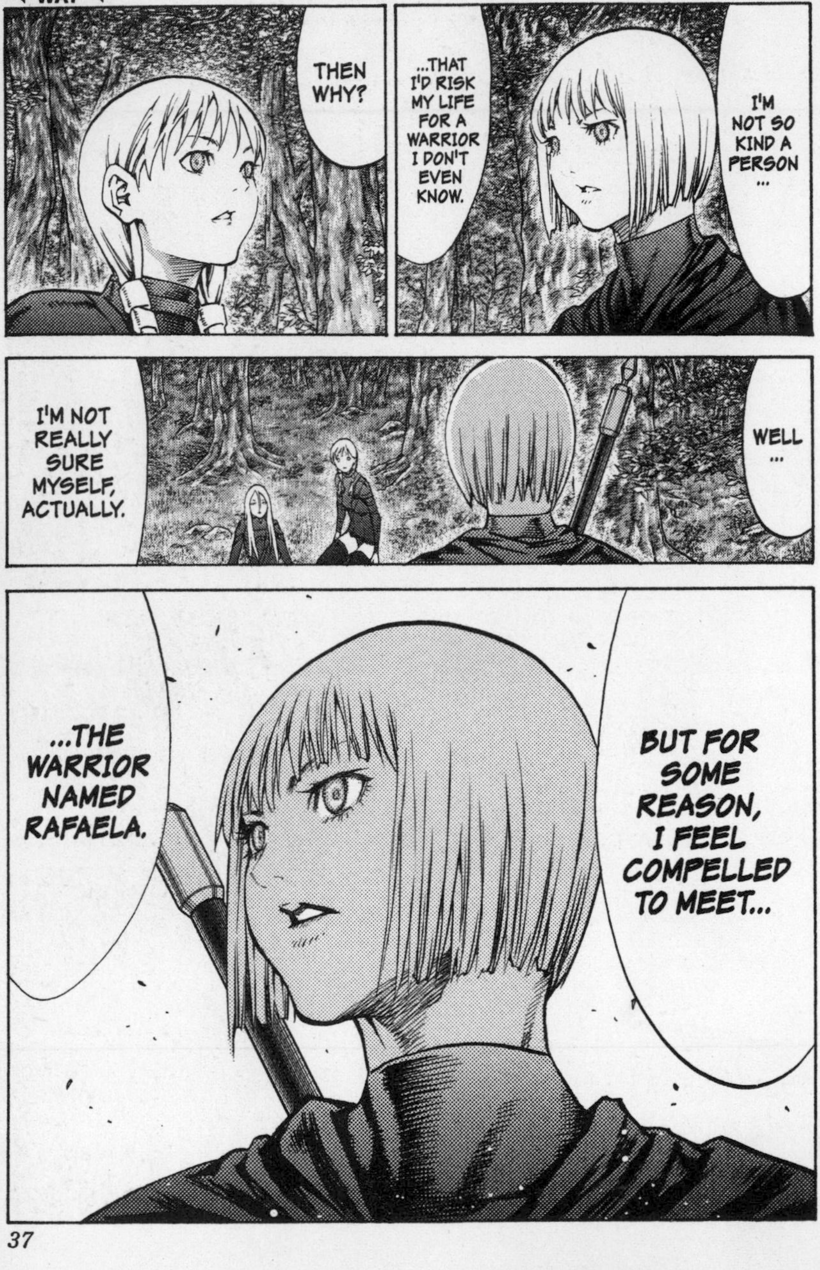
I'M NOT SO KIND A PERSON...
...THAT I'D RISK MY LIFE FOR A WARRIOR I DON'T EVEN KNOW.
THEN WHY?
WELL...
I'M NOT REALLY SURE MYSELF, ACTUALLY.
BUT FOR SOME REASON, I FEEL COMPELLED TO MEET...
...THE WARRIOR NAMED RAFAELA.

クレイモア

Claymore

Scene 91: The Claws of Memory, Part 2

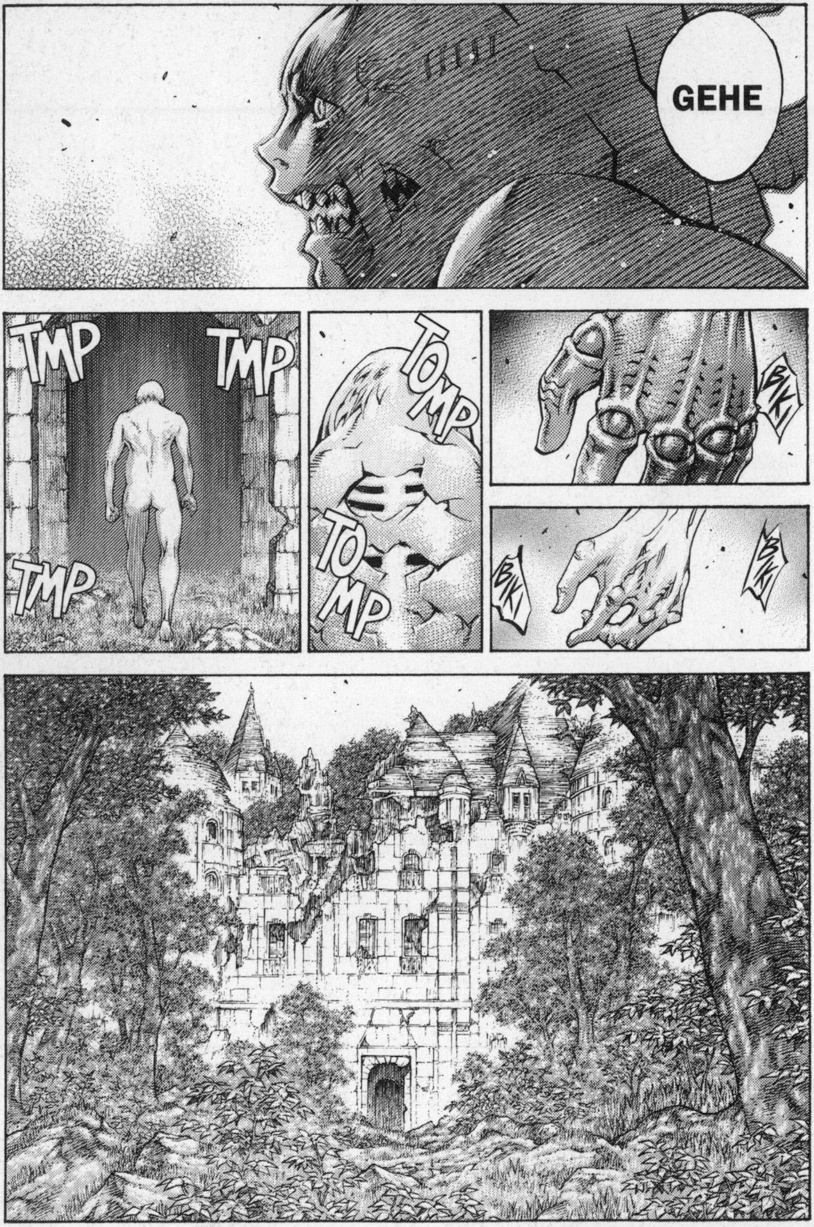
GEHE
BIKI
BIKI
BIKI
TOMP
TOMP
TMP
TMP
TMP

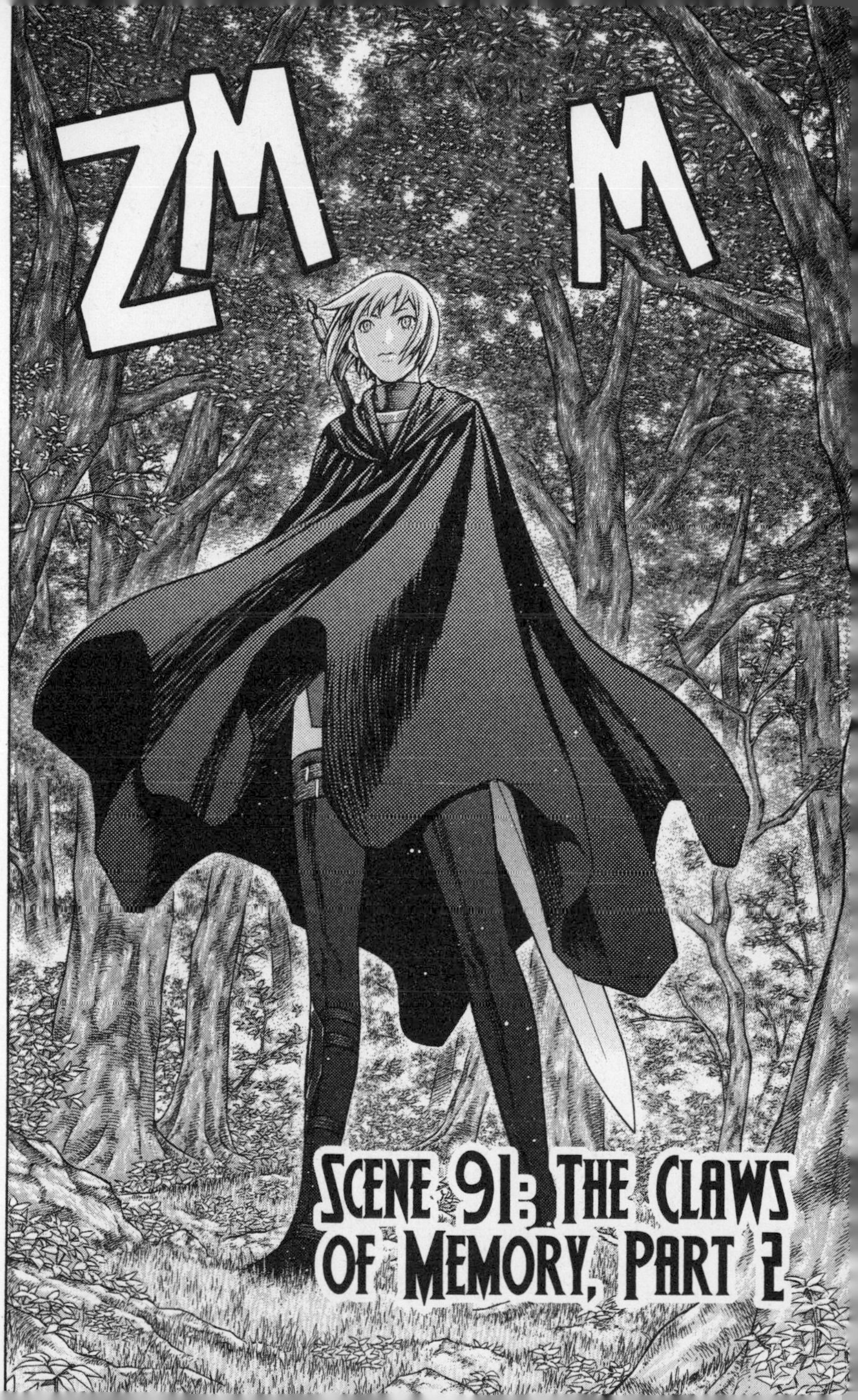
ZMM
SCENE 91: THE CLAWS OF MEMORY, PART 2

READ THIS WAY

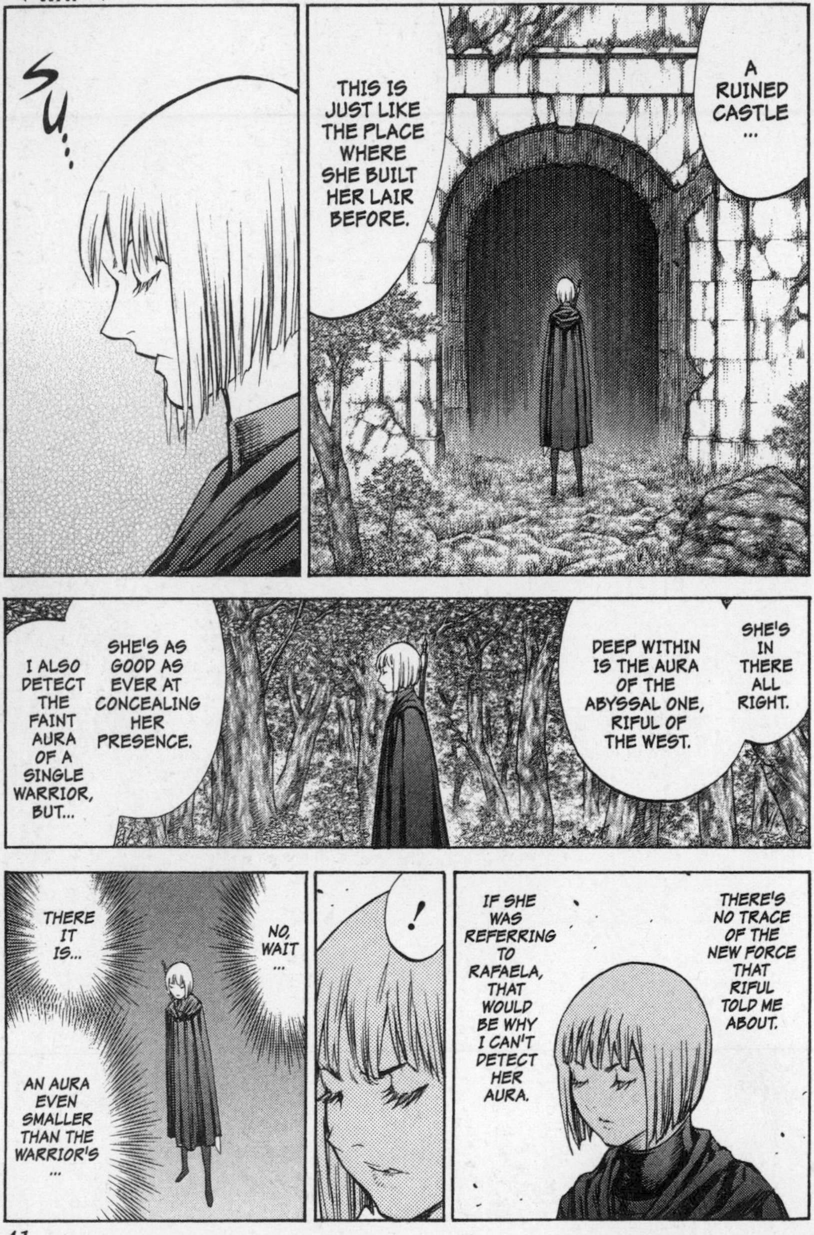
A RUINED CASTLE ...
THIS IS JUST LIKE THE PLACE WHERE SHE BUILT HER LAIR BEFORE.
SU...
SHE'S IN THERE ALL RIGHT.
DEEP WITHIN IS THE AURA OF THE ABYSSAL ONE, RIFUL OF THE WEST.
SHE'S AS GOOD AS EVER AT CONCEALING HER PRESENCE.
I ALSO DETECT THE FAINT AURA OF A SINGLE WARRIOR, BUT...
THERE'S NO TRACE OF THE NEW FORCE THAT RIFUL TOLD ME ABOUT.
IF SHE WAS REFERRING TO RAFAELA, THAT WOULD BE WHY I CAN'T DETECT HER AURA.
!
NO, WAIT ...
THERE IT IS...
AN AURA EVEN SMALLER THAN THE WARRIOR'S ...

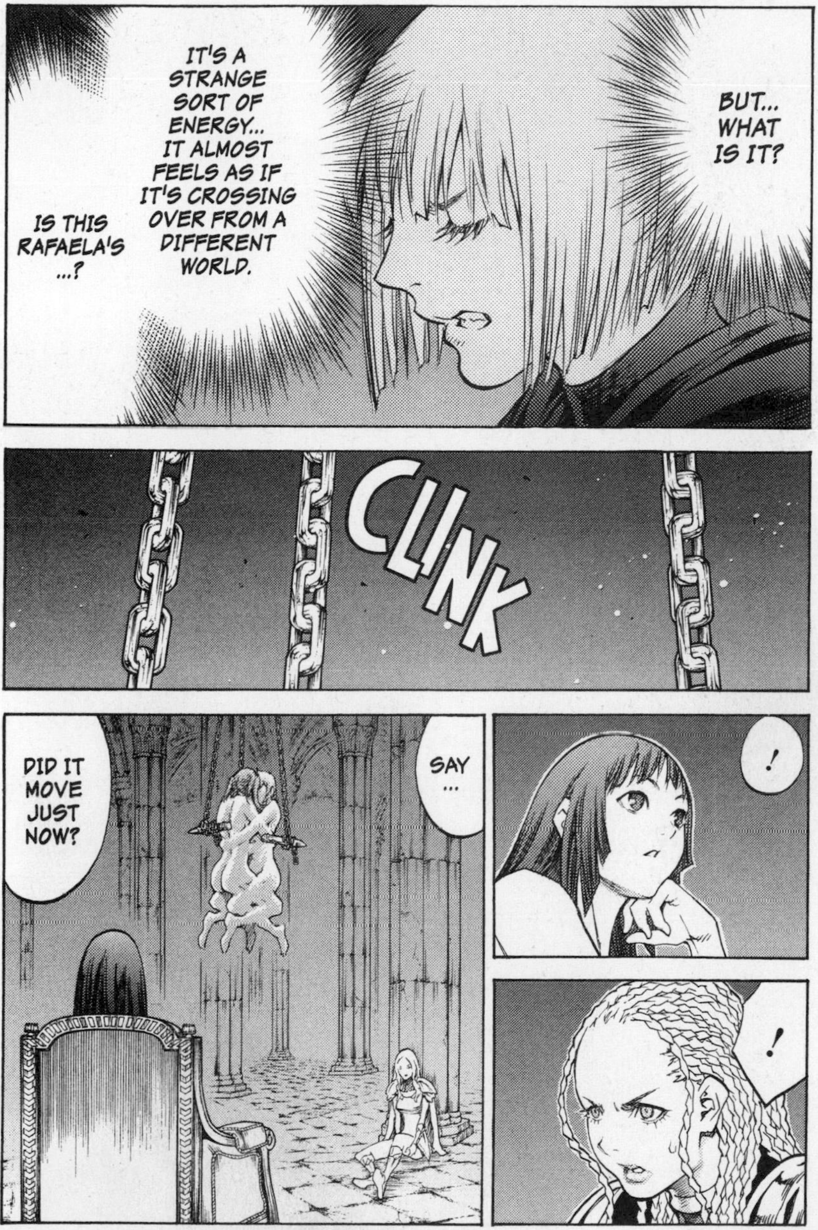
IS THIS RAFAELA'S ...?
IT'S A STRANGE SORT OF ENERGY... IT ALMOST FEELS AS IF IT'S CROSSING OVER FROM A DIFFERENT WORLD.
BUT... WHAT IS IT?
CLINK
DID IT MOVE JUST NOW?
SAY ...
!
!

READ THIS WAY

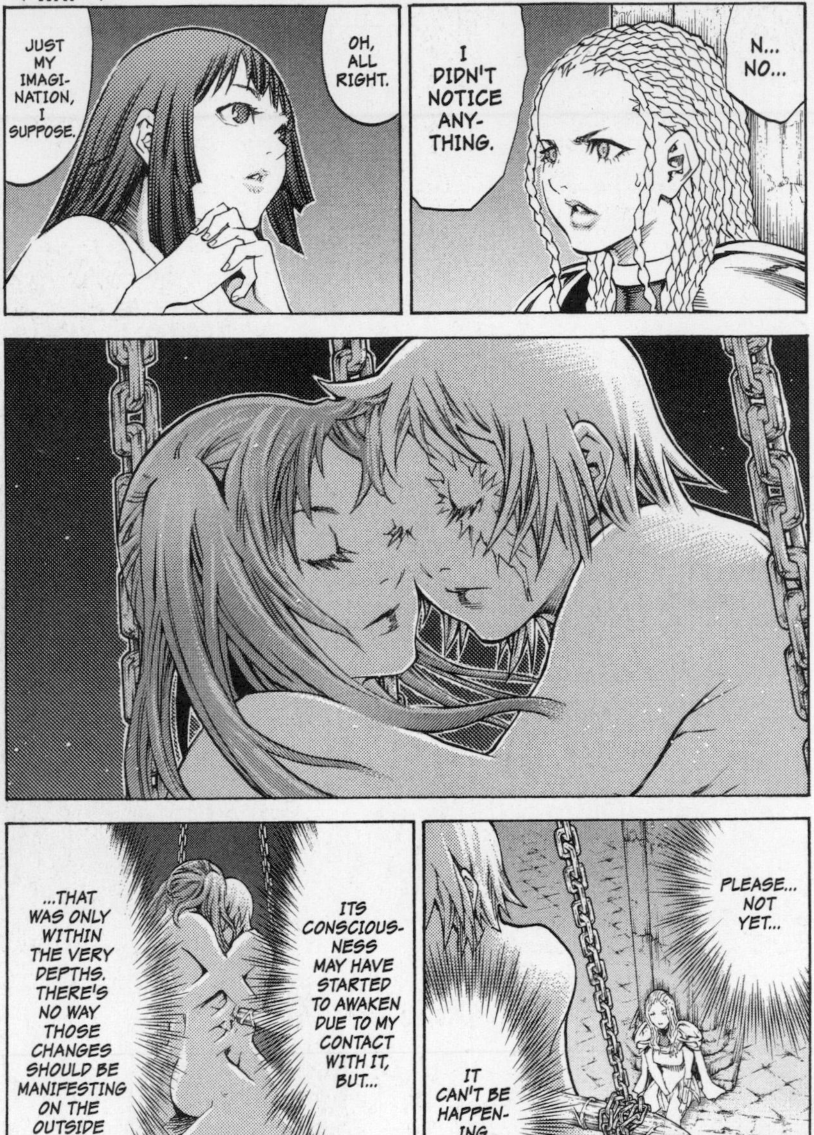
N... NO...
I DIDN'T NOTICE ANYTHING.
OH, ALL RIGHT.
JUST MY IMAGINATION, I SUPPOSE.
PLEASE... NOT YET...
IT CAN'T BE HAPPENING YET.
ITS CONSCIOUSNESS MAY HAVE STARTED TO AWAKEN DUE TO MY CONTACT WITH IT, BUT...
...THAT WAS ONLY WITHIN THE VERY DEPTHS. THERE'S NO WAY THOSE CHANGES SHOULD BE MANIFESTING ON THE OUTSIDE YET.

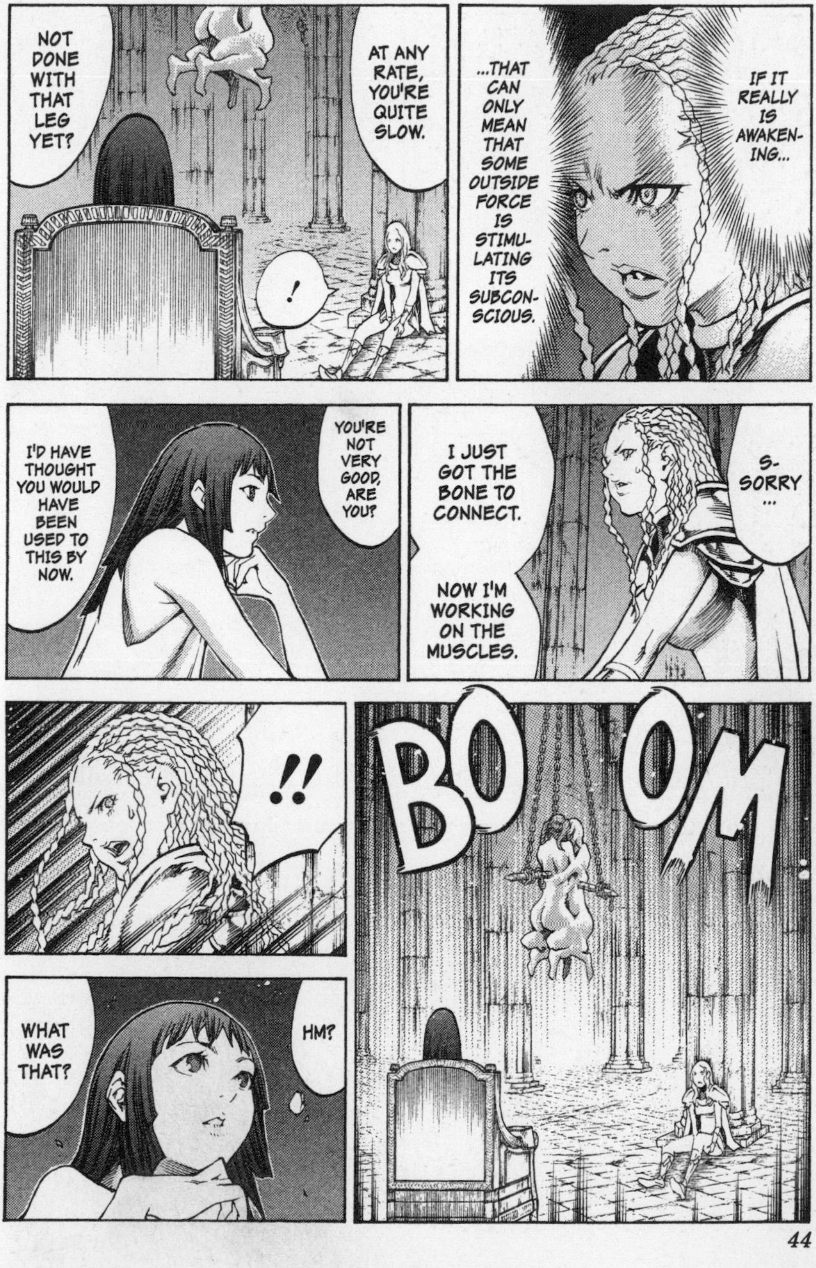
IF IT REALLY IS AWAKEN-ING...
...THAT CAN ONLY MEAN THAT SOME OUTSIDE FORCE IS STIMULATING ITS SUBCONSCIOUS.
AT ANY RATE, YOU'RE QUITE SLOW.
NOT DONE WITH THAT LEG YET?
!
S-SORRY...
I JUST GOT THE BONE TO CONNECT.
NOW I'M WORKING ON THE MUSCLES.
YOU'RE NOT VERY GOOD, ARE YOU?
I'D HAVE THOUGHT YOU WOULD HAVE BEEN USED TO THIS BY NOW.
BOOM
!!
HM?
WHAT WAS THAT?

READ THIS WAY

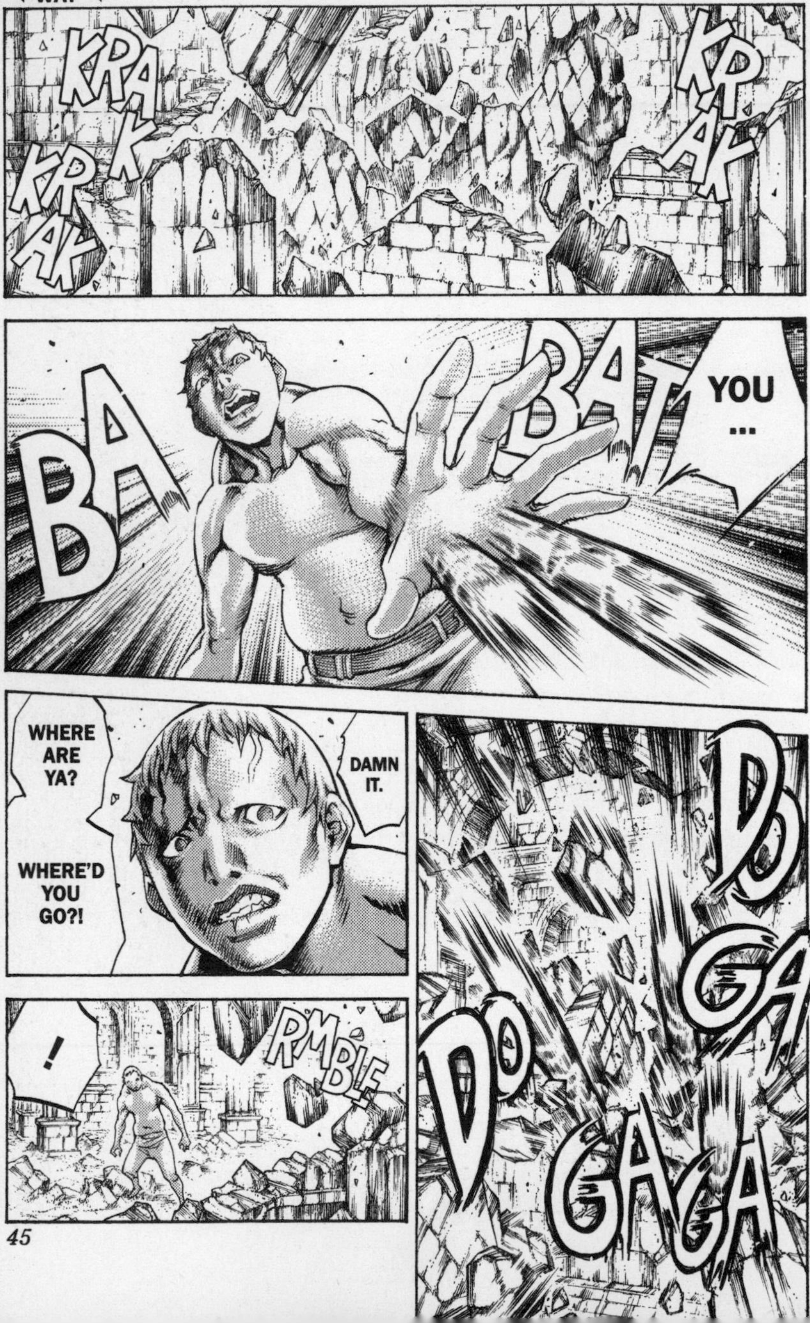
KRAK
KRAK
KRAK
BAT
BA
YOU ...
DOGA
DOGAGA
DAMN IT.
WHERE ARE YA?
WHERE'D YOU GO?!
RMBLE
!

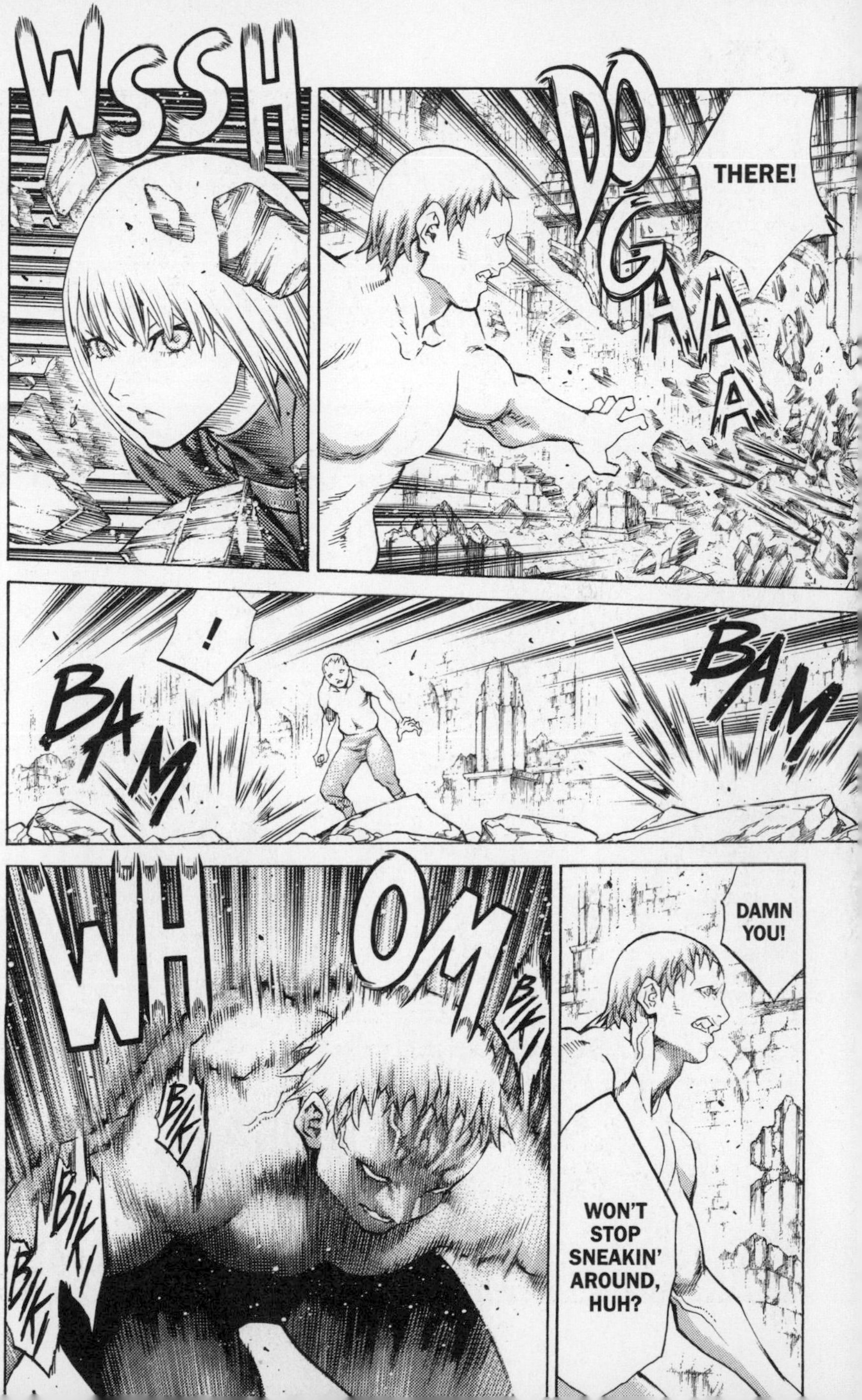
DOGAAA
THERE!
WSSH
BAM
!
BAM
DAMN YOU!
WON'T STOP SNEAKIN' AROUND, HUH?
WHOM
BIKI
BIKI
BIKI
BIKI

READ THIS WAY

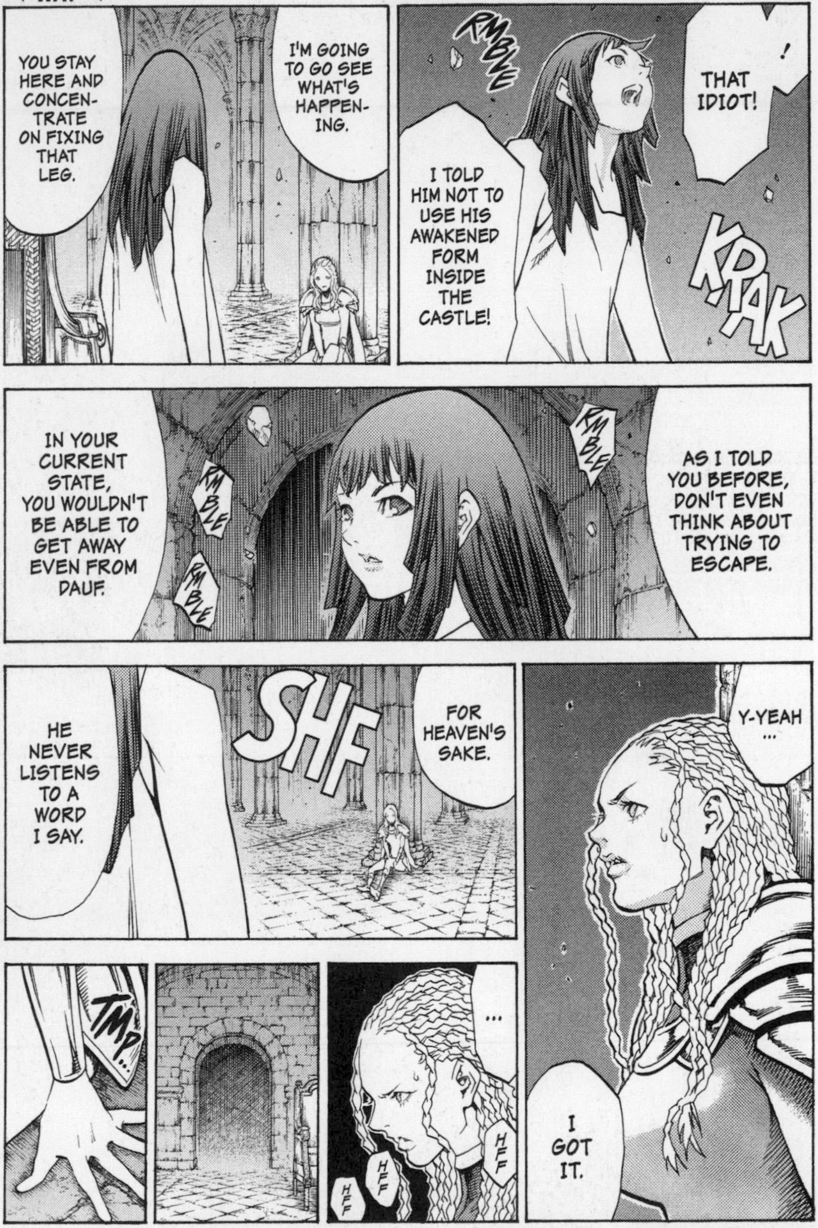
RMBLE
!
THAT IDIOT!
I TOLD HIM NOT TO USE HIS AWAKENED FORM INSIDE THE CASTLE!
KRAK
I'M GOING TO GO SEE WHAT'S HAPPENING.
YOU STAY HERE AND CONCENTRATE ON FIXING THAT LEG.
RMBLE
AS I TOLD YOU BEFORE, DON'T EVEN THINK ABOUT TRYING TO ESCAPE.
RMBLE
RMBLE
IN YOUR CURRENT STATE, YOU WOULDN'T BE ABLE TO GET AWAY EVEN FROM DAUF.
Y-YEAH ...
I GOT IT.
FOR HEAVEN'S SAKE.
SHF
HE NEVER LISTENS TO A WORD I SAY.
...
HFF
HFF
HFF
TMP...

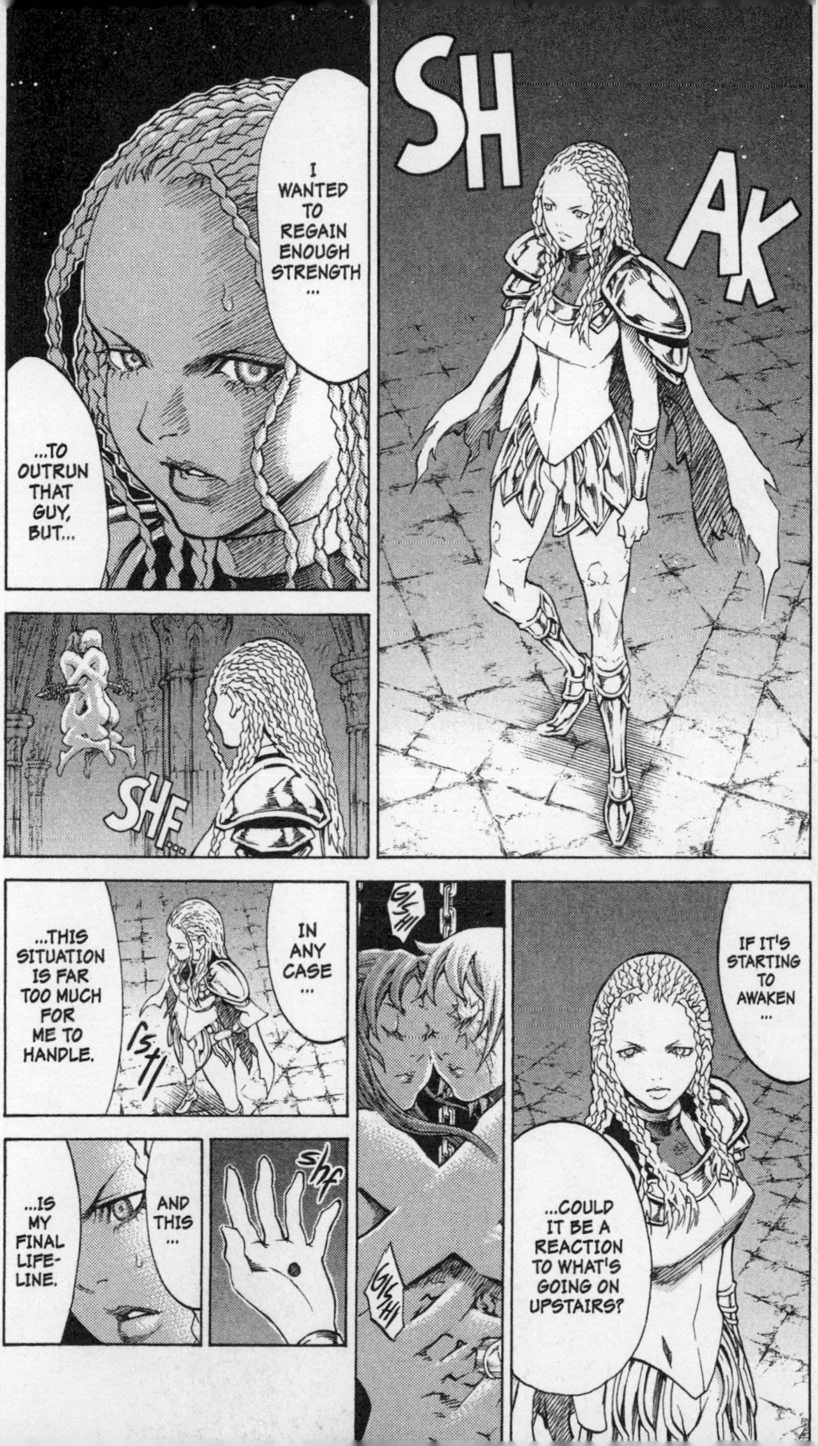
SH
AK
I WANTED TO REGAIN ENOUGH STRENGTH ...
...TO OUTRUN THAT GUY, BUT...
SHF...
IF IT'S STARTING TO AWAKEN ...
...COULD IT BE A REACTION TO WHAT'S GOING ON UPSTAIRS?
GISHI
GISHI
IN ANY CASE ...
...THIS SITUATION IS FAR TOO MUCH FOR ME TO HANDLE.
shf
AND THIS ...
...IS MY FINAL LIFE-LINE.

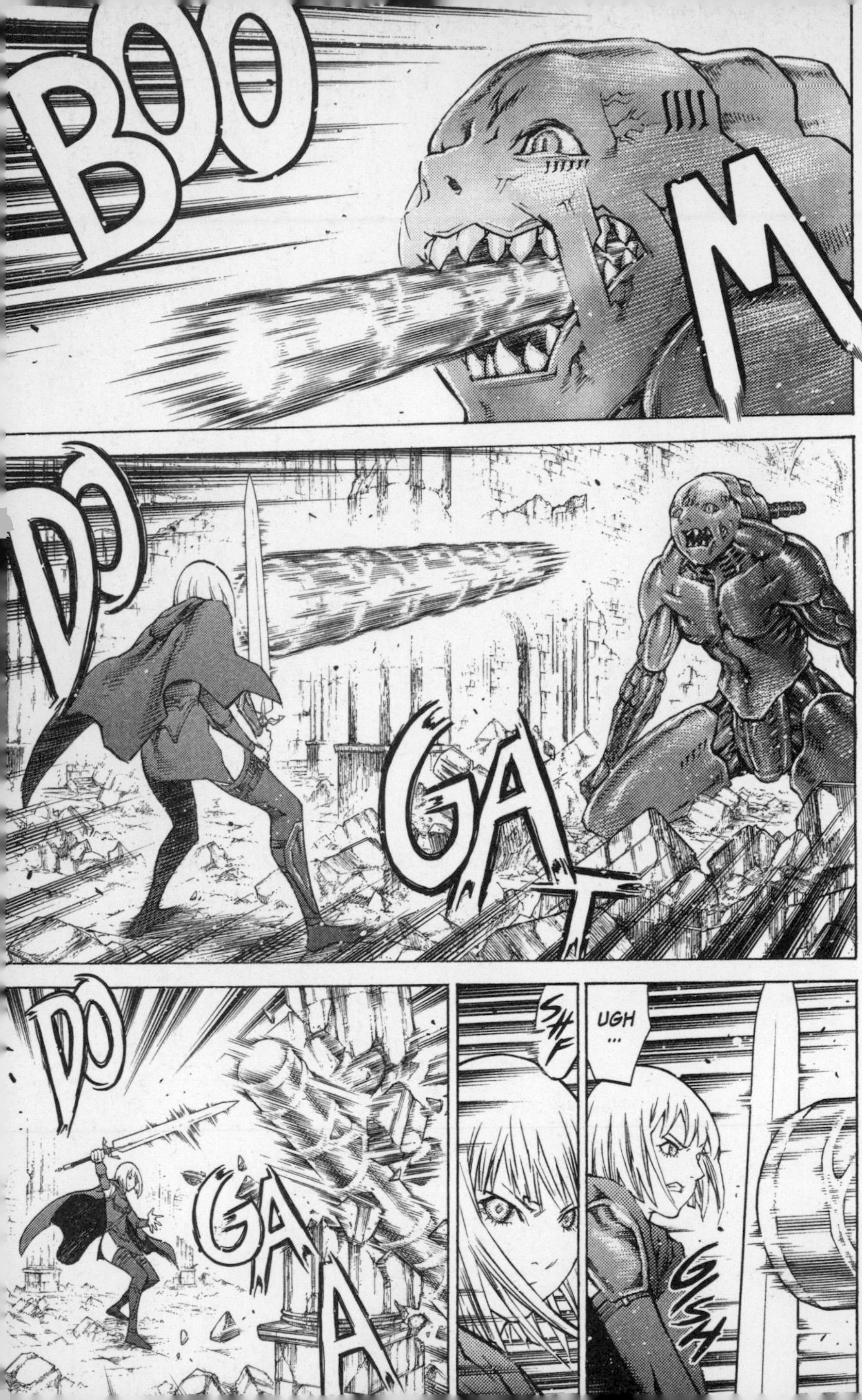
BOOOM
DOO
GAT
SHF
UGH...
GISH
DO
GAA

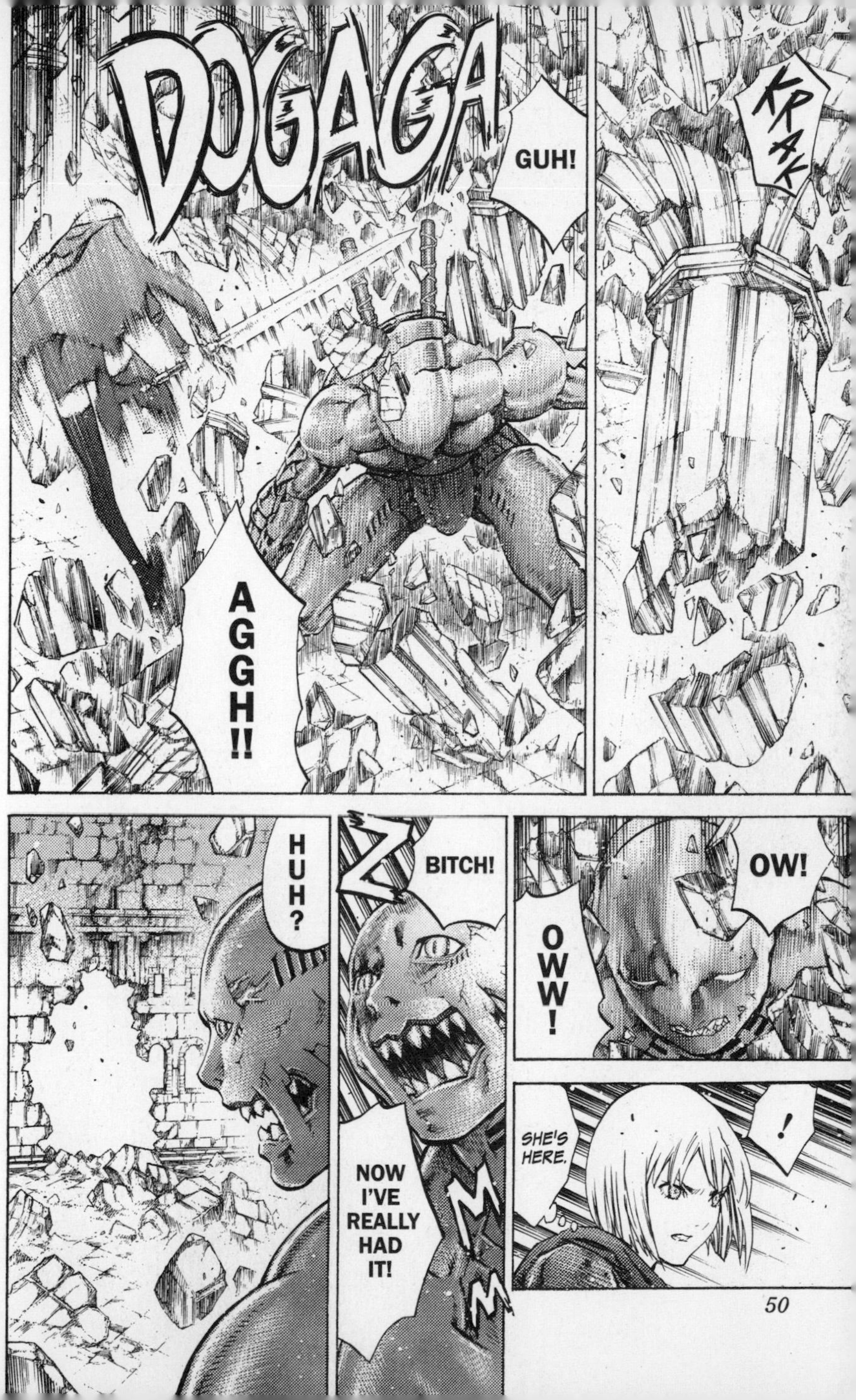
KRAK
DOGAGA
GUH!
AGGH!!
OW!
OWW!
!
SHE'S HERE.
Z
BITCH!
NOW I'VE REALLY HAD IT!
M
M
HUH?

READ THIS WAY

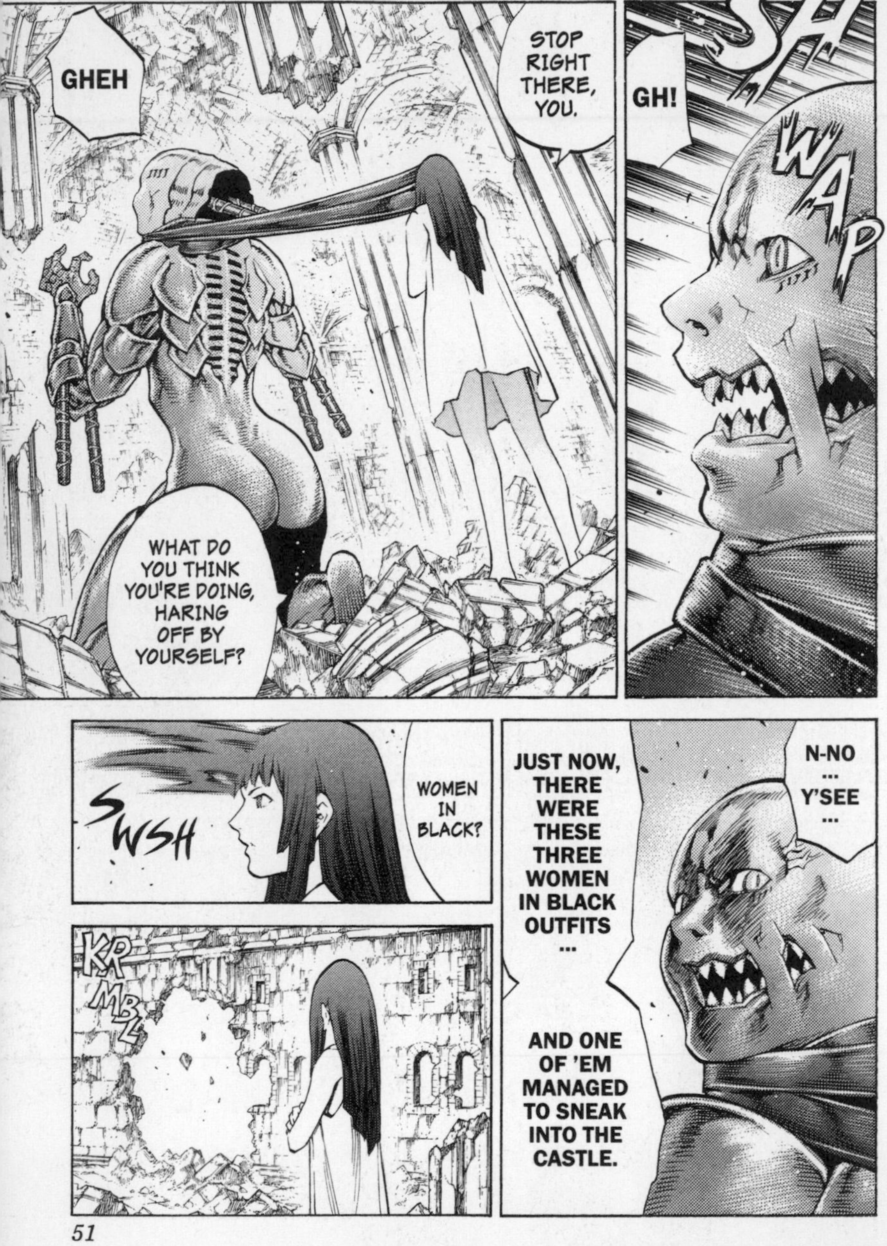
SH
WAP
GH!
STOP RIGHT THERE, YOU.
GHEH
WHAT DO YOU THINK YOU'RE DOING, HARING OFF BY YOURSELF?
N-NO ... Y'SEE ...
JUST NOW, THERE WERE THESE THREE WOMEN IN BLACK OUTFITS ...
AND ONE OF 'EM MANAGED TO SNEAK INTO THE CASTLE.
WOMEN IN BLACK?
SWSH
KRMBL

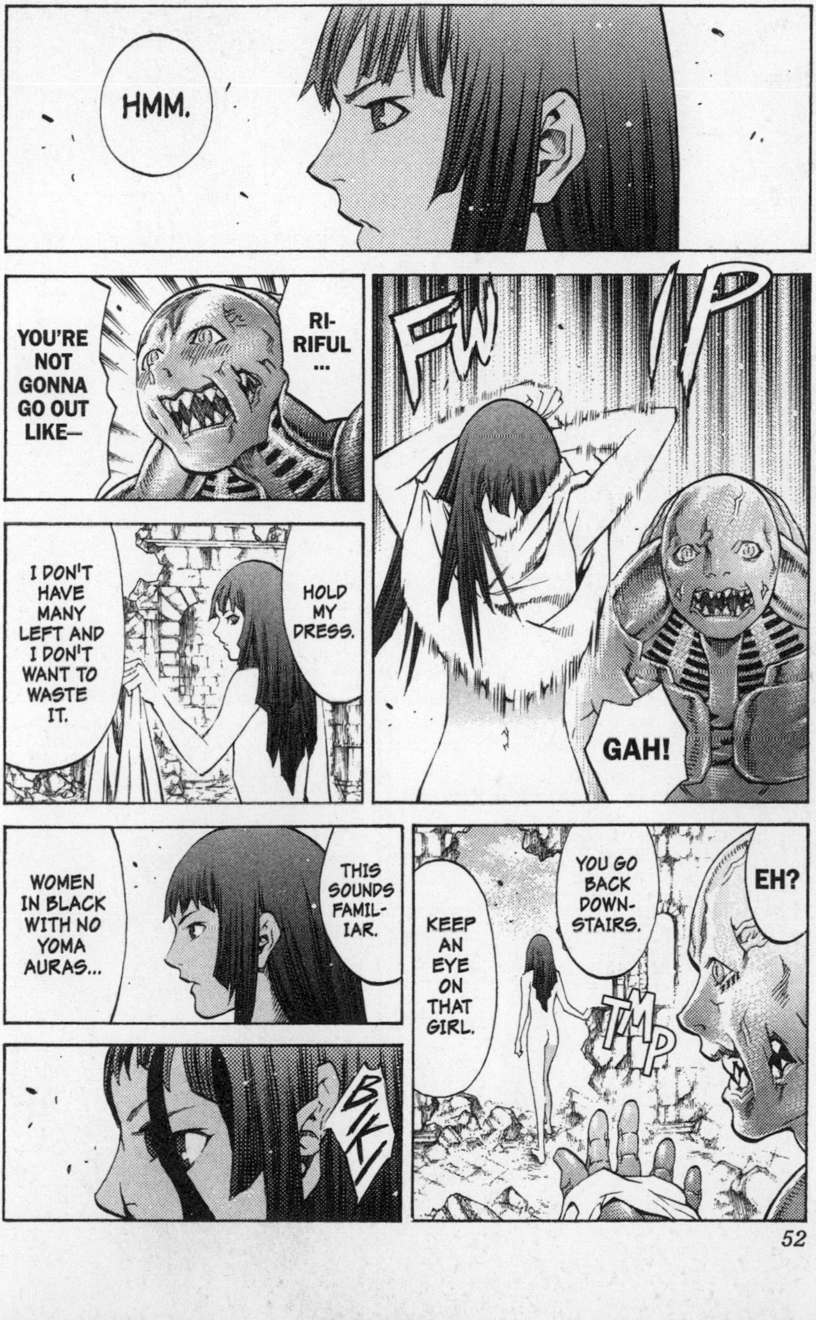
HMM.
FWIP
GAH!
RI-RIFUL...
YOU'RE NOT GONNA GO OUT LIKE—
HOLD MY DRESS.
I DON'T HAVE MANY LEFT AND I DON'T WANT TO WASTE IT.
EH?
YOU GO BACK DOWN-STAIRS.
KEEP AN EYE ON THAT GIRL.
TMP
THIS SOUNDS FAMIL-IAR.
WOMEN IN BLACK WITH NO YOMA AURAS...
BIKI

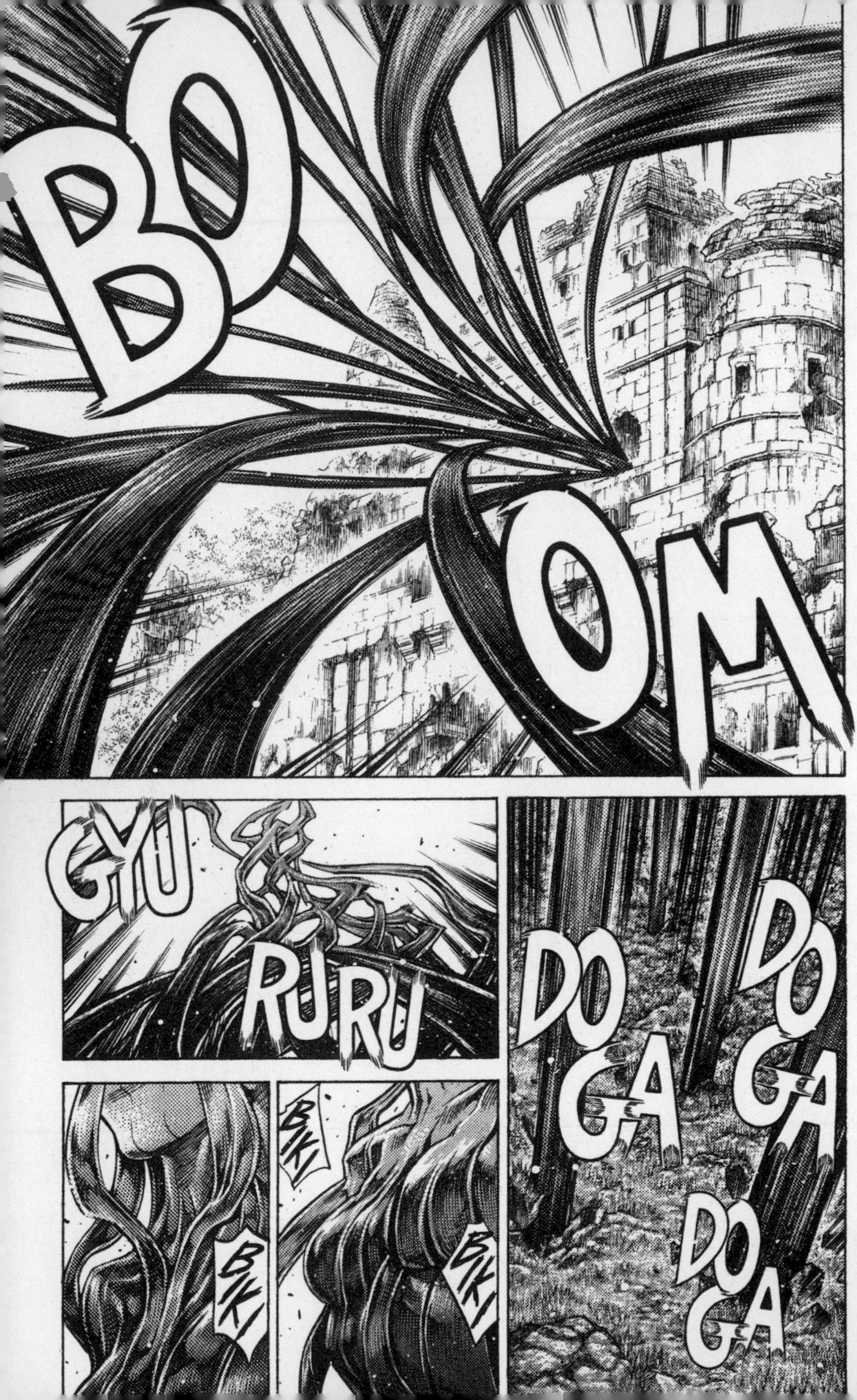
BOOM
DOGA
DOGA
DOGA
GYURURU
BIKI
BIKI
BIKI

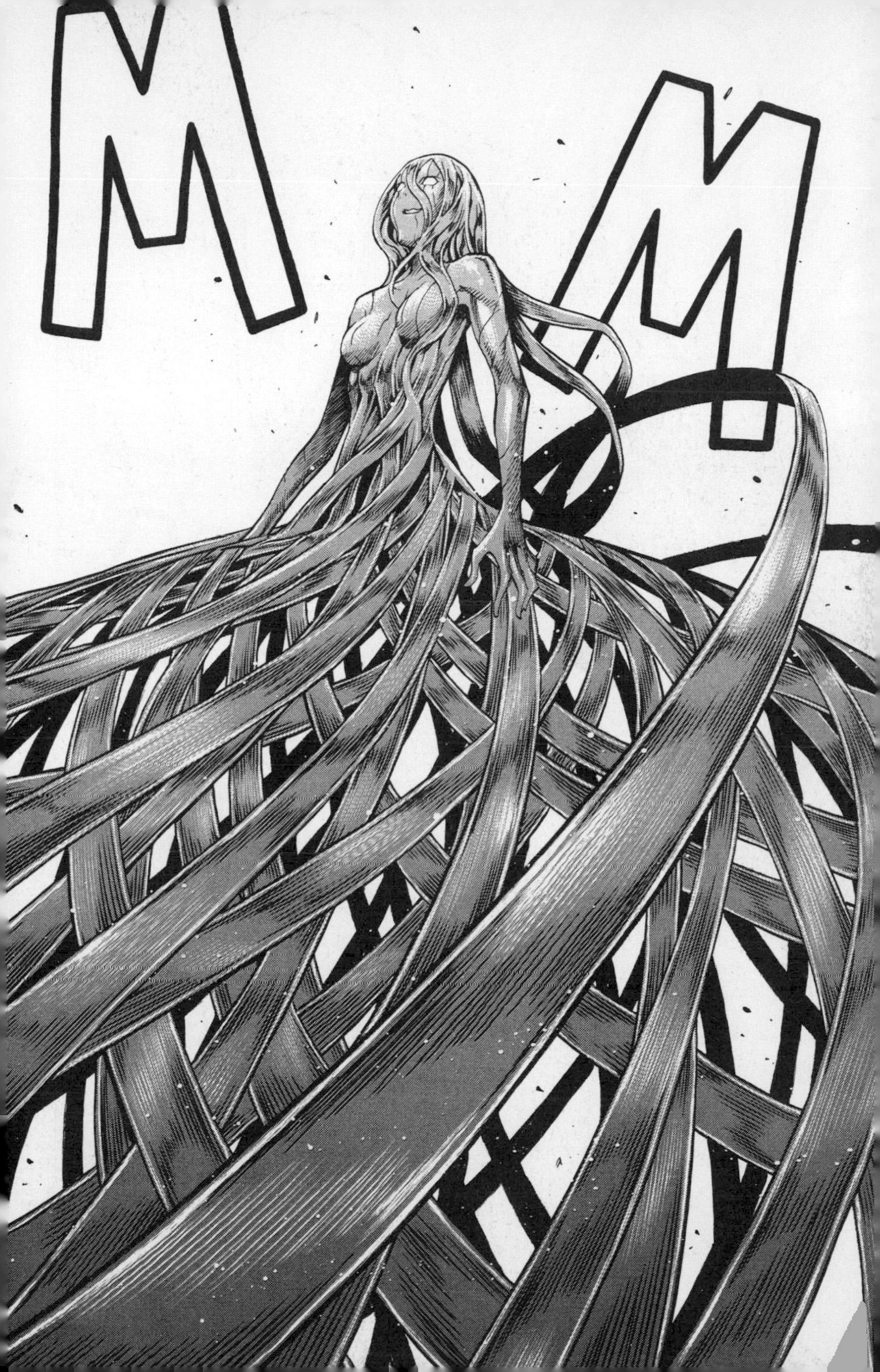
MM

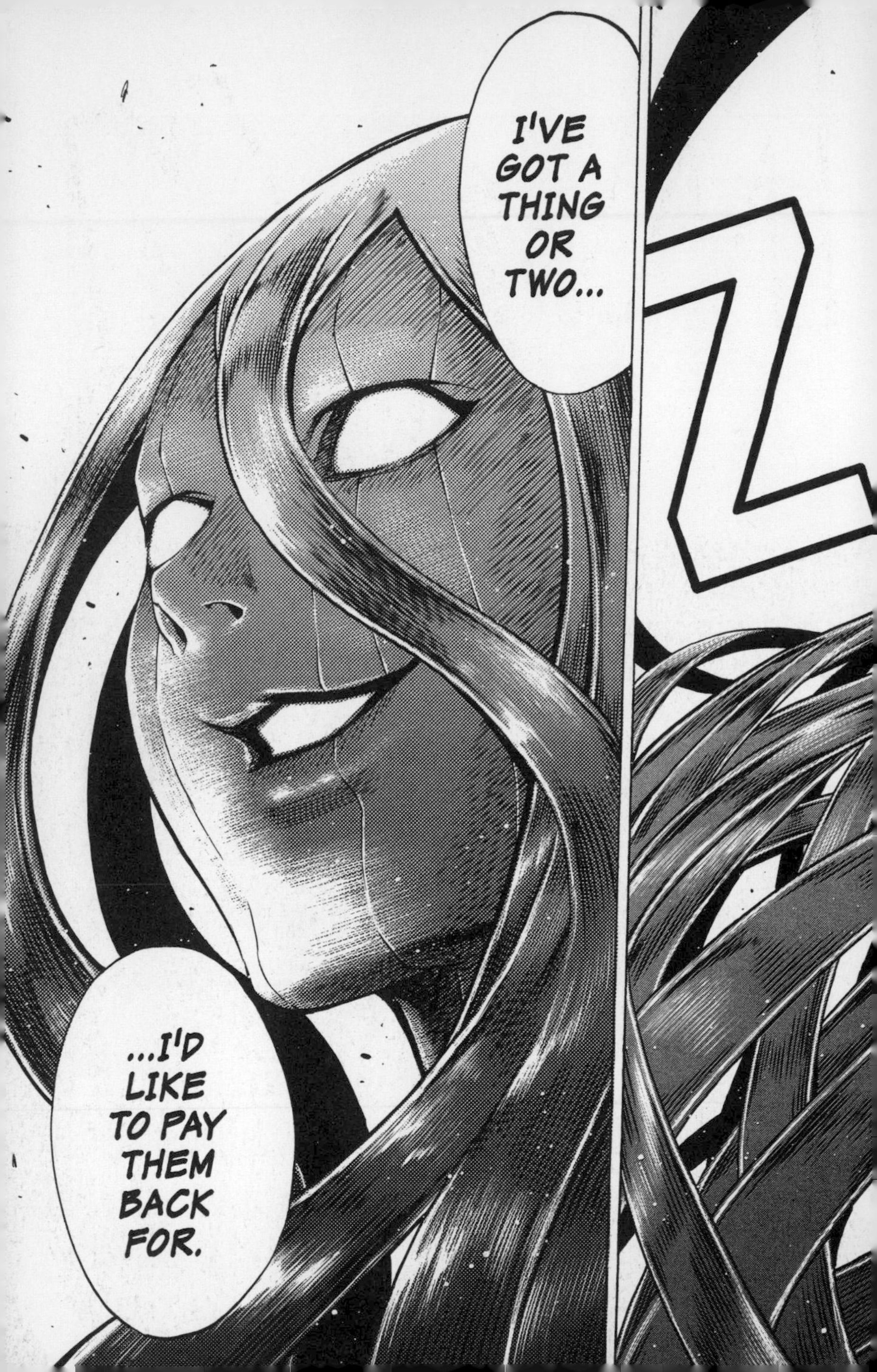
I'VE GOT A THING OR TWO...
...I'D LIKE TO PAY THEM BACK FOR.

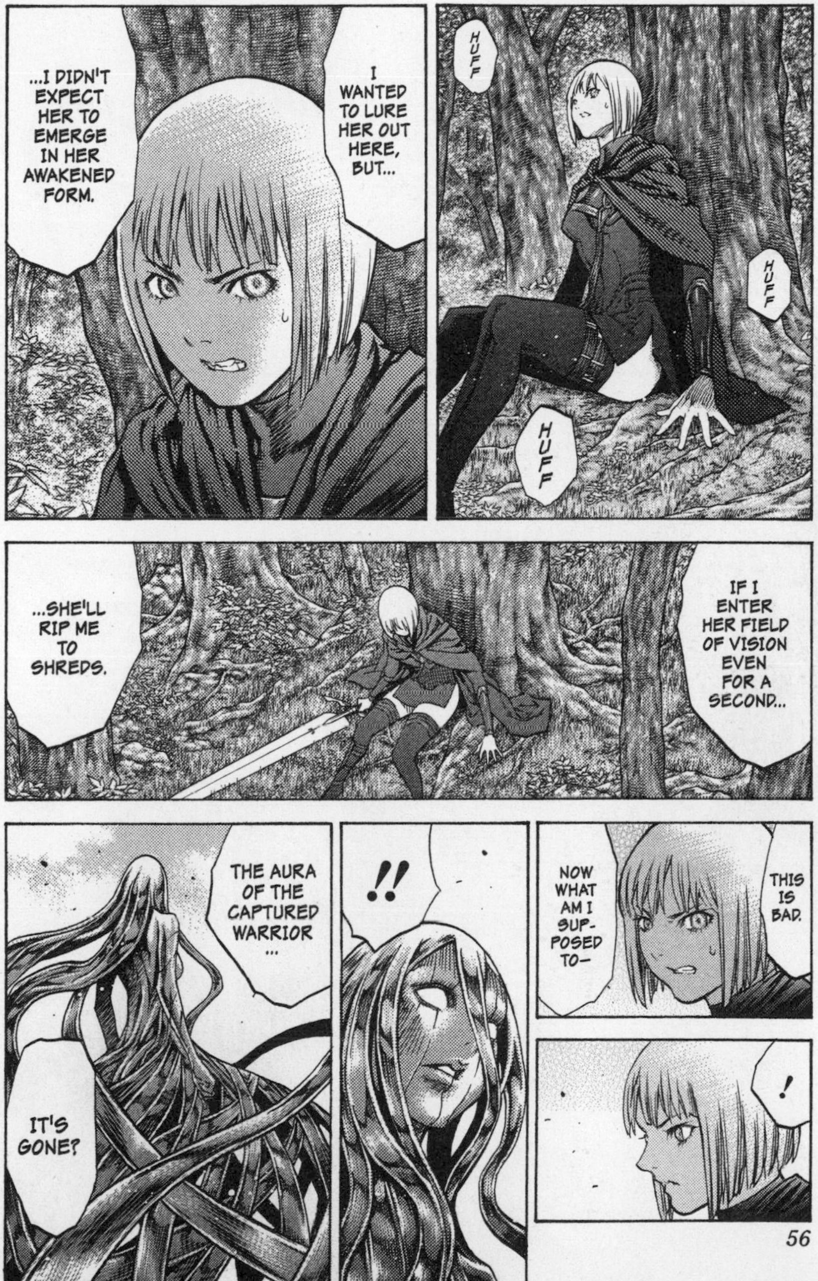
HUFF
HUFF
HUFF
I WANTED TO LURE HER OUT HERE, BUT...
...I DIDN'T EXPECT HER TO EMERGE IN HER AWAKENED FORM.
IF I ENTER HER FIELD OF VISION EVEN FOR A SECOND...
...SHE'LL RIP ME TO SHREDS.
THIS IS BAD.
NOW WHAT AM I SUP-POSED TO—
!
!!
THE AURA OF THE CAPTURED WARRIOR ...
IT'S GONE?

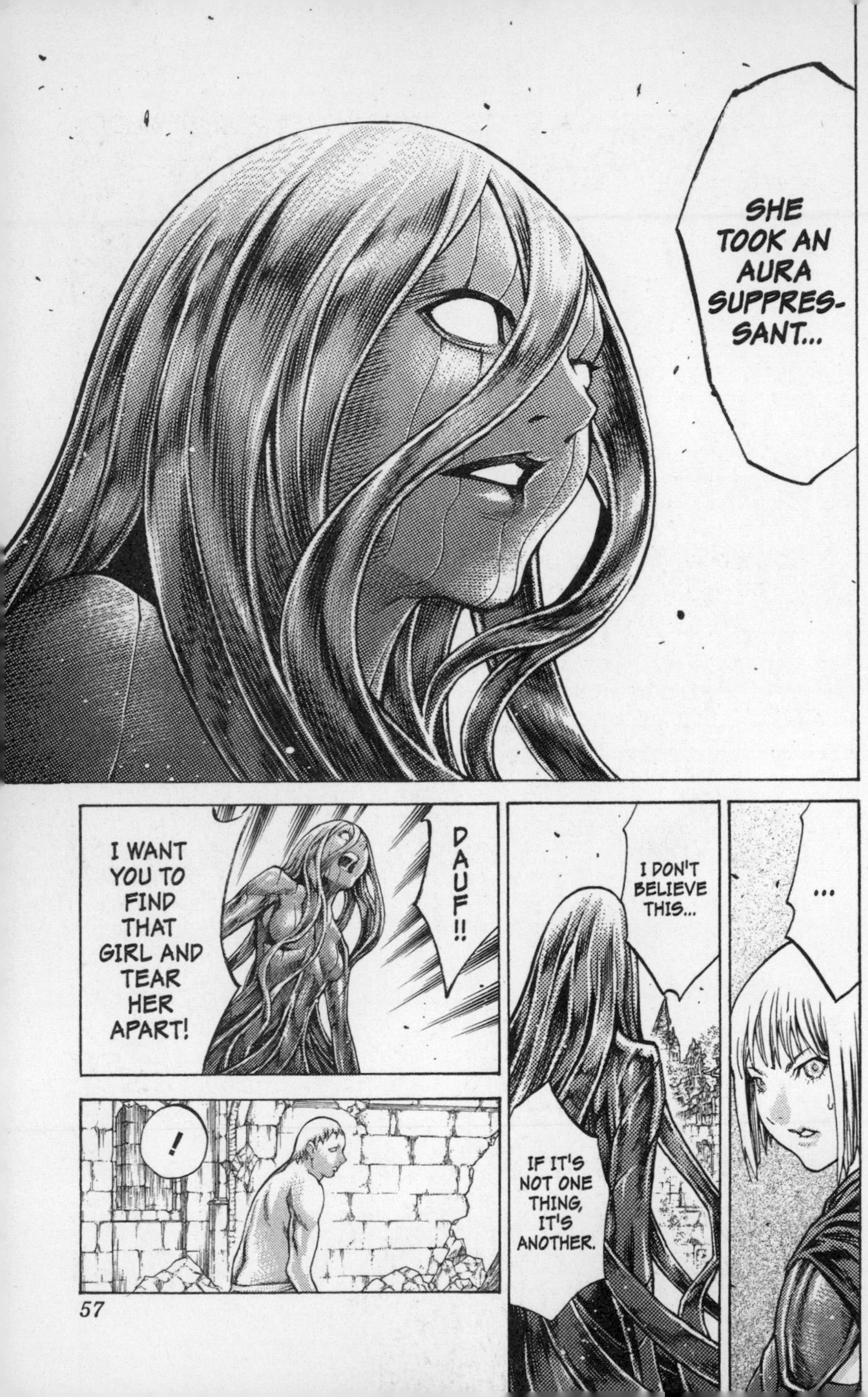
SHE TOOK AN AURA SUPPRES-SANT...
...
I DON'T BELIEVE THIS...
IF IT'S NOT ONE THING, IT'S ANOTHER.
DAUF!!
I WANT YOU TO FIND THAT GIRL AND TEAR HER APART!
!

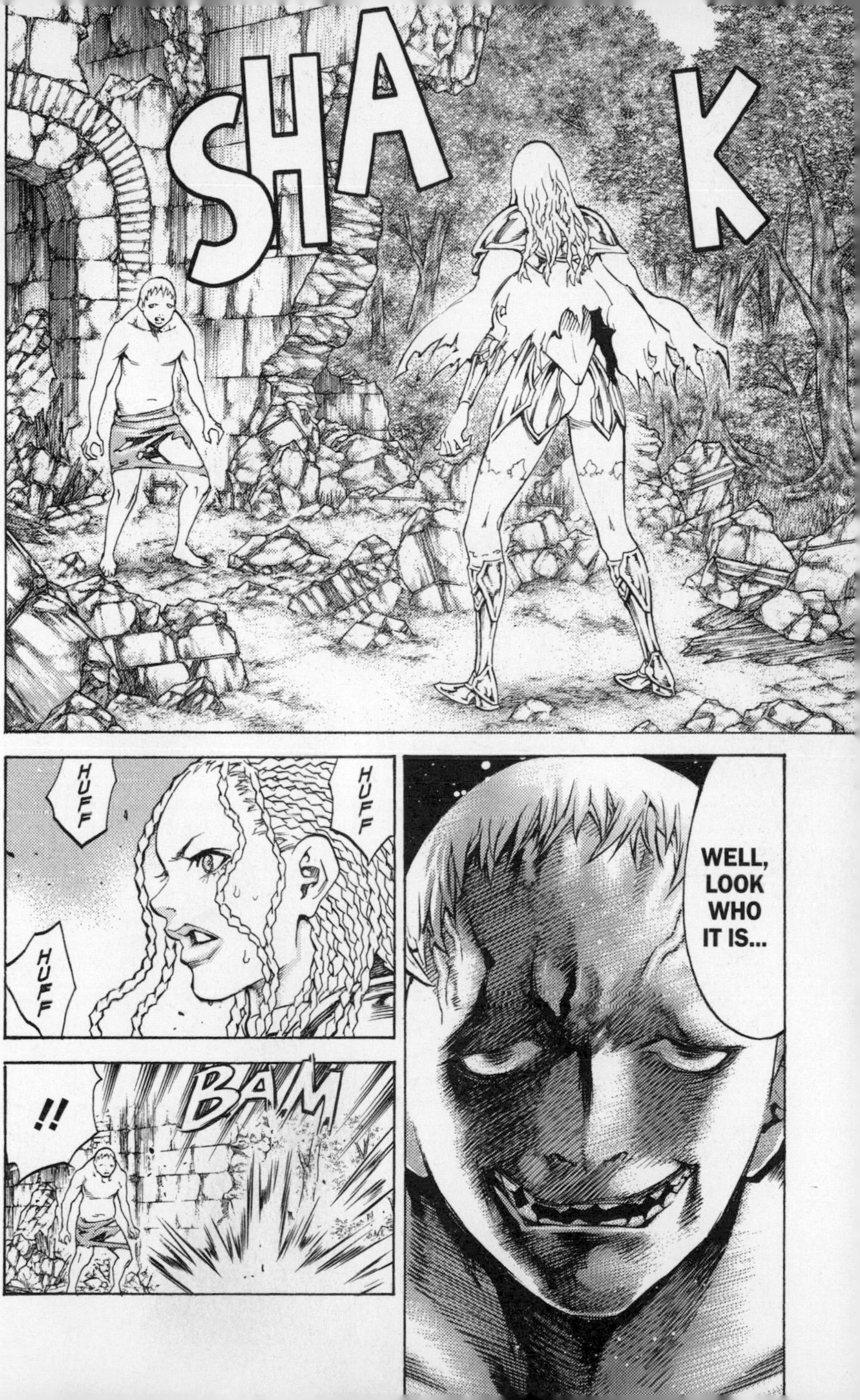
SHAK
WELL, LOOK WHO IT IS...
HUFF HUFF
HUFF HUFF
HUFF HUFF
!!
BAM

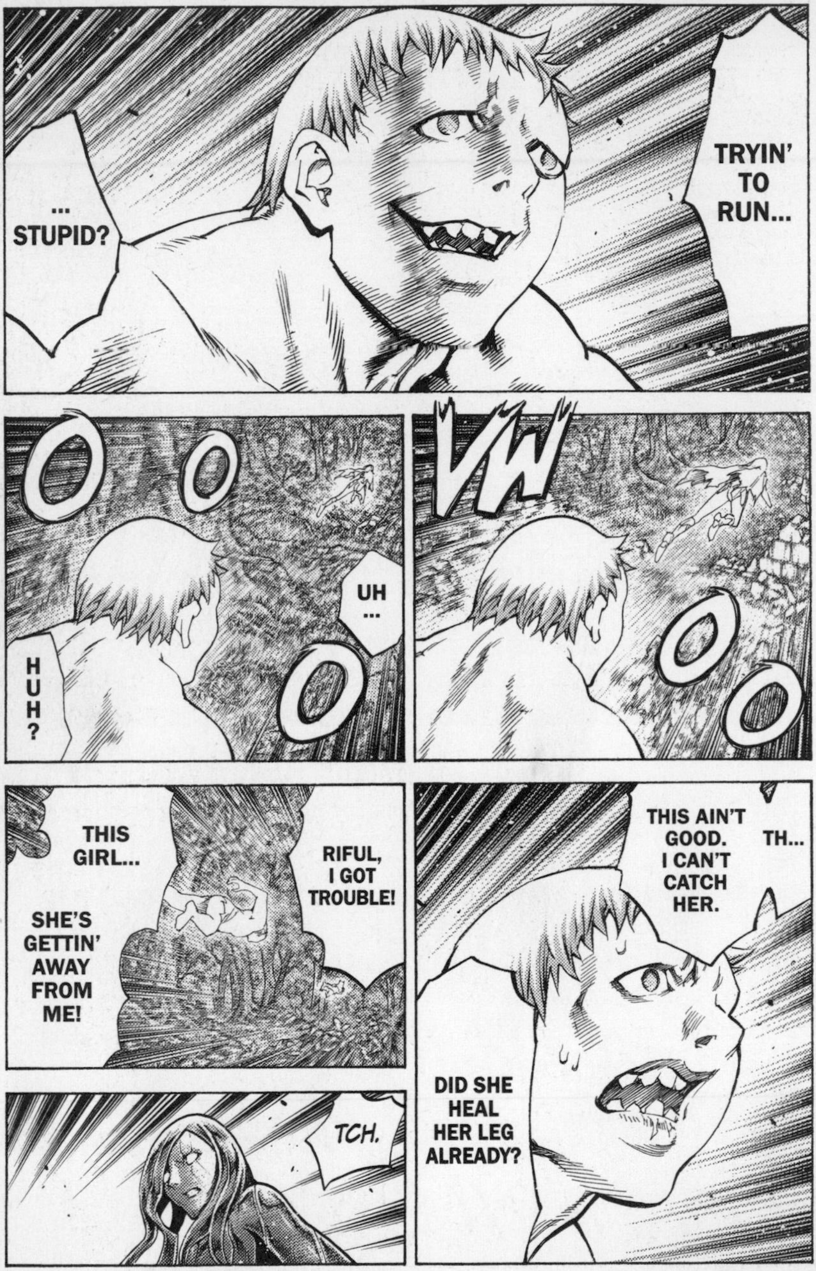
TRYIN' TO RUN...
... STUPID?
VW
OO
OO
OO
UH ...
HUH?
O
TH...
THIS AIN'T GOOD. I CAN'T CATCH HER.
DID SHE HEAL HER LEG ALREADY?
RIFUL, I GOT TROUBLE!
THIS GIRL...
SHE'S GETTIN' AWAY FROM ME!
TCH.

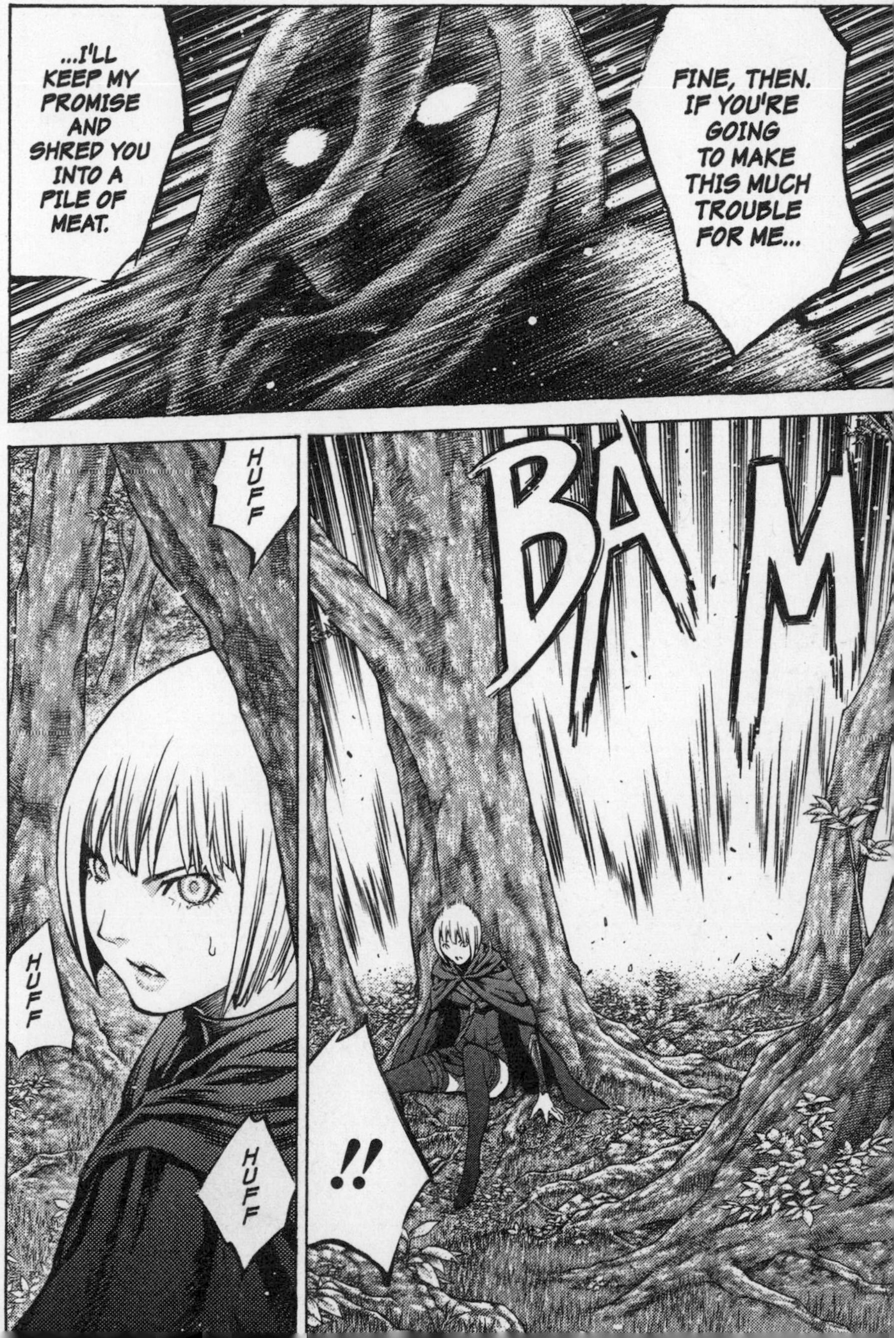
FINE, THEN. IF YOU'RE GOING TO MAKE THIS MUCH TROUBLE FOR ME...
...I'LL KEEP MY PROMISE AND SHRED YOU INTO A PILE OF MEAT.
BAM
!!
HUFF
HUFF
HUFF

READ THIS WAY

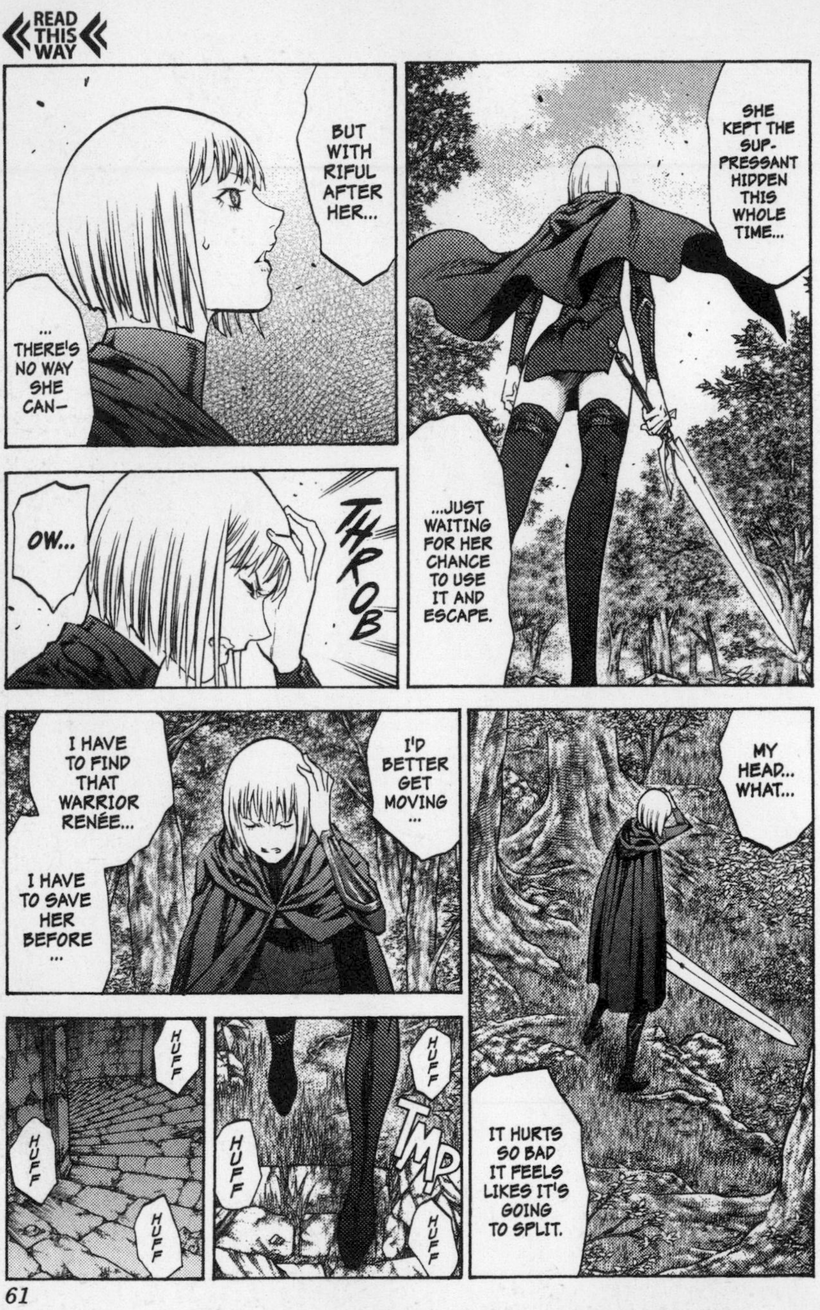
SHE KEPT THE SUP-PRESSANT HIDDEN THIS WHOLE TIME...
...JUST WAITING FOR HER CHANCE TO USE IT AND ESCAPE.
BUT WITH RIFUL AFTER HER...
...THERE'S NO WAY SHE CAN—
THROB
OW...
MY HEAD... WHAT...
IT HURTS SO BAD IT FEELS LIKES IT'S GOING TO SPLIT.
I'D BETTER GET MOVING...
I HAVE TO FIND THAT WARRIOR RENÉE...
I HAVE TO SAVE HER BEFORE...
HUFF
TMP
HUFF
HUFF
HUFF
HUFF
HUFF

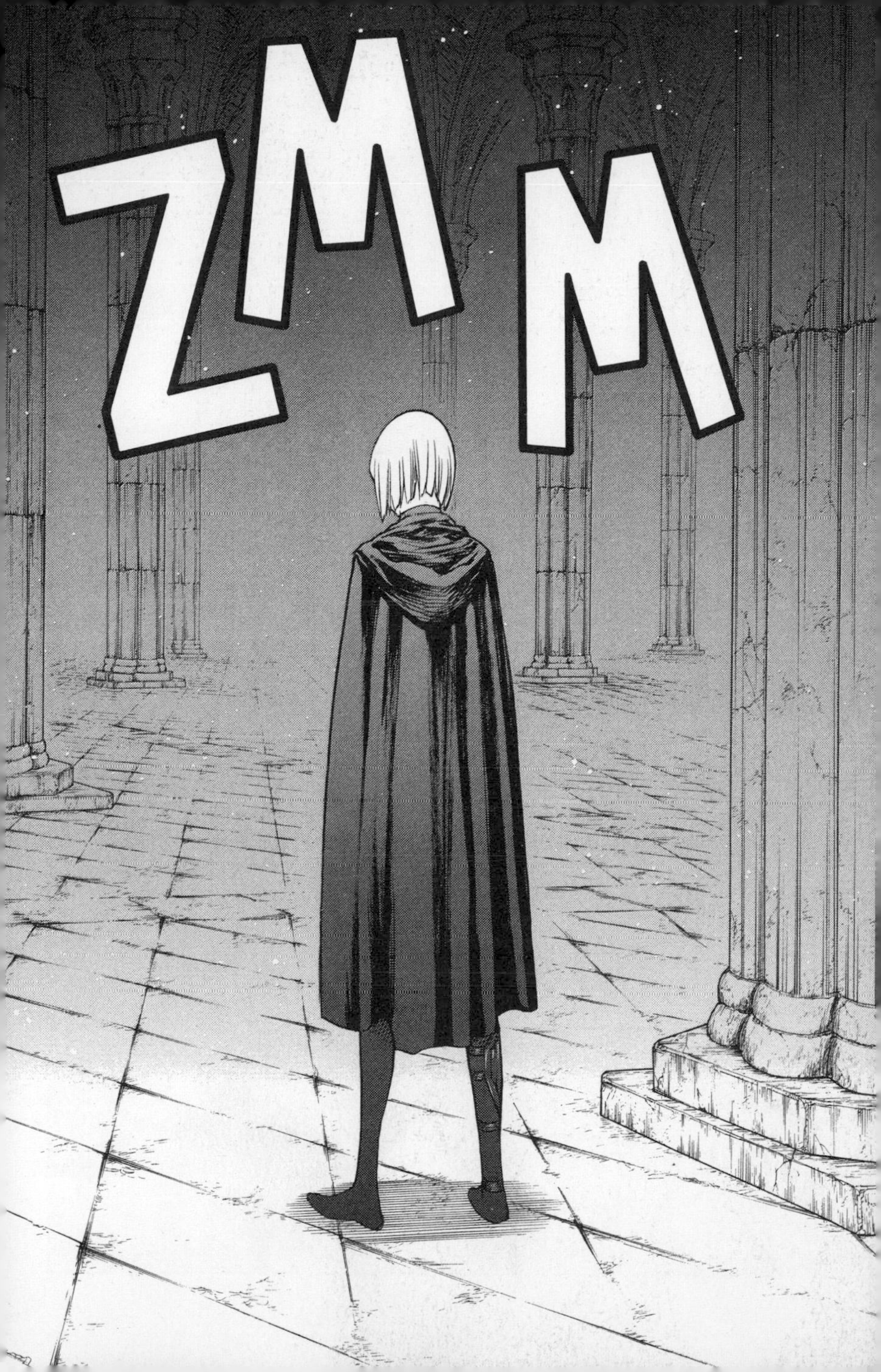
ZMM

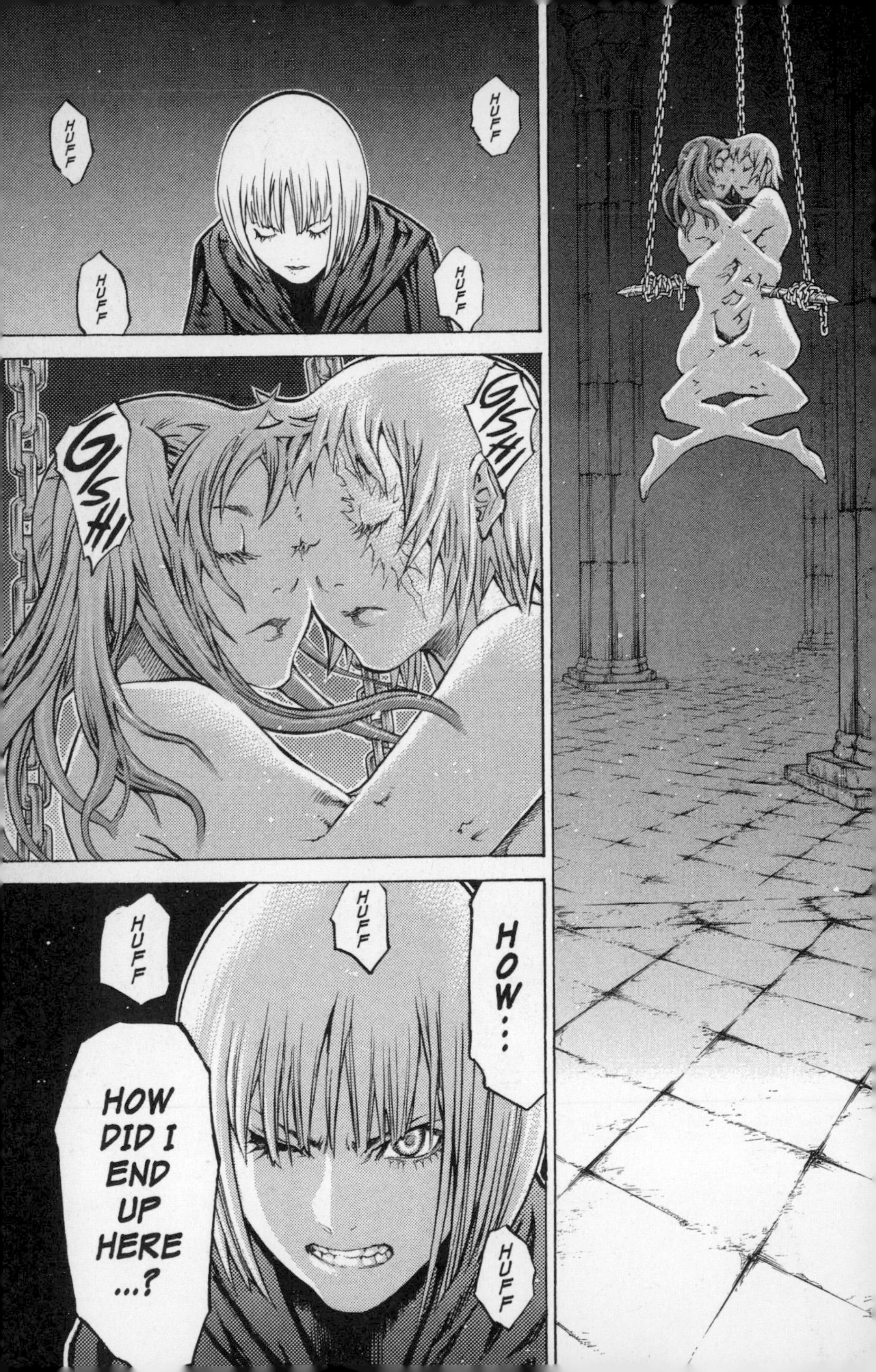
HUFF
HUFF
HUFF
HUFF
GISHI
GISHI
HUFF
HUFF
HOW...
HOW DID I END UP HERE ...?
HUFF

クレイモア
Claymore

SCENE 92: THE CLAWS OF MEMORY, PART 3

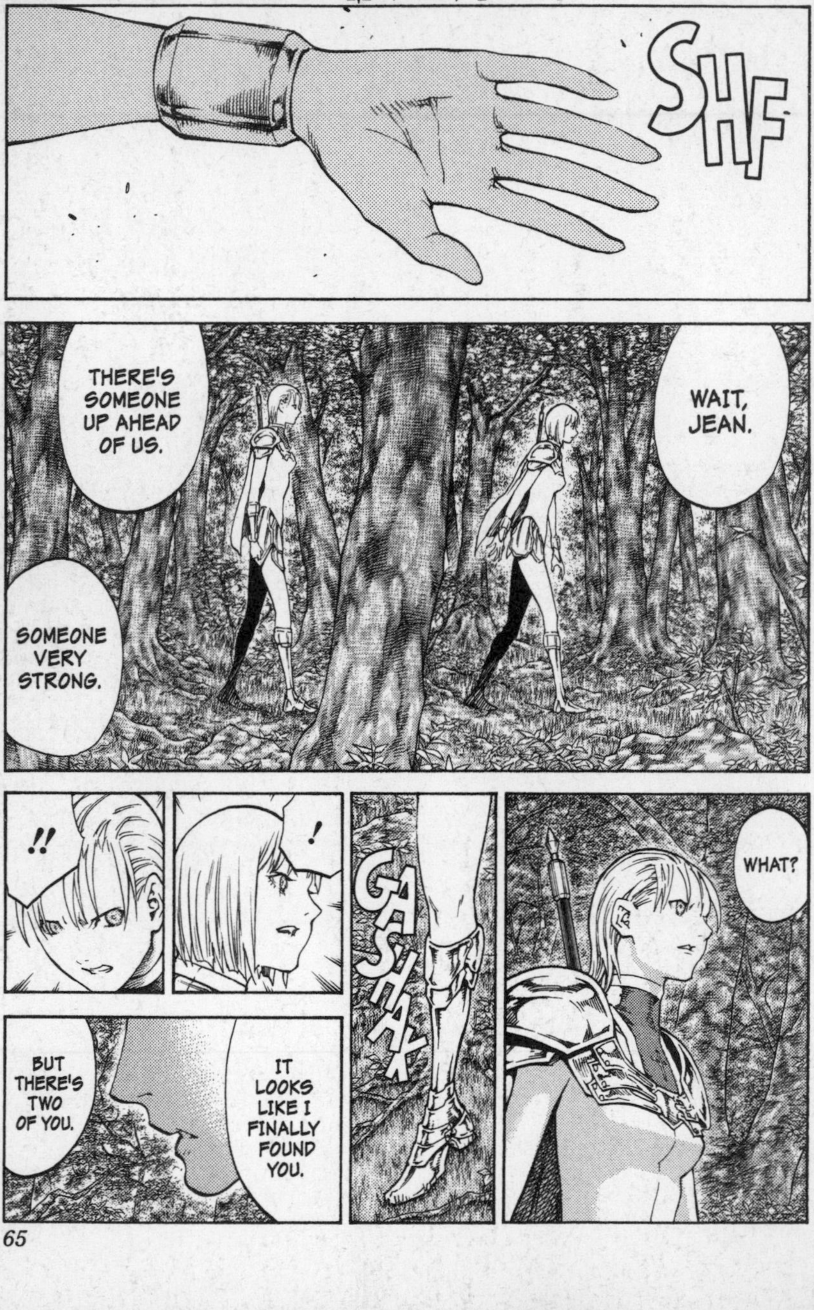
SHF
WAIT, JEAN.
THERE'S SOMEONE UP AHEAD OF US.
SOMEONE VERY STRONG.
WHAT?
GASHAK
!
!!
IT LOOKS LIKE I FINALLY FOUND YOU.
BUT THERE'S TWO OF YOU.

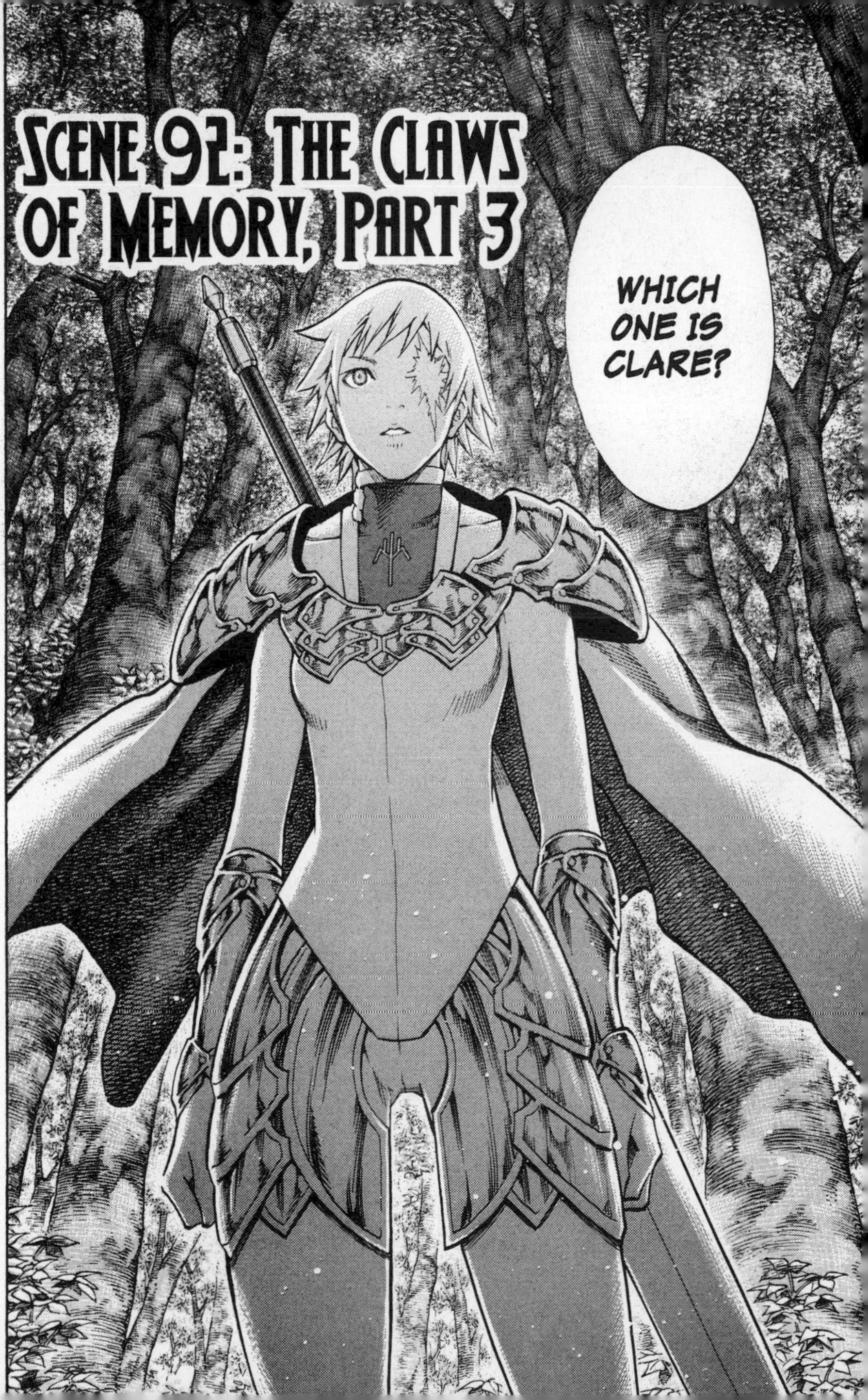
SCENE 92: THE CLAWS OF MEMORY, PART 3
WHICH ONE IS CLARE?

READ THIS WAY

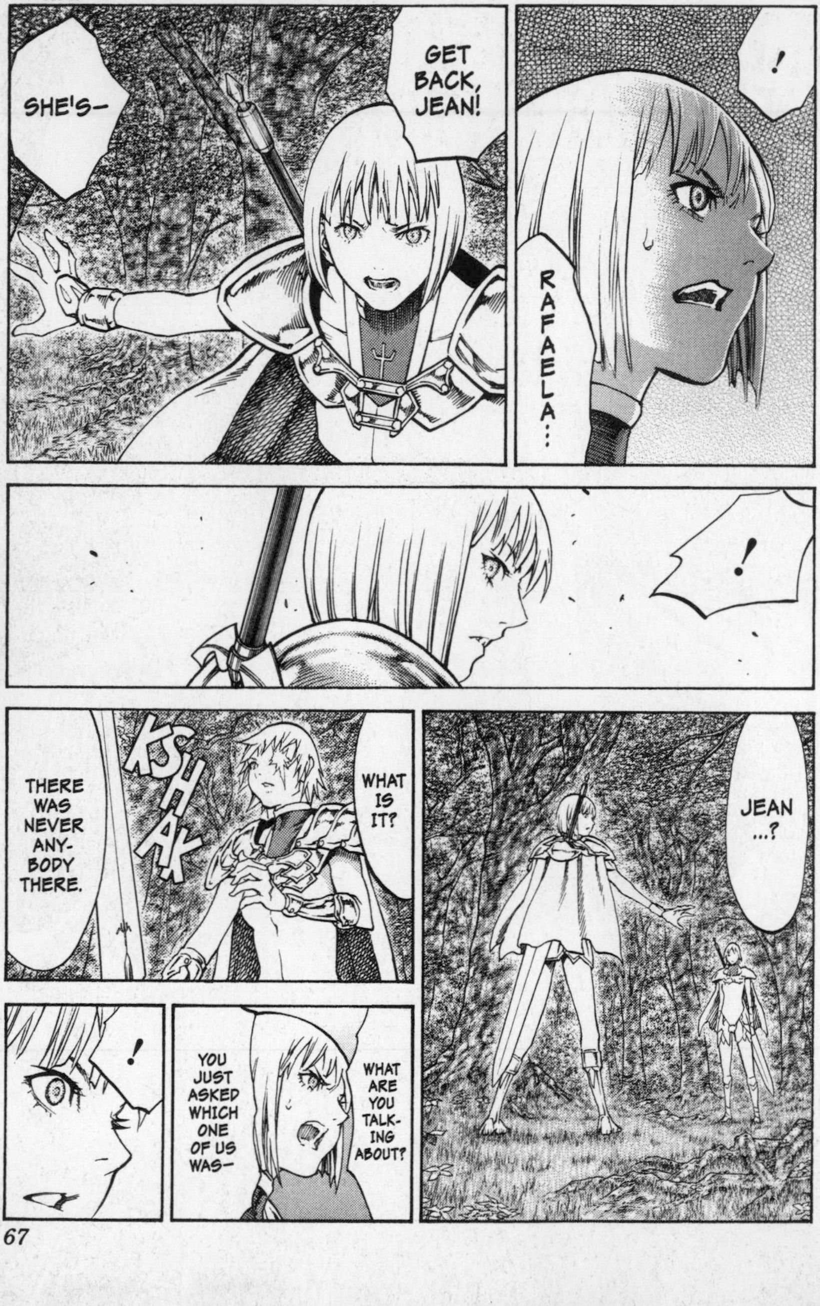
!
RAFAELA...
GET BACK, JEAN!
SHE'S—
!
JEAN ...?
WHAT IS IT?
KSHAK
THERE WAS NEVER ANY-BODY THERE.
WHAT ARE YOU TALK-ING ABOUT?
YOU JUST ASKED WHICH ONE OF US WAS—
!

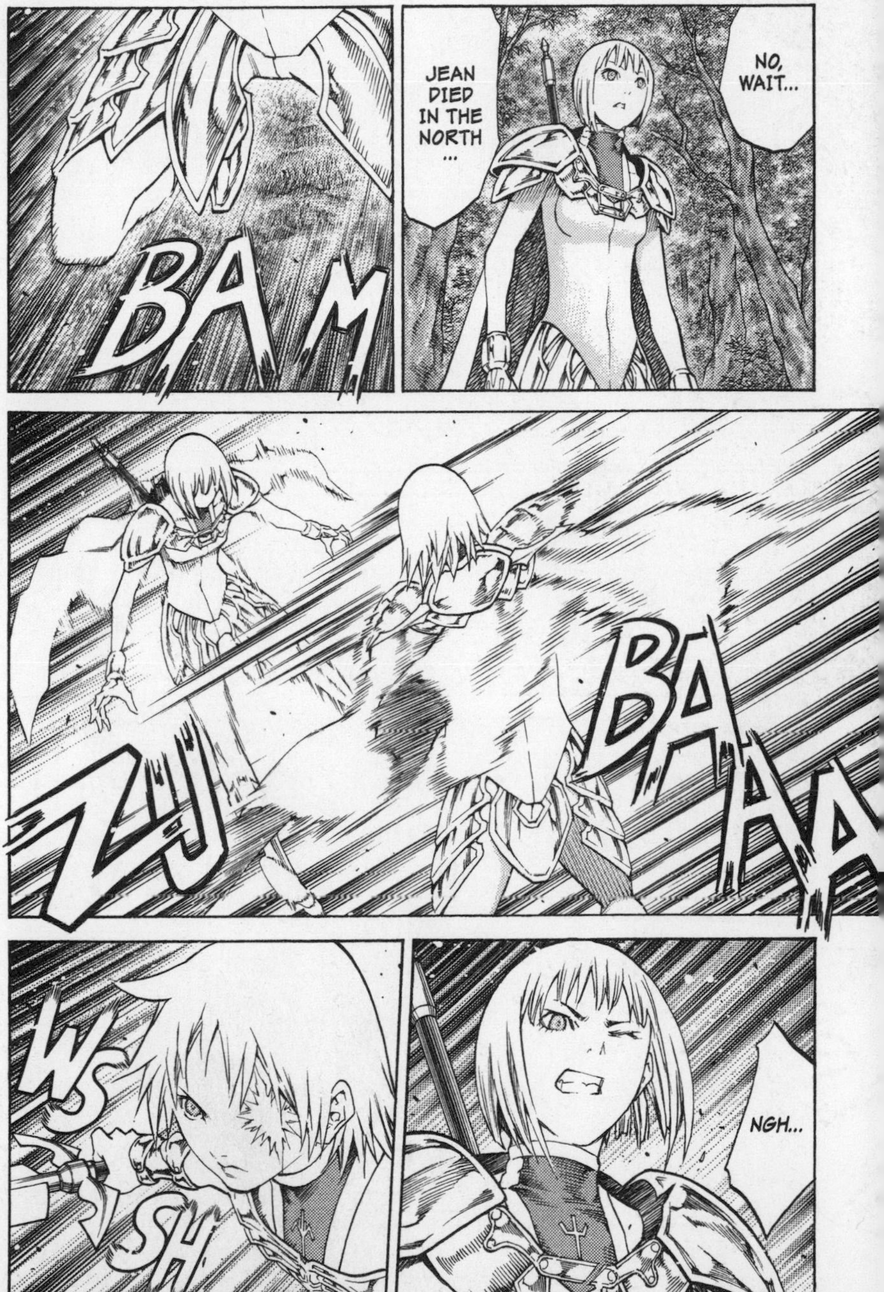
NO, WAIT...
JEAN DIED IN THE NORTH ...
BAM
BAAA
ZUJ
NGH...
WSSH

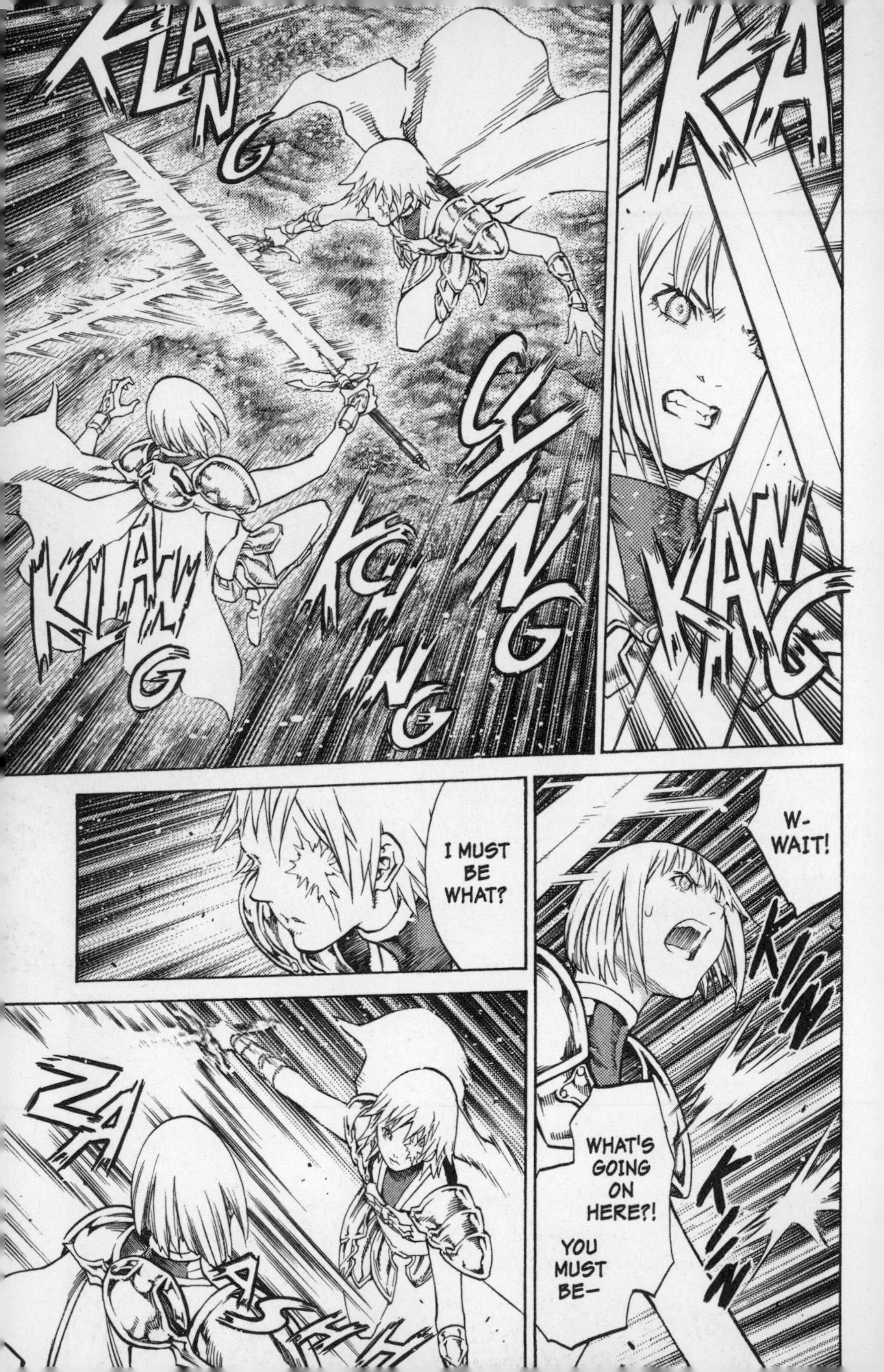
KLANG
W-WAIT!
WHAT'S GOING ON HERE?!
YOU MUST BE—
I MUST BE WHAT?

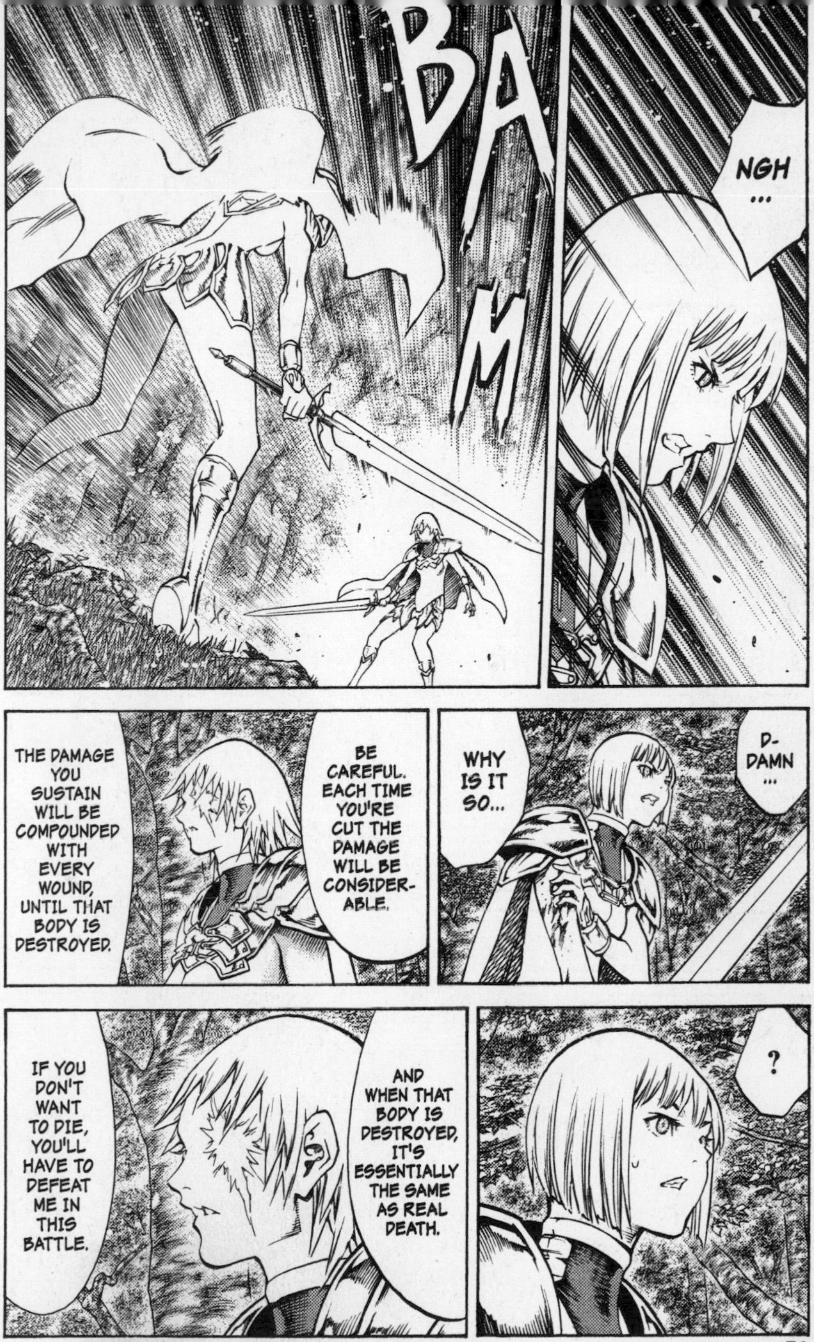
NGH ...
BAM
D-DAMN ...
WHY IS IT SO...
BE CAREFUL. EACH TIME YOU'RE CUT THE DAMAGE WILL BE CONSIDERABLE.
THE DAMAGE YOU SUSTAIN WILL BE COMPOUNDED WITH EVERY WOUND, UNTIL THAT BODY IS DESTROYED.
?
AND WHEN THAT BODY IS DESTROYED, IT'S ESSENTIALLY THE SAME AS REAL DEATH.
IF YOU DON'T WANT TO DIE, YOU'LL HAVE TO DEFEAT ME IN THIS BATTLE.

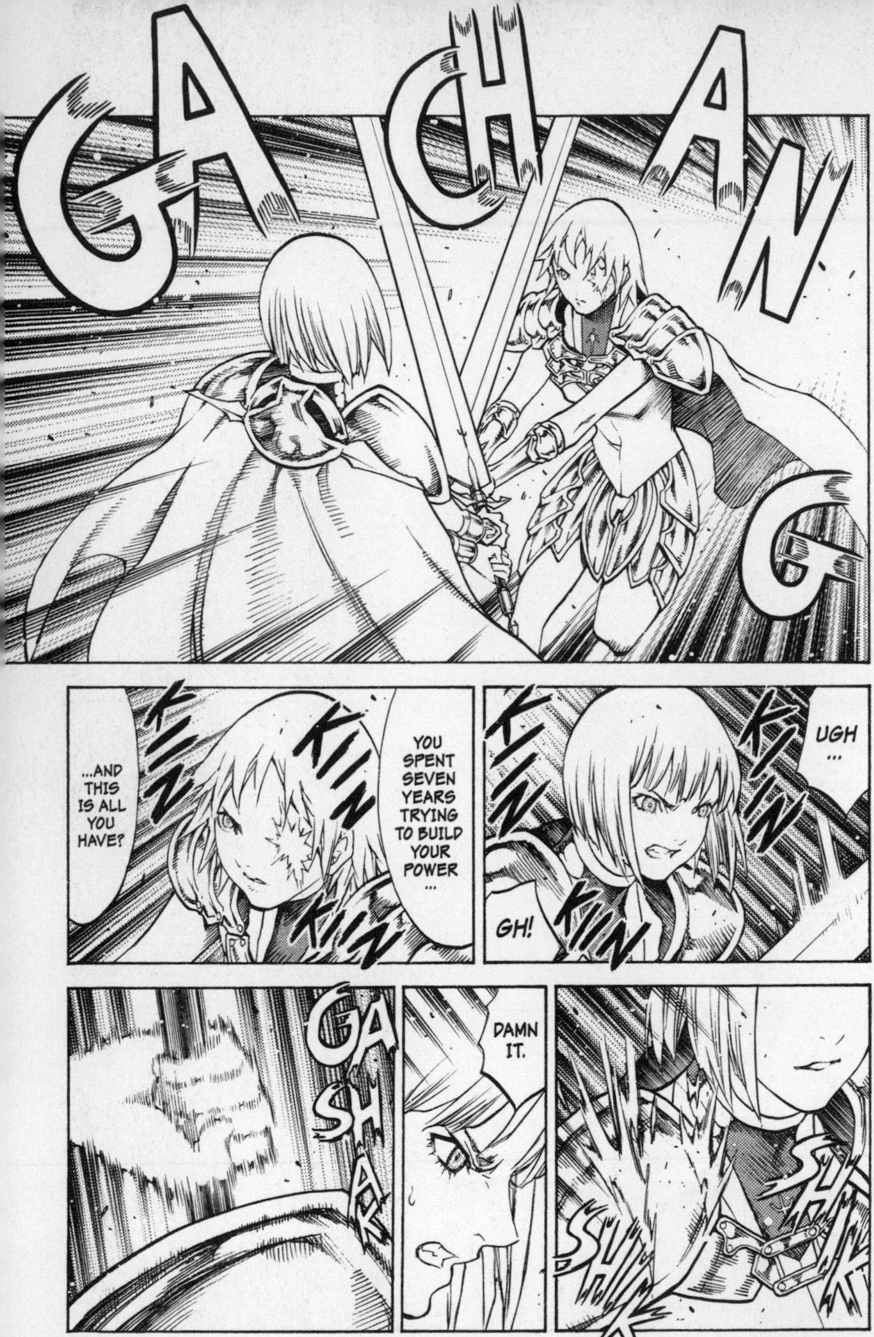
GACHAN
G
UGH...
KIIN
KIIN
GH!
YOU SPENT SEVEN YEARS TRYING TO BUILD YOUR POWER...
...AND THIS IS ALL YOU HAVE?
KIIN
KIIN
KIIN
SHK
SHK
DAMN IT.
GASHAK

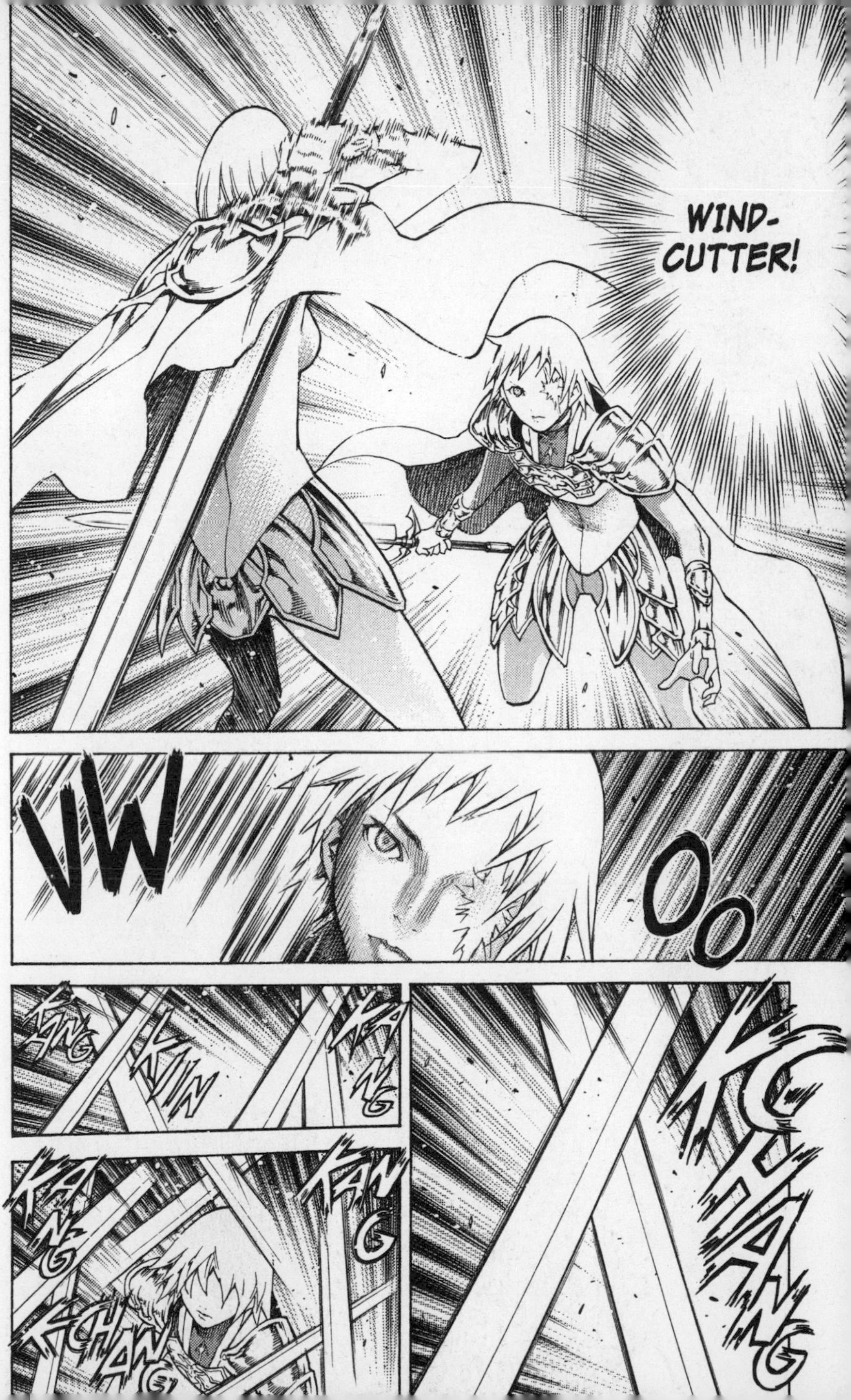
WIND-CUTTER!
VW
OO
KCHAANG
KANG
KIIN
KANG
KANG
KANG
KCHANG

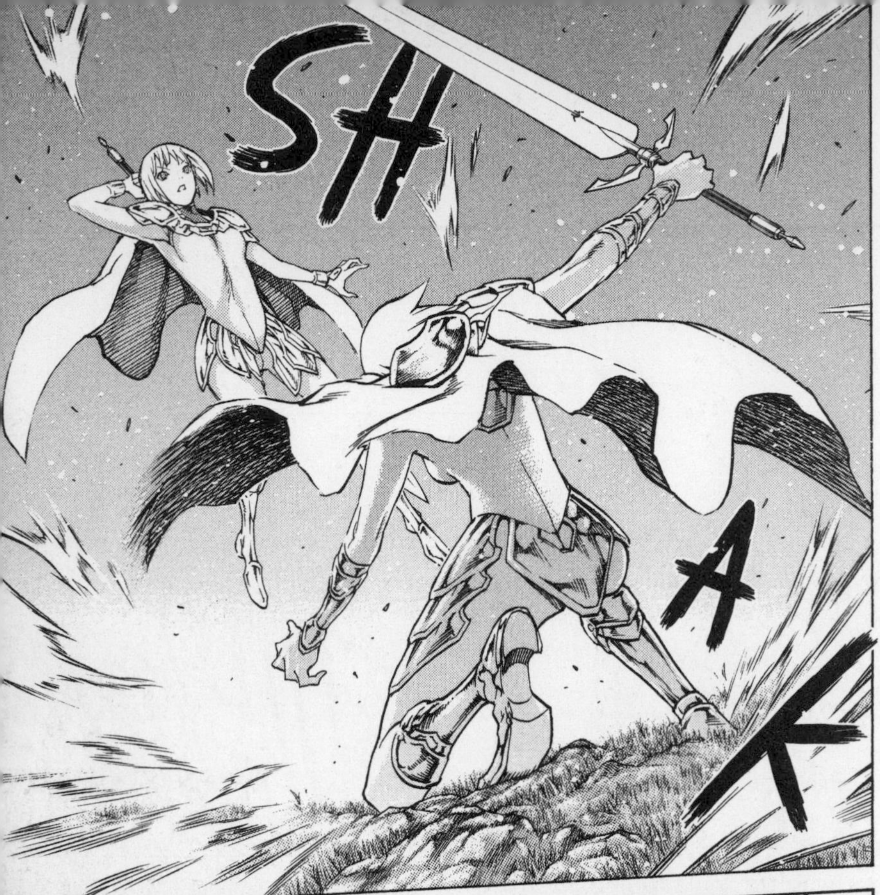
SHAK
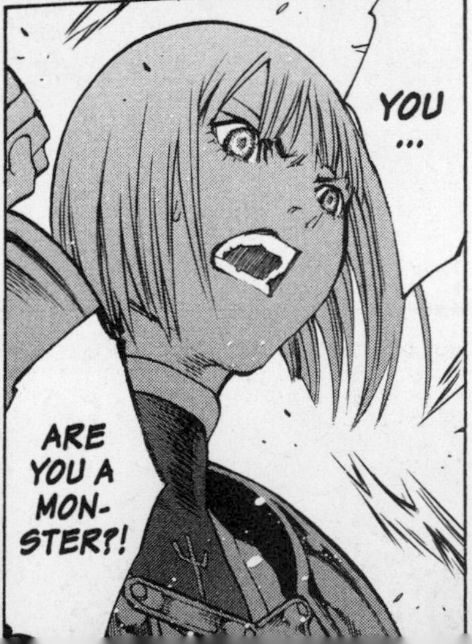
YOU ...
ARE YOU A MONSTER?!
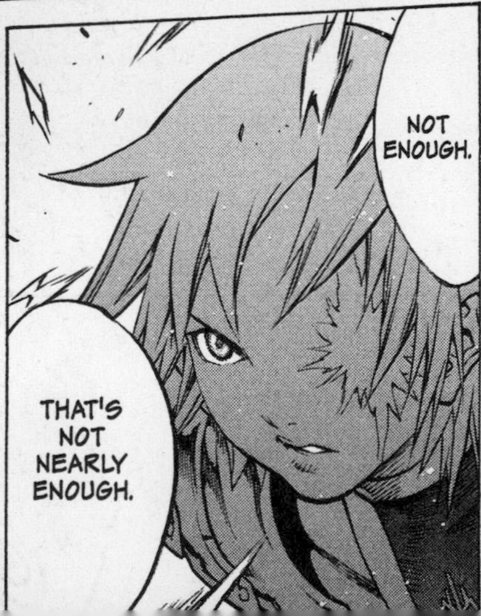
NOT ENOUGH.
THAT'S NOT NEARLY ENOUGH.

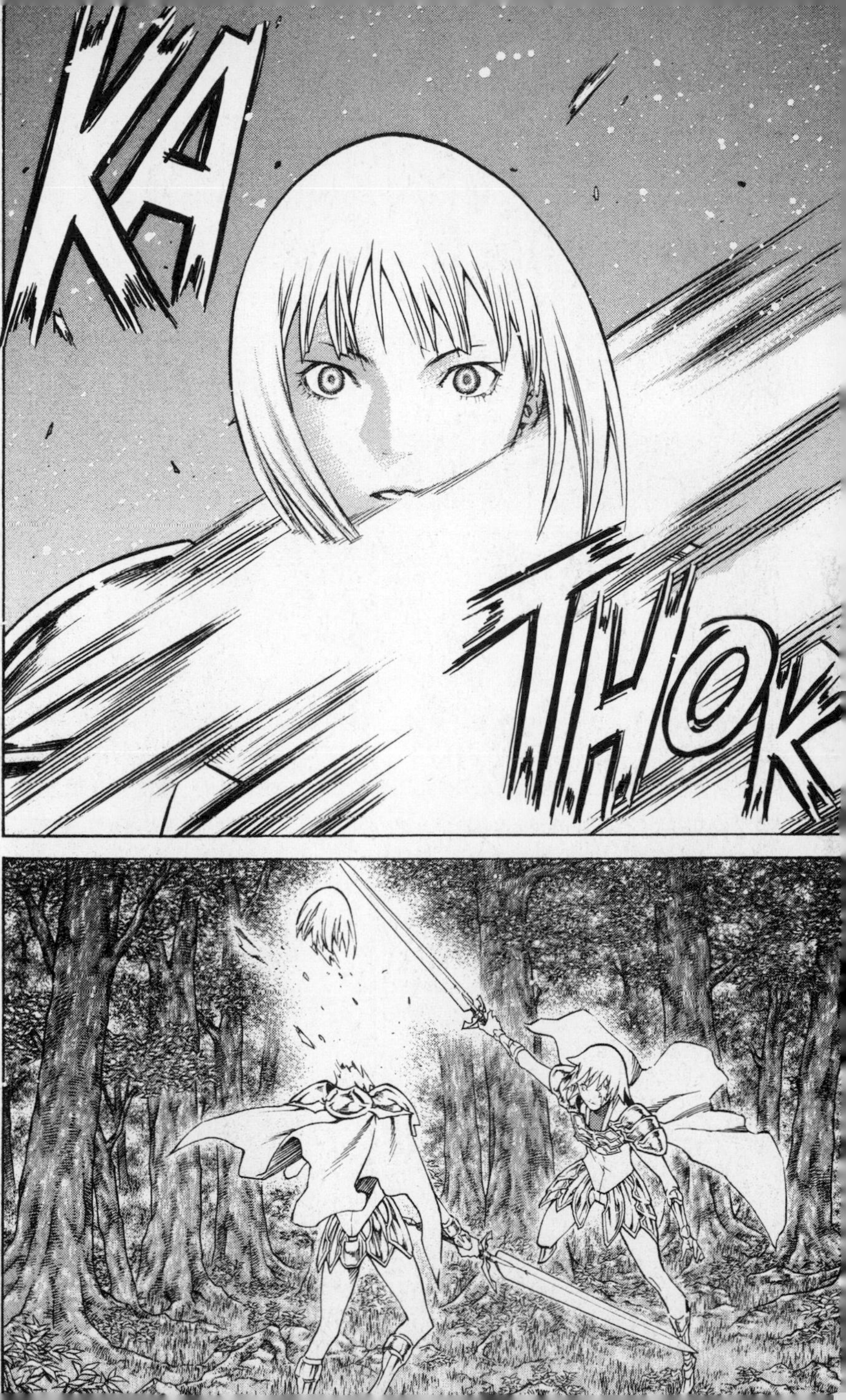
KA
THOK

READ THIS WAY

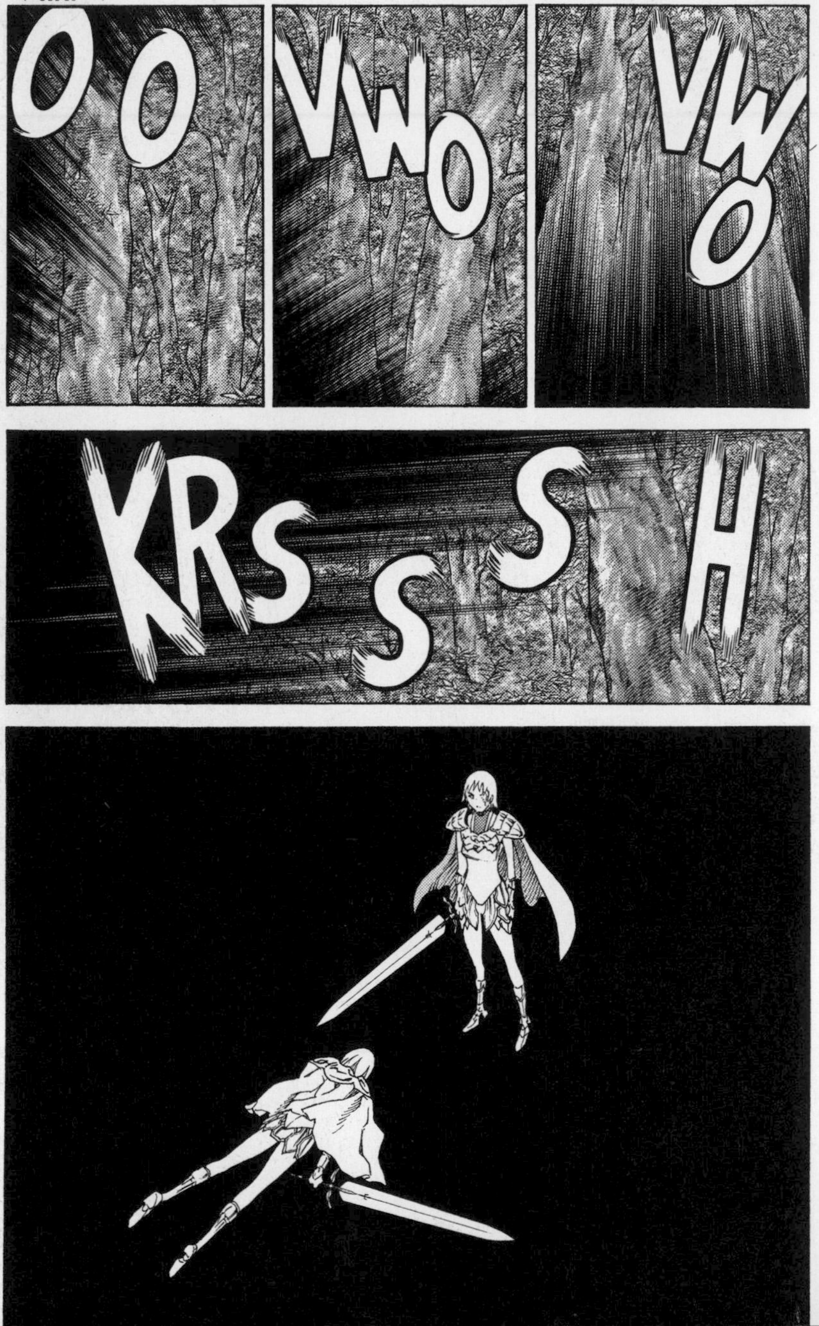
VWO
VWO
OO
KRSSSH

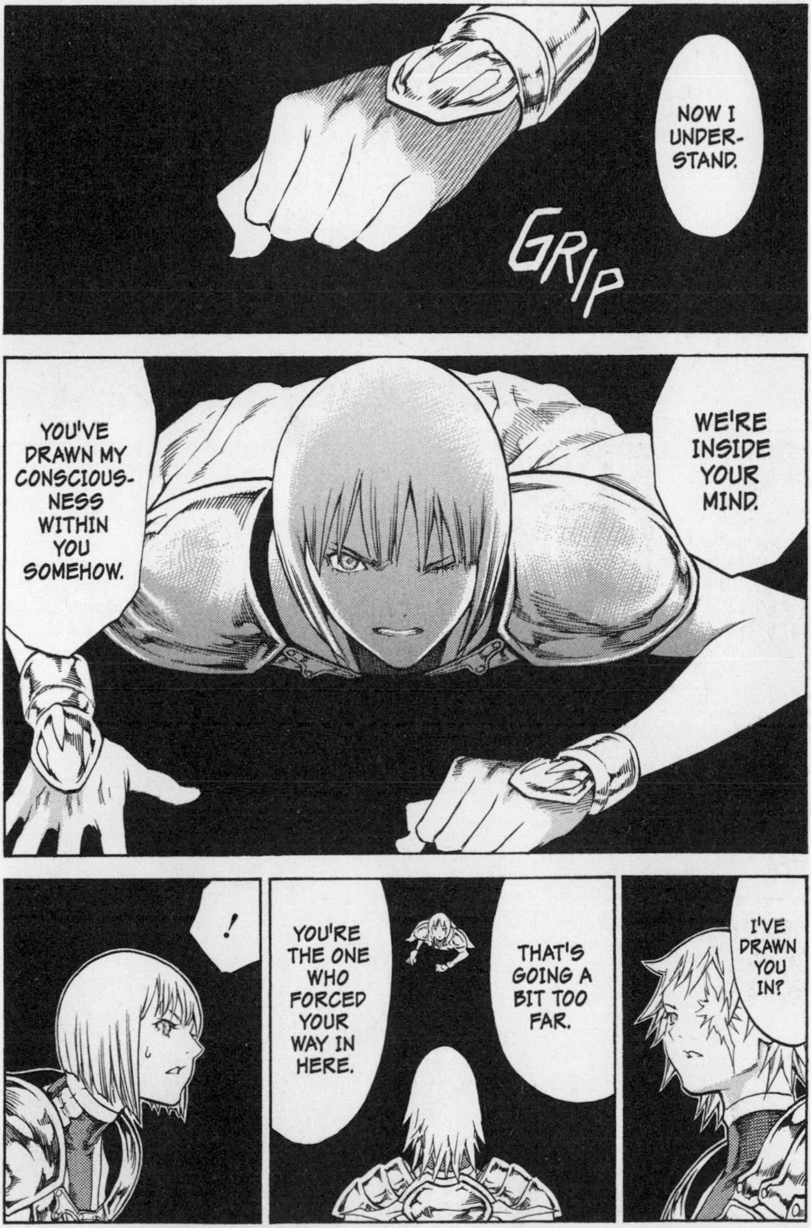
NOW I UNDER-STAND.
GRIP
WE'RE INSIDE YOUR MIND.
YOU'VE DRAWN MY CONSCIOUS-NESS WITHIN YOU SOMEHOW.
I'VE DRAWN YOU IN?
THAT'S GOING A BIT TOO FAR.
YOU'RE THE ONE WHO FORCED YOUR WAY IN HERE.
!

READ THIS WAY

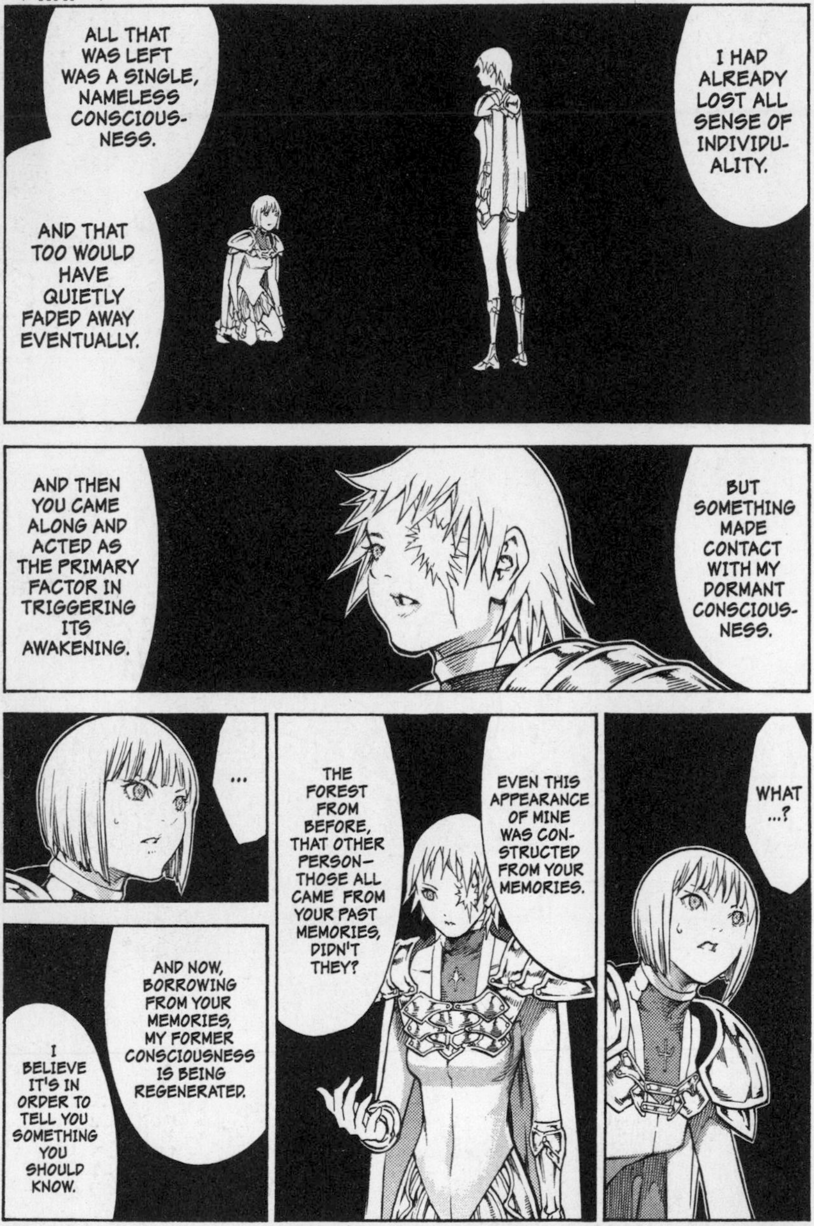

I HAD ALREADY LOST ALL SENSE OF INDIVIDU-ALITY.
ALL THAT WAS LEFT WAS A SINGLE, NAMELESS CONSCIOUS-NESS.
AND THAT TOO WOULD HAVE QUIETLY FADED AWAY EVENTUALLY.
BUT SOMETHING MADE CONTACT WITH MY DORMANT CONSCIOUS-NESS.
AND THEN YOU CAME ALONG AND ACTED AS THE PRIMARY FACTOR IN TRIGGERING ITS AWAKENING.
WHAT ...?
EVEN THIS APPEARANCE OF MINE WAS CON-STRUCTED FROM YOUR MEMORIES.
THE FOREST FROM BEFORE, THAT OTHER PERSON— THOSE ALL CAME FROM YOUR PAST MEMORIES, DIDN'T THEY?
...
AND NOW, BORROWING FROM YOUR MEMORIES, MY FORMER CONSCIOUSNESS IS BEING REGENERATED.
I BELIEVE IT'S IN ORDER TO TELL YOU SOMETHING YOU SHOULD KNOW.

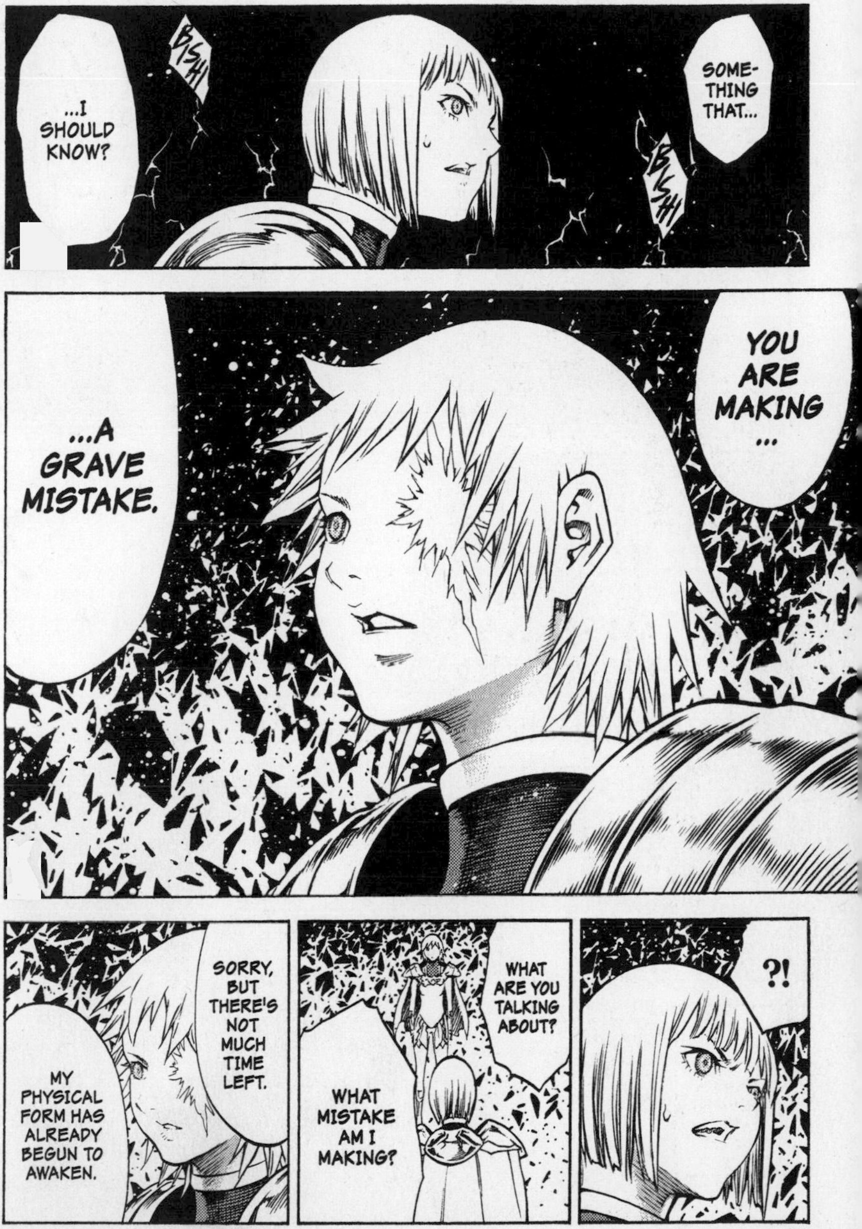
SOMETHING THAT...
BISHI
...I SHOULD KNOW?
BISHI
YOU ARE MAKING...
...A GRAVE MISTAKE.
?!
WHAT ARE YOU TALKING ABOUT?
WHAT MISTAKE AM I MAKING?
SORRY, BUT THERE'S NOT MUCH TIME LEFT.
MY PHYSICAL FORM HAS ALREADY BEGUN TO AWAKEN.

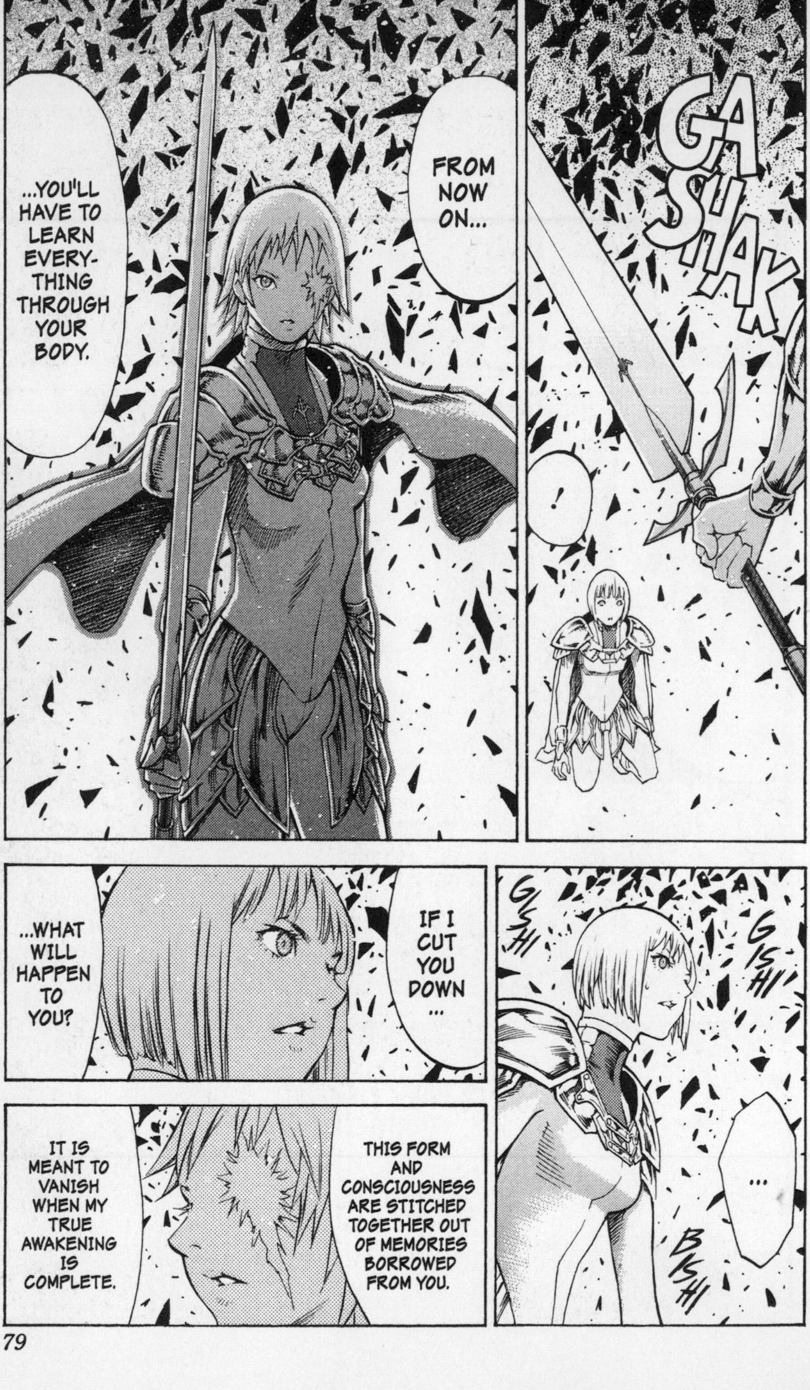
GA SHAK
!
FROM NOW ON...
...YOU'LL HAVE TO LEARN EVERY-THING THROUGH YOUR BODY.
GISHI
GISHI
...
BISHI
IF I CUT YOU DOWN ...
...WHAT WILL HAPPEN TO YOU?
THIS FORM AND CONSCIOUSNESS ARE STITCHED TOGETHER OUT OF MEMORIES BORROWED FROM YOU.
IT IS MEANT TO VANISH WHEN MY TRUE AWAKENING IS COMPLETE.

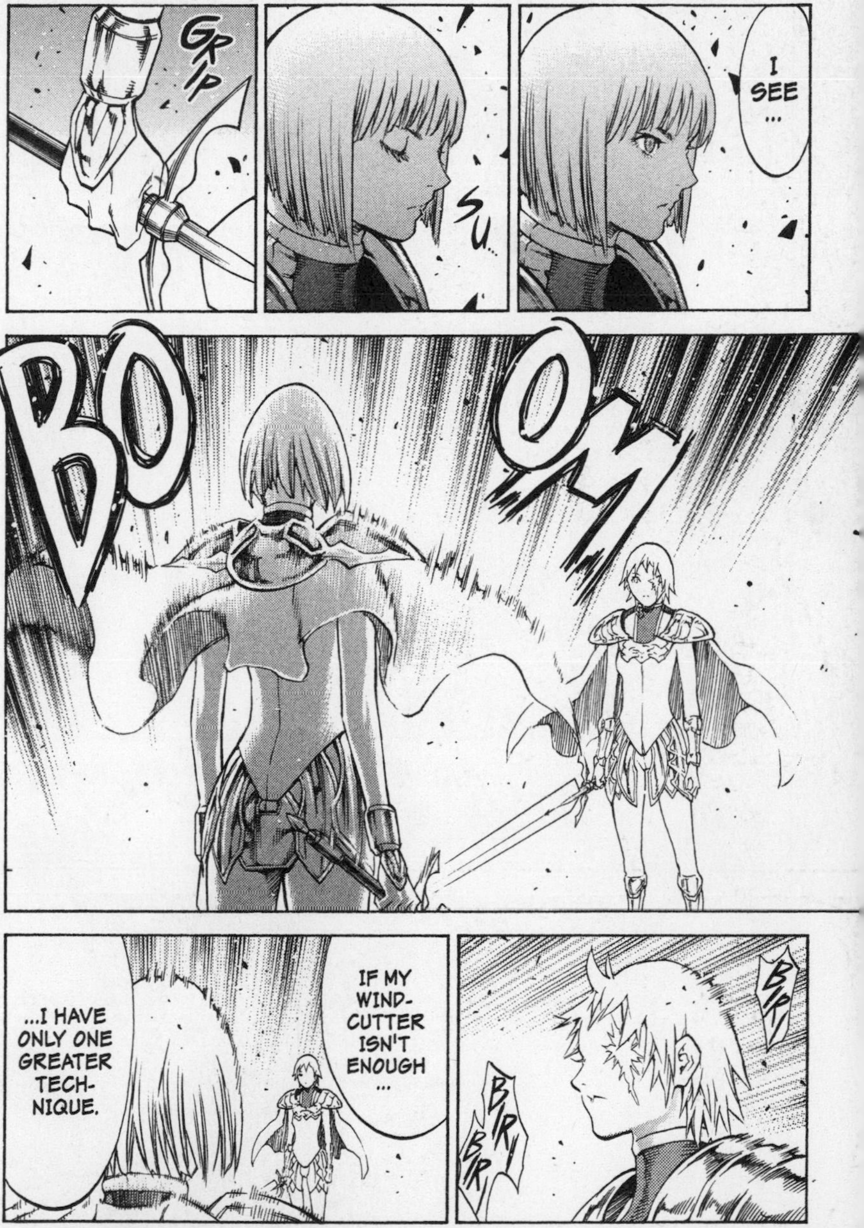
I SEE ...
SU...
GRIP
BOOM
BIRI
BIRI
BIRI
IF MY WIND-CUTTER ISN'T ENOUGH ...
...I HAVE ONLY ONE GREATER TECH-NIQUE.

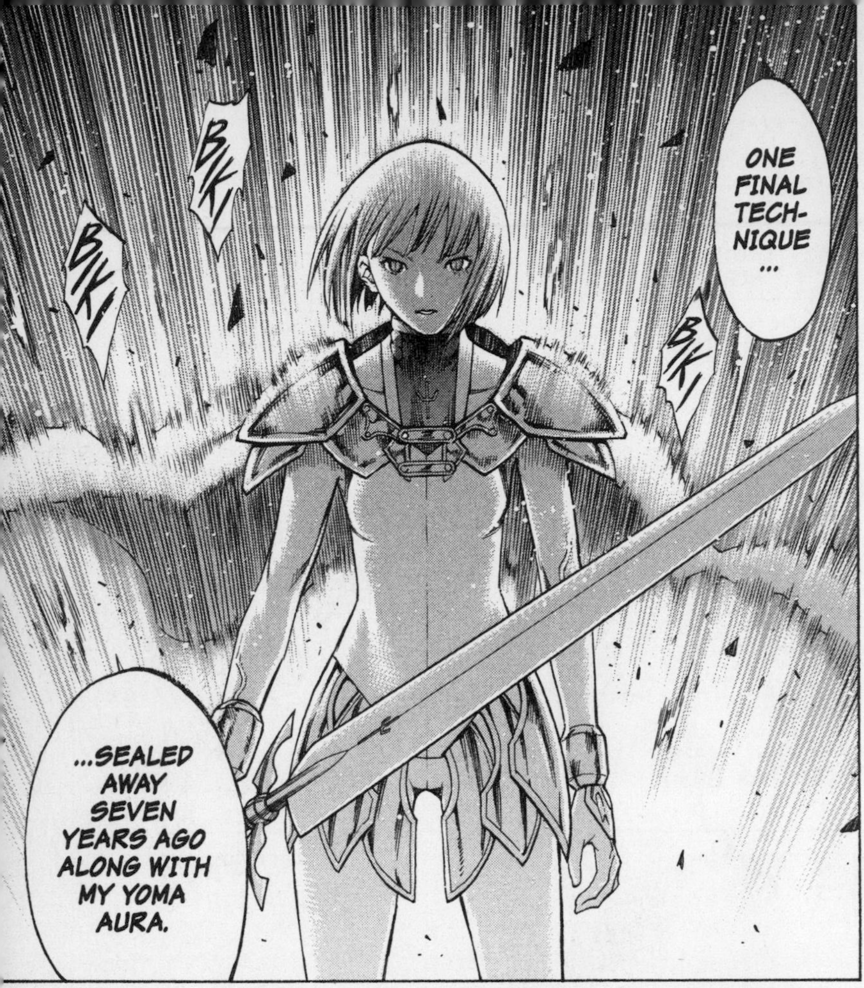
ONE FINAL TECH-NIQUE ...
BIKI
BIKI
BIKI
...SEALED AWAY SEVEN YEARS AGO ALONG WITH MY YOMA AURA.
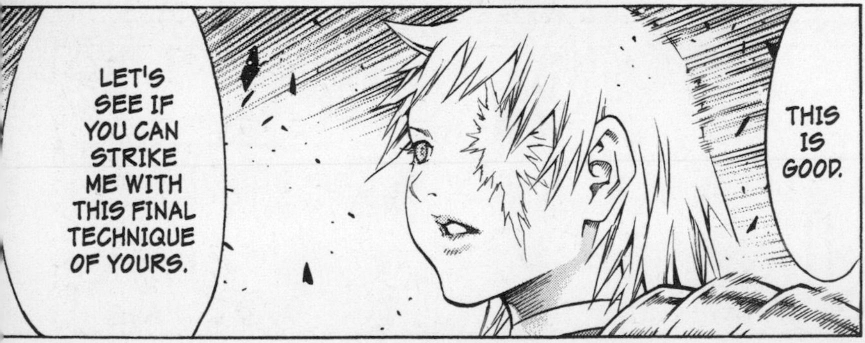
THIS IS GOOD.
LET'S SEE IF YOU CAN STRIKE ME WITH THIS FINAL TECHNIQUE OF YOURS.

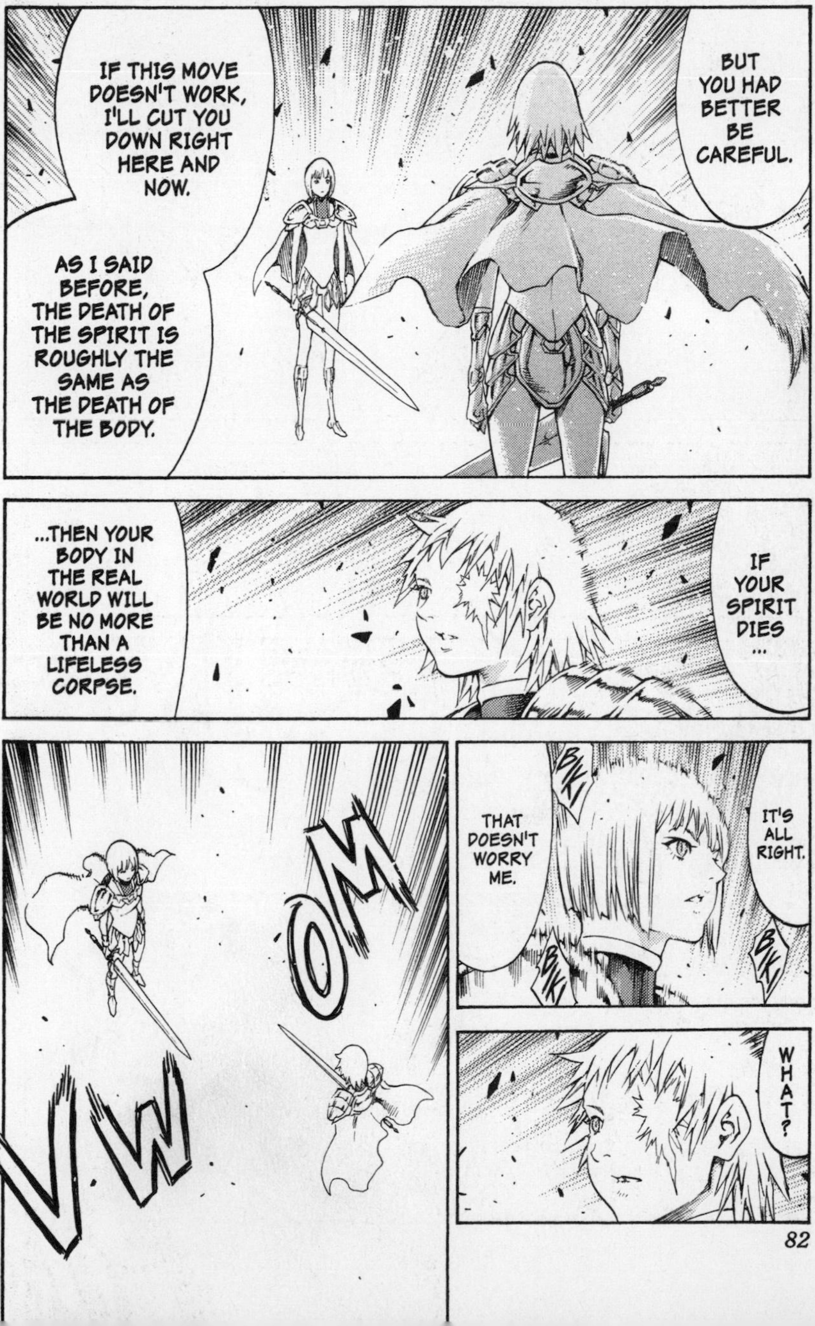
BUT YOU HAD BETTER BE CAREFUL.
IF THIS MOVE DOESN'T WORK, I'LL CUT YOU DOWN RIGHT HERE AND NOW.
AS I SAID BEFORE, THE DEATH OF THE SPIRIT IS ROUGHLY THE SAME AS THE DEATH OF THE BODY.
IF YOUR SPIRIT DIES...
...THEN YOUR BODY IN THE REAL WORLD WILL BE NO MORE THAN A LIFELESS CORPSE.
BKI
IT'S ALL RIGHT.
THAT DOESN'T WORRY ME.
BKI
BKI
WHAT?
VWOM

READ THIS WAY

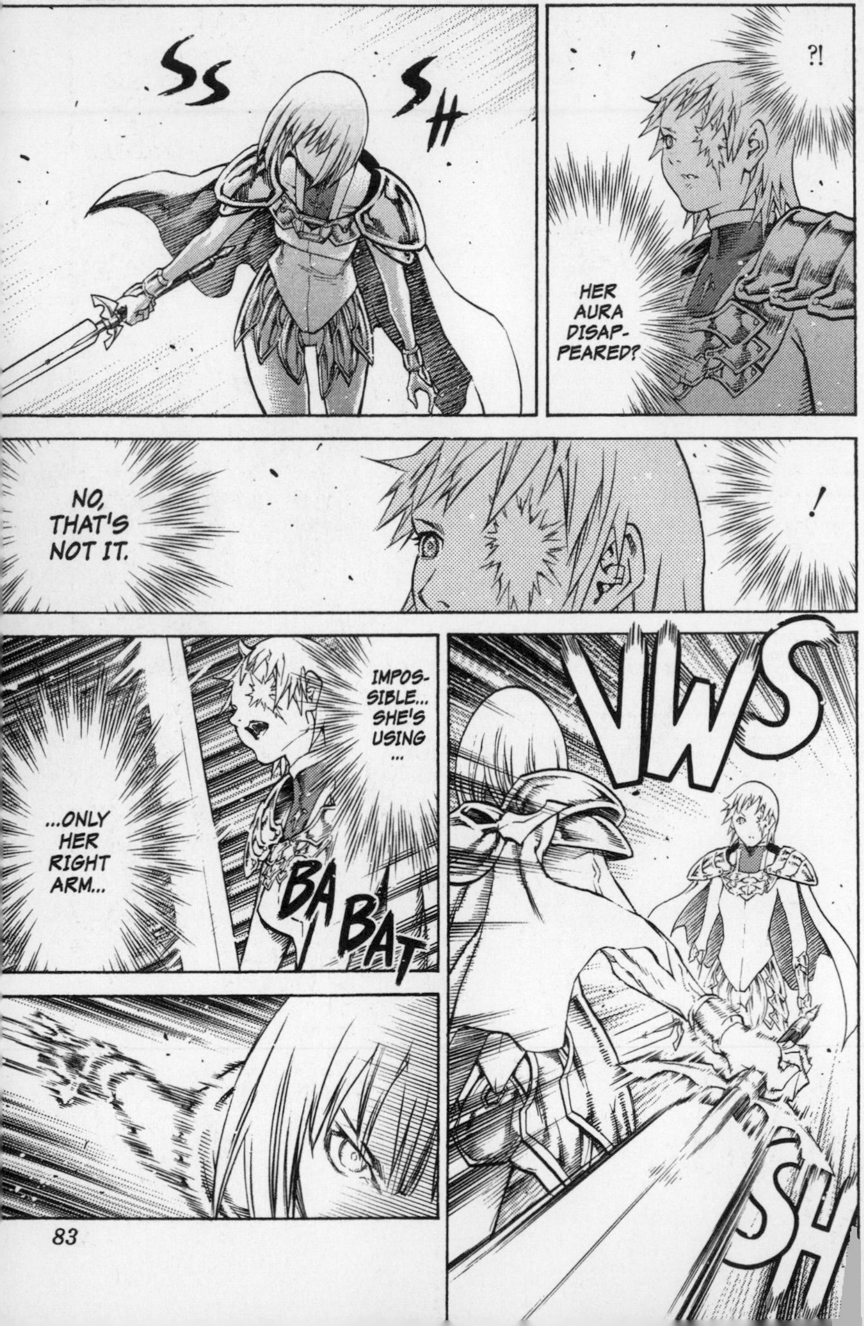
?!
HER AURA DISAP-PEARED?
SS SH
!
NO, THAT'S NOT IT.
VWS
SH
IMPOS-SIBLE... SHE'S USING ...
...ONLY HER RIGHT ARM...
BA BA BAT

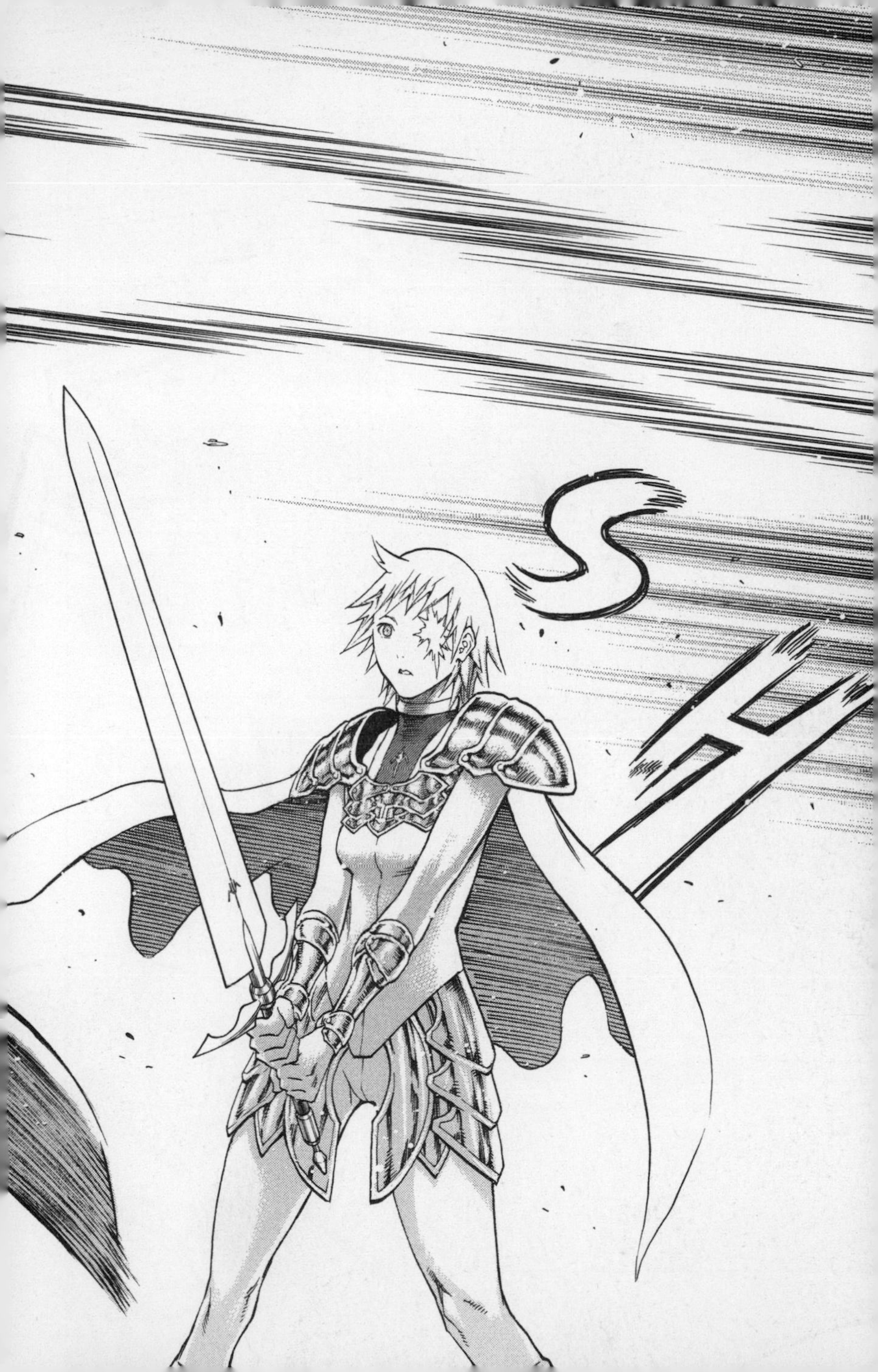
SH

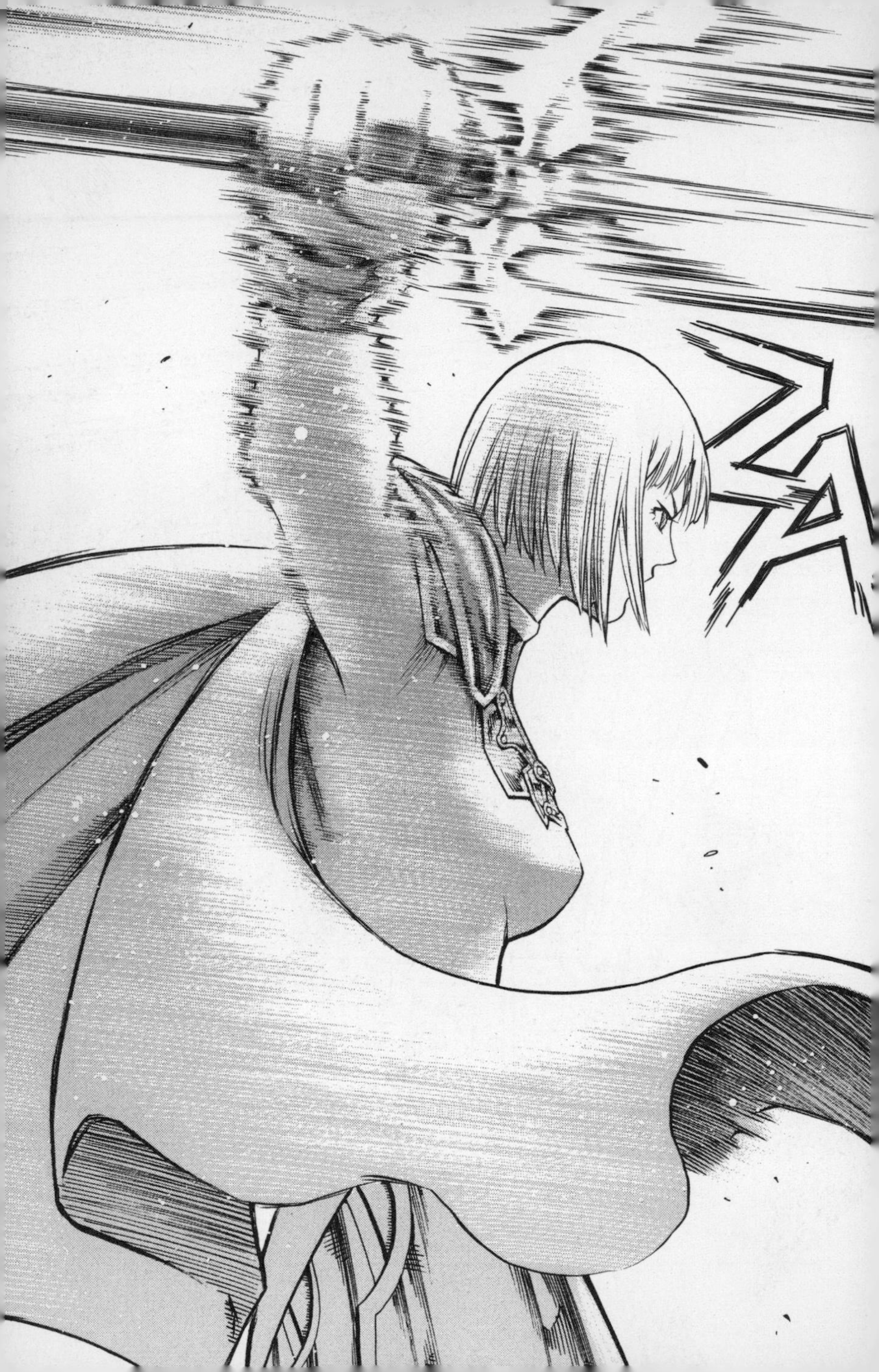
ZAA

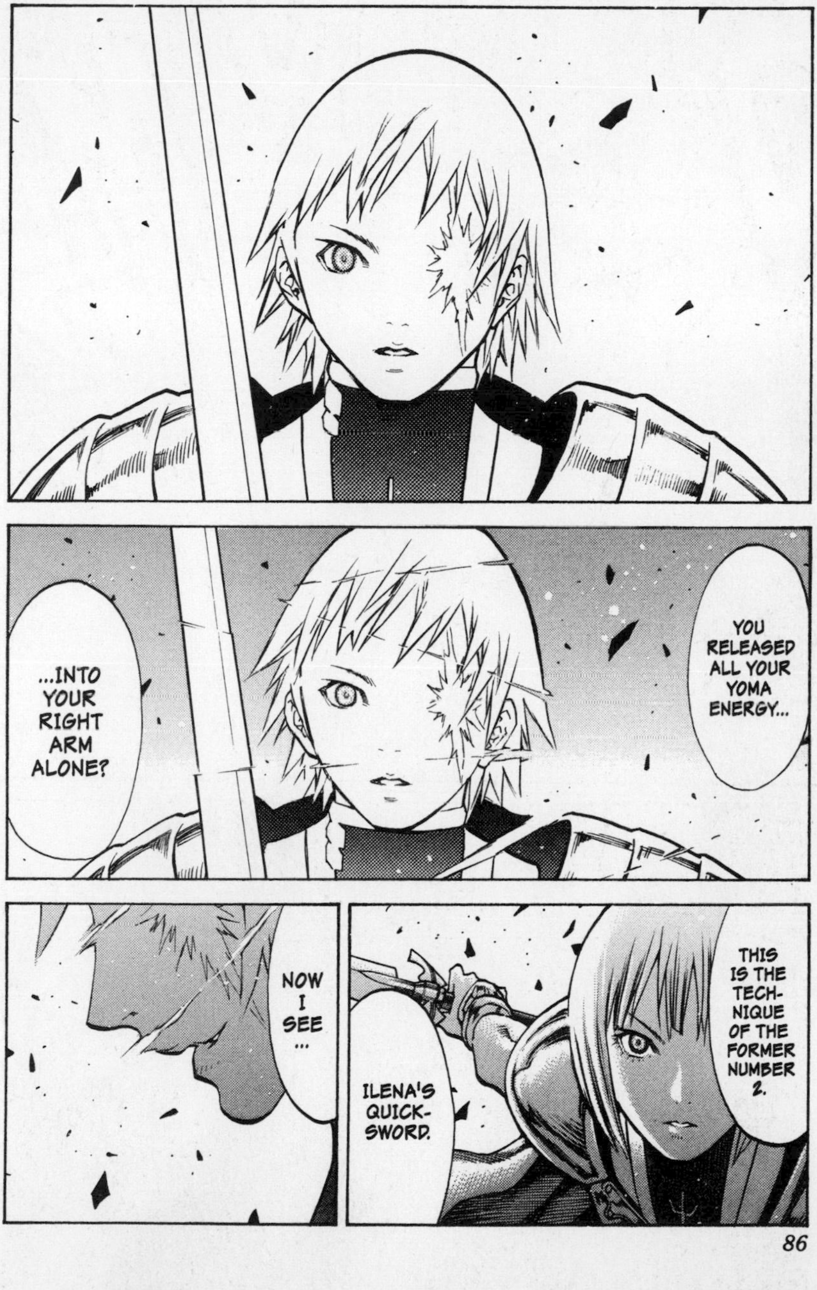
YOU RELEASED ALL YOUR YOMA ENERGY...
...INTO YOUR RIGHT ARM ALONE?
THIS IS THE TECH-NIQUE OF THE FORMER NUMBER 2.
ILENA'S QUICK-SWORD.
NOW I SEE ...

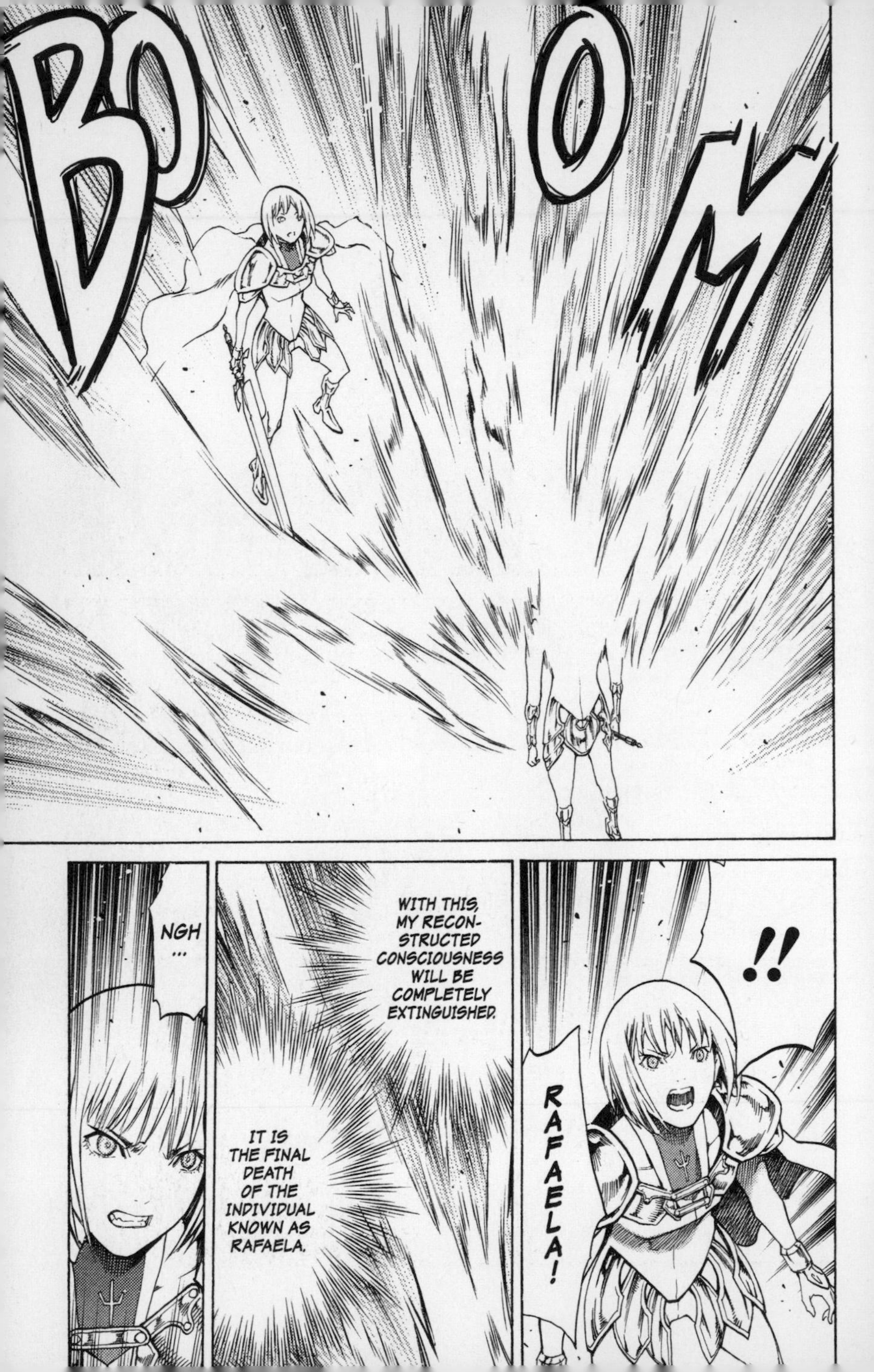
BOOOM
!!
RAFAELA!
WITH THIS, MY RECONSTRUCTED CONSCIOUSNESS WILL BE COMPLETELY EXTINGUISHED.
IT IS THE FINAL DEATH OF THE INDIVIDUAL KNOWN AS RAFAELA.
NGH...

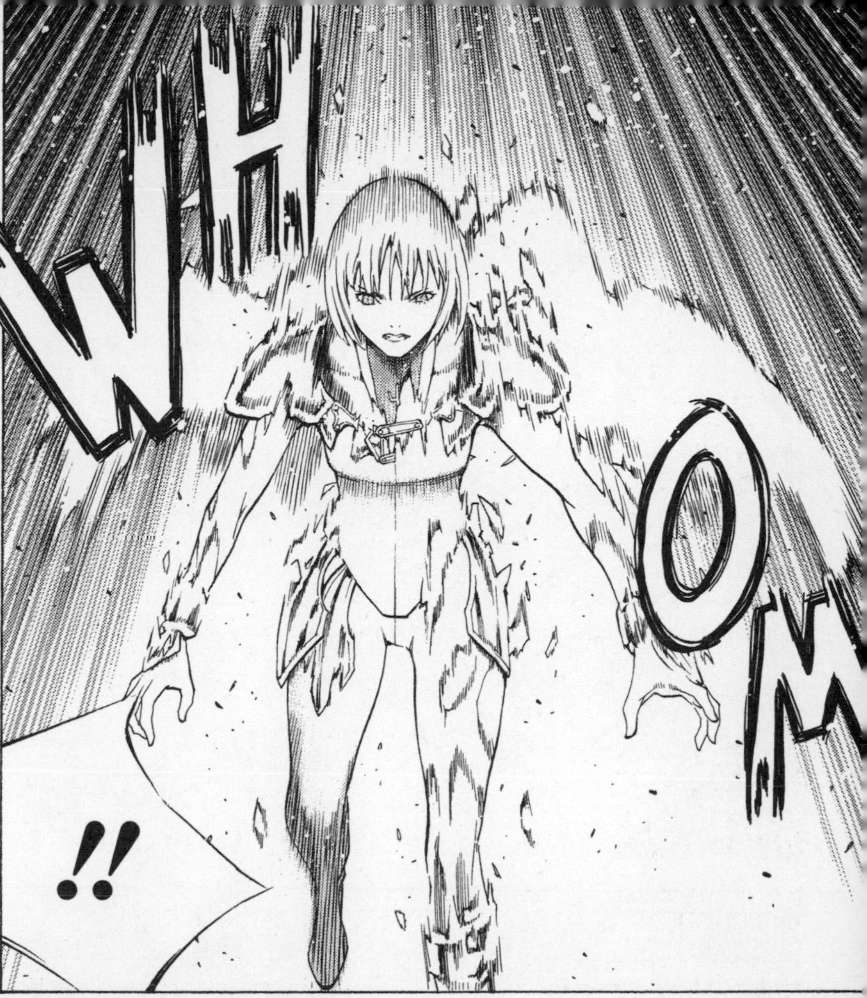
WHOOM
!!
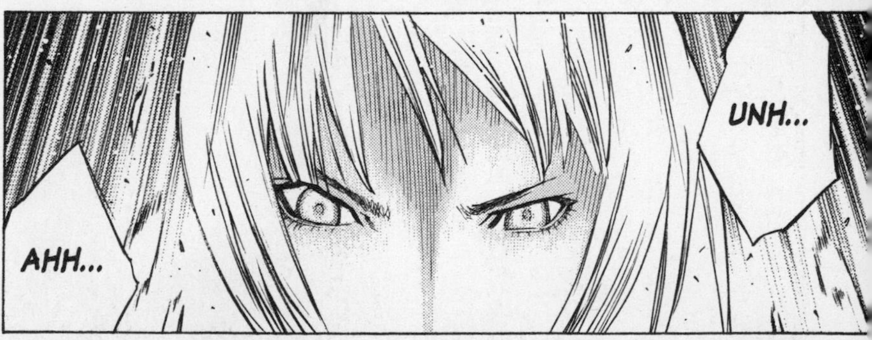
UNH...
AHH...

READ THIS WAY

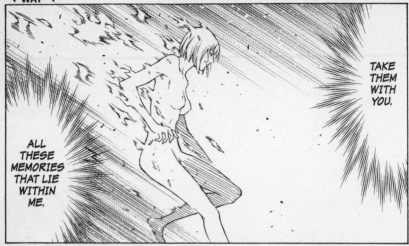

TAKE THEM WITH YOU.
ALL THESE MEMORIES THAT LIE WITHIN ME.
THE JOY... THE SORROW... THE ANGER...
THE LOVE TWINNED WITH HATRED.
SOME-WHERE IN ALL THESE EMOTIONS YOU WILL FIND...
...THE THING THAT YOU MUST KNOW.
UGH ...
RAFAELA...
YOU ...
UH ...

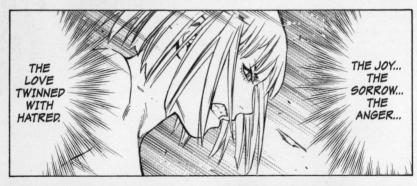

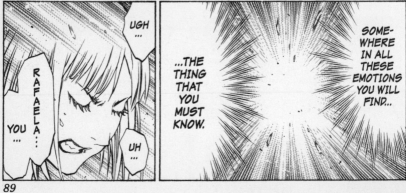

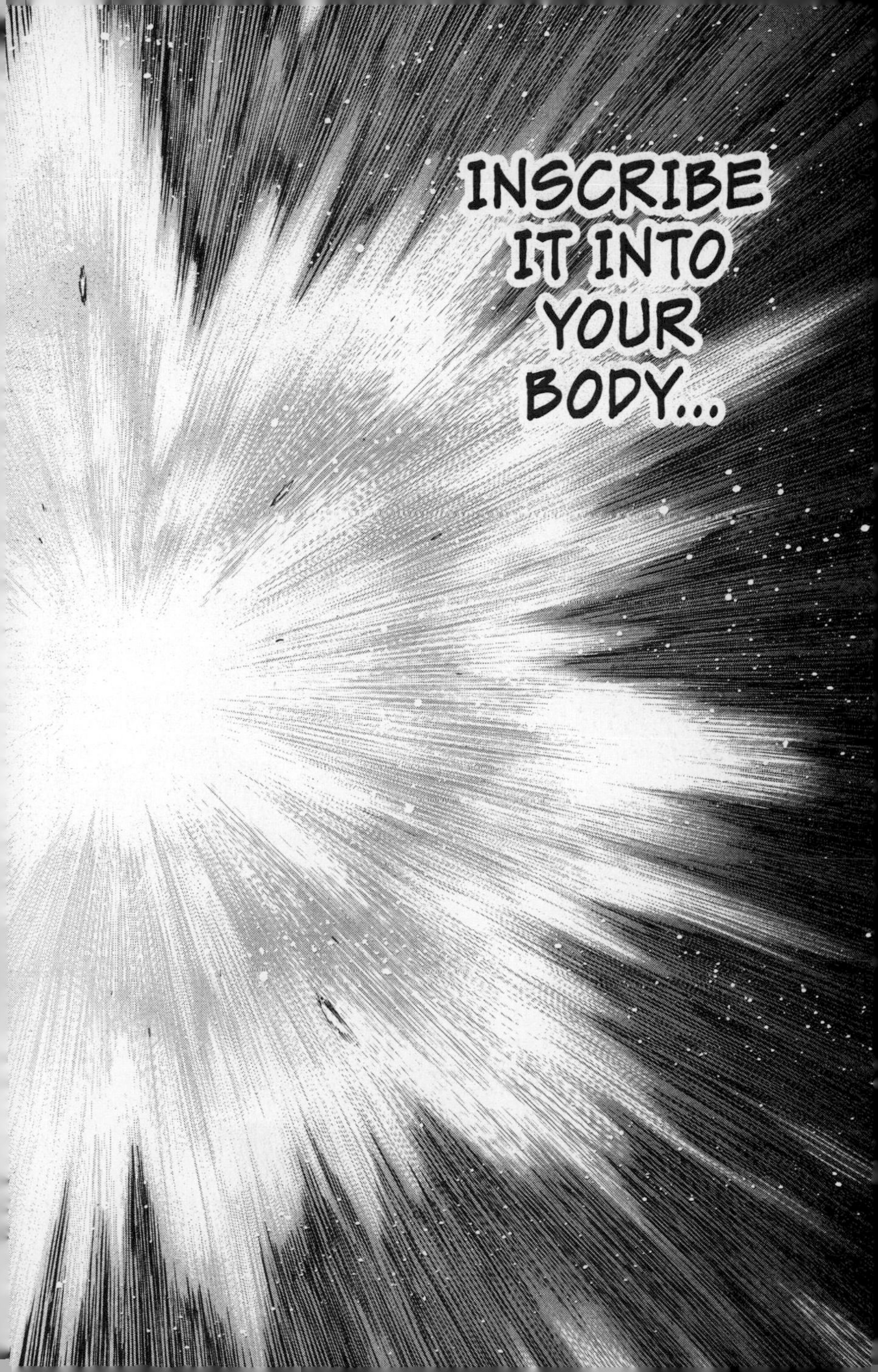
INSCRIBE IT INTO YOUR BODY...

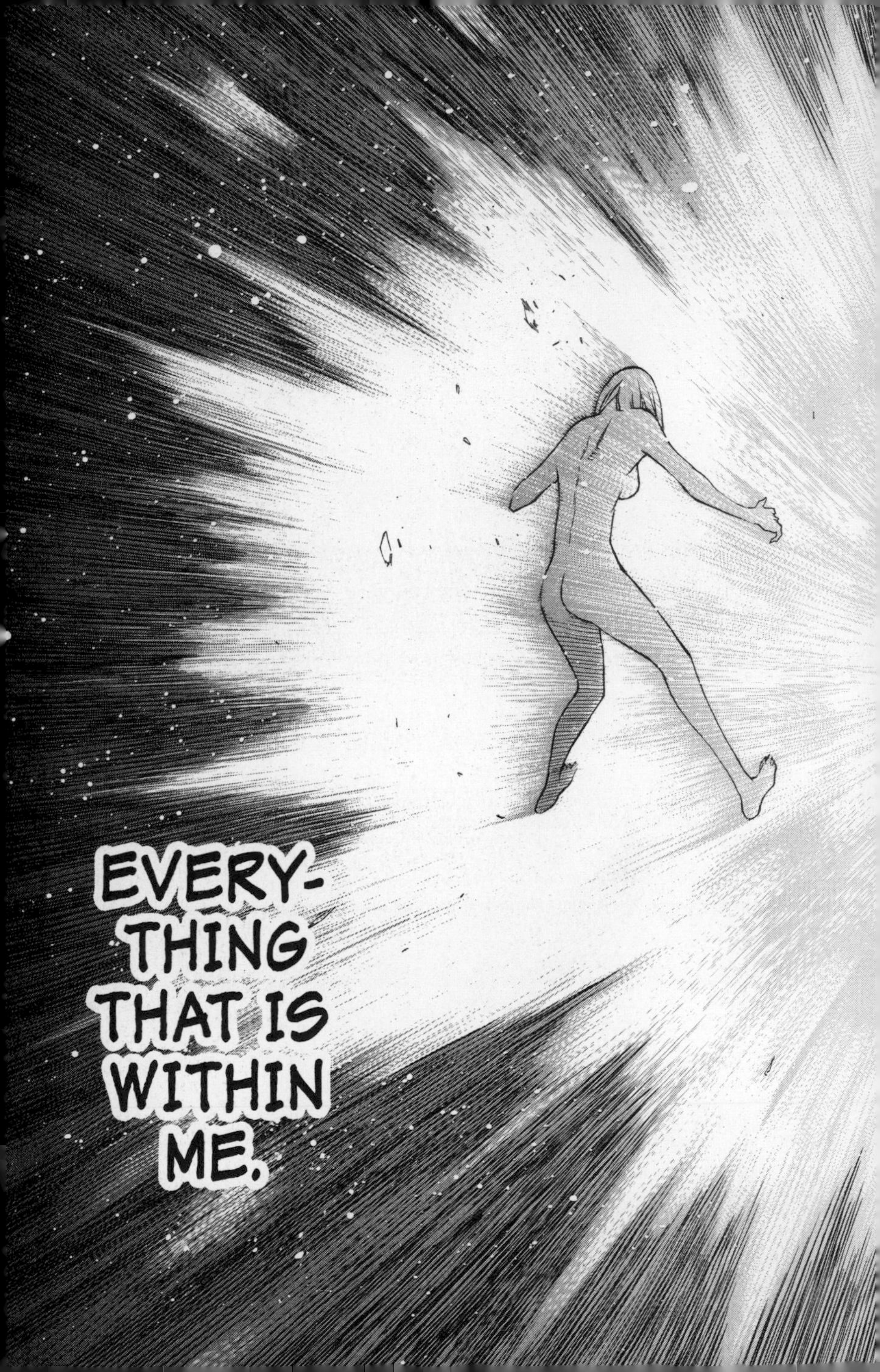
EVERY-THING THAT IS WITHIN ME.

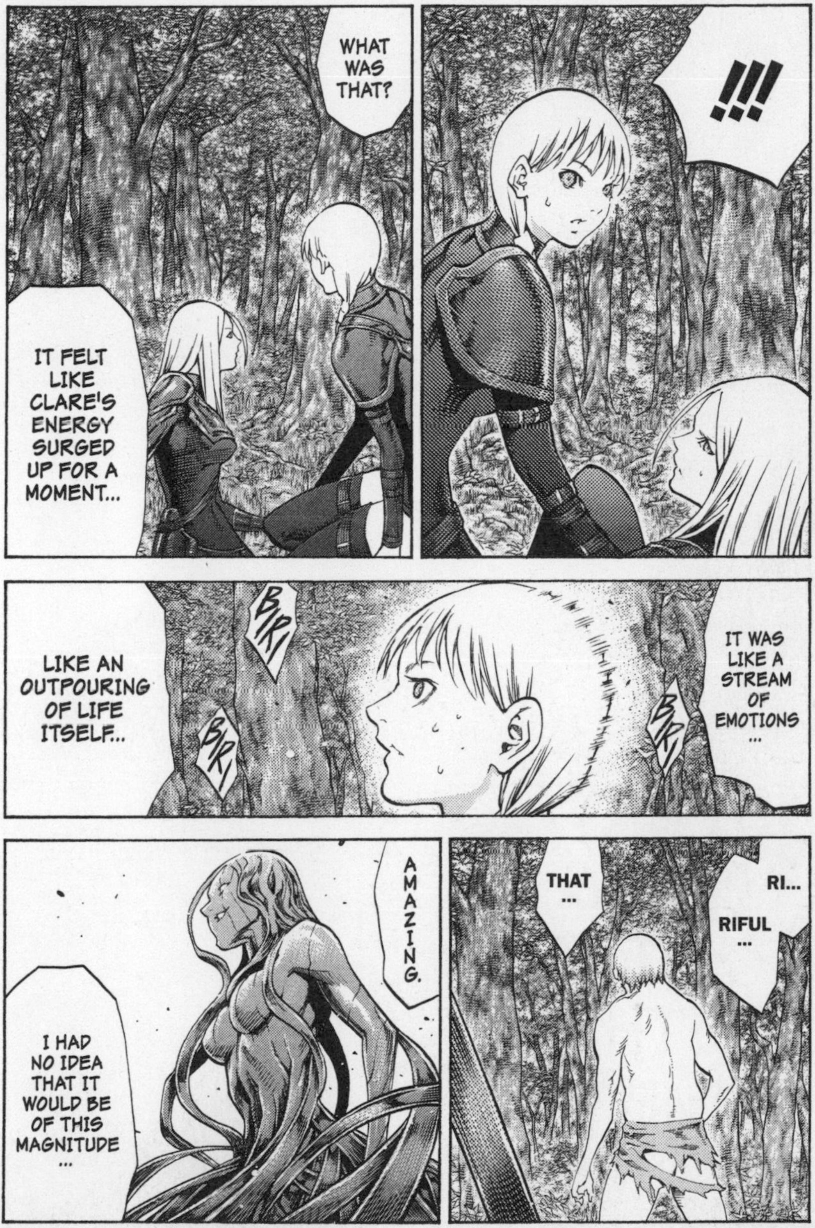
!!!
WHAT WAS THAT?
IT FELT LIKE CLARE'S ENERGY SURGED UP FOR A MOMENT...
IT WAS LIKE A STREAM OF EMOTIONS ...
BIRI
BIRI
LIKE AN OUTPOURING OF LIFE ITSELF...
RI...
RIFUL ...
THAT ...
AMAZING.
I HAD NO IDEA THAT IT WOULD BE OF THIS MAGNITUDE ...

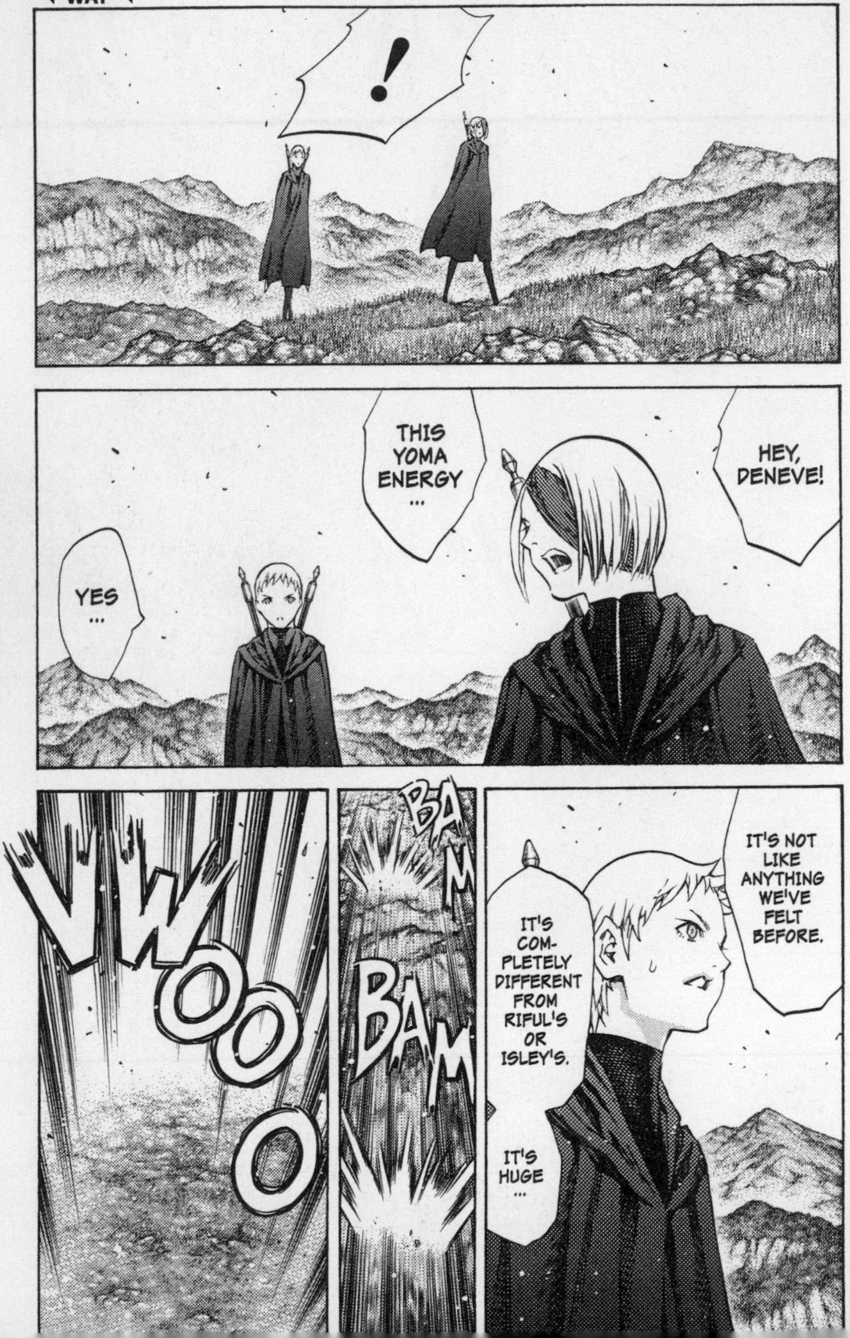
!
HEY, DENEVE!
THIS YOMA ENERGY ...
YES ...
IT'S NOT LIKE ANYTHING WE'VE FELT BEFORE.
IT'S COMPLETELY DIFFERENT FROM RIFUL'S OR ISLEY'S.
IT'S HUGE ...
BAM
BAM
VWOOOO

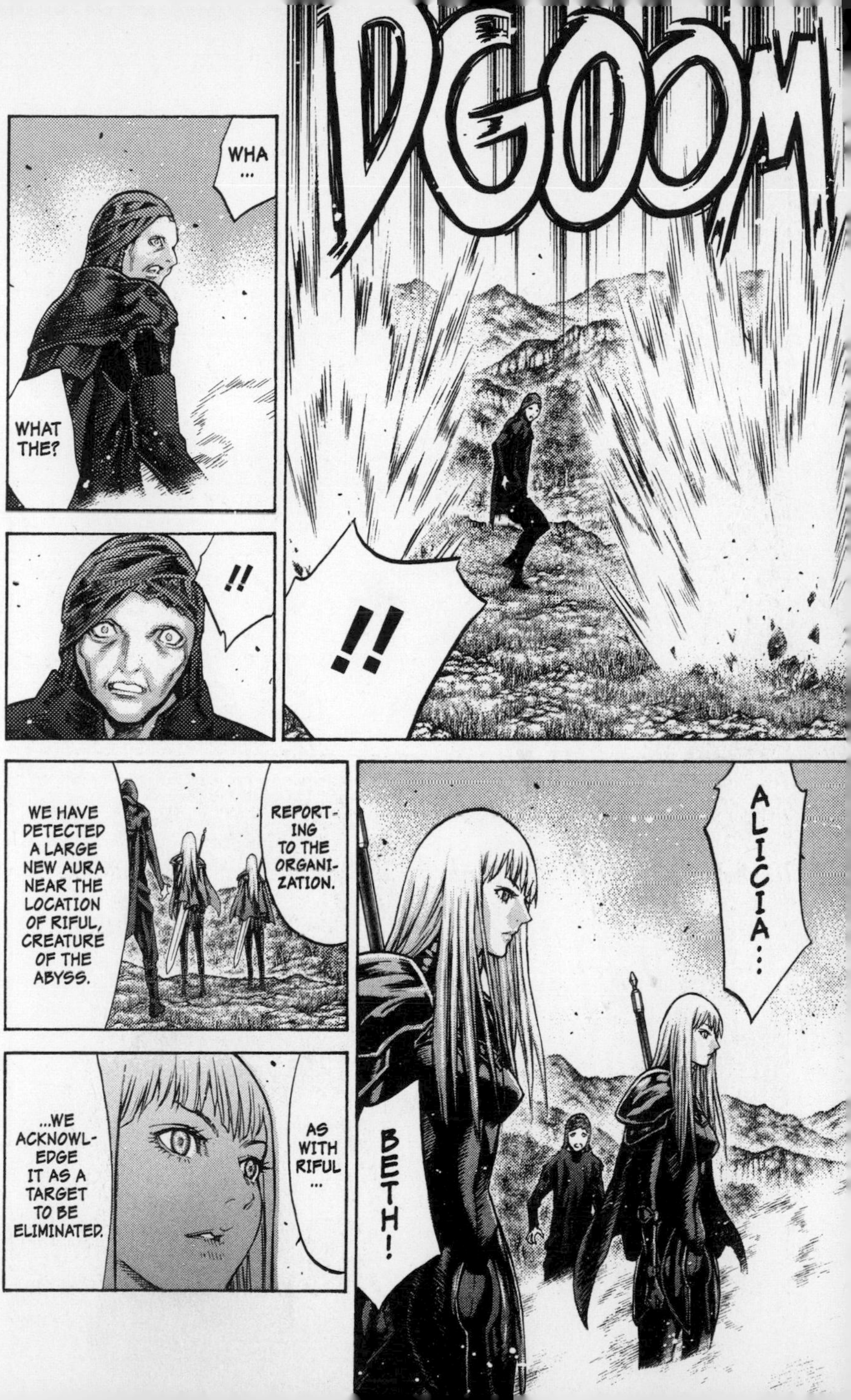
DGOOM
!!
WHA ...
WHAT THE?
!!
ALICIA...
BETH!
REPORTING TO THE ORGANIZATION.
WE HAVE DETECTED A LARGE NEW AURA NEAR THE LOCATION OF RIFUL, CREATURE OF THE ABYSS.
AS WITH RIFUL ...
...WE ACKNOWLEDGE IT AS A TARGET TO BE ELIMINATED.

READ THIS WAY

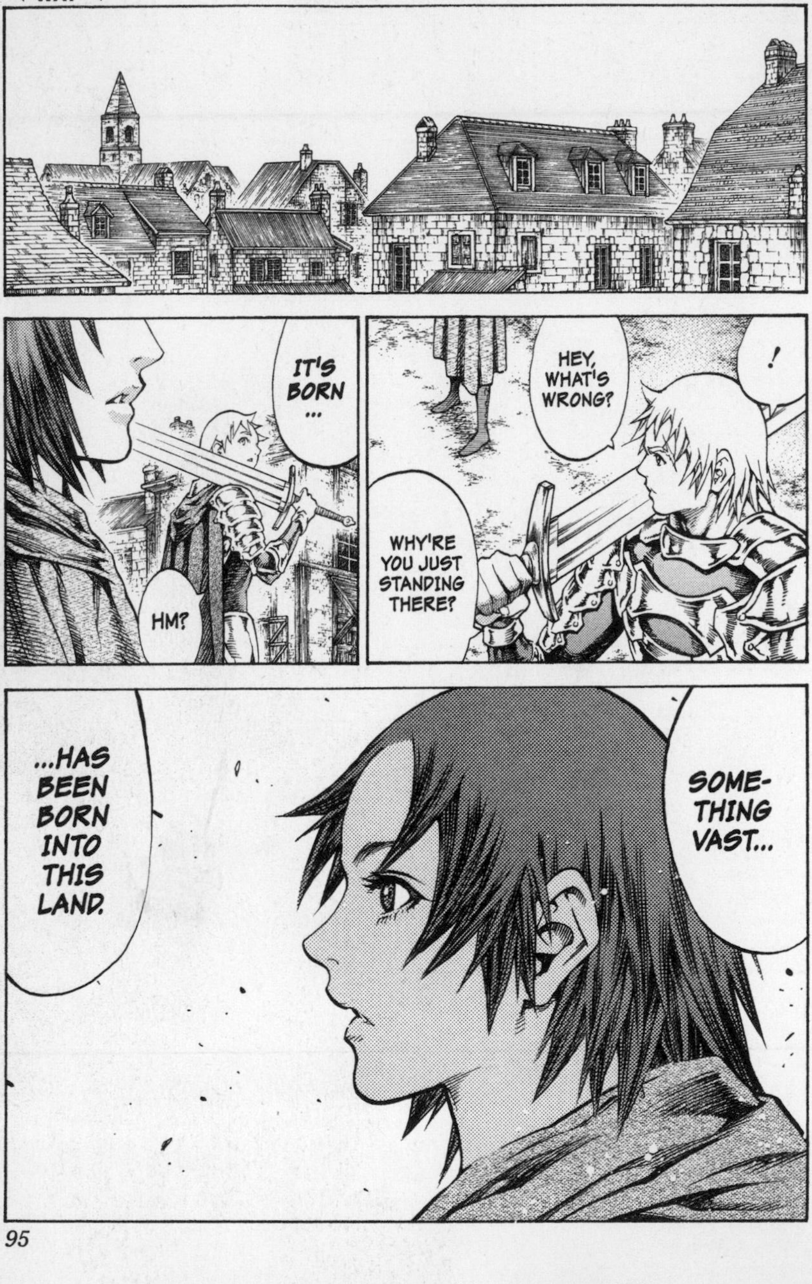
!
HEY, WHAT'S WRONG?
WHY'RE YOU JUST STANDING THERE?
IT'S BORN ...
HM?
SOME-THING VAST...
...HAS BEEN BORN INTO THIS LAND.

Claymore
クレイモア

Scene 93: The Claws of Memory, Part 4

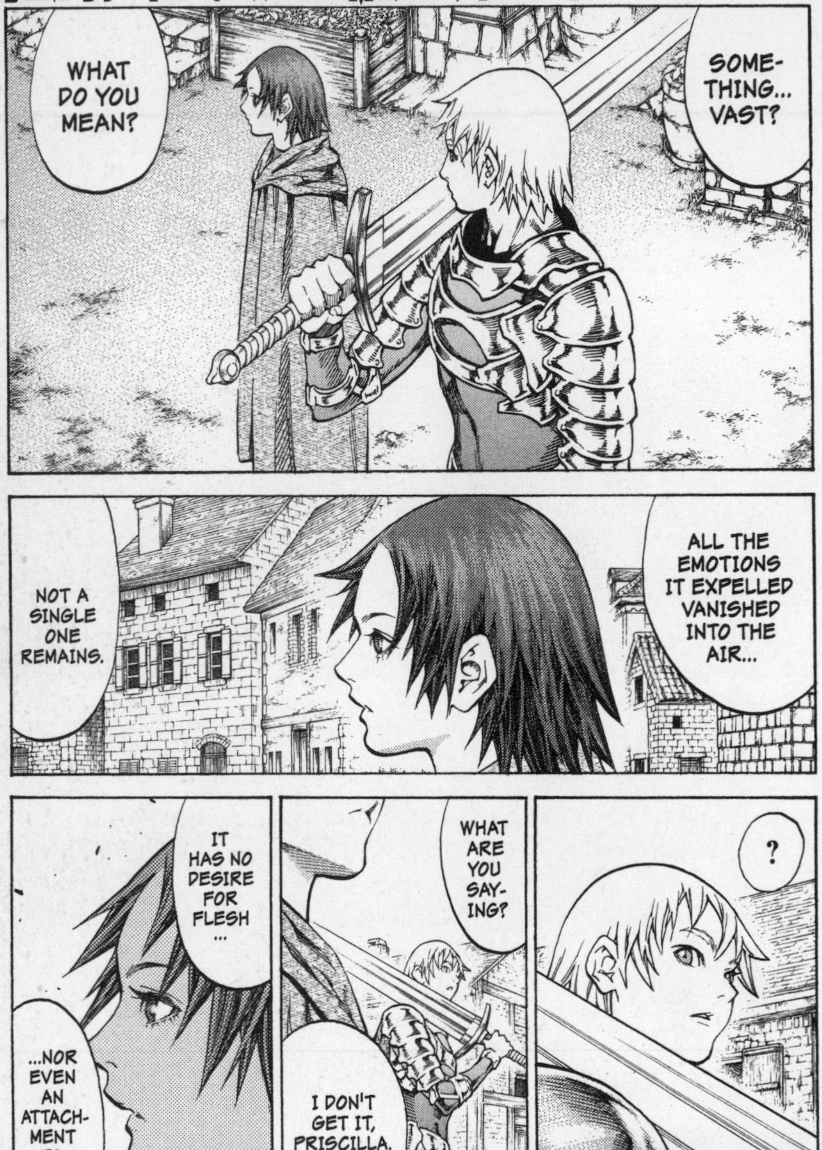
SOME-THING... VAST?
WHAT DO YOU MEAN?
ALL THE EMOTIONS IT EXPELLED VANISHED INTO THE AIR...
NOT A SINGLE ONE REMAINS.
?
WHAT ARE YOU SAYING?
I DON'T GET IT, PRISCILLA.
IT HAS NO DESIRE FOR FLESH ...
...NOR EVEN AN ATTACHMENT TO LIFE.

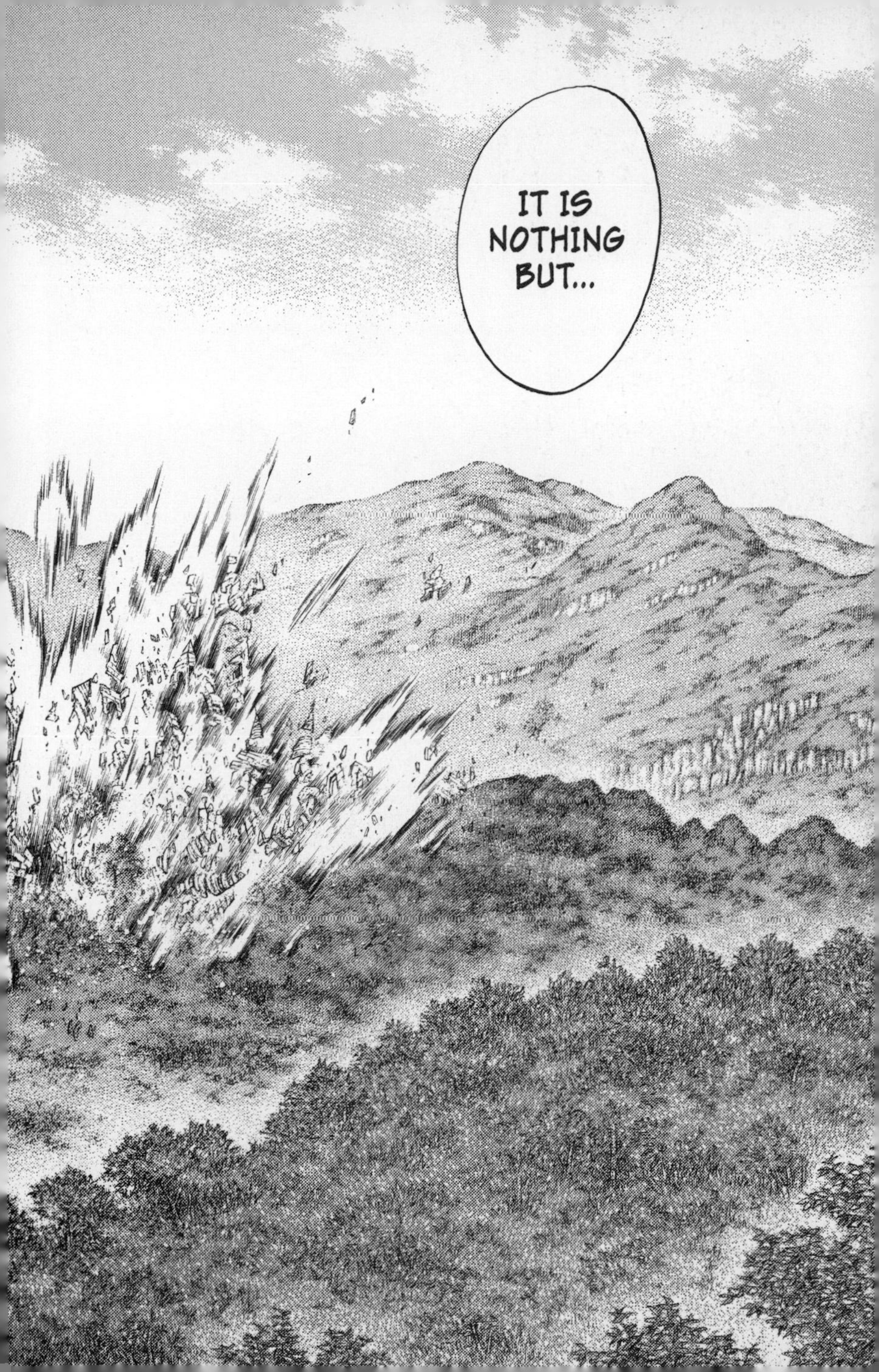
IT IS NOTHING BUT...

Scene 93: The Claws of Memory, Part 4

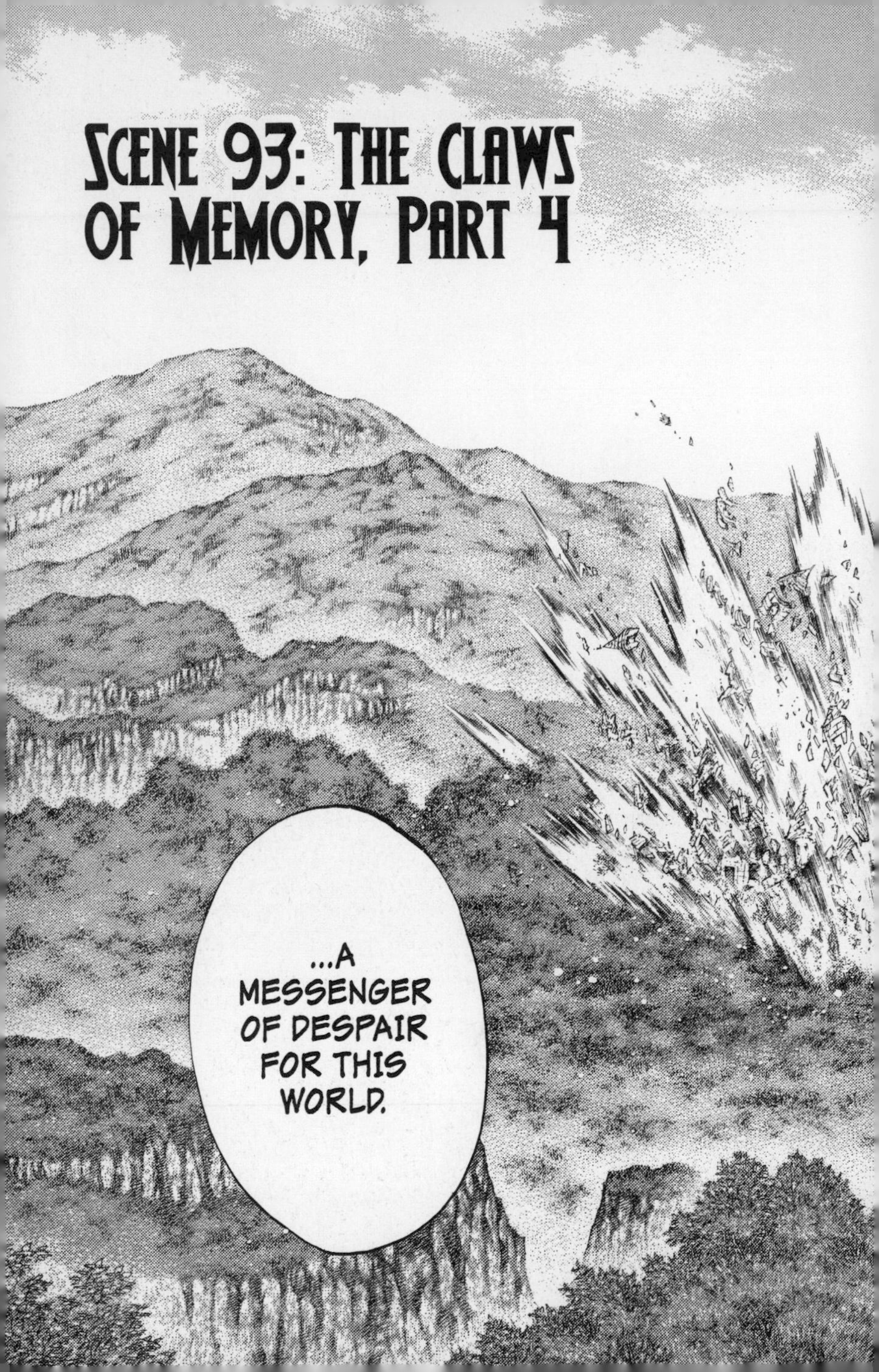
...A MESSENGER OF DESPAIR FOR THIS WORLD.

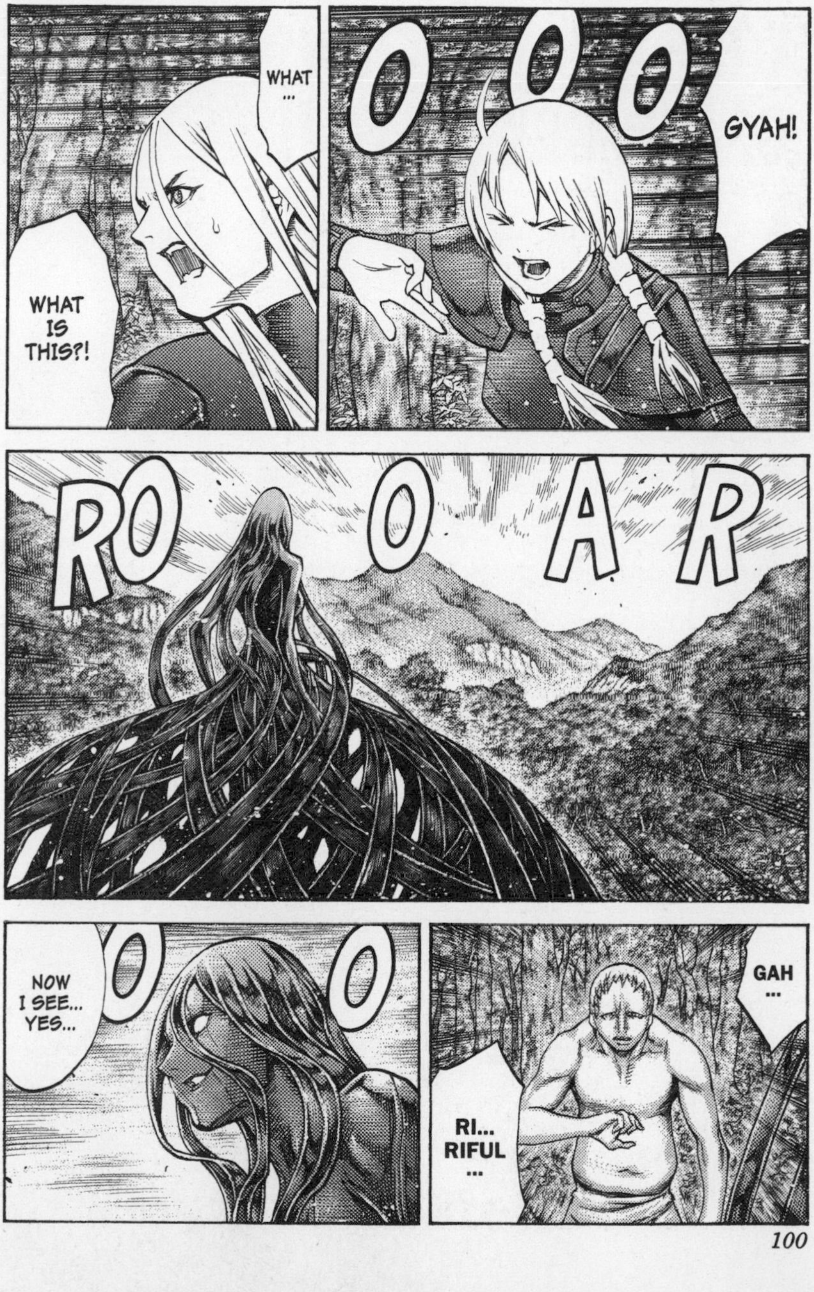
OOO
GYAH!
WHAT ...
WHAT IS THIS?!
ROOAR
GAH ...
RI... RIFUL ...
OO
NOW I SEE... YES...

READ THIS WAY

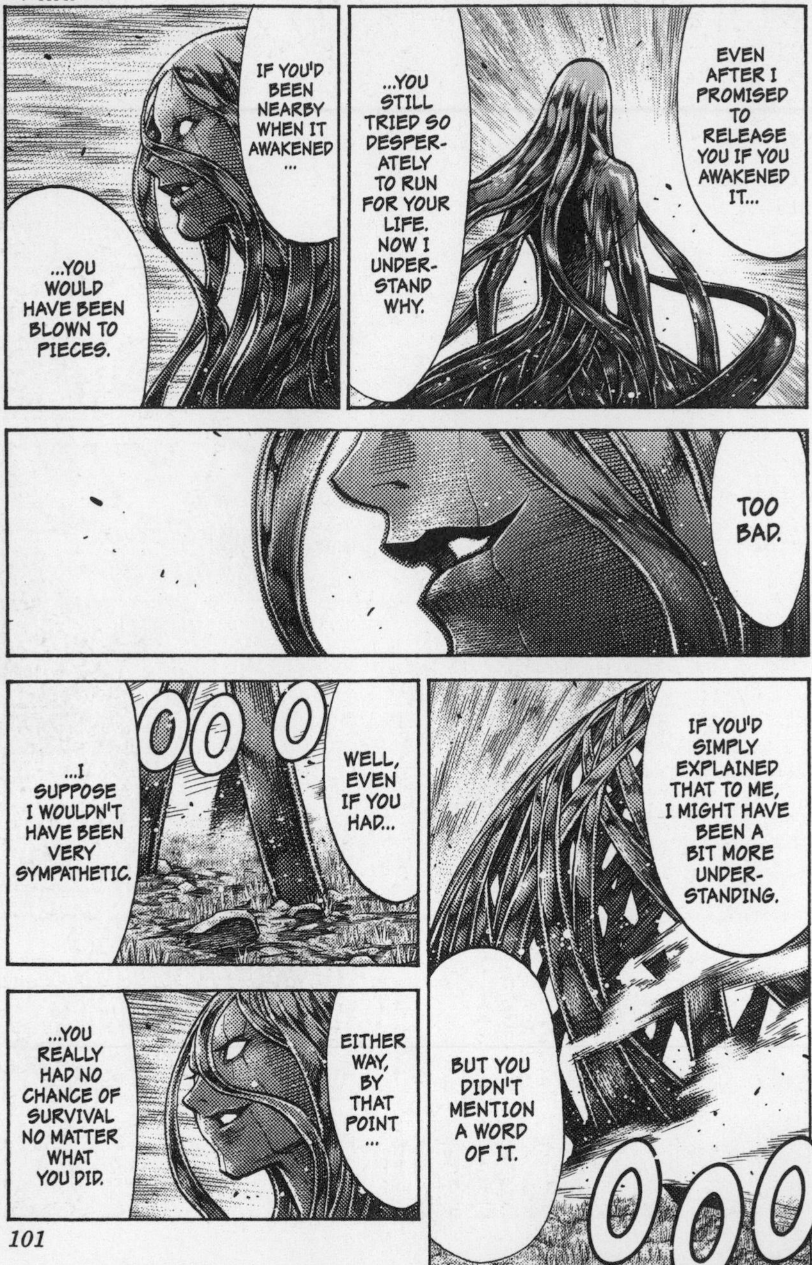
EVEN AFTER I PROMISED TO RELEASE YOU IF YOU AWAKENED IT...
...YOU STILL TRIED SO DESPER-ATELY TO RUN FOR YOUR LIFE. NOW I UNDER-STAND WHY.
IF YOU'D BEEN NEARBY WHEN IT AWAKENED ...
...YOU WOULD HAVE BEEN BLOWN TO PIECES.
TOO BAD.
IF YOU'D SIMPLY EXPLAINED THAT TO ME, I MIGHT HAVE BEEN A BIT MORE UNDER-STANDING.
BUT YOU DIDN'T MENTION A WORD OF IT.
OOO
OOO
WELL, EVEN IF YOU HAD...
...I SUPPOSE I WOULDN'T HAVE BEEN VERY SYMPATHETIC.
EITHER WAY, BY THAT POINT ...
...YOU REALLY HAD NO CHANCE OF SURVIVAL NO MATTER WHAT YOU DID.

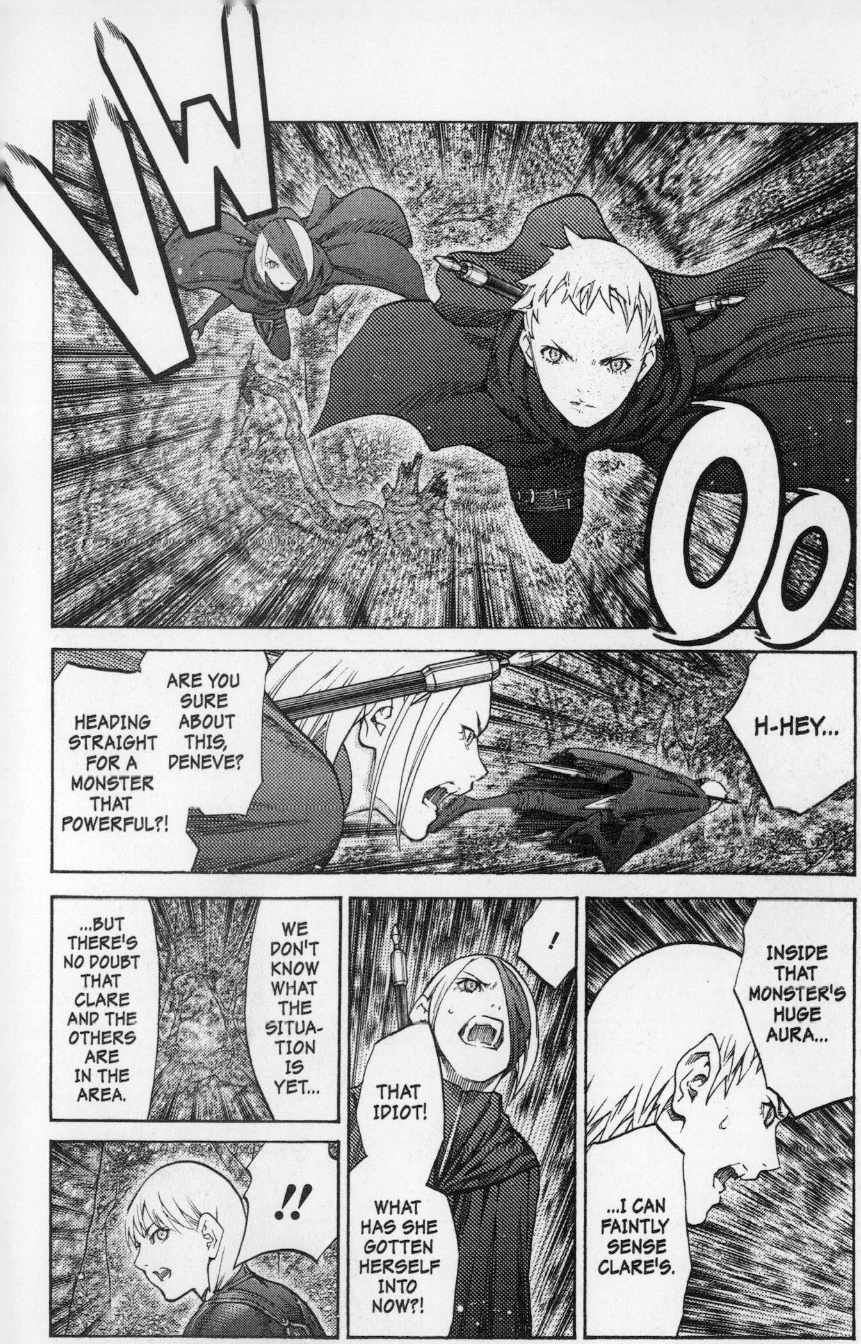
VWOO
H-HEY...
ARE YOU SURE ABOUT THIS, DENEVE?
HEADING STRAIGHT FOR A MONSTER THAT POWERFUL?!
INSIDE THAT MONSTER'S HUGE AURA...
...I CAN FAINTLY SENSE CLARE'S.
!
THAT IDIOT!
WHAT HAS SHE GOTTEN HERSELF INTO NOW?!
WE DON'T KNOW WHAT THE SITUATION IS YET...
...BUT THERE'S NO DOUBT THAT CLARE AND THE OTHERS ARE IN THE AREA.
!!

READ THIS WAY

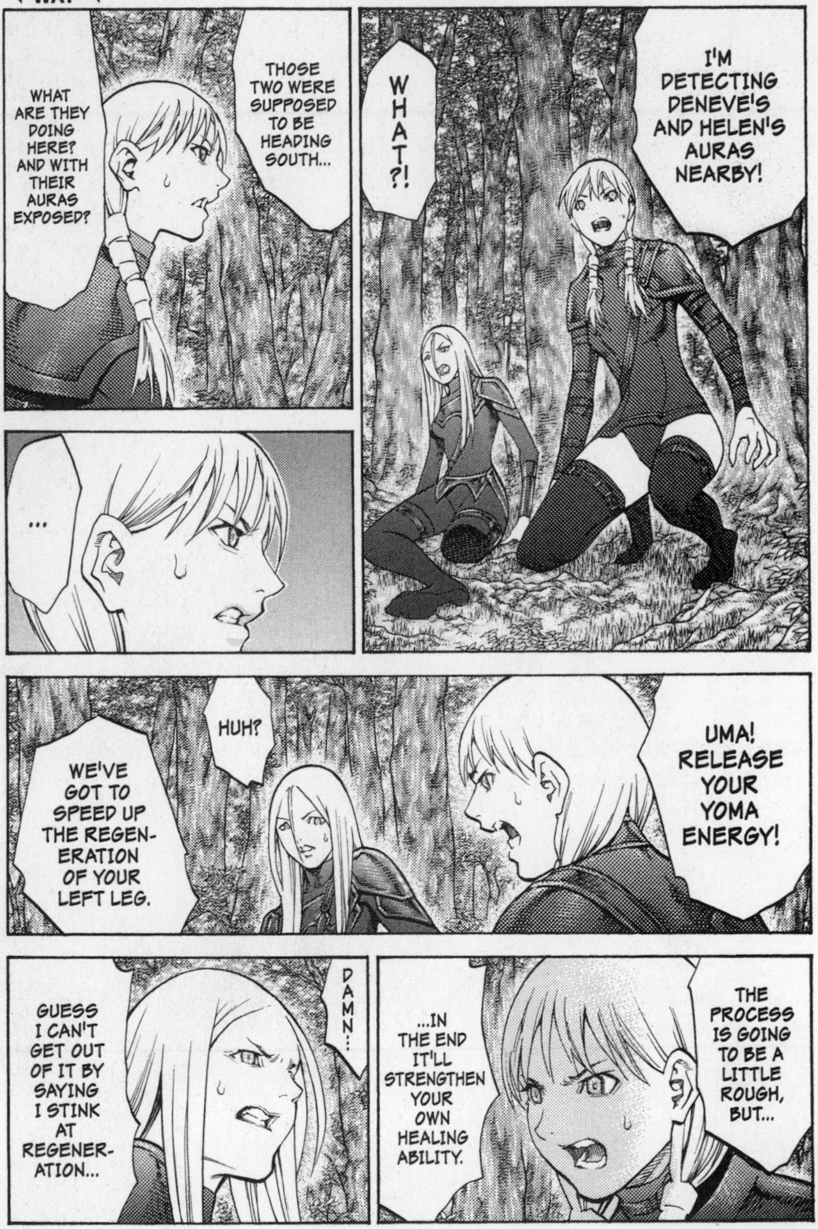
I'M DETECTING DENEVE'S AND HELEN'S AURAS NEARBY!
WHAT?!
THOSE TWO WERE SUPPOSED TO BE HEADING SOUTH...
WHAT ARE THEY DOING HERE? AND WITH THEIR AURAS EXPOSED?
...
UMA! RELEASE YOUR YOMA ENERGY!
HUH?
WE'VE GOT TO SPEED UP THE REGEN-ERATION OF YOUR LEFT LEG.
THE PROCESS IS GOING TO BE A LITTLE ROUGH, BUT...
...IN THE END IT'LL STRENGTHEN YOUR OWN HEALING ABILITY.
DAMN...
GUESS I CAN'T GET OUT OF IT BY SAYING I STINK AT REGENER-ATION...

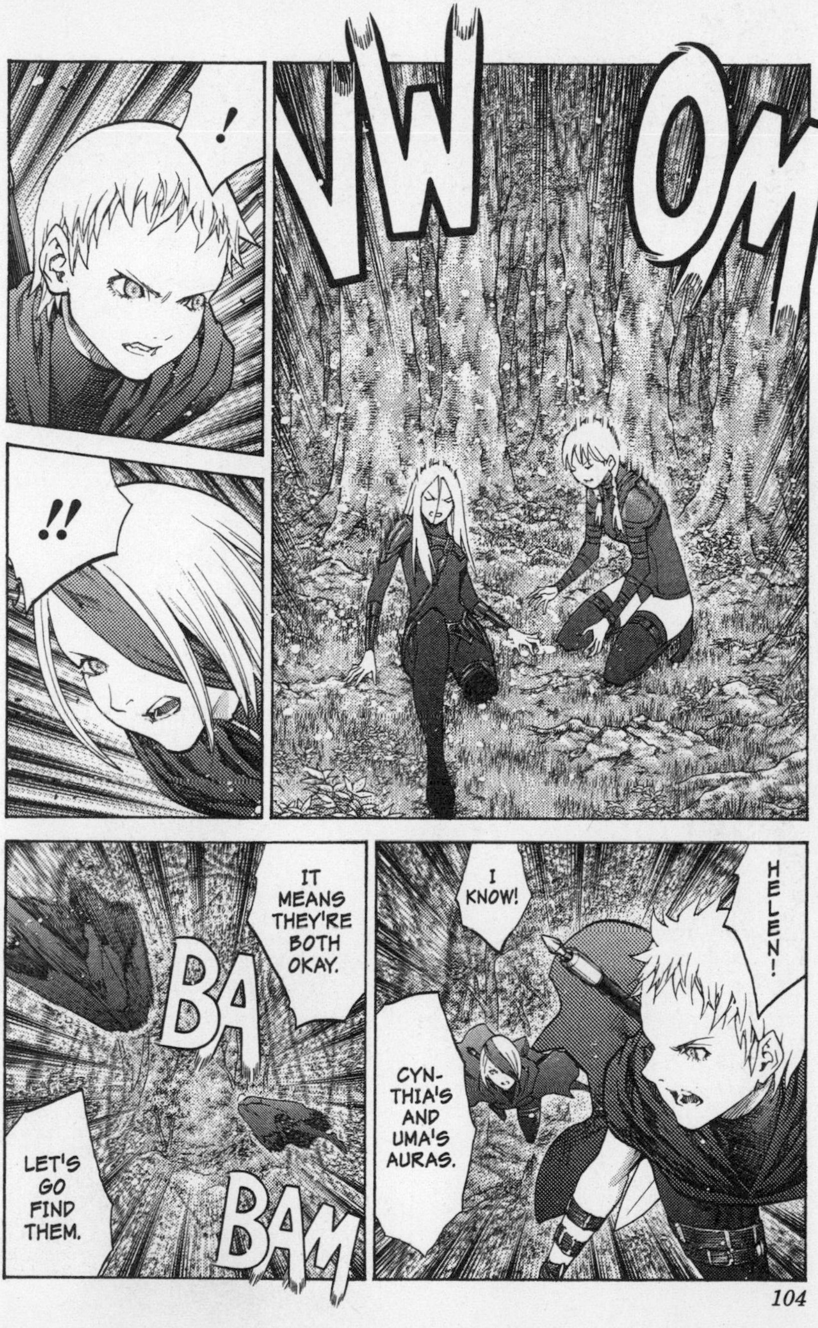
VWOM
!
!!
HELEN!
I KNOW!
CYN-THIA'S AND UMA'S AURAS.
IT MEANS THEY'RE BOTH OKAY.
BA BAM
LET'S GO FIND THEM.

READ THIS WAY

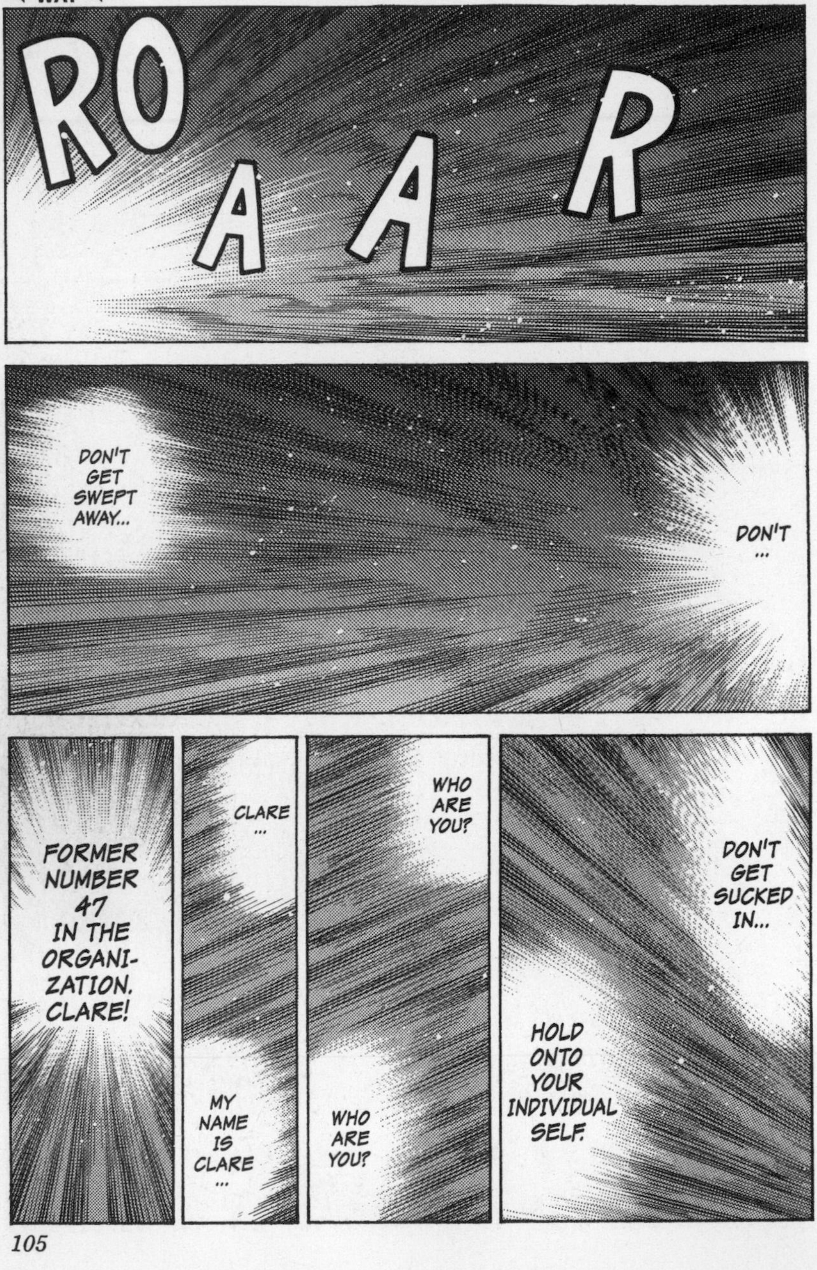
ROAAAR
DON'T ...
DON'T GET SWEPT AWAY...
DON'T GET SUCKED IN...
HOLD ONTO YOUR INDIVIDUAL SELF.
WHO ARE YOU?
WHO ARE YOU?
CLARE ...
MY NAME IS CLARE ...
FORMER NUMBER 47 IN THE ORGANIZATION. CLARE!

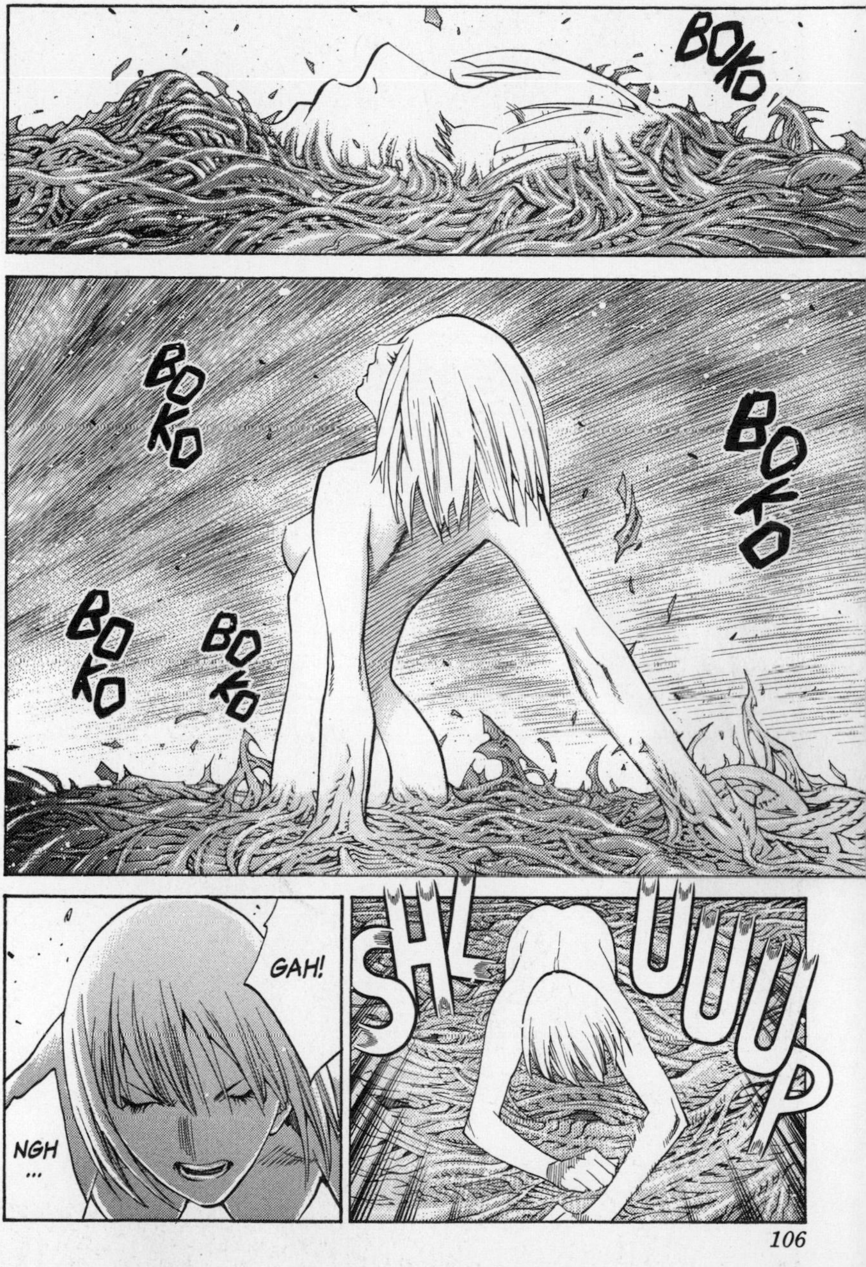
BOKO
BOKO
BOKO
BOKO
BOKO
SHLUUUP
GAH!
NGH
...

READ THIS WAY

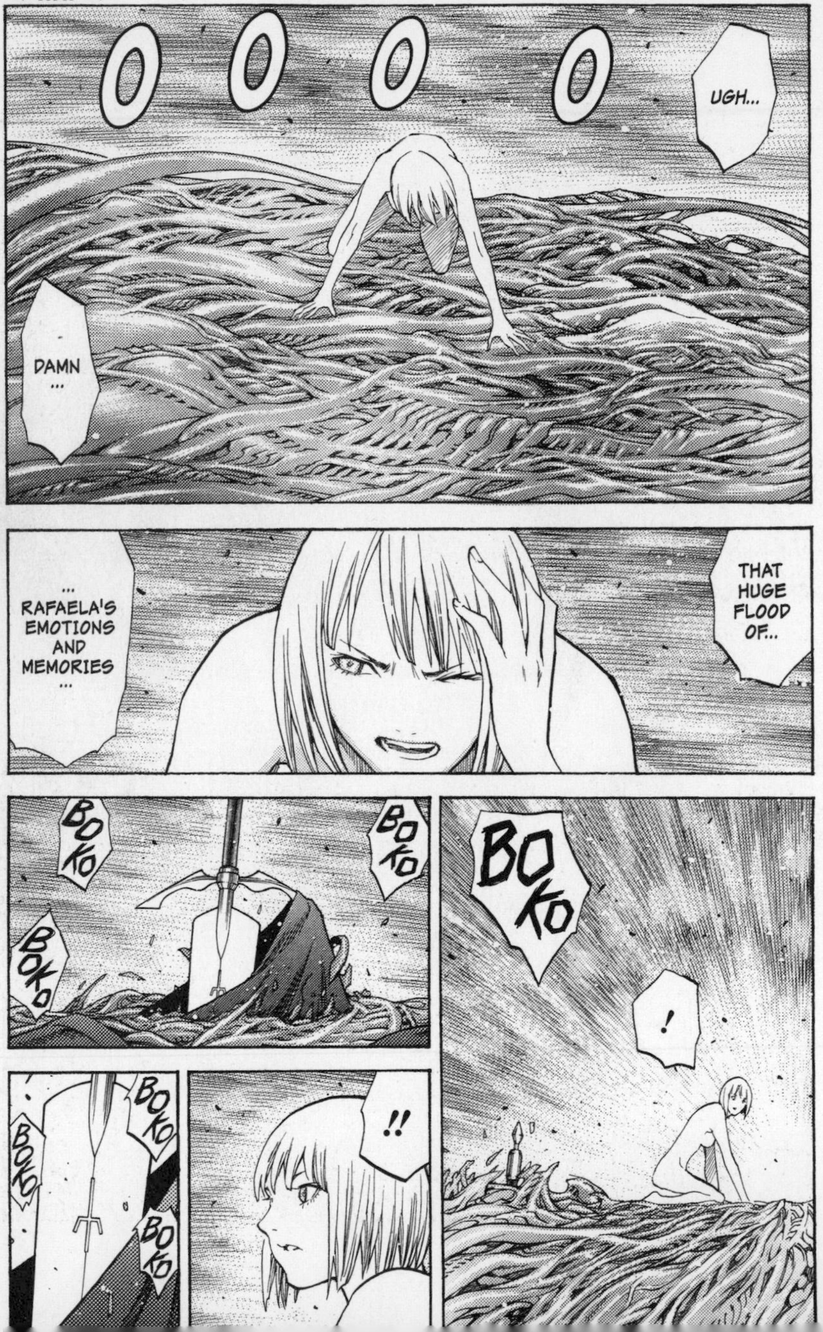

UGH...
O O O O
DAMN ...
THAT HUGE FLOOD OF...
... RAFAELA'S EMOTIONS AND MEMORIES ...
BOKO
!
BOKO
BOKO
BOKO
!!
BOKO
BOKO
BOKO

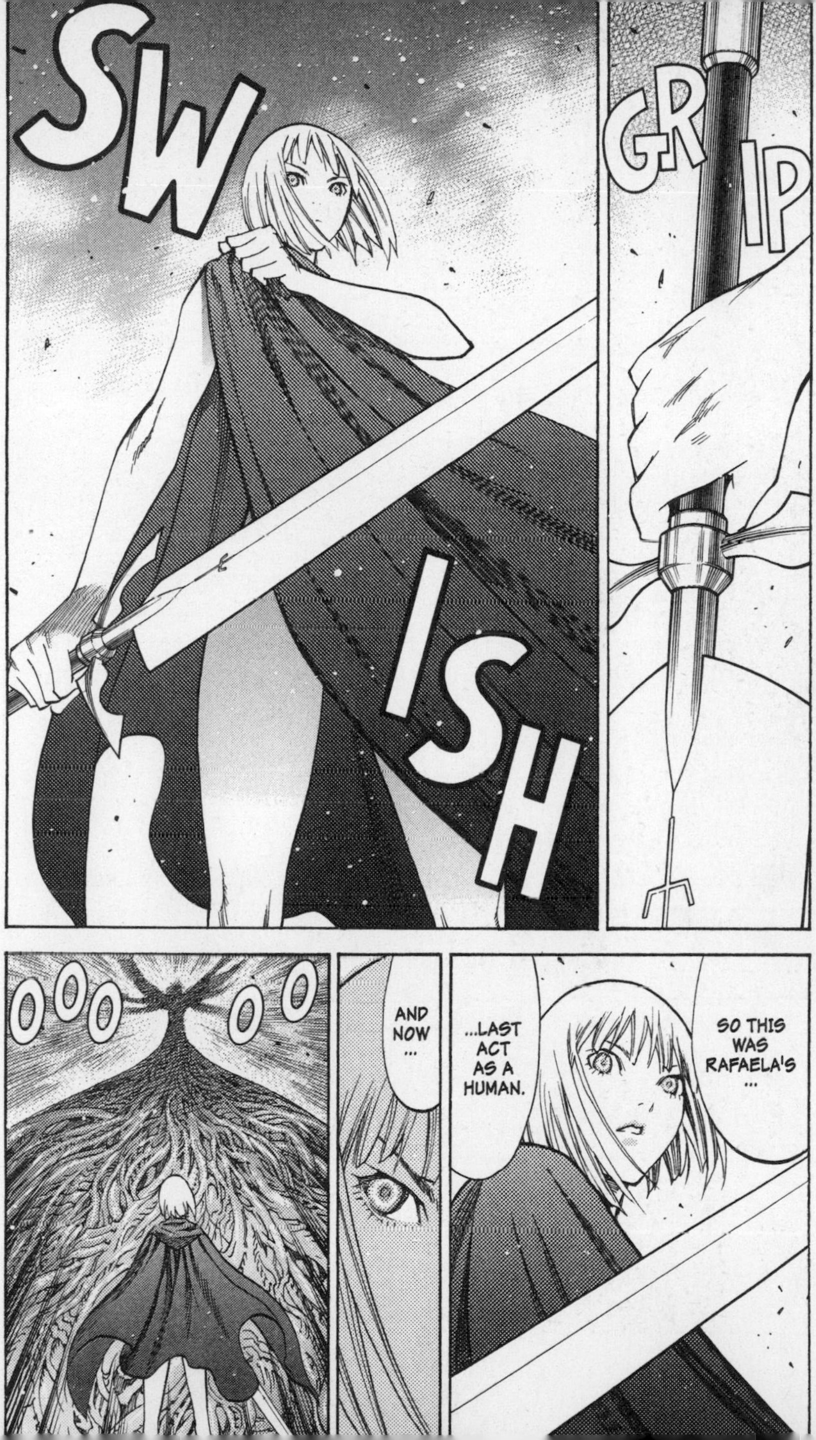
GRIP
SWISH
SO THIS WAS RAFAELA'S ...
...LAST ACT AS A HUMAN.
AND NOW ...
OOOO
OO

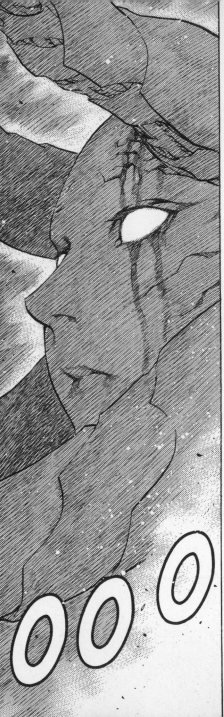

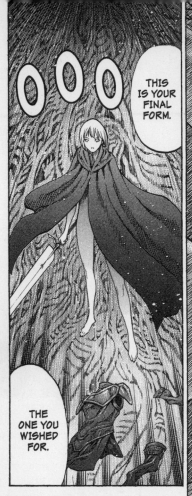

THIS IS YOUR FINAL FORM.

THE ONE YOU WISHED FOR.

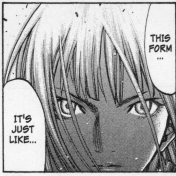

THIS FORM...

IT'S JUST LIKE...

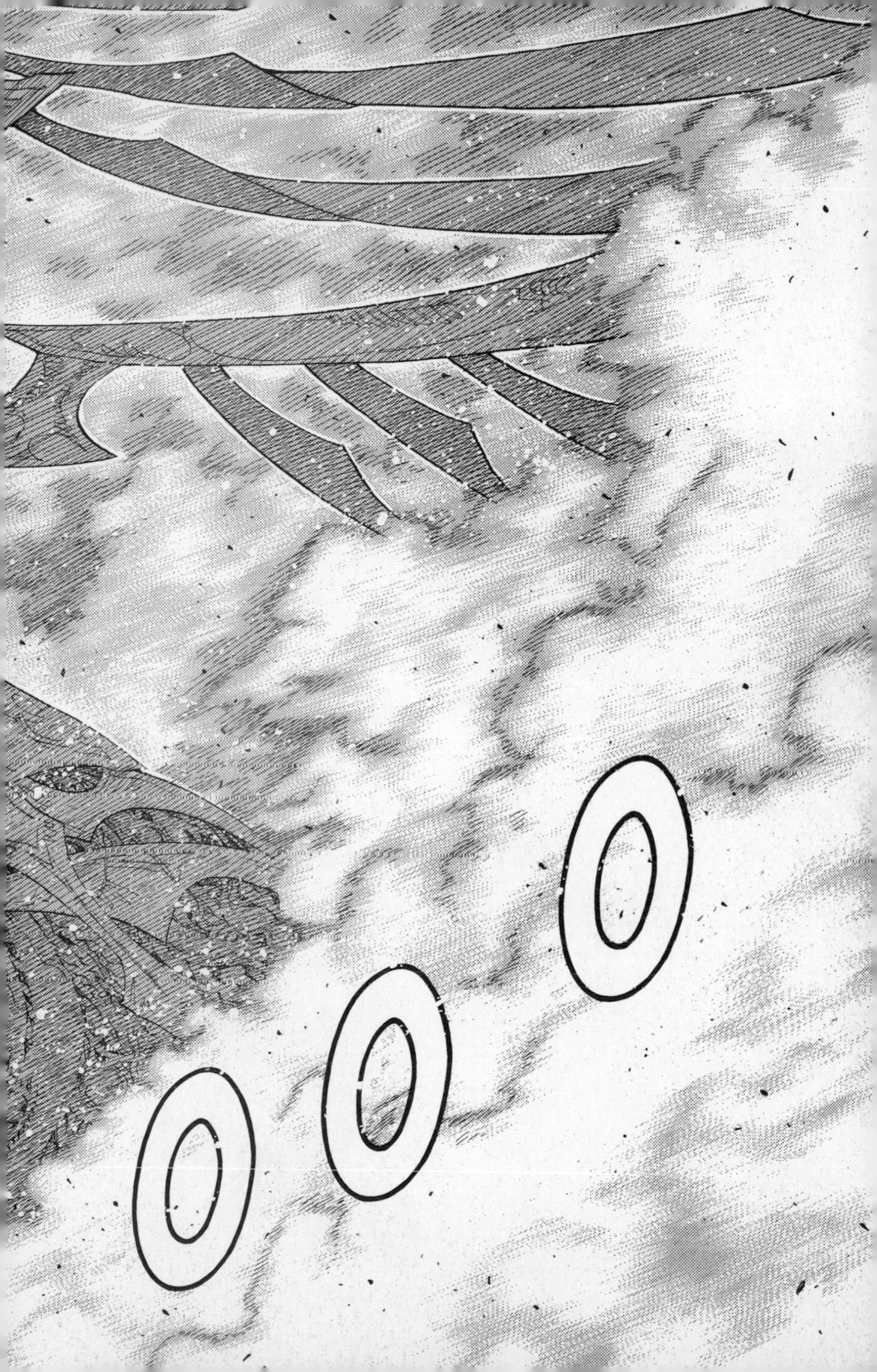

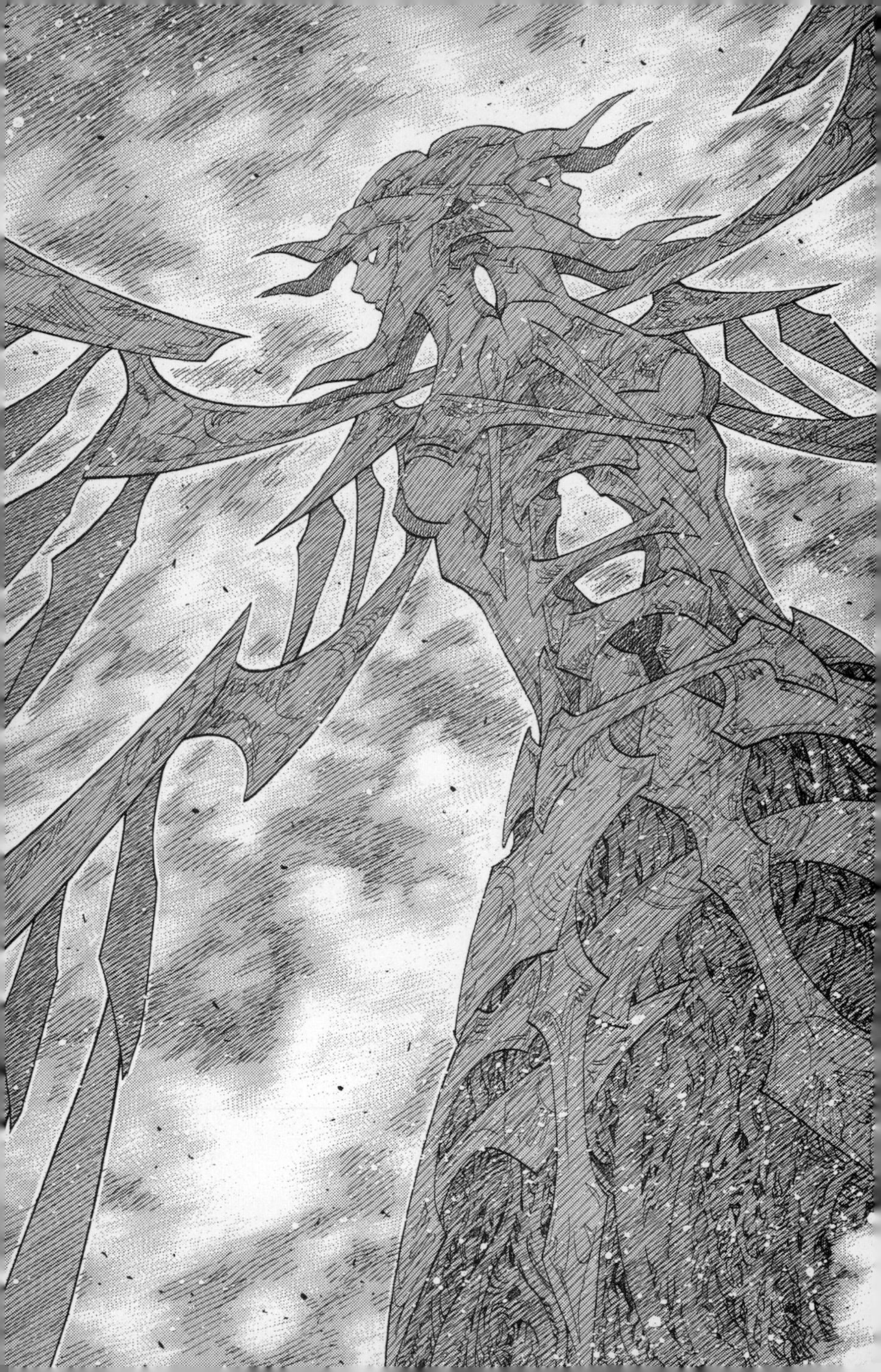

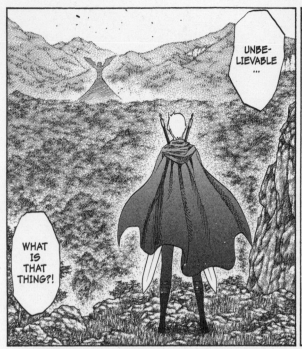

TCH.
UNBE-LIEVABLE ...
WHAT IS THAT THING?!
JUDGING FROM ITS AURA ALONE...
BIRI
BIRI
...IT EASILY SURPASSES RIFUL OR ISLEY.
BIRI
CYNTHIA! ARE YOU DONE YET?!
UH... ALMOST!
JUST A LITTLE MORE!
BIKI
BIKI
BIKI
SHHP

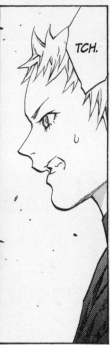

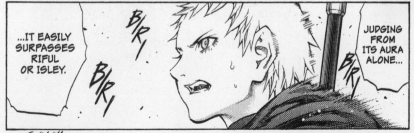

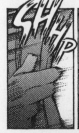

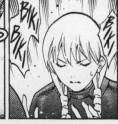

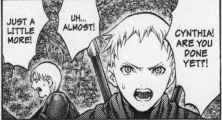

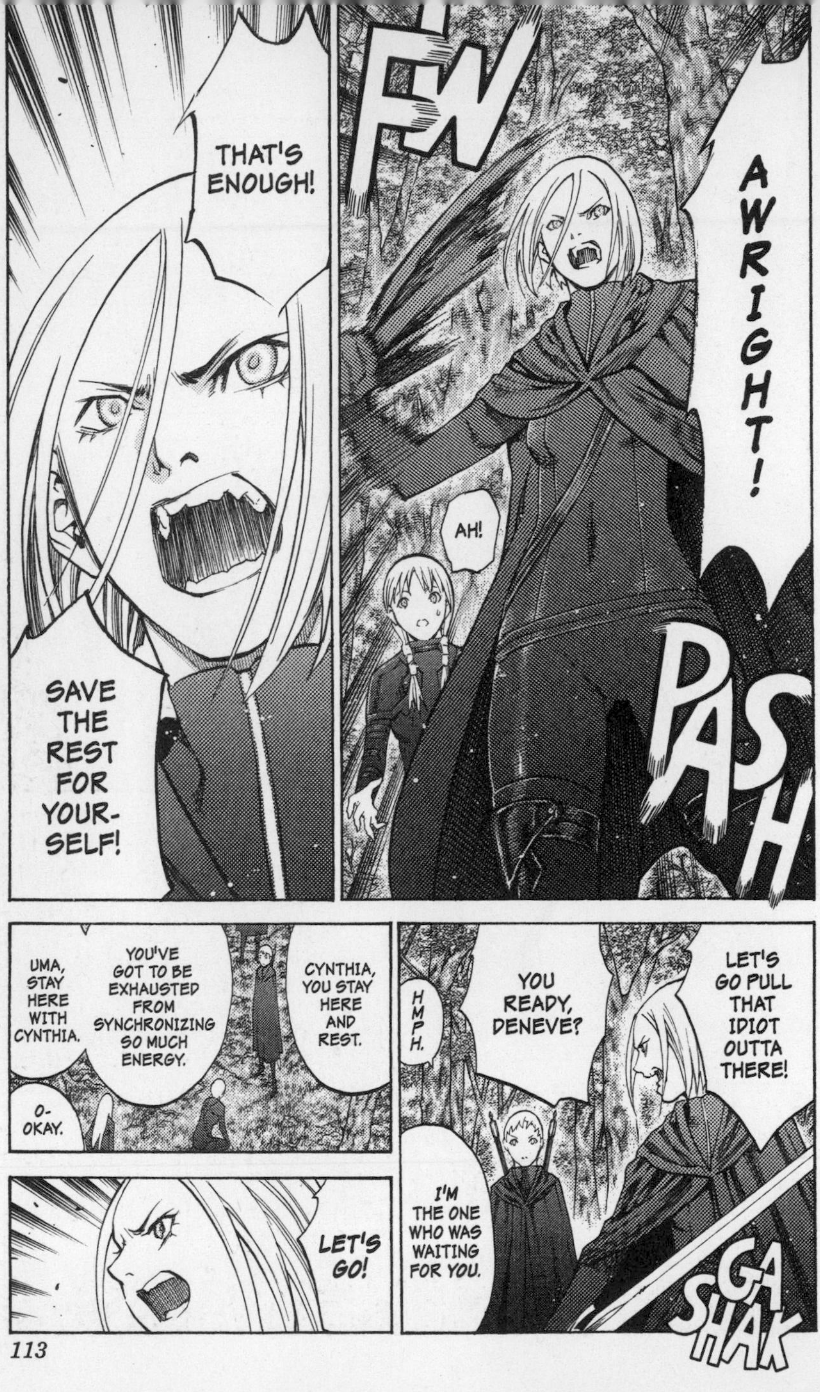
FW
AWRIGHT!
AH!
PASH
THAT'S ENOUGH!
SAVE THE REST FOR YOUR-SELF!
LET'S GO PULL THAT IDIOT OUTTA THERE!
YOU READY, DENEVE?
HMPH.
I'M THE ONE WHO WAS WAITING FOR YOU.
GA SHAK
CYNTHIA, YOU STAY HERE AND REST.
YOU'VE GOT TO BE EXHAUSTED FROM SYNCHRONIZING SO MUCH ENERGY.
UMA, STAY HERE WITH CYNTHIA.
O-OKAY.
LET'S GO!

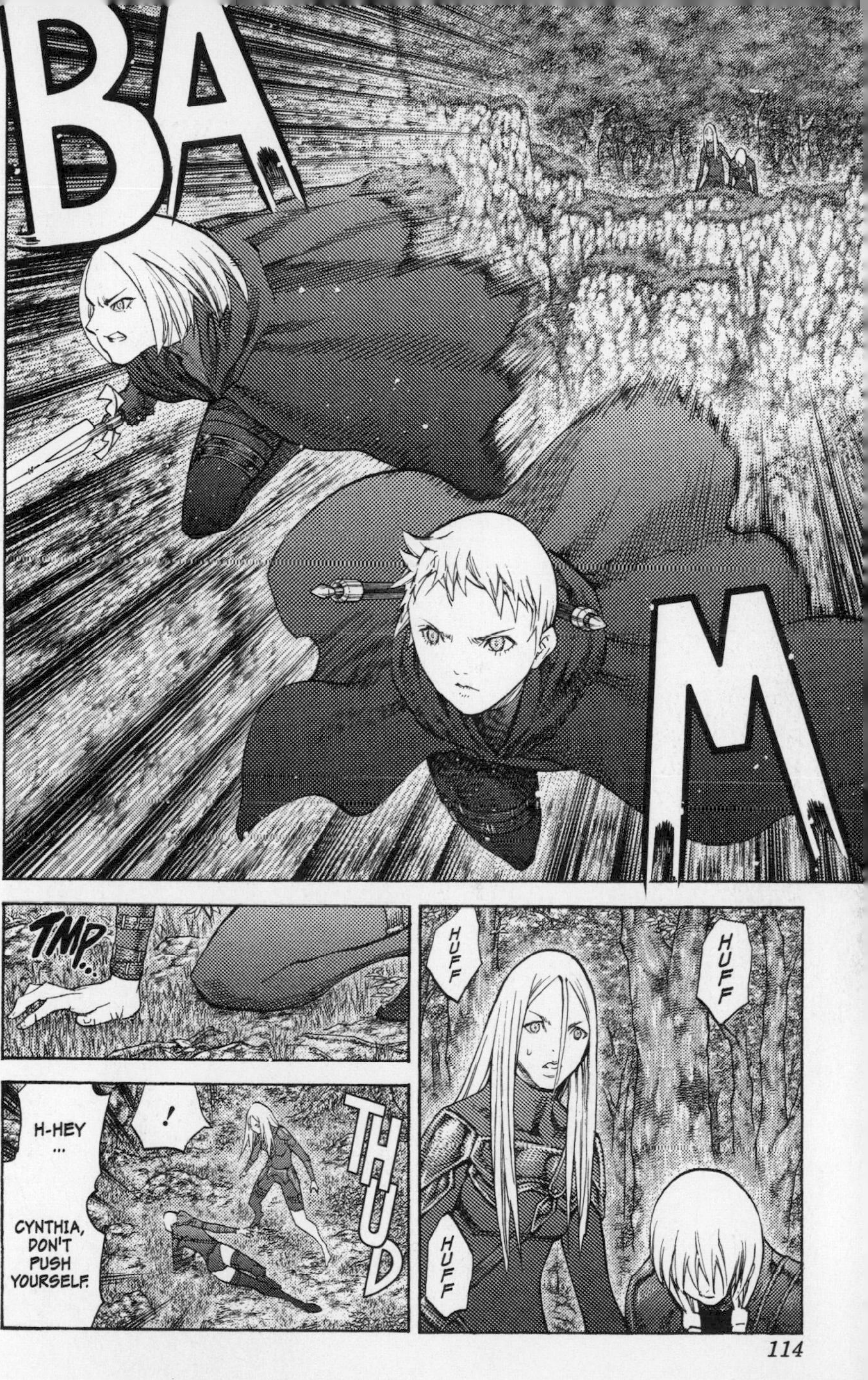
BA
M
HUFF
HUFF
HUFF
TMP...
THUD
!
H-HEY...
CYNTHIA, DON'T PUSH YOURSELF.

READ THIS WAY

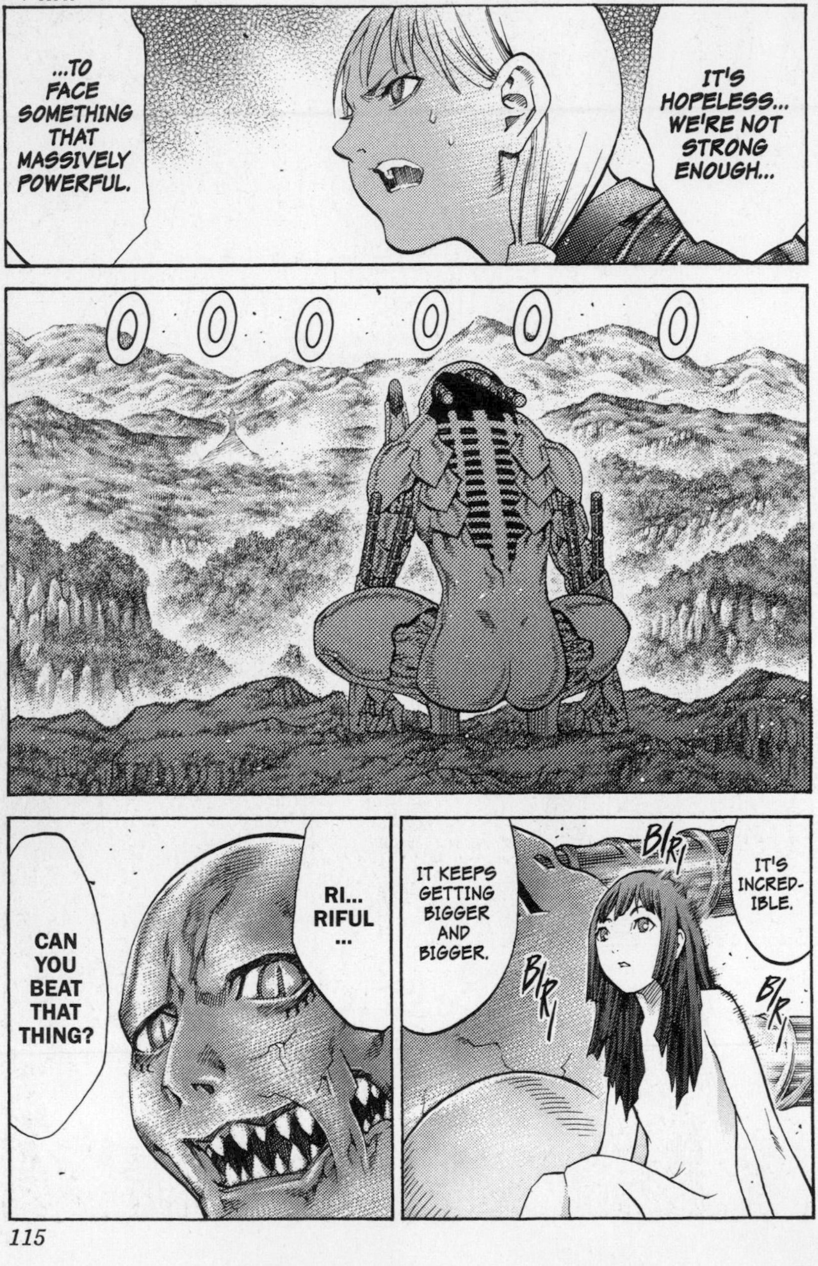
IT'S HOPELESS... WE'RE NOT STRONG ENOUGH...
...TO FACE SOMETHING THAT MASSIVELY POWERFUL.
O O O O O O
BIRI
IT'S INCRED-IBLE.
BIRI
BIRI
IT KEEPS GETTING BIGGER AND BIGGER.
RI... RIFUL ...
CAN YOU BEAT THAT THING?

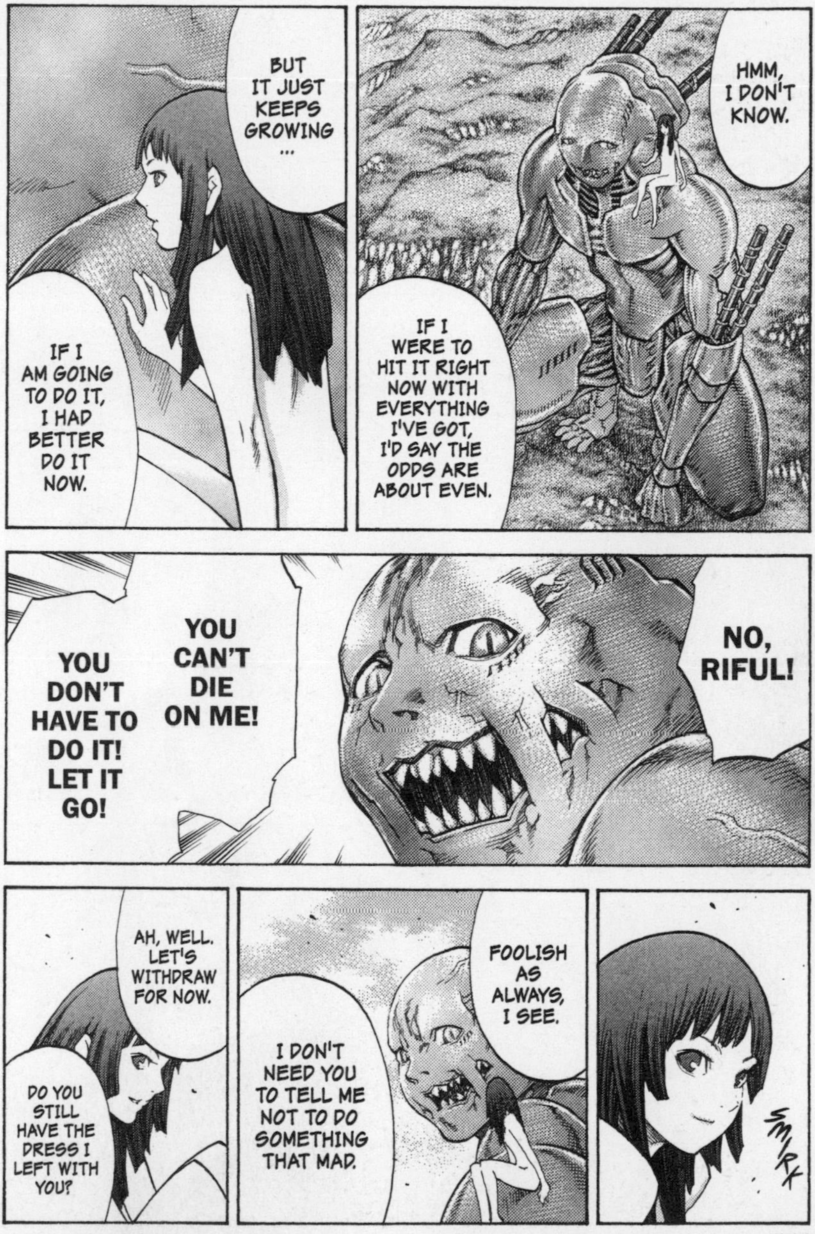
HMM, I DON'T KNOW.
IF I WERE TO HIT IT RIGHT NOW WITH EVERYTHING I'VE GOT, I'D SAY THE ODDS ARE ABOUT EVEN.
BUT IT JUST KEEPS GROWING ...
IF I AM GOING TO DO IT, I HAD BETTER DO IT NOW.
NO, RIFUL!
YOU CAN'T DIE ON ME!
YOU DON'T HAVE TO DO IT! LET IT GO!
...
SMIRK
FOOLISH AS ALWAYS, I SEE.
I DON'T NEED YOU TO TELL ME NOT TO DO SOMETHING THAT MAD.
AH, WELL. LET'S WITHDRAW FOR NOW.
DO YOU STILL HAVE THE DRESS I LEFT WITH YOU?

READ THIS WAY

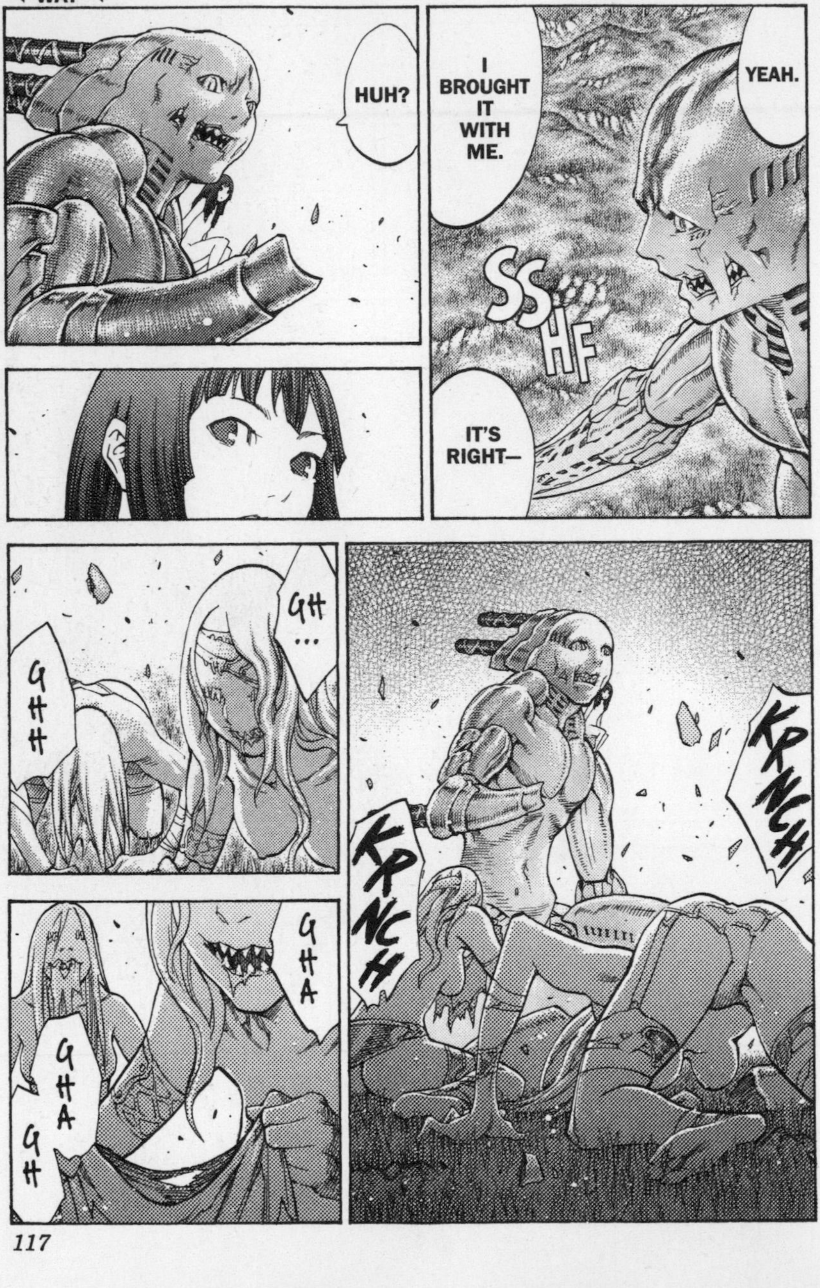
YEAH.
I BROUGHT IT WITH ME.
SSHF
IT'S RIGHT—
HUH?
KRNCH
KRNCH
GH...
GHH
GHA
GHA GH

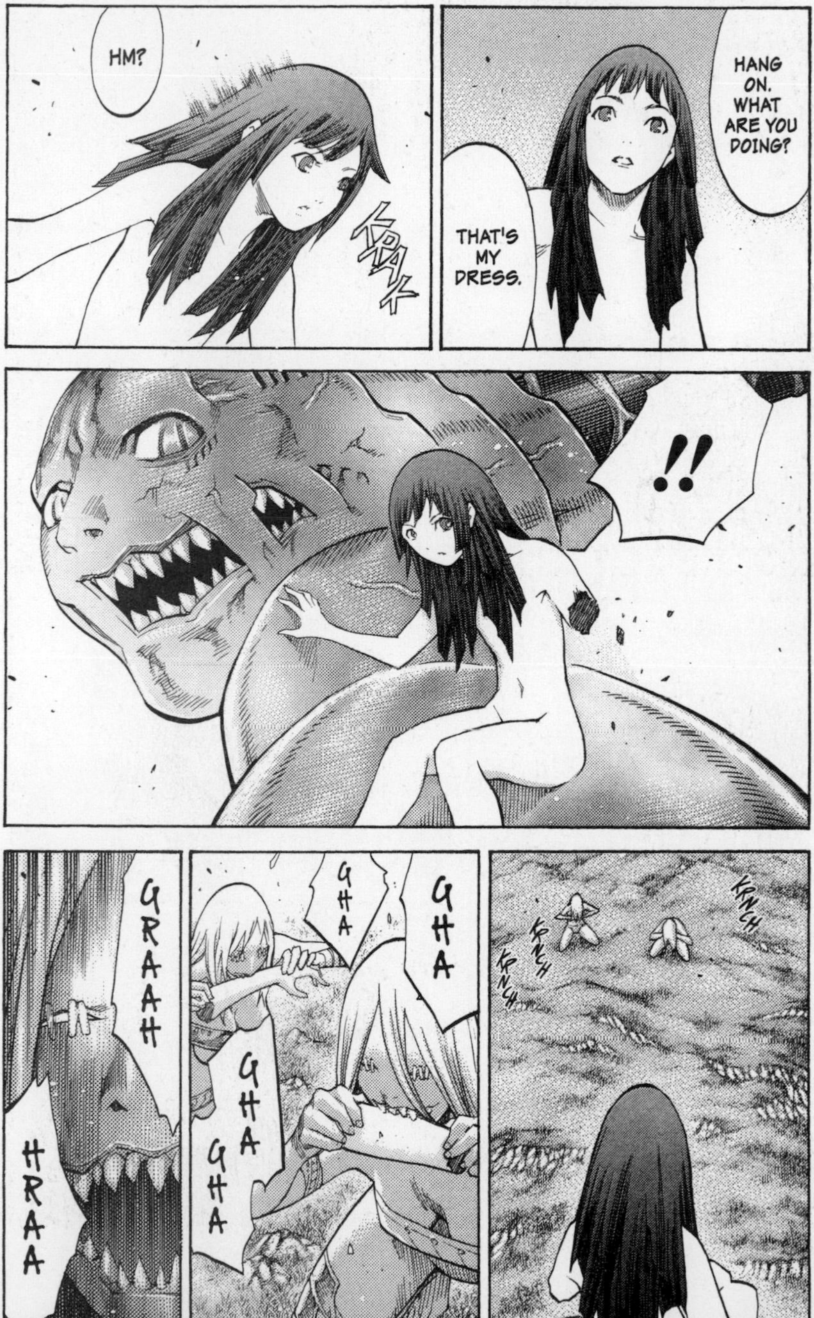
HANG ON. WHAT ARE YOU DOING?
THAT'S MY DRESS.
KRAK
HM?
!!
KRNCH
KRNCH
KRNCH
GHA
GHA
GHA
GHA
GRAAAH
HRAA

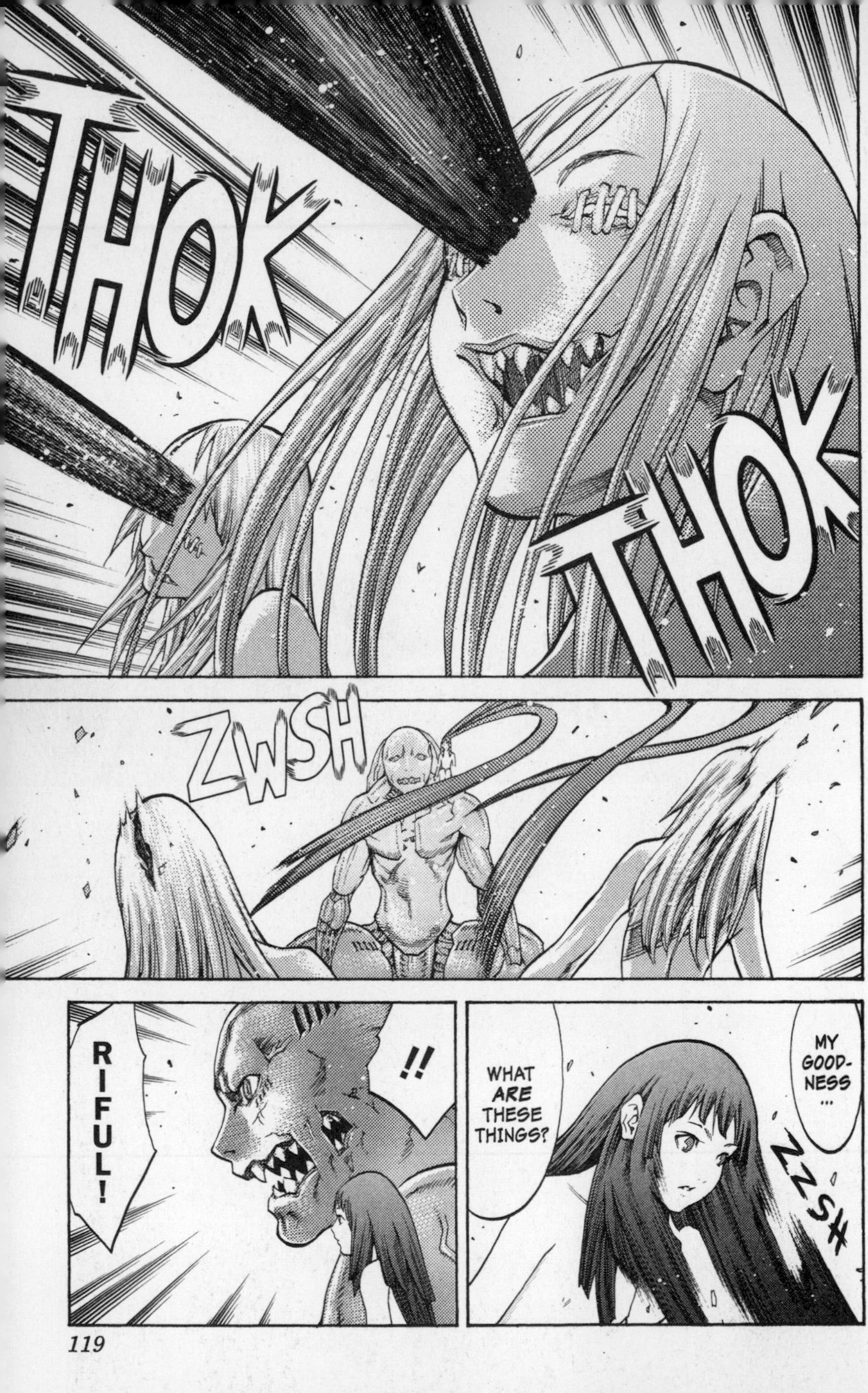
THOK
THOK
ZWSH
MY GOODNESS...
WHAT ARE THESE THINGS?
ZZSH
!!
RIFUL!

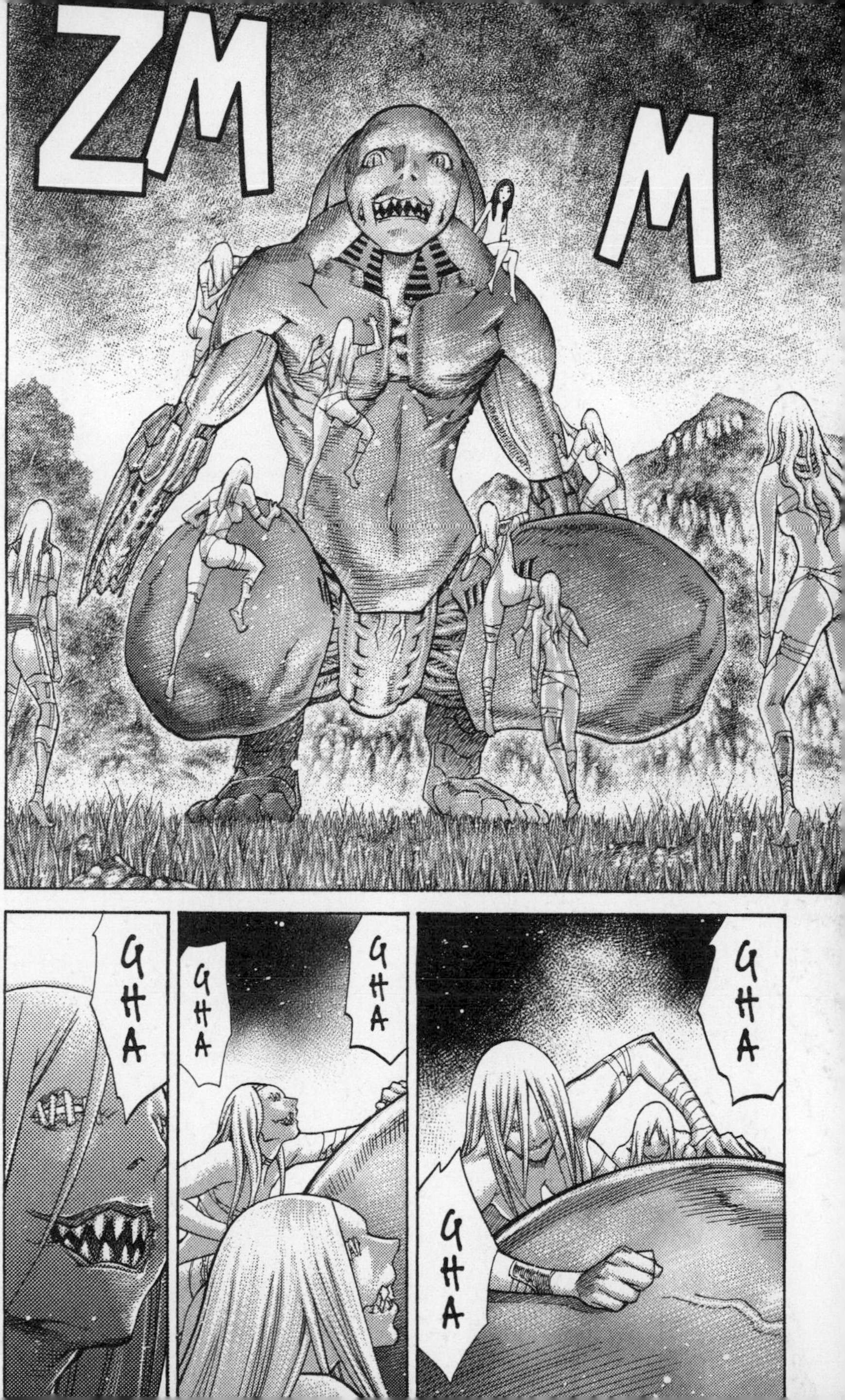
ZM
M
GHA
GHA
GHA
GHA
GHA

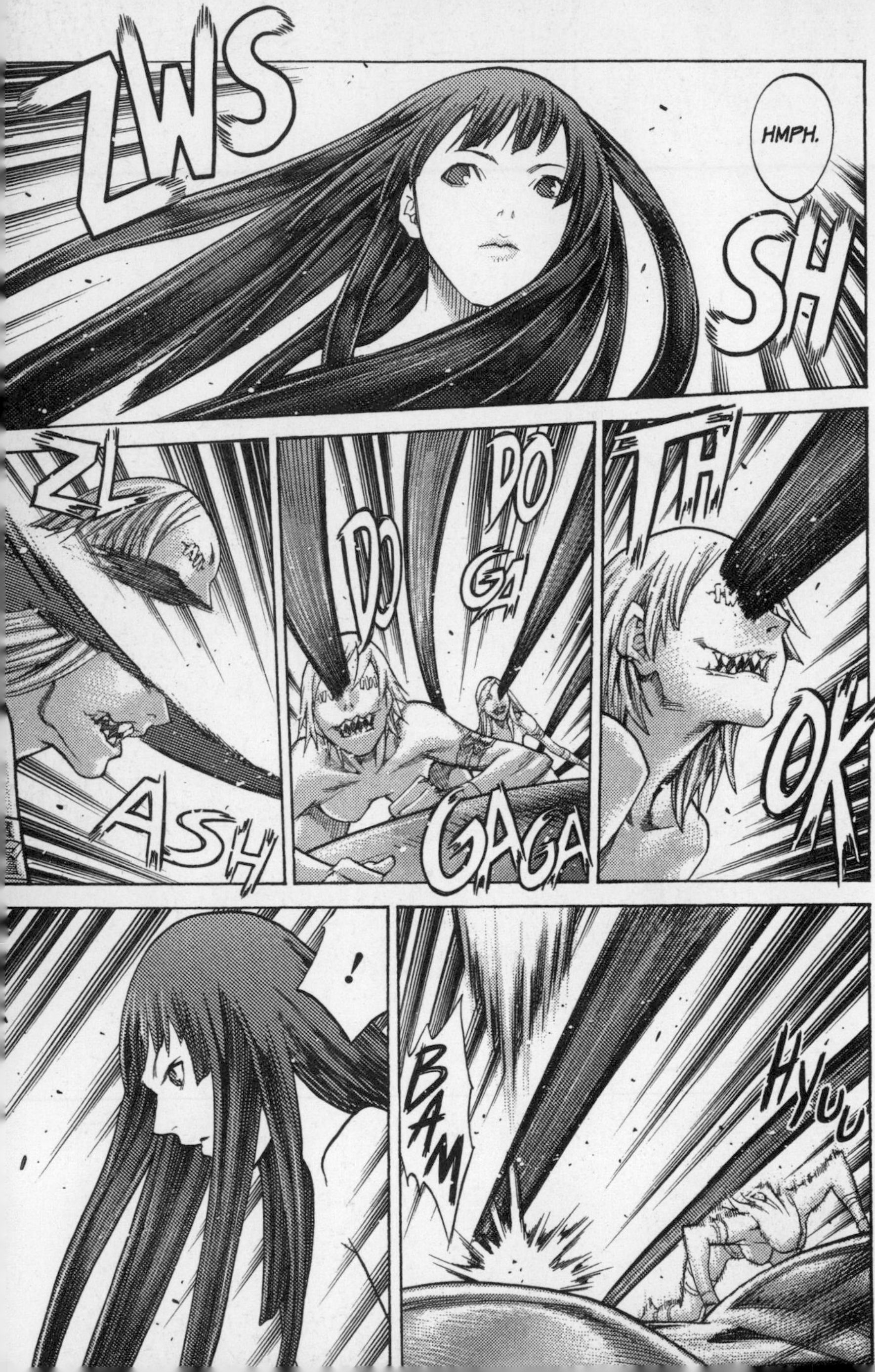
HMPH.
ZWS
SH
TH
OK
DO
DO
GA
GAGA
ZL
ASH
HYUU
BAM
!

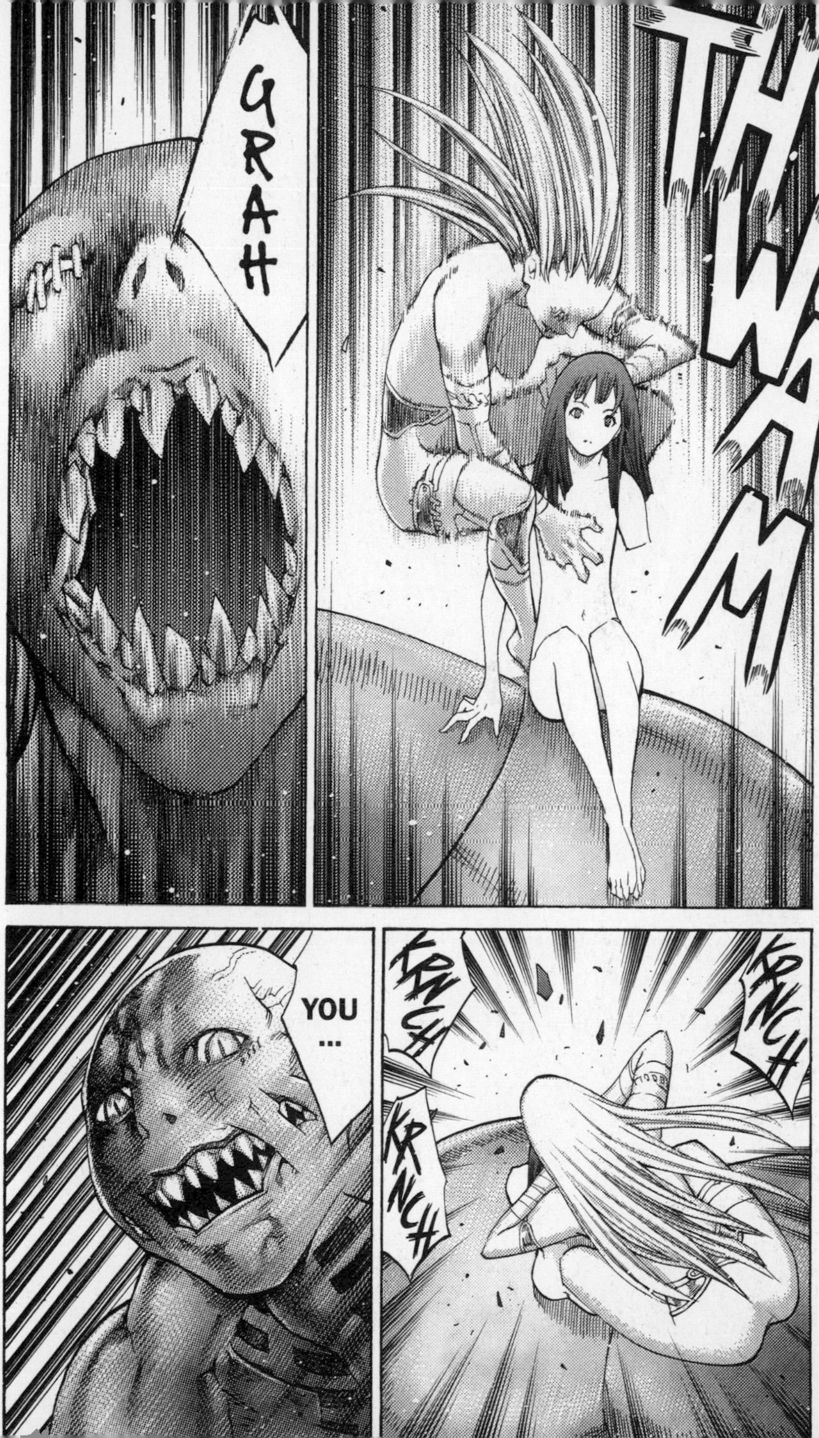
THWAMM
GRAH
KRNCH
KRNCH
KRNCH
YOU ...

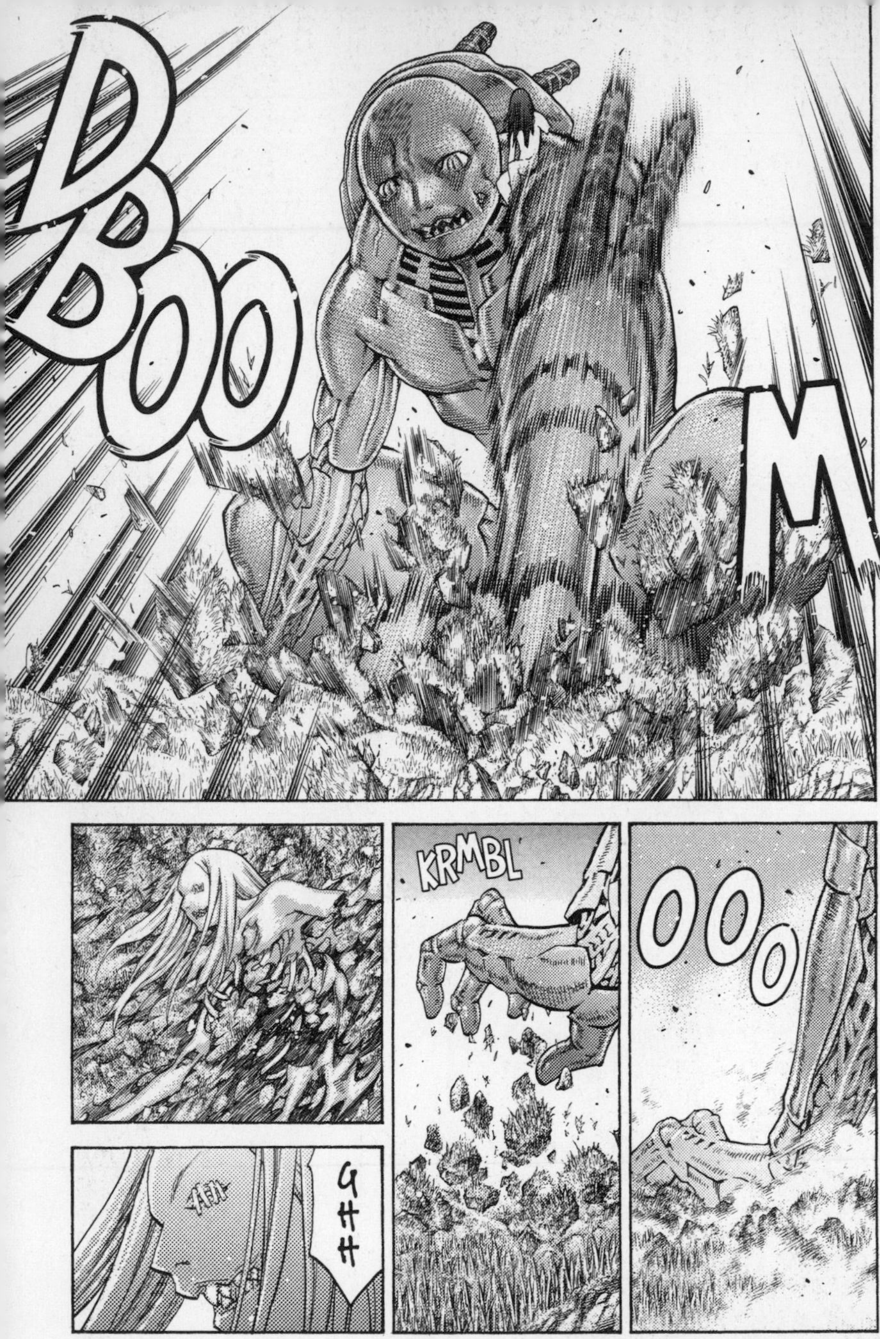
DBOOOM
OOO
KRMBL
GHH

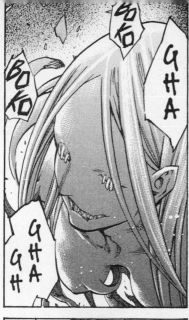

BO KO

BO KO

GHA

GHA

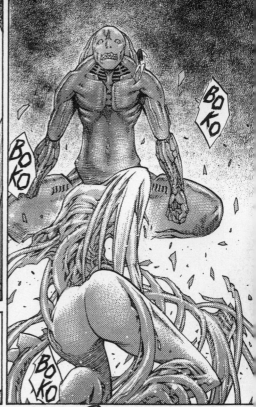

BO KO

BO KO

BO KO

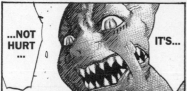

...NOT HURT...

IT'S...

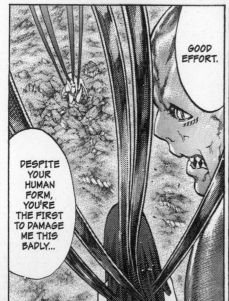

GOOD EFFORT.

DESPITE YOUR HUMAN FORM, YOU'RE THE FIRST TO DAMAGE ME THIS BADLY...

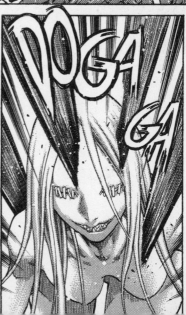

DOGA

GA

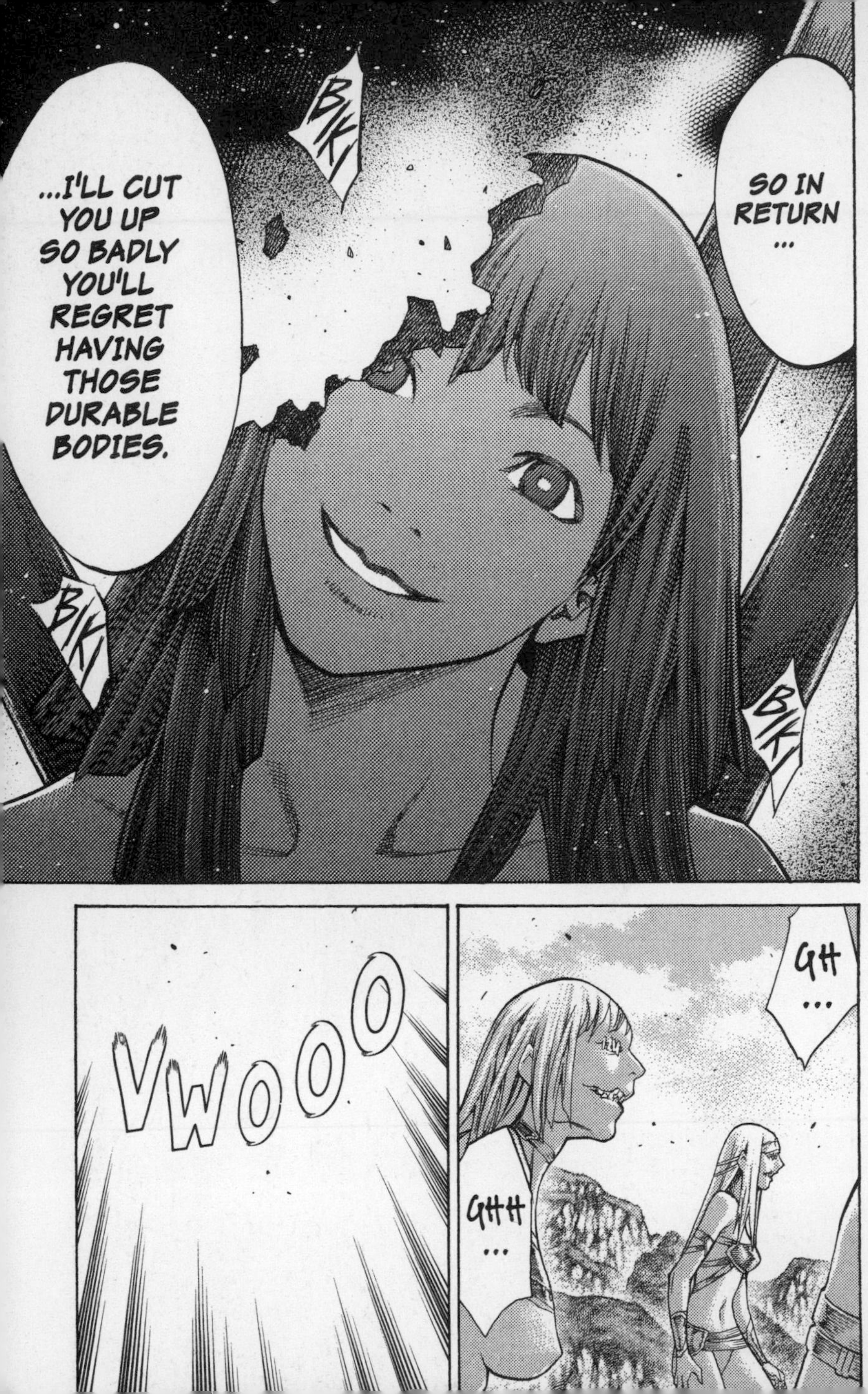
SO IN RETURN ...
BIKI
...I'LL CUT YOU UP SO BADLY YOU'LL REGRET HAVING THOSE DURABLE BODIES.
BIKI
BIKI
GH ...
GHH ...
VWOOO

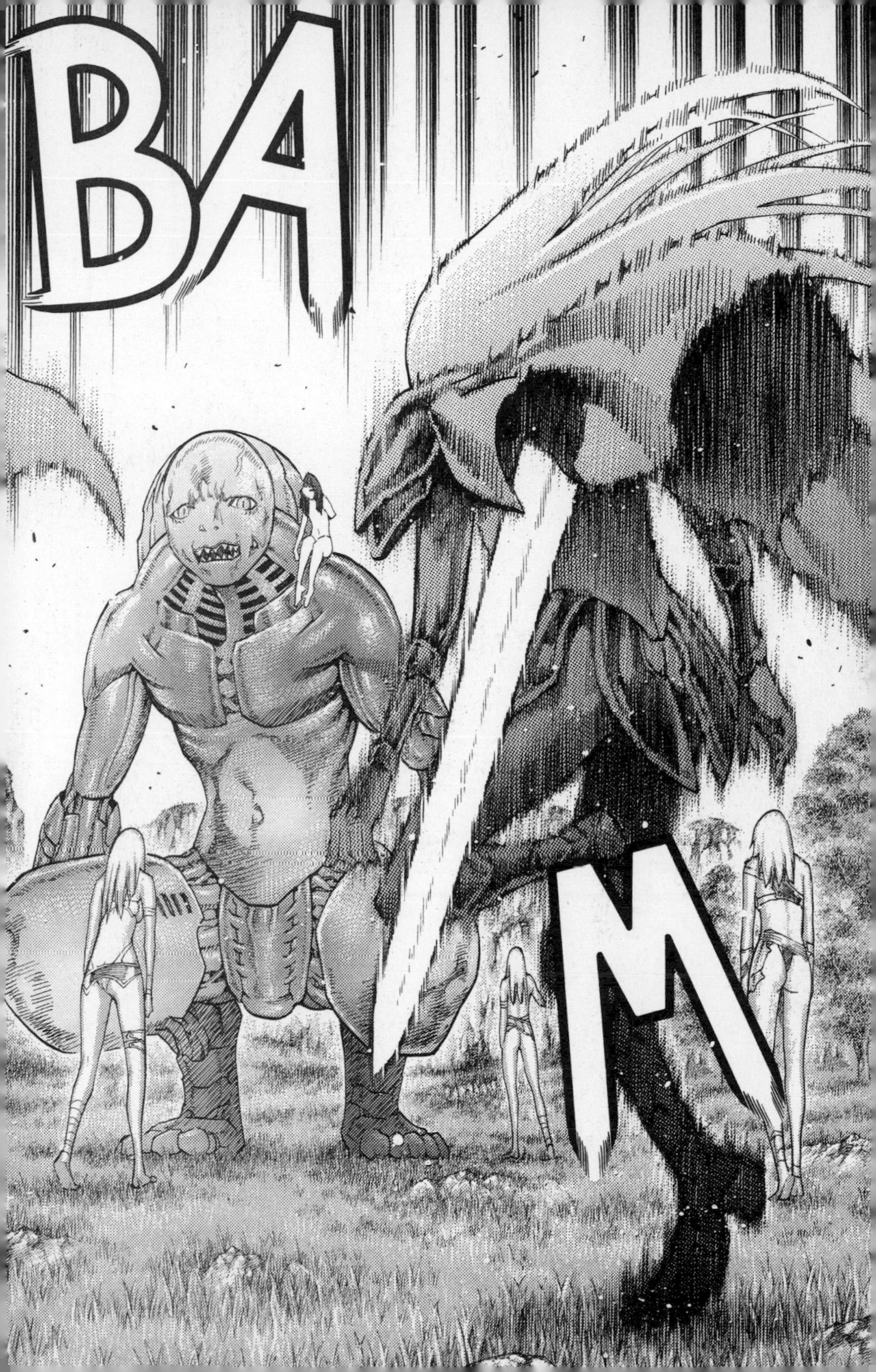
BA
M

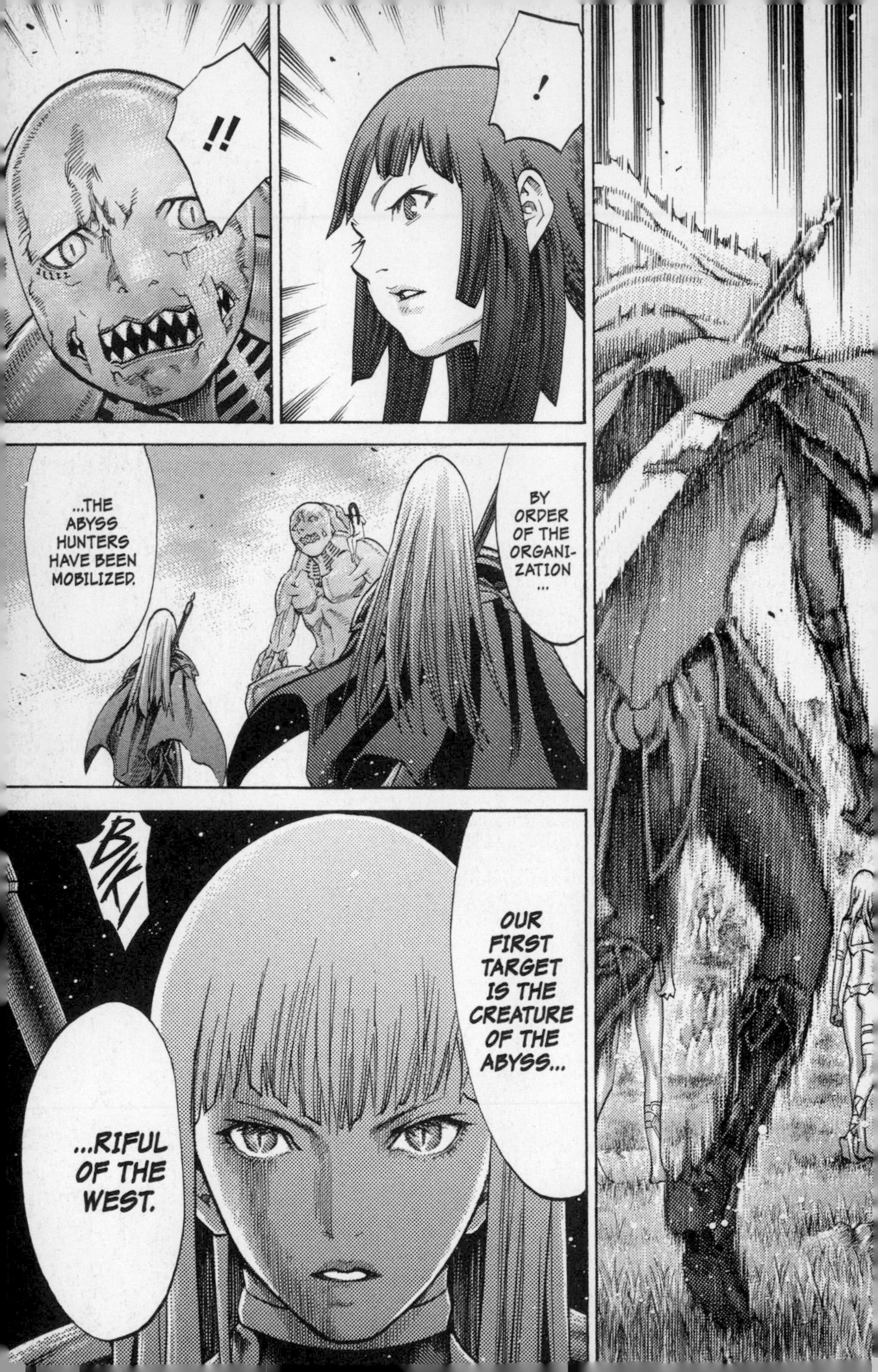
!
!!
BY ORDER OF THE ORGANIZATION ...
...THE ABYSS HUNTERS HAVE BEEN MOBILIZED.
BIKI
OUR FIRST TARGET IS THE CREATURE OF THE ABYSS...
...RIFUL OF THE WEST.

クレイモア
Claymore

SCENE 94: THE CLAWS OF MEMORY, PART 5

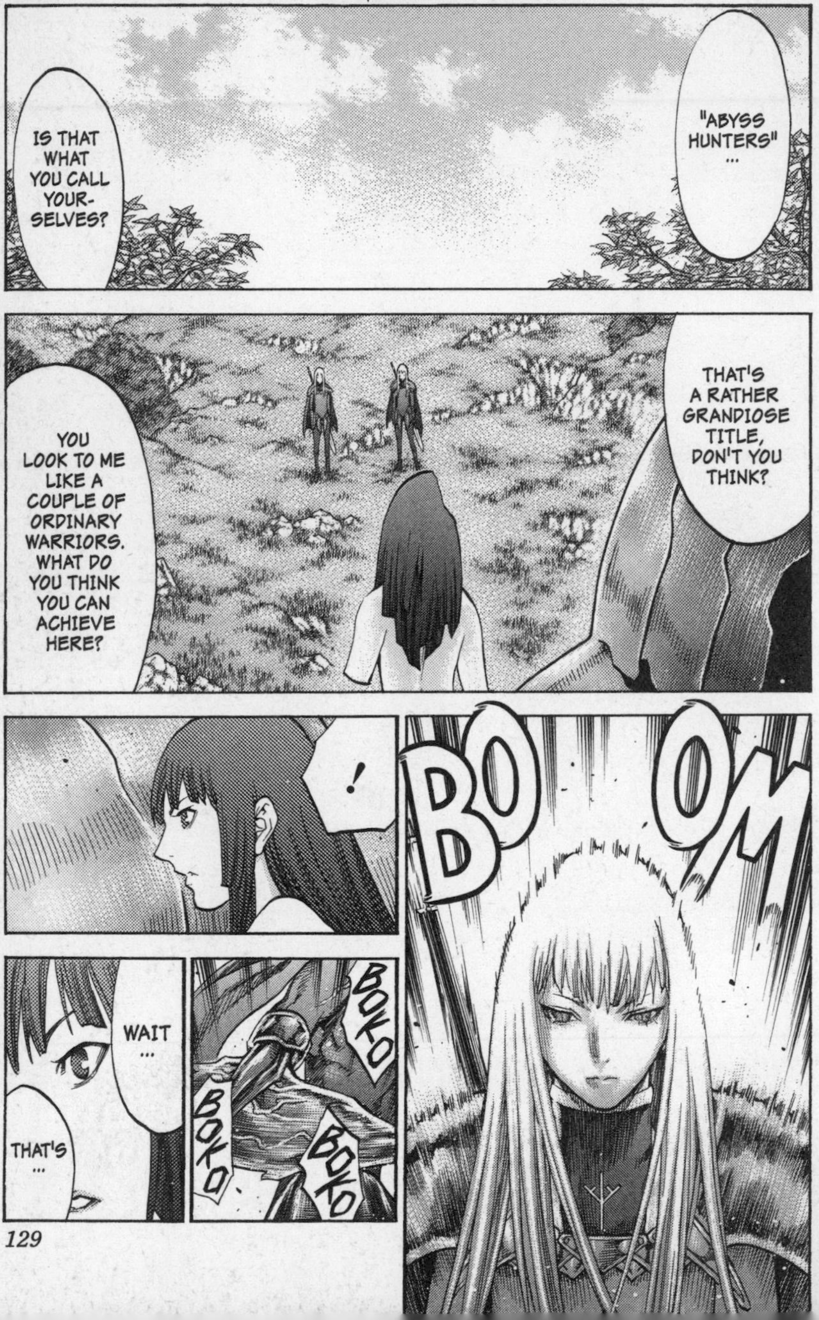
"ABYSS HUNTERS" ...
IS THAT WHAT YOU CALL YOUR-SELVES?
THAT'S A RATHER GRANDIOSE TITLE, DON'T YOU THINK?
YOU LOOK TO ME LIKE A COUPLE OF ORDINARY WARRIORS. WHAT DO YOU THINK YOU CAN ACHIEVE HERE?
BOOM
!
BOKO
BOKO
BOKO
WAIT ...
THAT'S ...

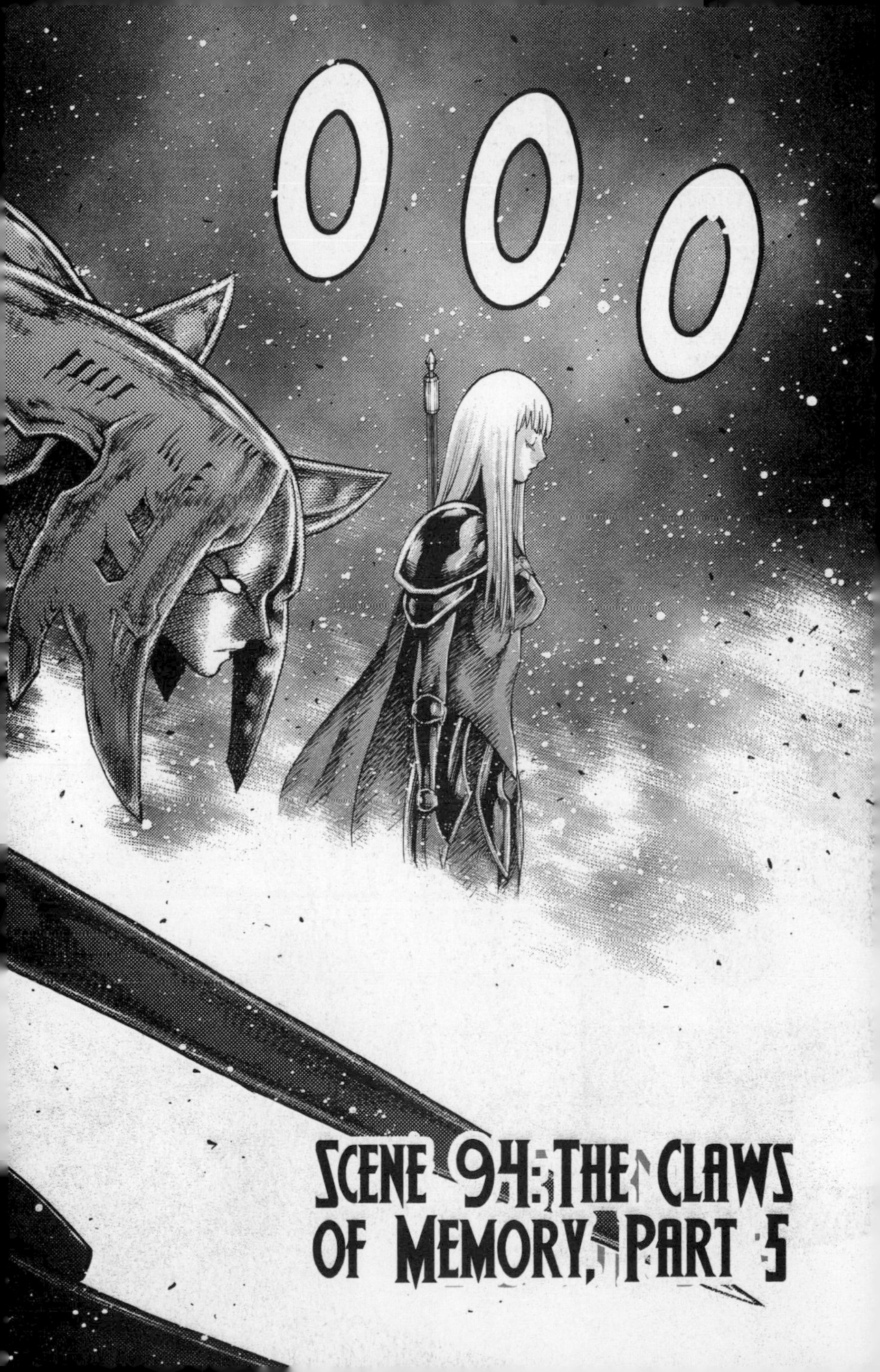

OOO
SCENE 94: THE CLAWS OF MEMORY, PART 5

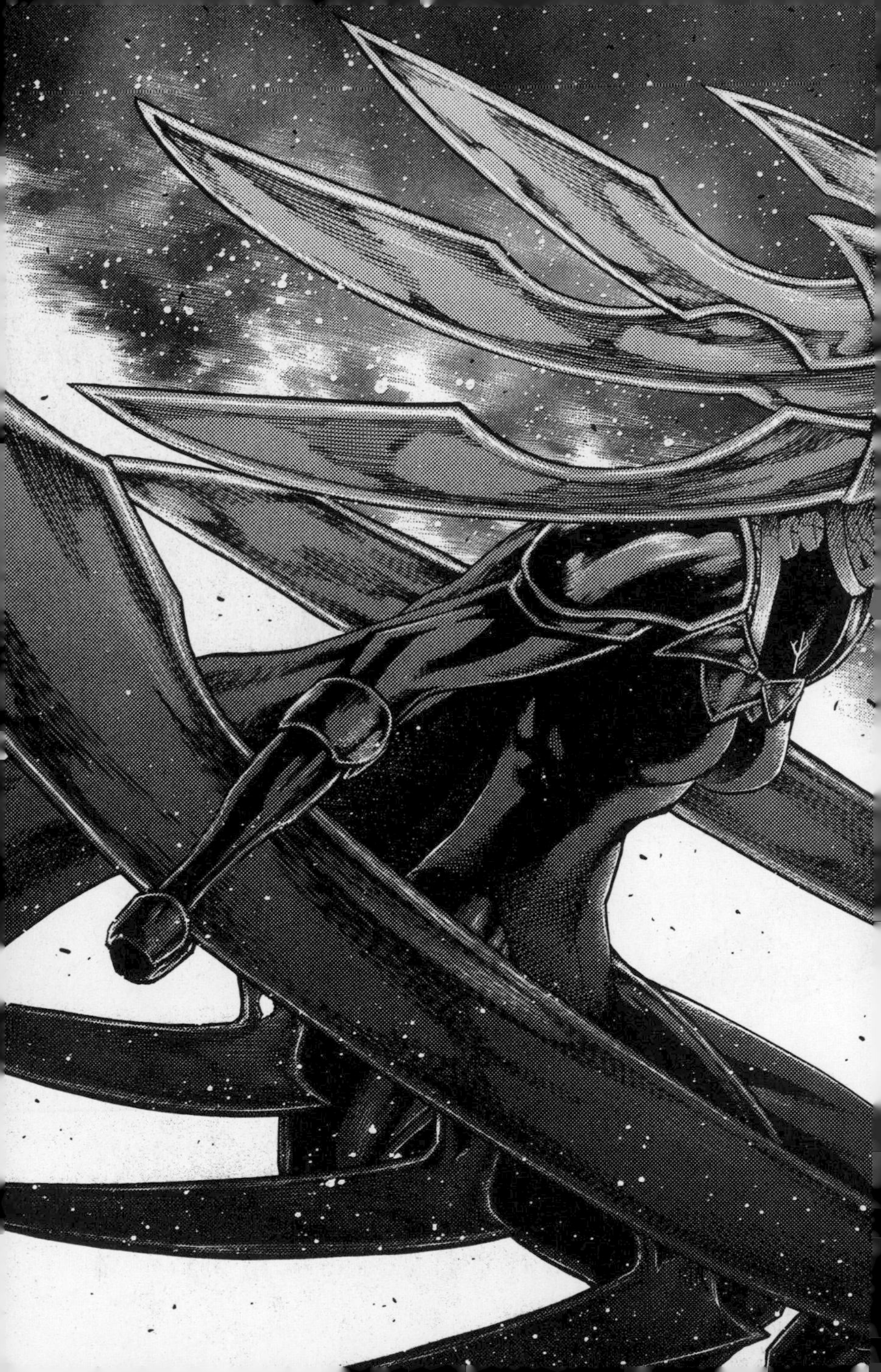

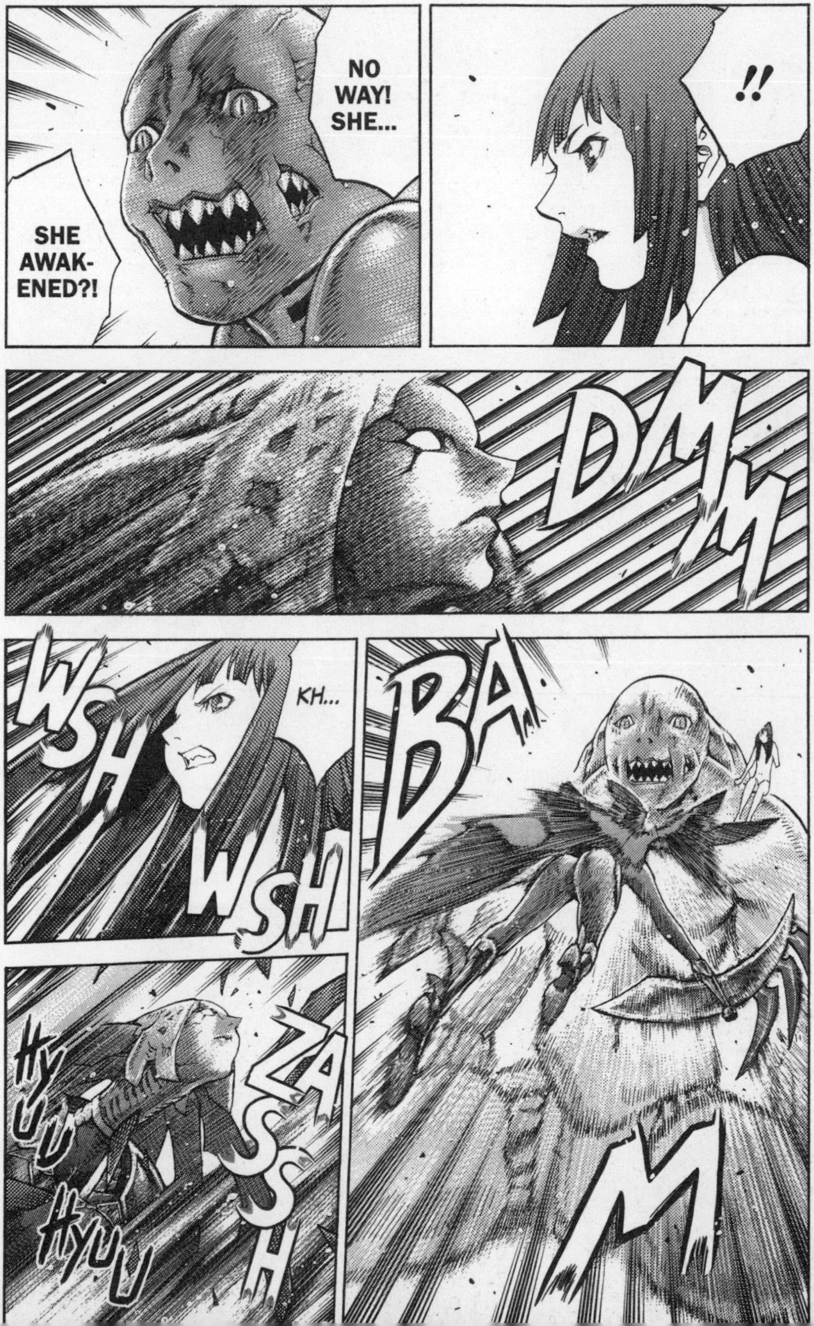
!!
NO WAY! SHE...
SHE AWAKENED?!
DMMM
BAM
KH...
WSH
WSH
HYUU
HYUU
ZASSH

READ THIS WAY

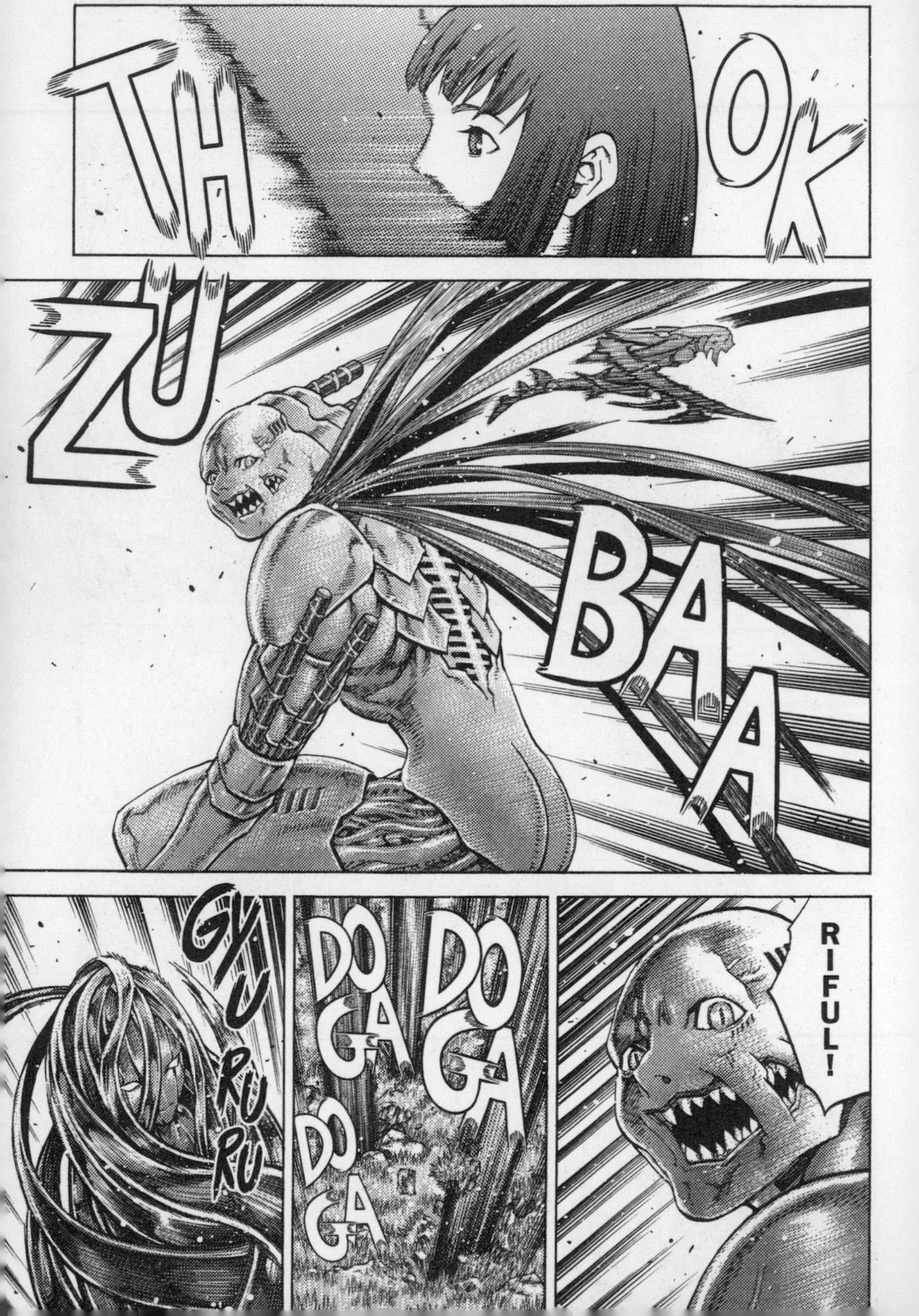

THOK
ZU
BAA
RIFUL!
DO GA
DO GA
DO GA
GYURURU

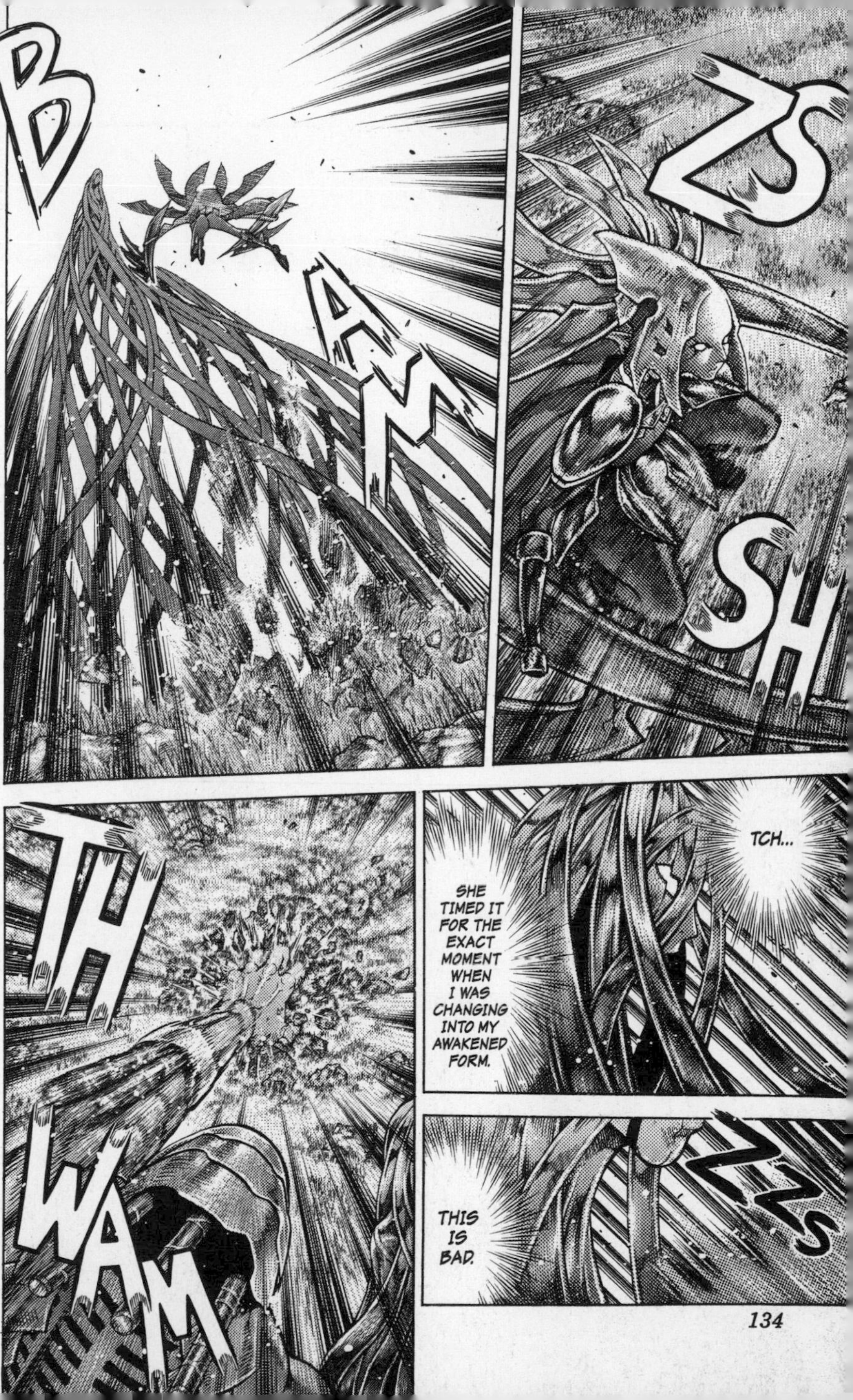
ZS
SH
BAM
TCH...
SHE TIMED IT FOR THE EXACT MOMENT WHEN I WAS CHANGING INTO MY AWAKENED FORM.
ZZS
THIS IS BAD.
TH
WAM

READ THIS WAY

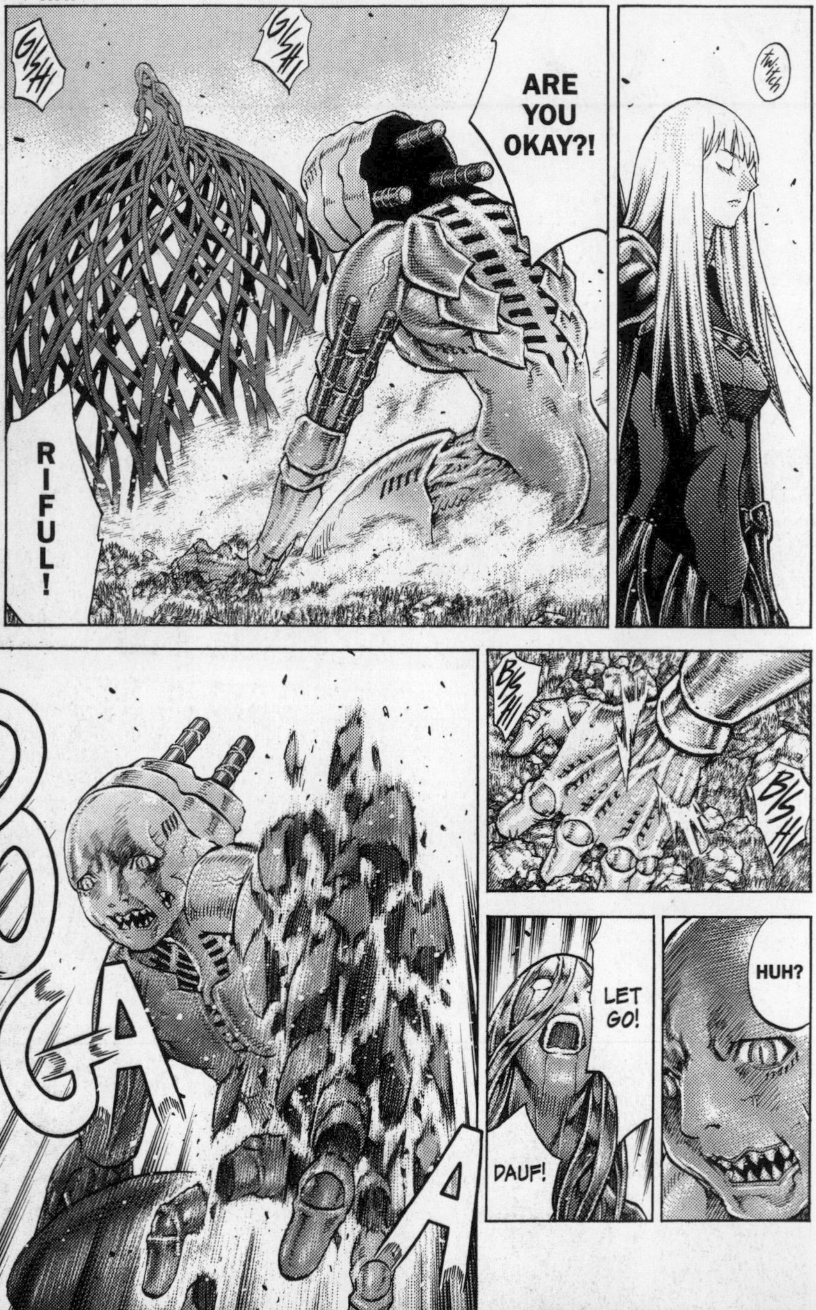
twitch
GISHI
ARE YOU OKAY?!
GISHI
RIFUL!
BISHI
BISHI
HUH?
LET GO!
DAUF!
DOGA
A

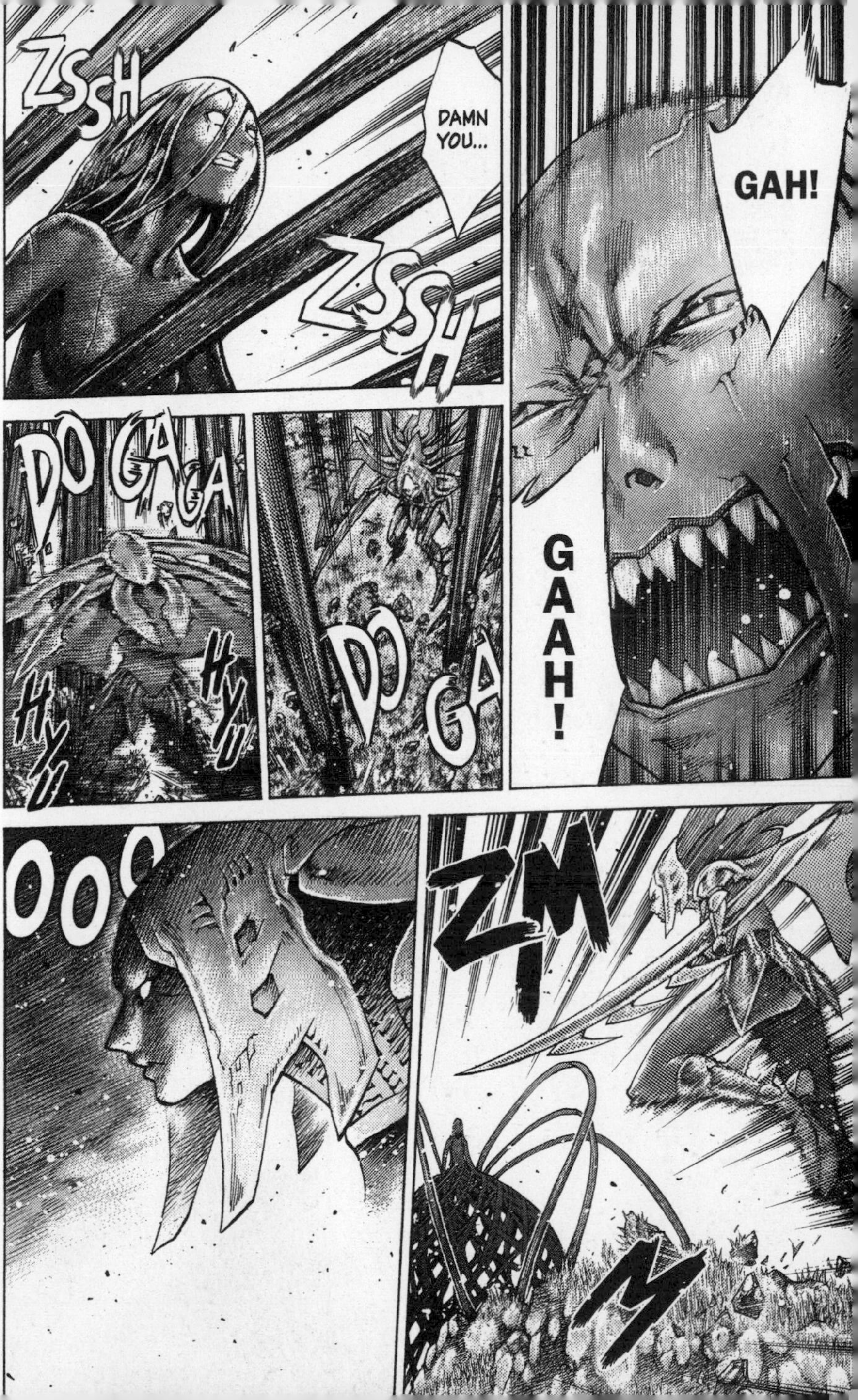
GAH!
GAAAH!
DAMN YOU...
ZSSH
ZSSH
DOGA
DOGAGA
HYU
HYU
ZM
M
OOO

READ THIS WAY

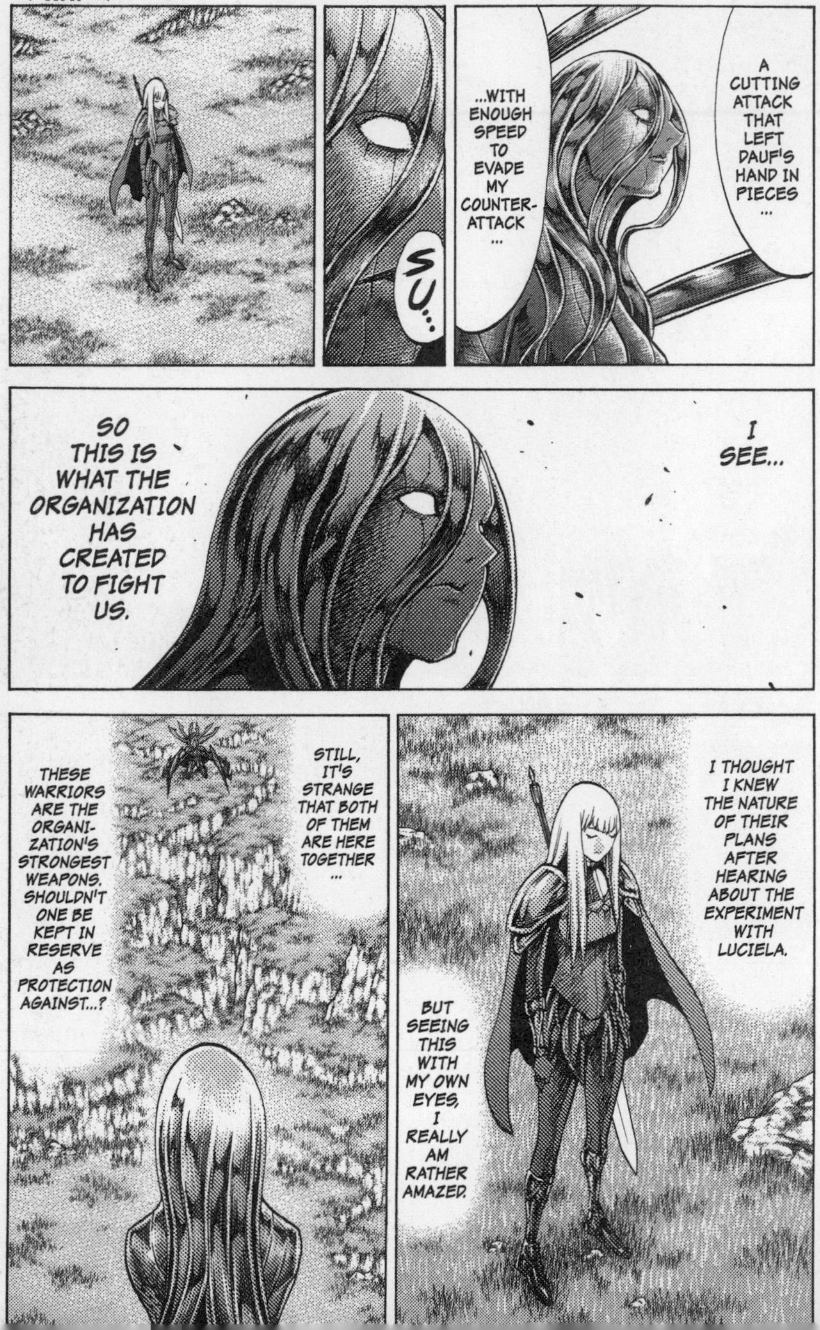
A CUTTING ATTACK THAT LEFT DAUF'S HAND IN PIECES ...
...WITH ENOUGH SPEED TO EVADE MY COUNTER-ATTACK ...
SU...
I SEE...
SO THIS IS WHAT THE ORGANIZATION HAS CREATED TO FIGHT US.
I THOUGHT I KNEW THE NATURE OF THEIR PLANS AFTER HEARING ABOUT THE EXPERIMENT WITH LUCIELA.
BUT SEEING THIS WITH MY OWN EYES, I REALLY AM RATHER AMAZED.
STILL, IT'S STRANGE THAT BOTH OF THEM ARE HERE TOGETHER ...
THESE WARRIORS ARE THE ORGANIZATION'S STRONGEST WEAPONS. SHOULDN'T ONE BE KEPT IN RESERVE AS PROTECTION AGAINST...?

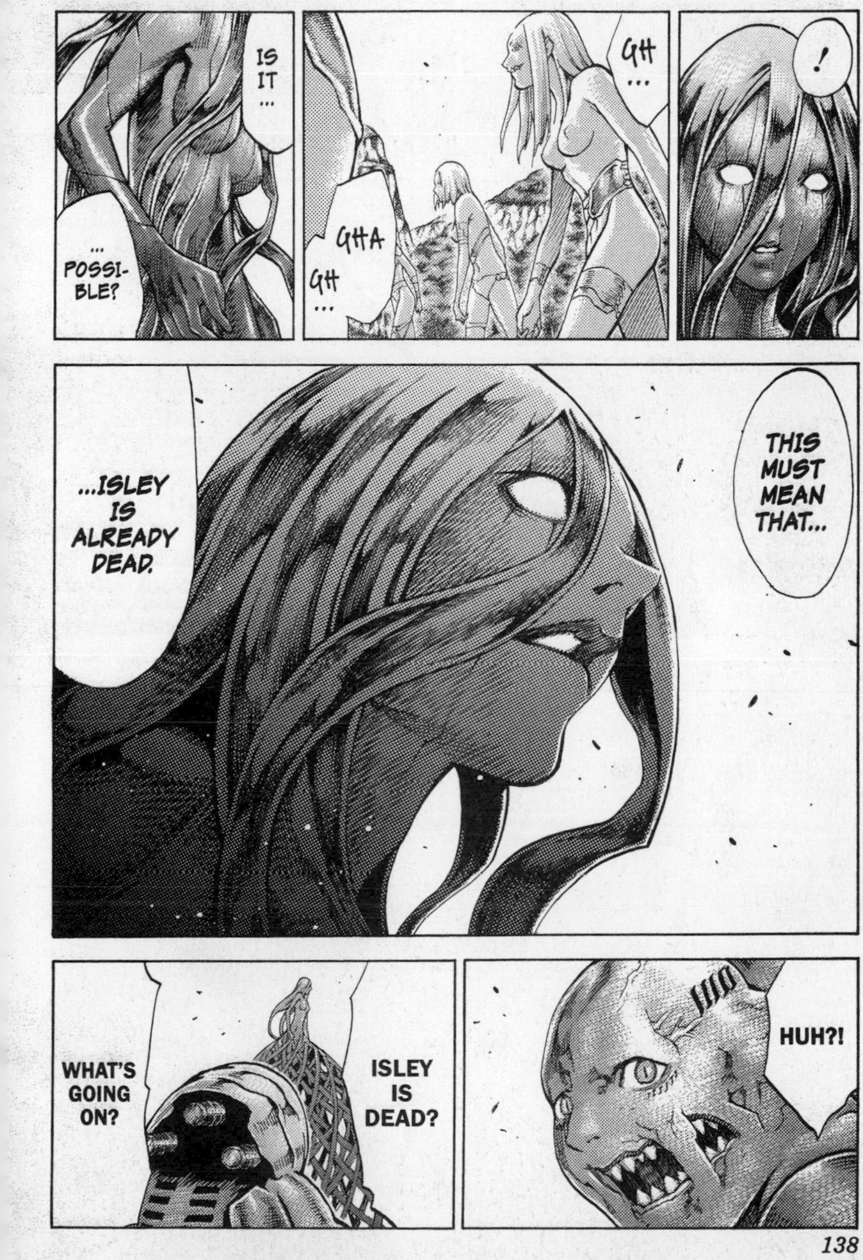
!
GH ...
GHA
GH ...
IS IT ...
... POSSI-BLE?
THIS MUST MEAN THAT...
...ISLEY IS ALREADY DEAD.
HUH?!
ISLEY IS DEAD?
WHAT'S GOING ON?

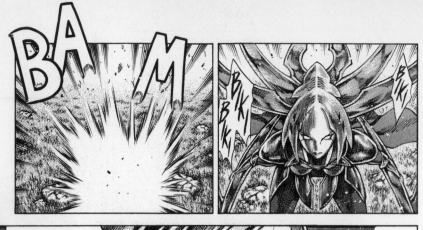

BAM M

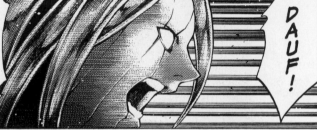

CRUSH THE ONE THAT'S NOT MOVING!

DAUF!

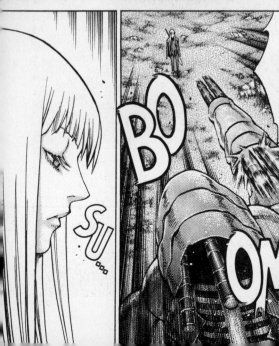

BO

GRAAH!

SU...

OM

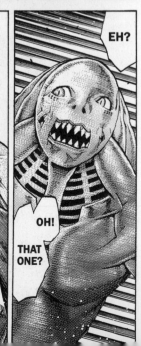

EH?

OH! THAT ONE?

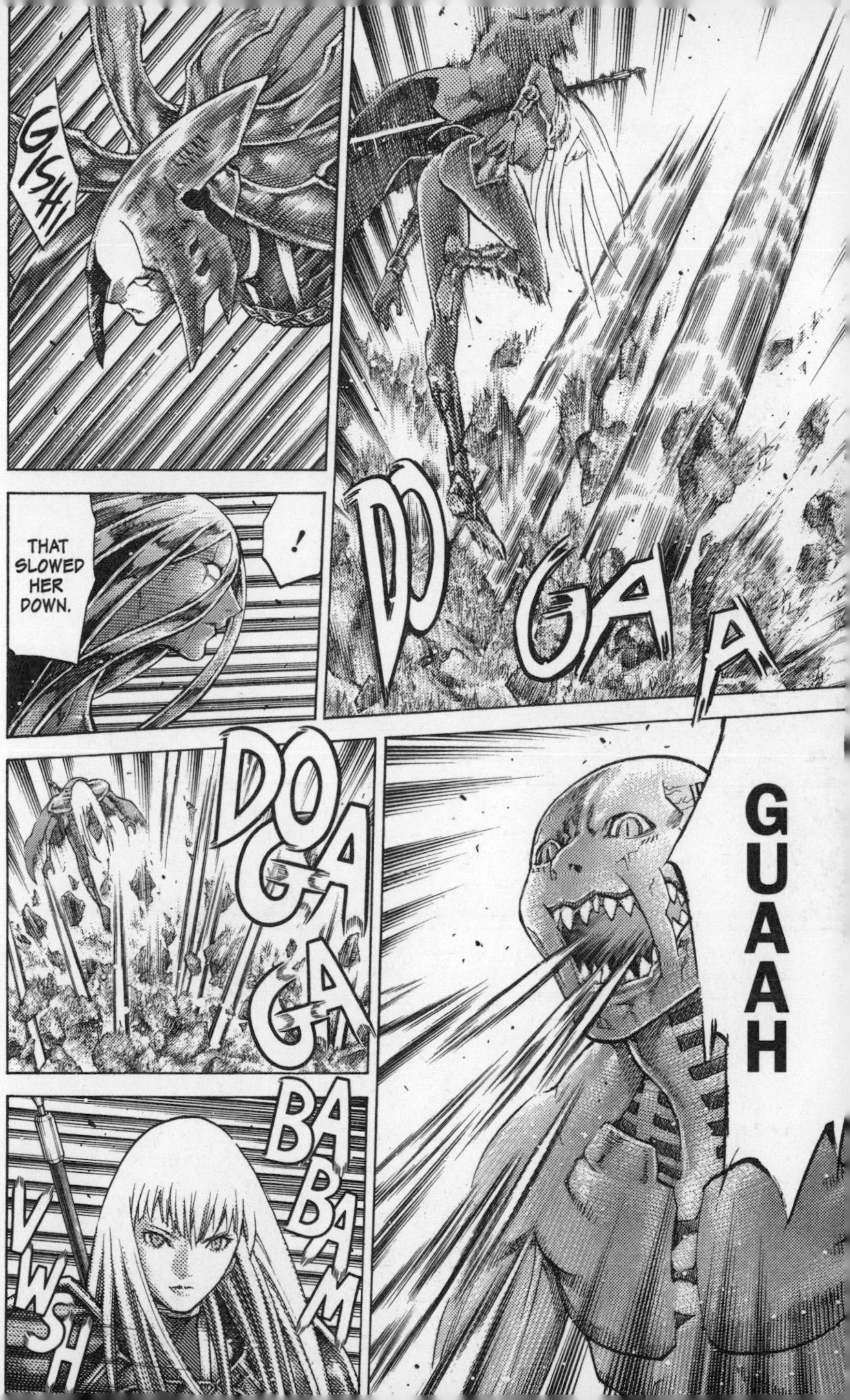
DOGAA
GISHI
THAT SLOWED HER DOWN.
!
GUAAH
DOGAGA
BABABAM
VWSH

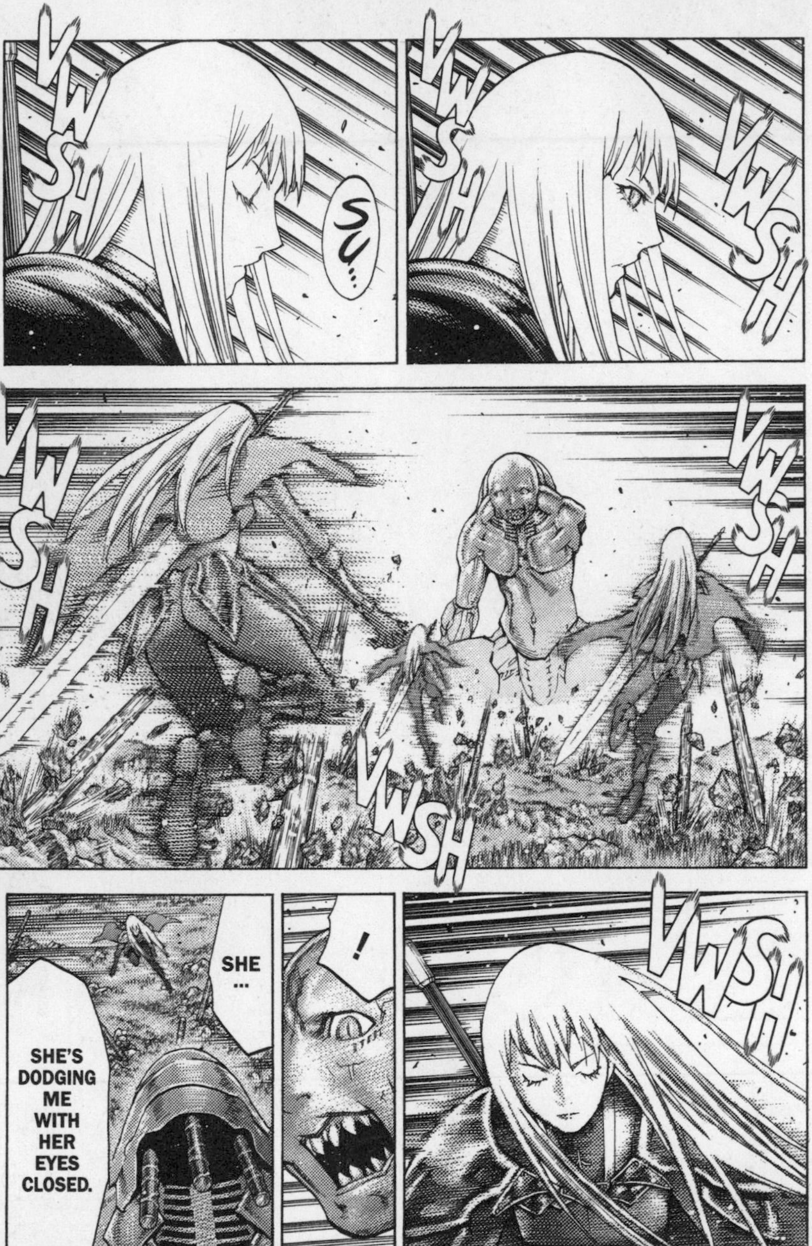
VWSH
VWSH
VWSH
SU...
VWSH
VWSH
VWSH
VWSH
!
SHE ...
SHE'S DODGING ME WITH HER EYES CLOSED.

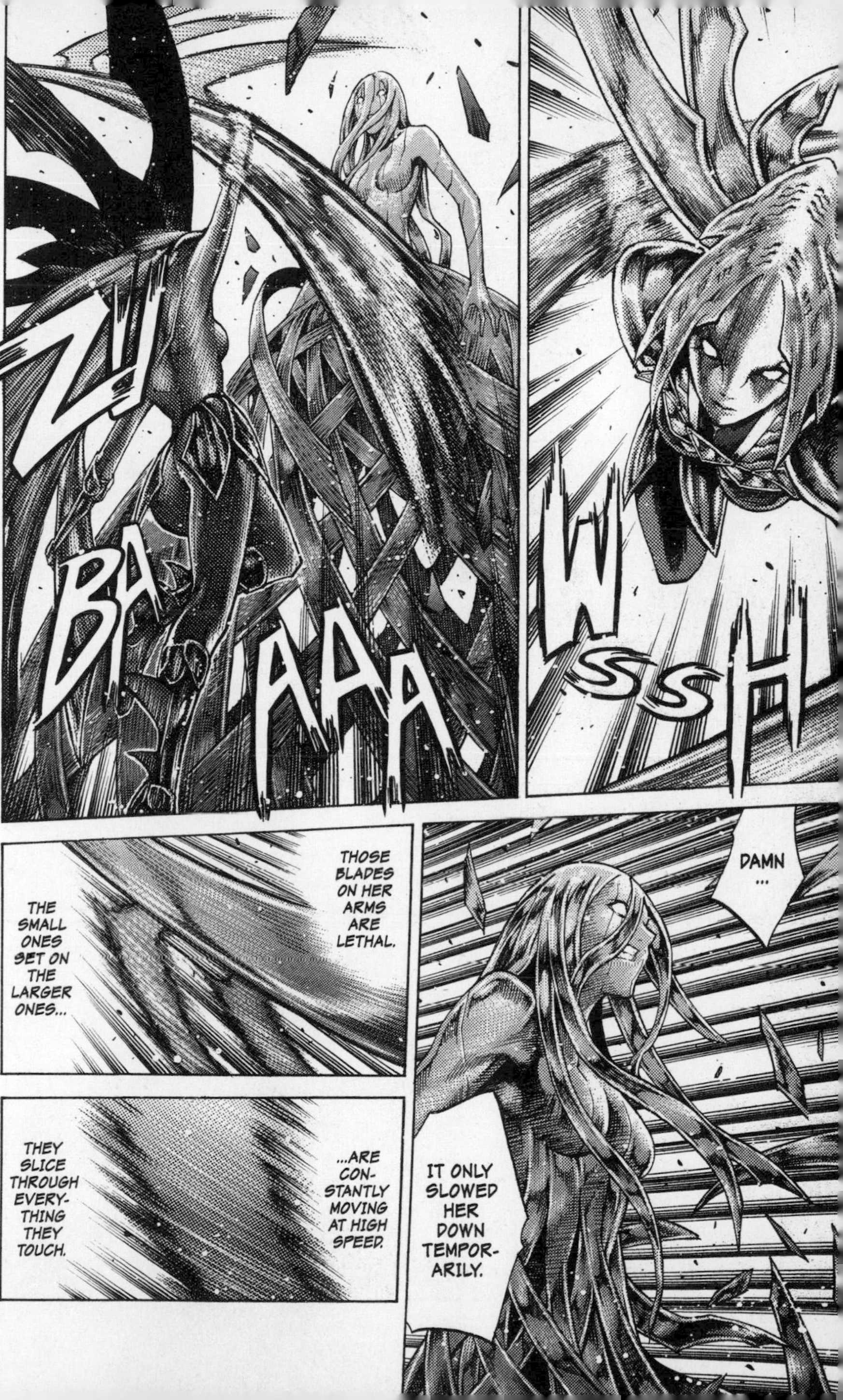
WSSH
BA
AAA
DAMN ...
IT ONLY SLOWED HER DOWN TEMPOR-ARILY.
THOSE BLADES ON HER ARMS ARE LETHAL.
THE SMALL ONES SET ON THE LARGER ONES...
...ARE CON-STANTLY MOVING AT HIGH SPEED.
THEY SLICE THROUGH EVERY-THING THEY TOUCH.

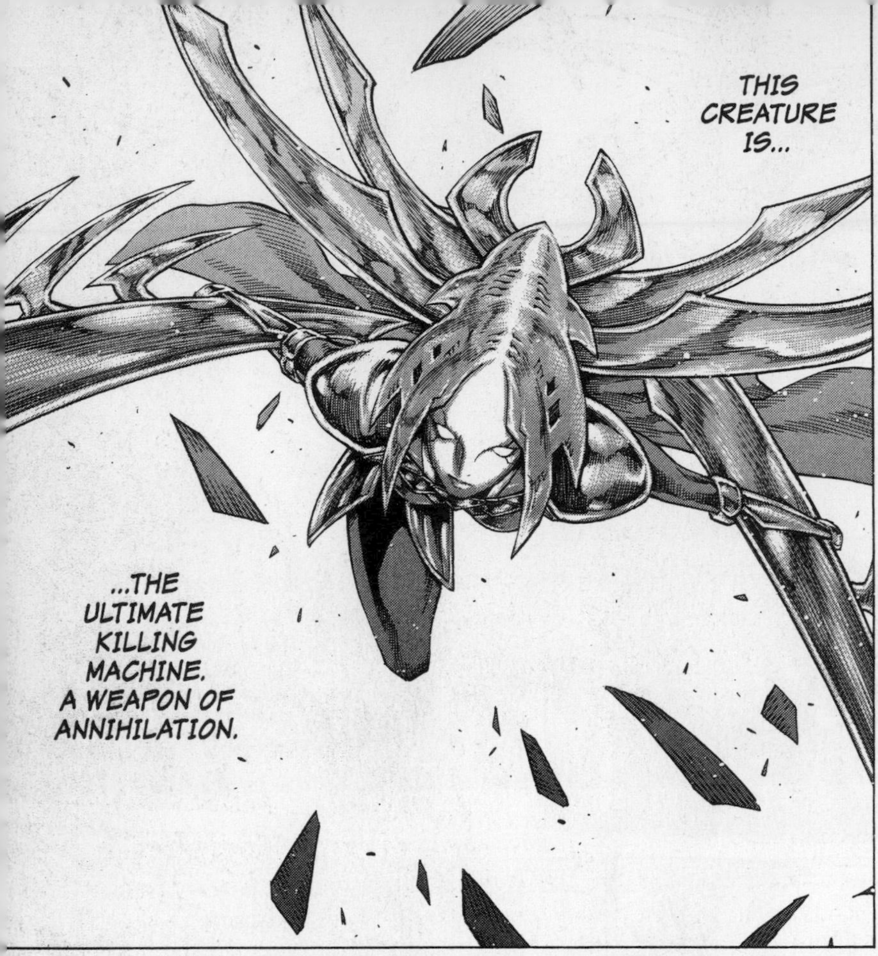
THIS CREATURE IS...
...THE ULTIMATE KILLING MACHINE. A WEAPON OF ANNIHILATION.
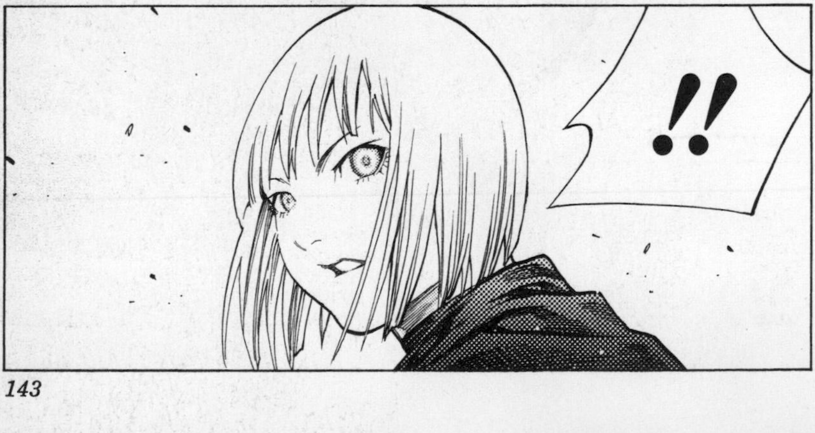
!!

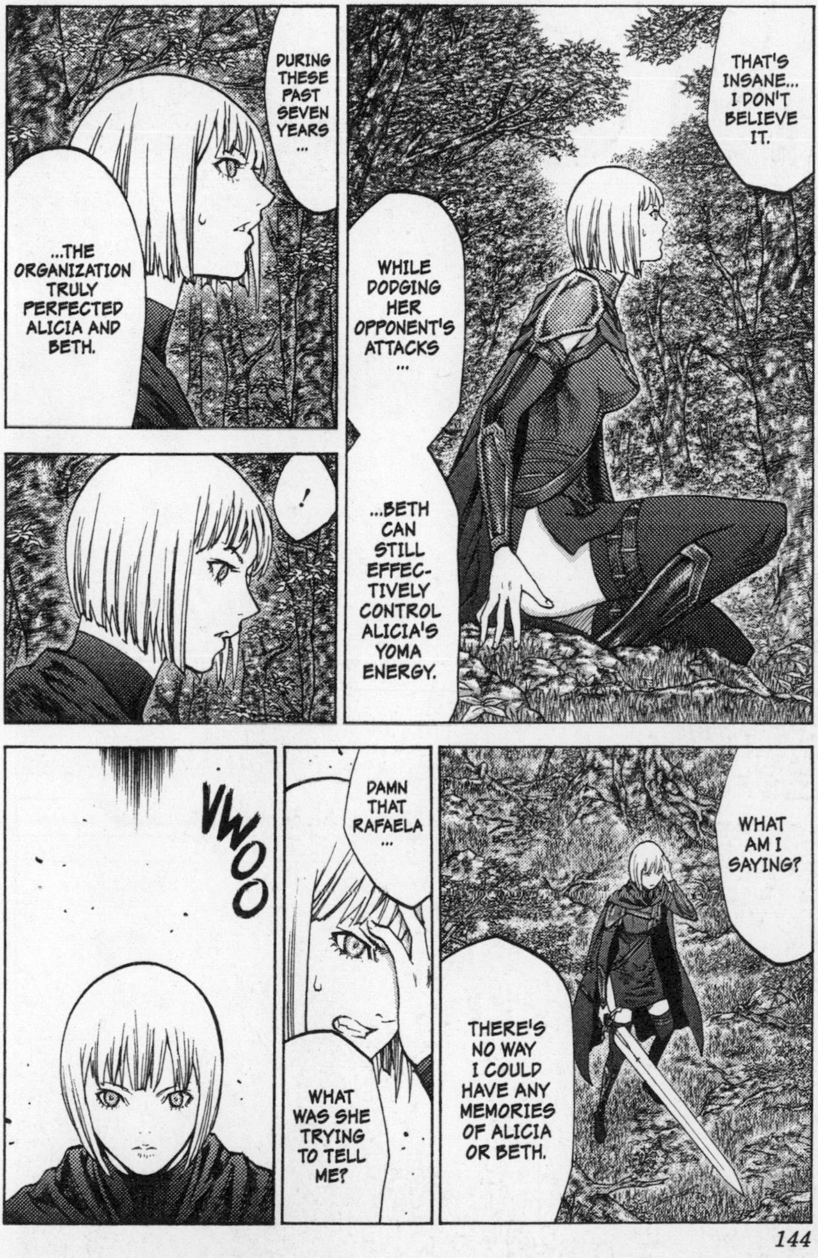
DURING THESE PAST SEVEN YEARS ...
...THE ORGANIZATION TRULY PERFECTED ALICIA AND BETH.
!
THAT'S INSANE... I DON'T BELIEVE IT.
WHILE DODGING HER OPPONENT'S ATTACKS ...
...BETH CAN STILL EFFEC-TIVELY CONTROL ALICIA'S YOMA ENERGY.
VWOO
DAMN THAT RAFAELA ...
WHAT WAS SHE TRYING TO TELL ME?
WHAT AM I SAYING?
THERE'S NO WAY I COULD HAVE ANY MEMORIES OF ALICIA OR BETH.

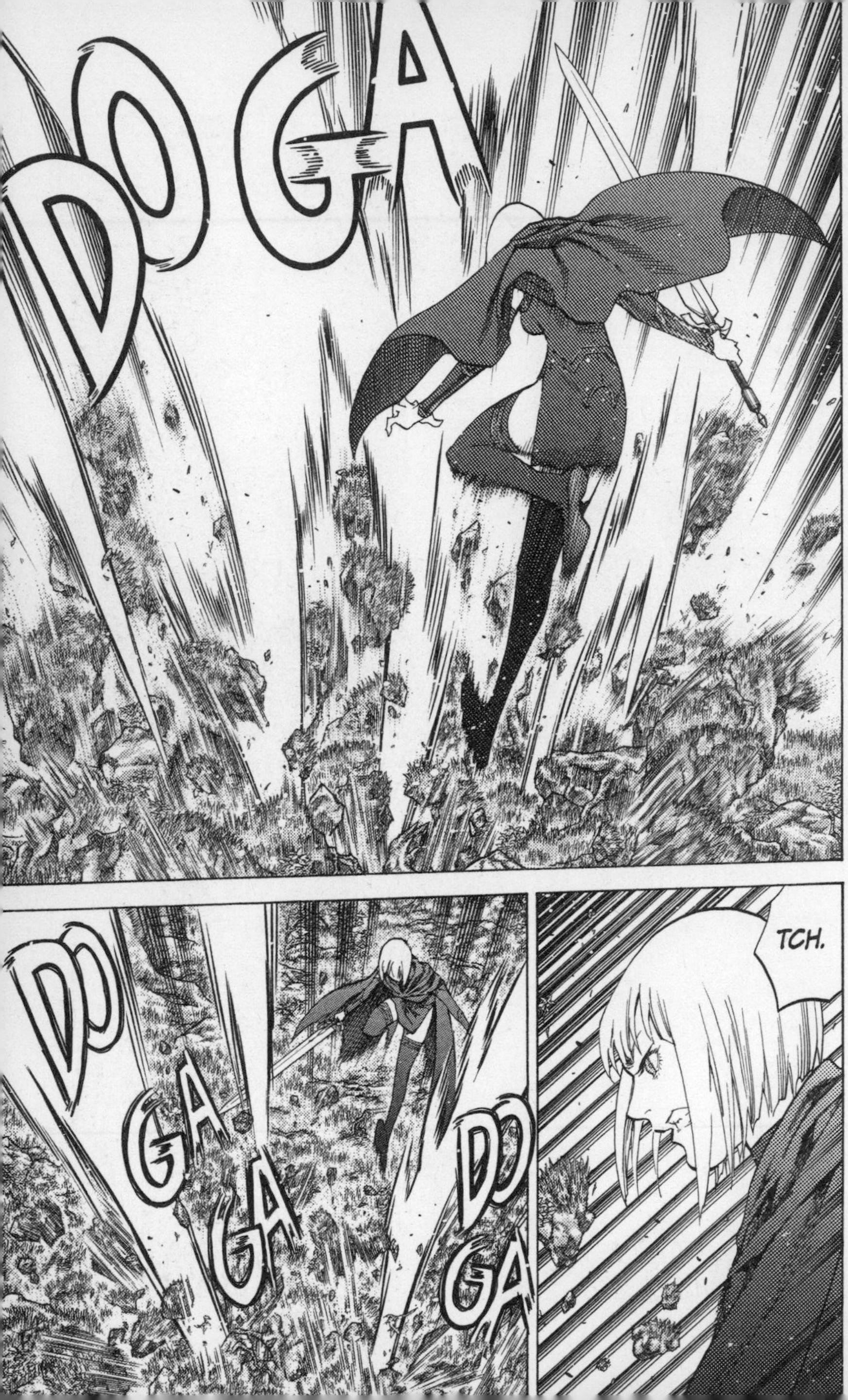
DOGA
TCH.
DO
GA
GA
DO
GA

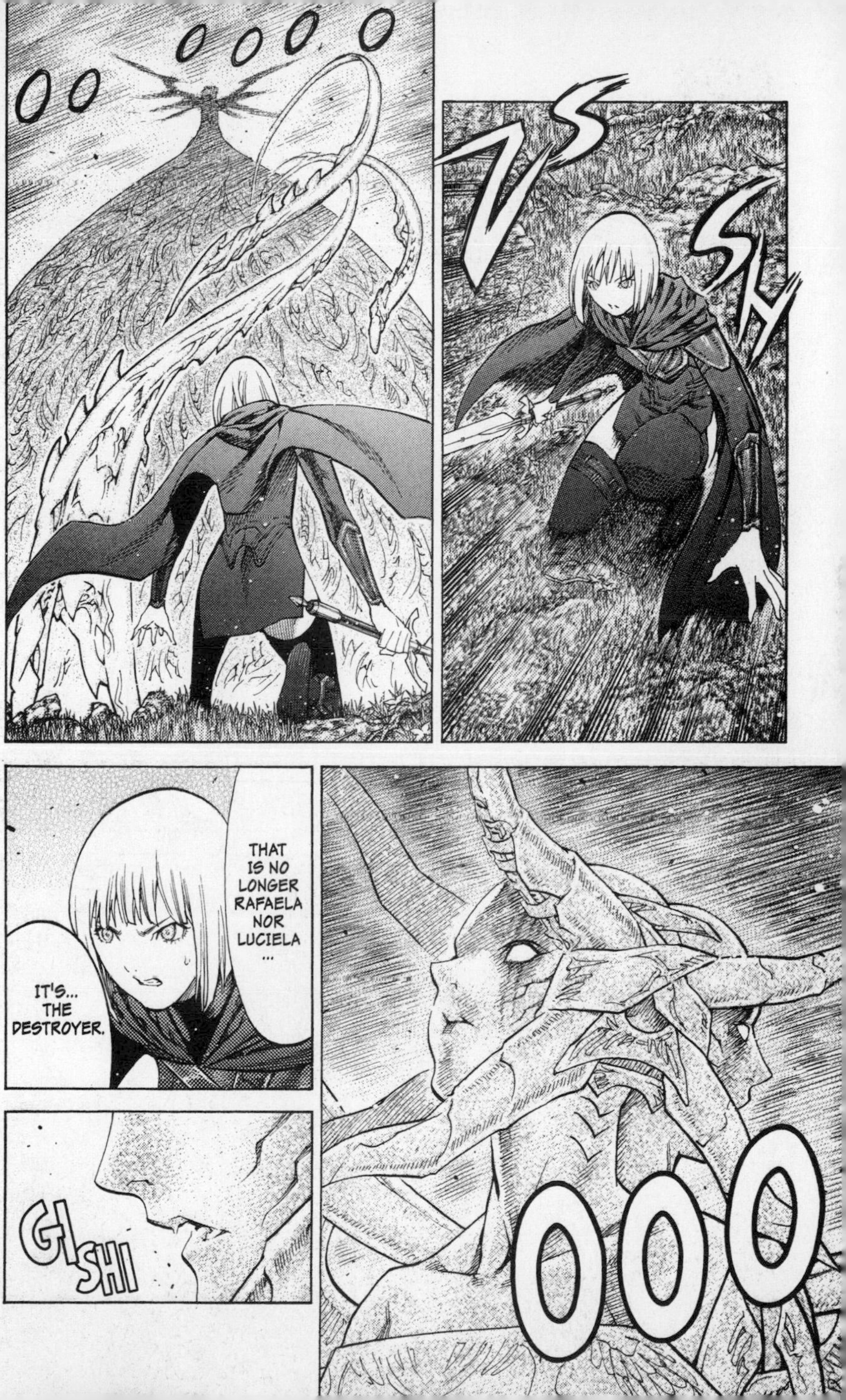
ZSSH
OOOOOO
OOO
THAT IS NO LONGER RAFAELA NOR LUCIELA ...
IT'S... THE DESTROYER.
GISHI

READ THIS WAY

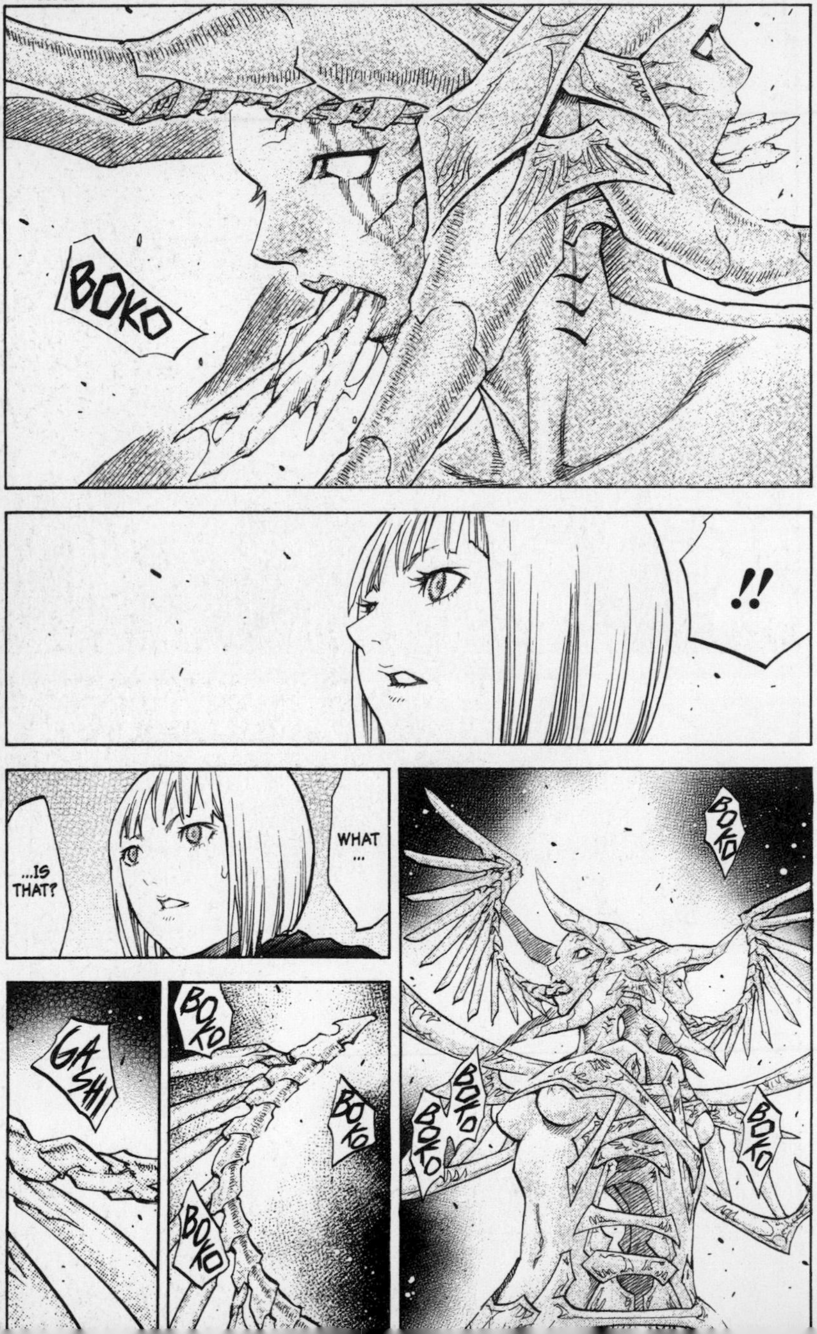
BOKO
!!
BOKO
BOKO
BOKO
BOKO
BOKO
WHAT ...
...IS THAT?
BOKO
BOKO
BOKO
GASHI

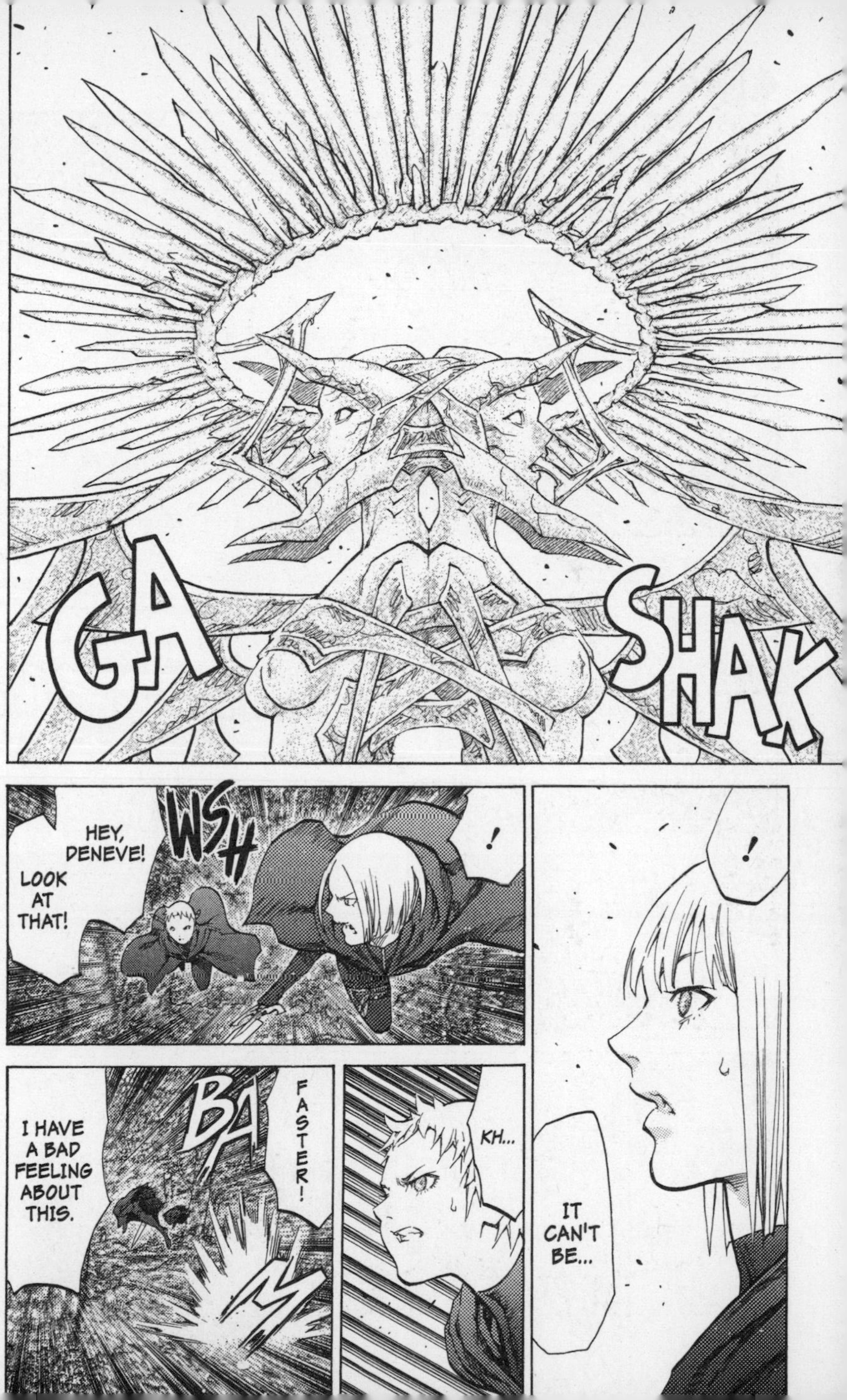
GA SHAK
!
IT CAN'T BE...
WSH
!
HEY, DENEVE!
LOOK AT THAT!
KH...
FASTER!
BAM
I HAVE A BAD FEELING ABOUT THIS.

READ THIS WAY

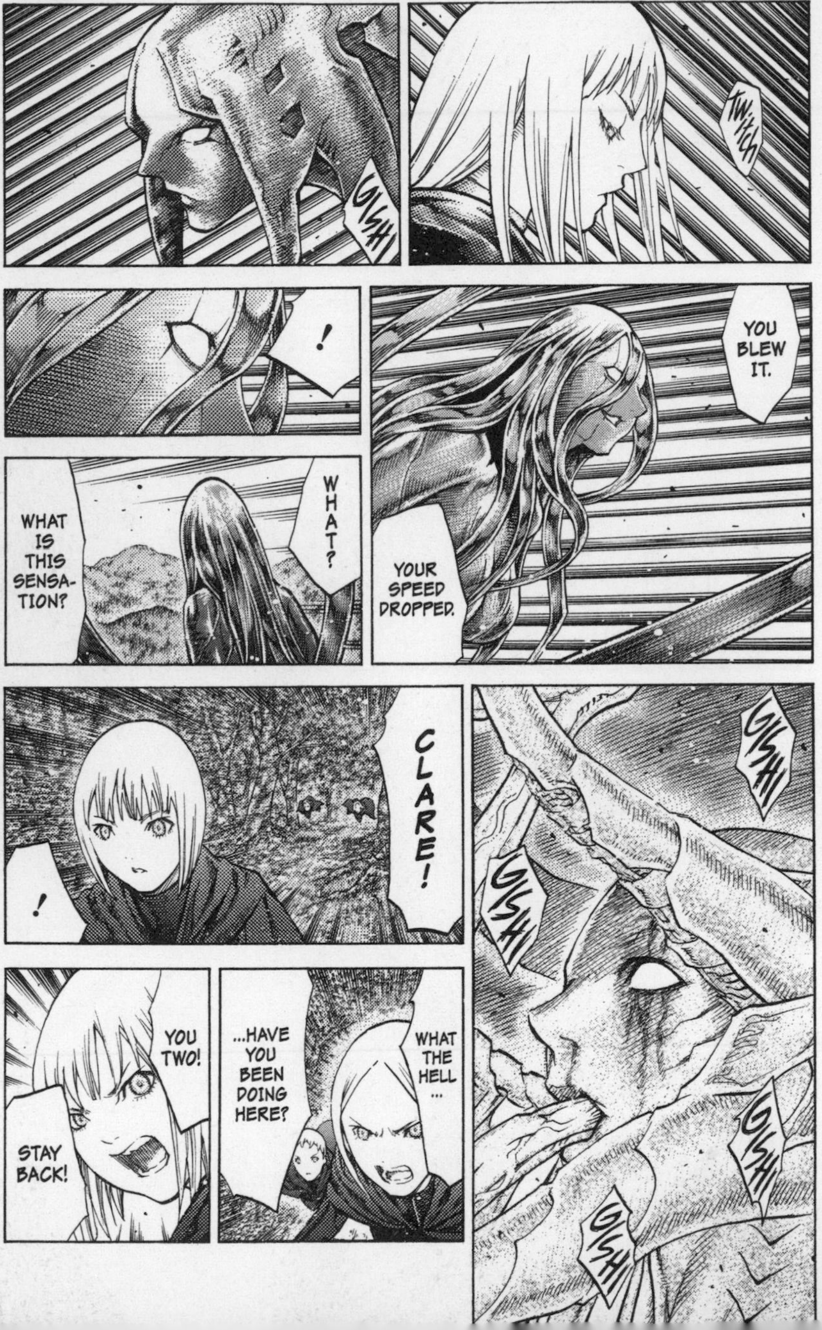
TWITCH
GISH
YOU BLEW IT.
YOUR SPEED DROPPED.
!
WHAT?
WHAT IS THIS SENSATION?
GISH
GISH
GISH
GISH
CLARE!
!
WHAT THE HELL...
...HAVE YOU BEEN DOING HERE?
YOU TWO!
STAY BACK!

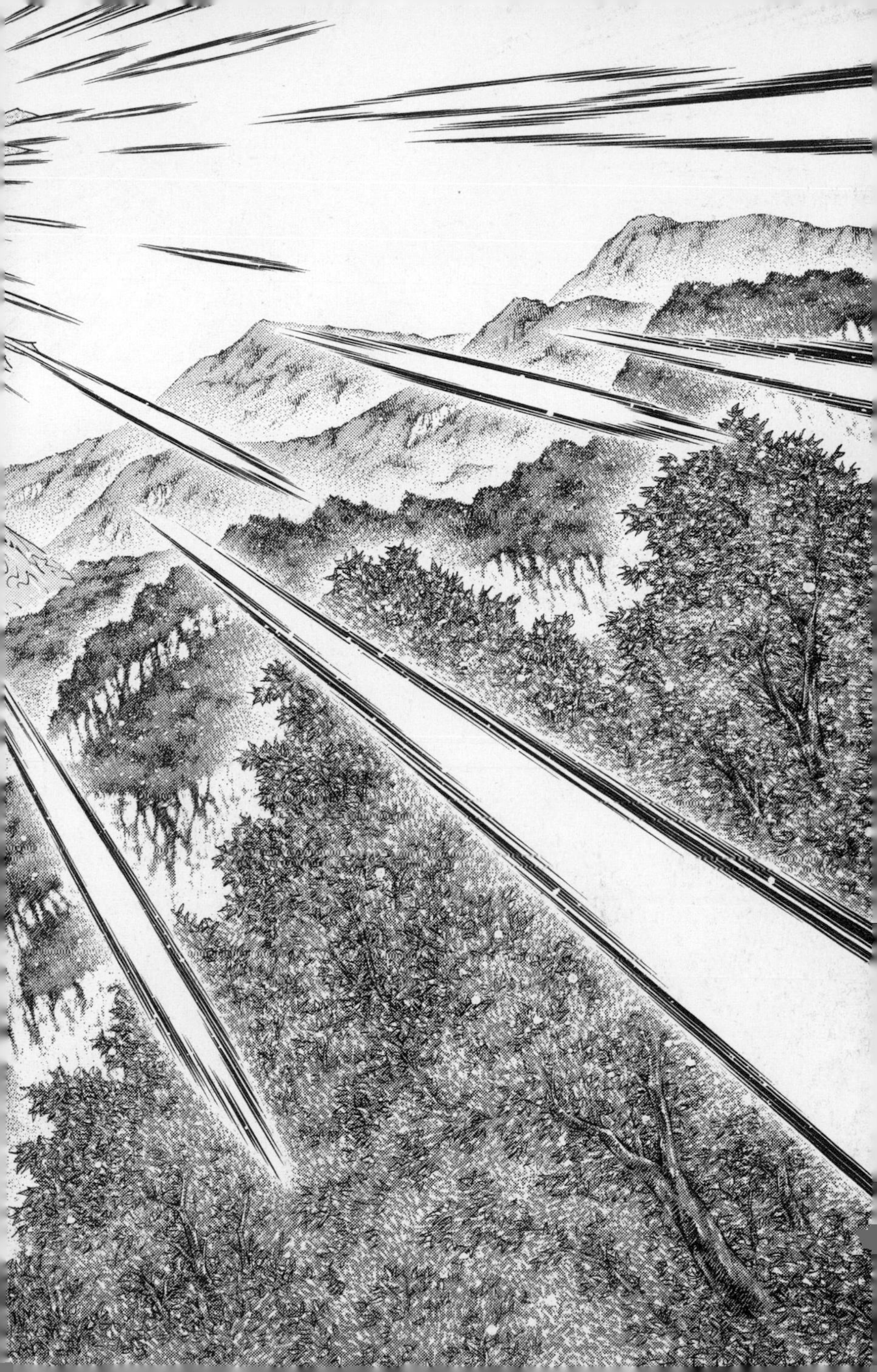

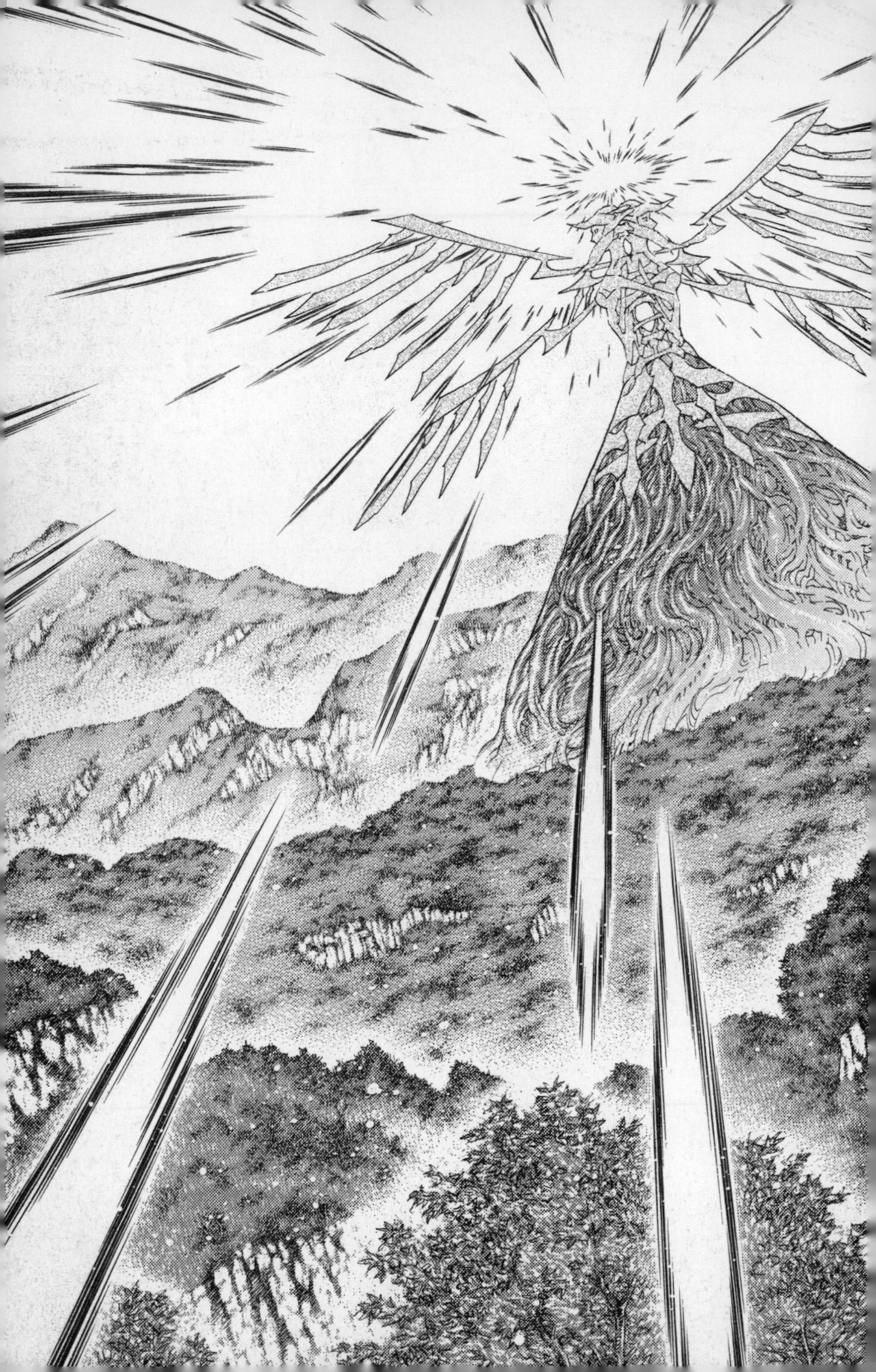

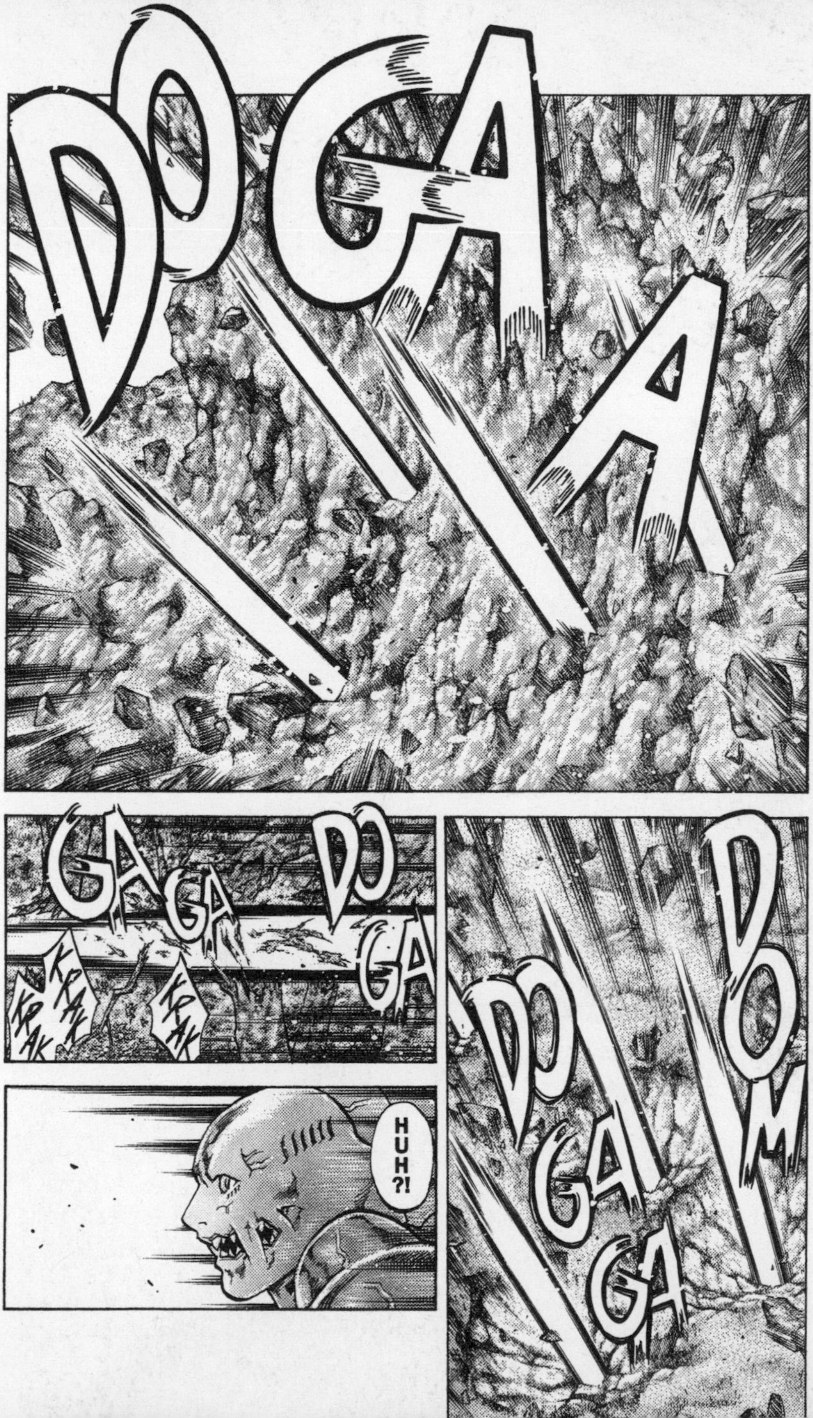
DOGAA
DOM
DOGAGA
DOGA
GAGA
KRAK
KRAKKRAK
HUH?!

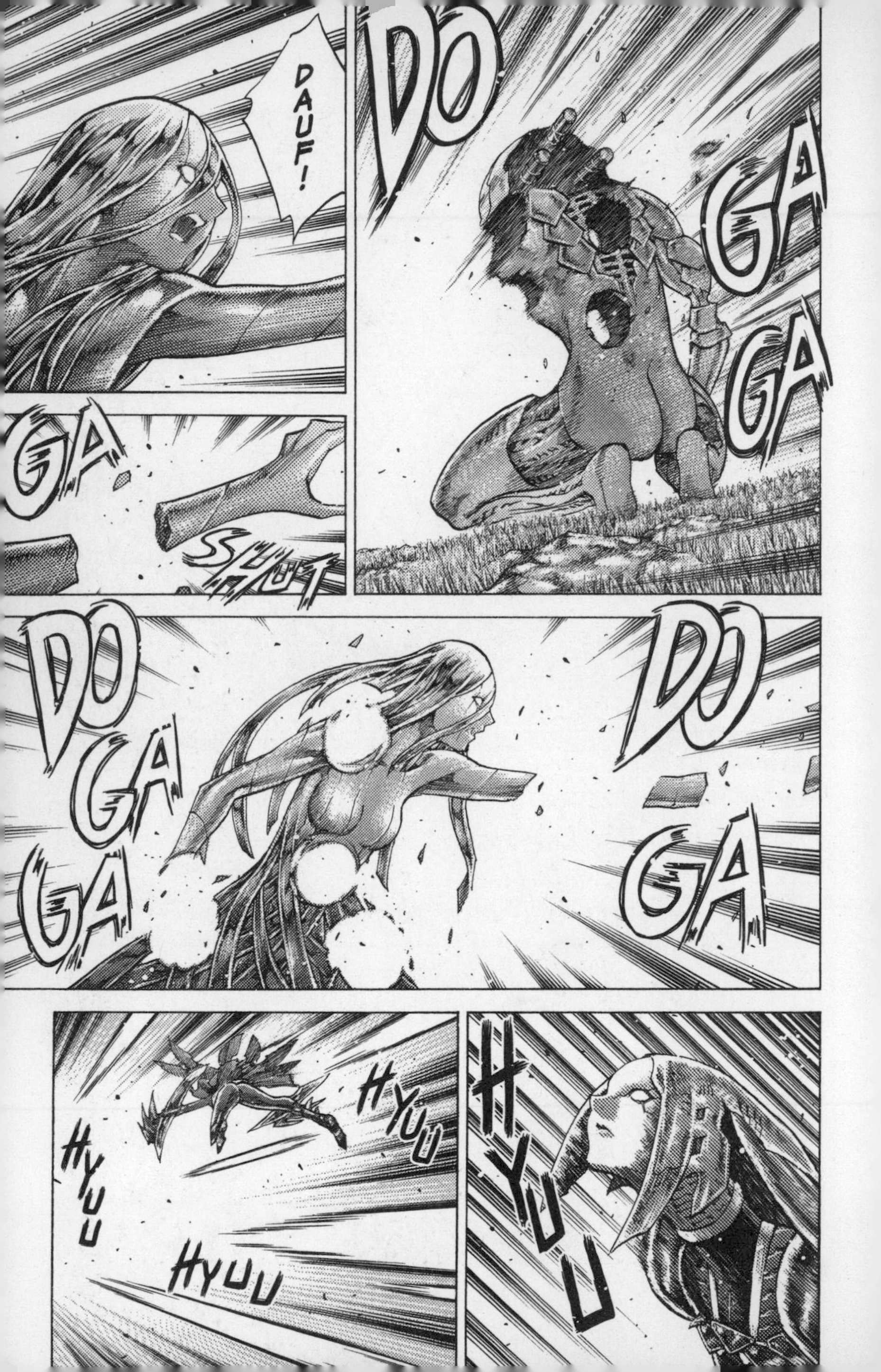
DO
GA
GA
DAUF!
GA
SHUT
DO
GA
GA
DO
GA
GA
HYUUU
HYUU
HYUU
HYUU

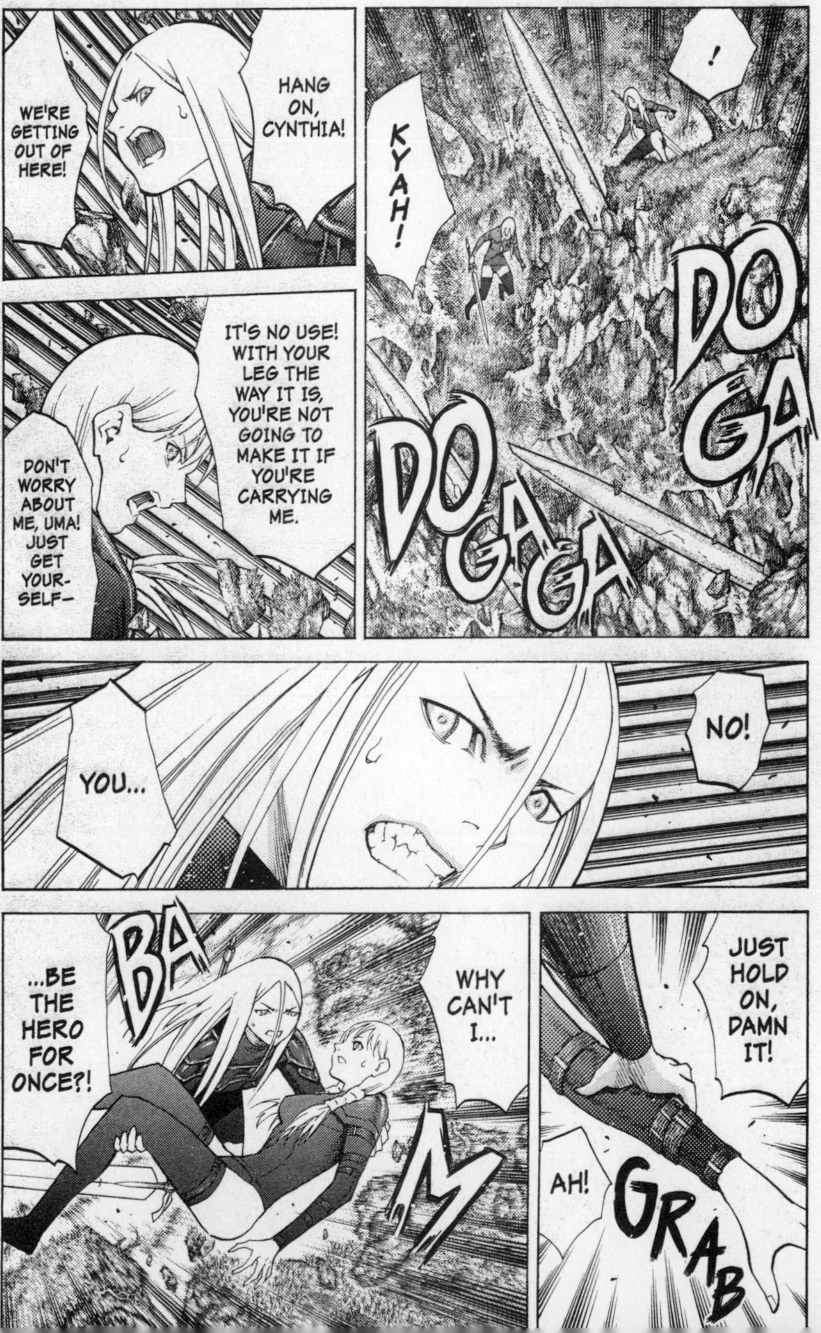
!
KYAH!
DOGA
DOGAGA
HANG ON, CYNTHIA!
WE'RE GETTING OUT OF HERE!
IT'S NO USE! WITH YOUR LEG THE WAY IT IS, YOU'RE NOT GOING TO MAKE IT IF YOU'RE CARRYING ME.
DON'T WORRY ABOUT ME, UMA! JUST GET YOUR-SELF—
NO!
YOU...
JUST HOLD ON, DAMN IT!
AH!
GRAB
WHY CAN'T I...
...BE THE HERO FOR ONCE?!
BAM

READ THIS WAY

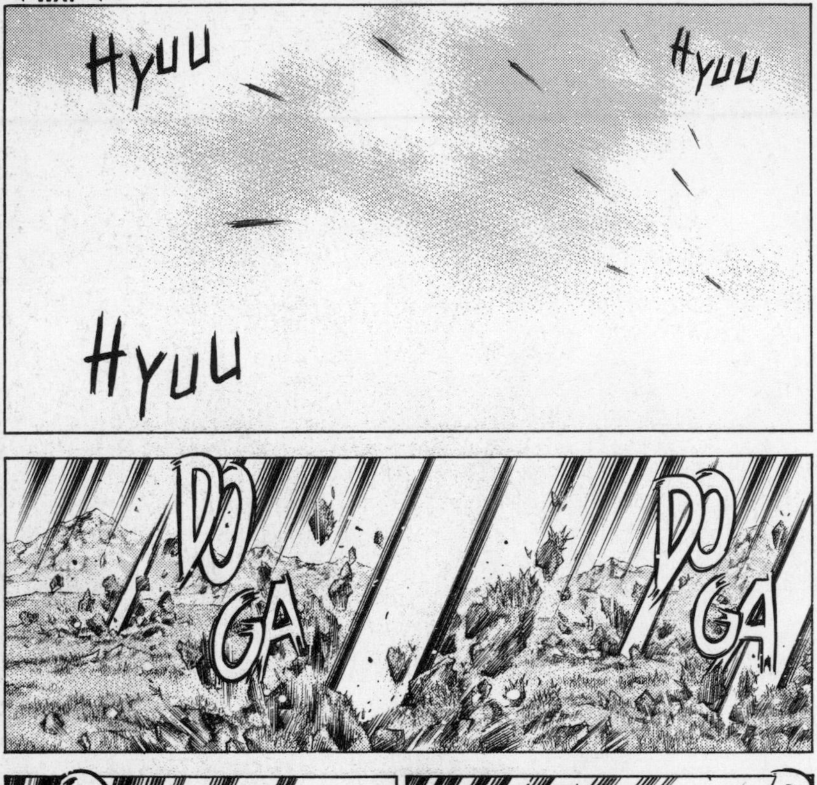
Hyuu
Hyuu
Hyuu
DOGA
DOGA
DOGA
DOGA
DOGAAA

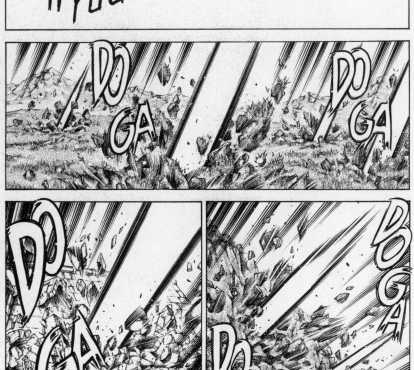

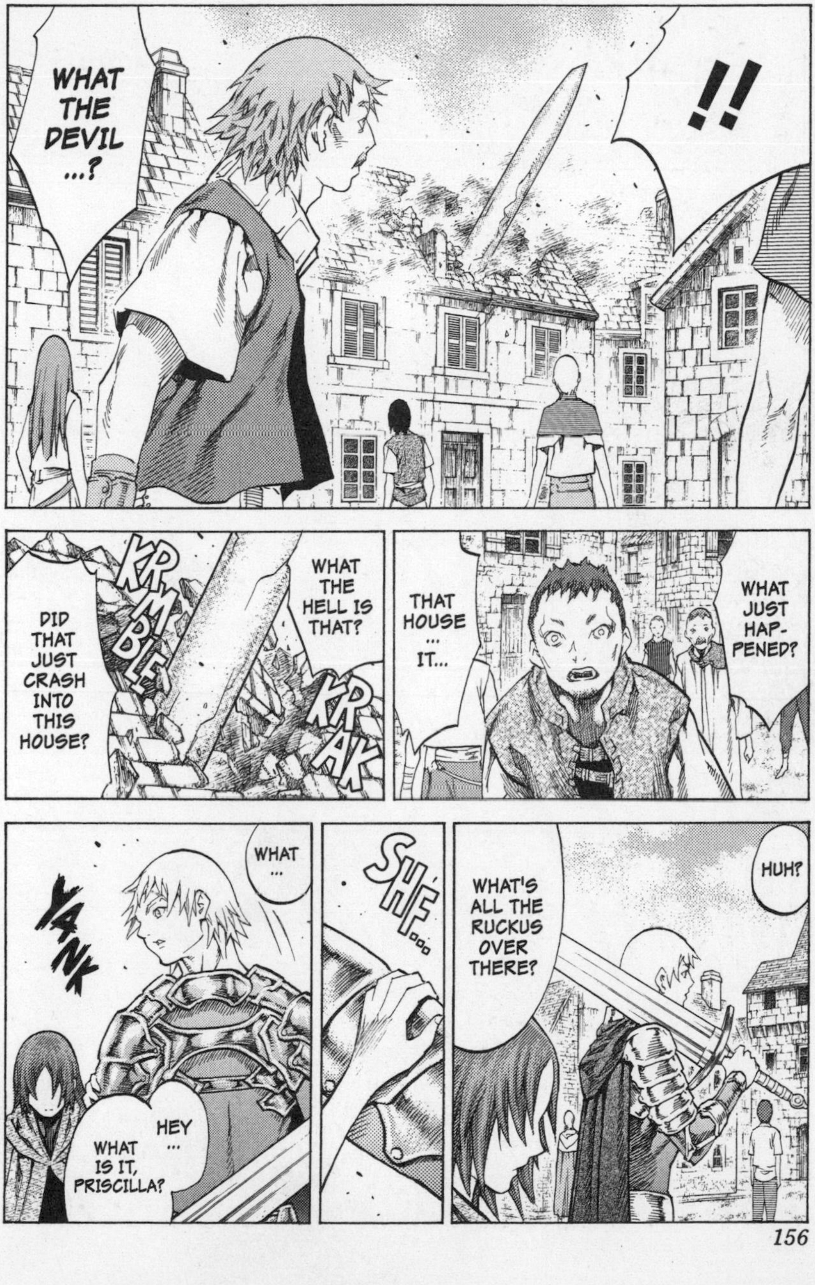
!!
WHAT THE DEVIL ...?
WHAT JUST HAP-PENED?
THAT HOUSE ... IT...
WHAT THE HELL IS THAT?
KRAK
KRMBLE
DID THAT JUST CRASH INTO THIS HOUSE?
HUH?
WHAT'S ALL THE RUCKUS OVER THERE?
SHF...
WHAT ...
YANK
HEY ...
WHAT IS IT, PRISCILLA?

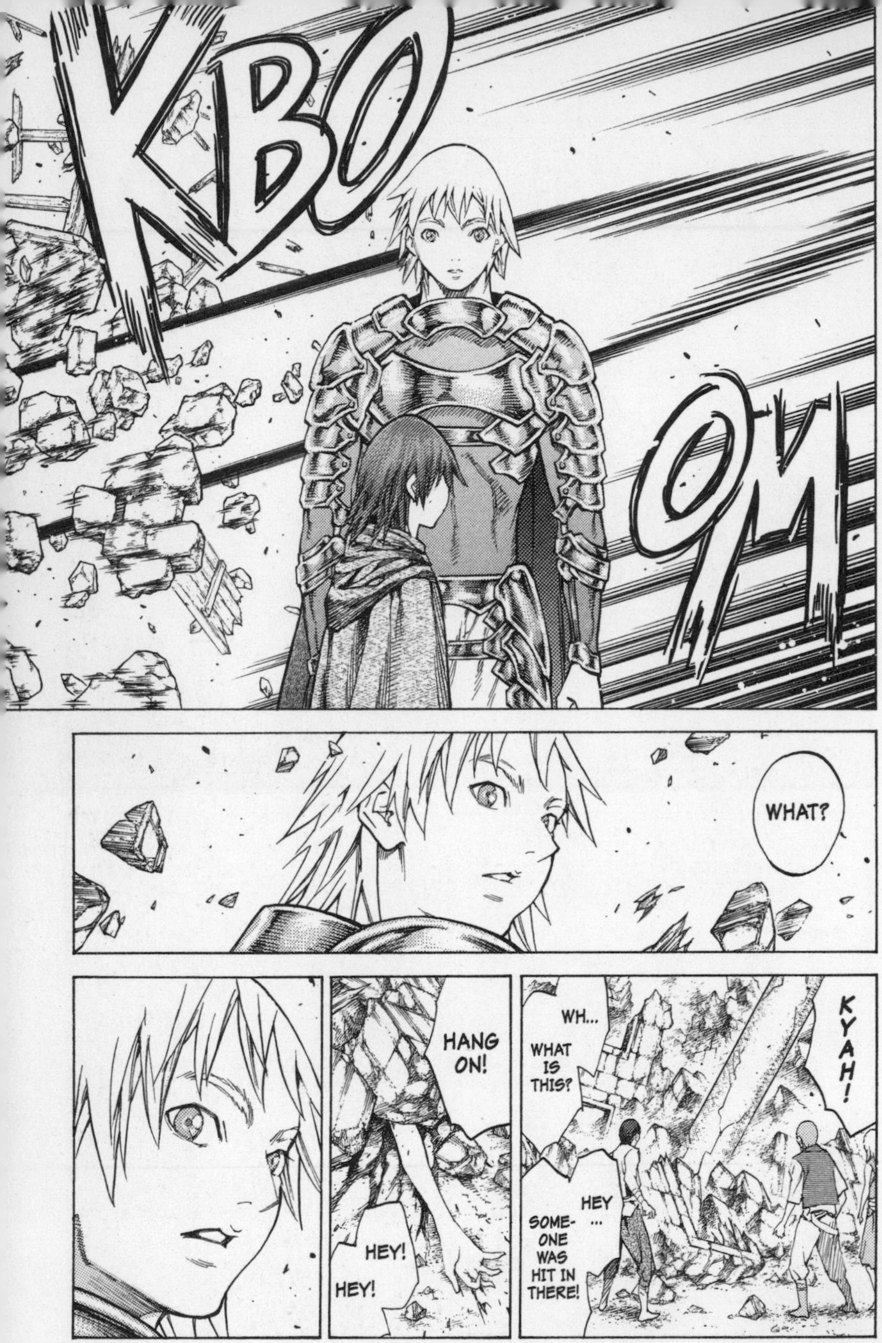
KBOOM
WHAT?
KYAH!
WH...
WHAT IS THIS?
HEY ...
SOME-ONE WAS HIT IN THERE!
HANG ON!
HEY!
HEY!

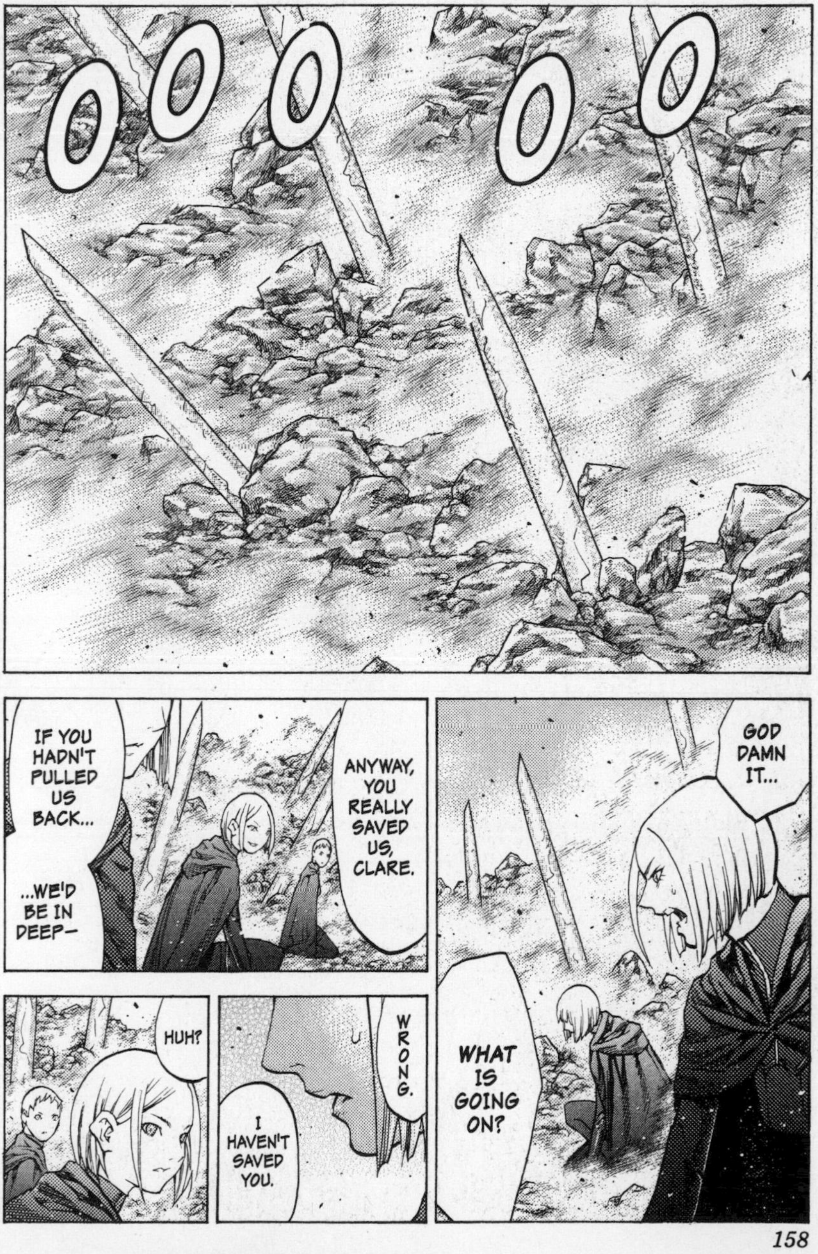
OOOOO
GOD DAMN IT...
WHAT IS GOING ON?
ANYWAY, YOU REALLY SAVED US, CLARE.
IF YOU HADN'T PULLED US BACK...
...WE'D BE IN DEEP—
WRONG.
I HAVEN'T SAVED YOU.
HUH?

READ THIS WAY

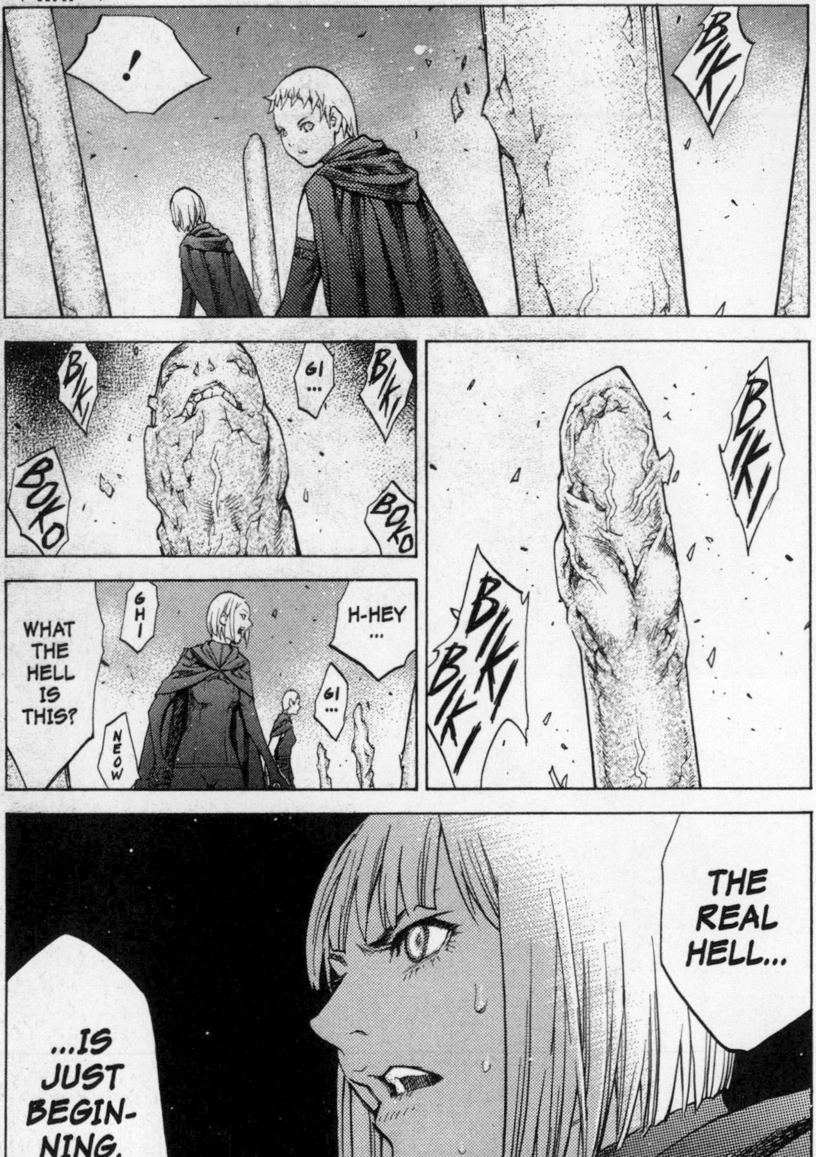
BIKI
!
BIKI
BIKI BIKI
BIKI
BOKO
GI...
BIKI
BOKO
H-HEY...
GI...
GHI
NEOW
WHAT THE HELL IS THIS?
THE REAL HELL...
...IS JUST BEGIN-NING.

クレイモア

Claymore

Scene 95: The Claws of Memory, Part 6

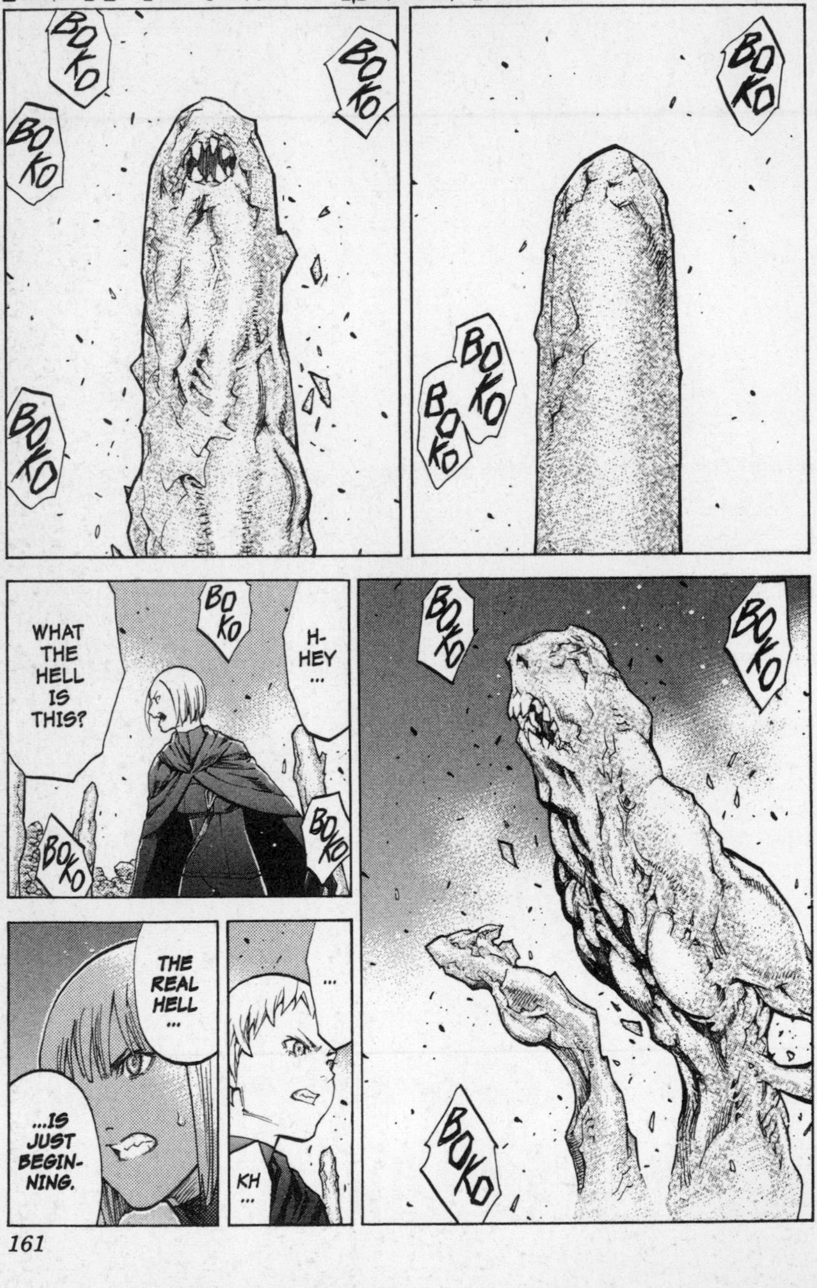
BOKO
BOKO
BOKO
BOKO
BOKO
BOKO
BOKO
BOKO
BOKO
BOKO
BOKO
BOKO
H-HEY ...
WHAT THE HELL IS THIS?
BOKO
BOKO
...
KH ...
THE REAL HELL ...
...IS JUST BEGINNING.

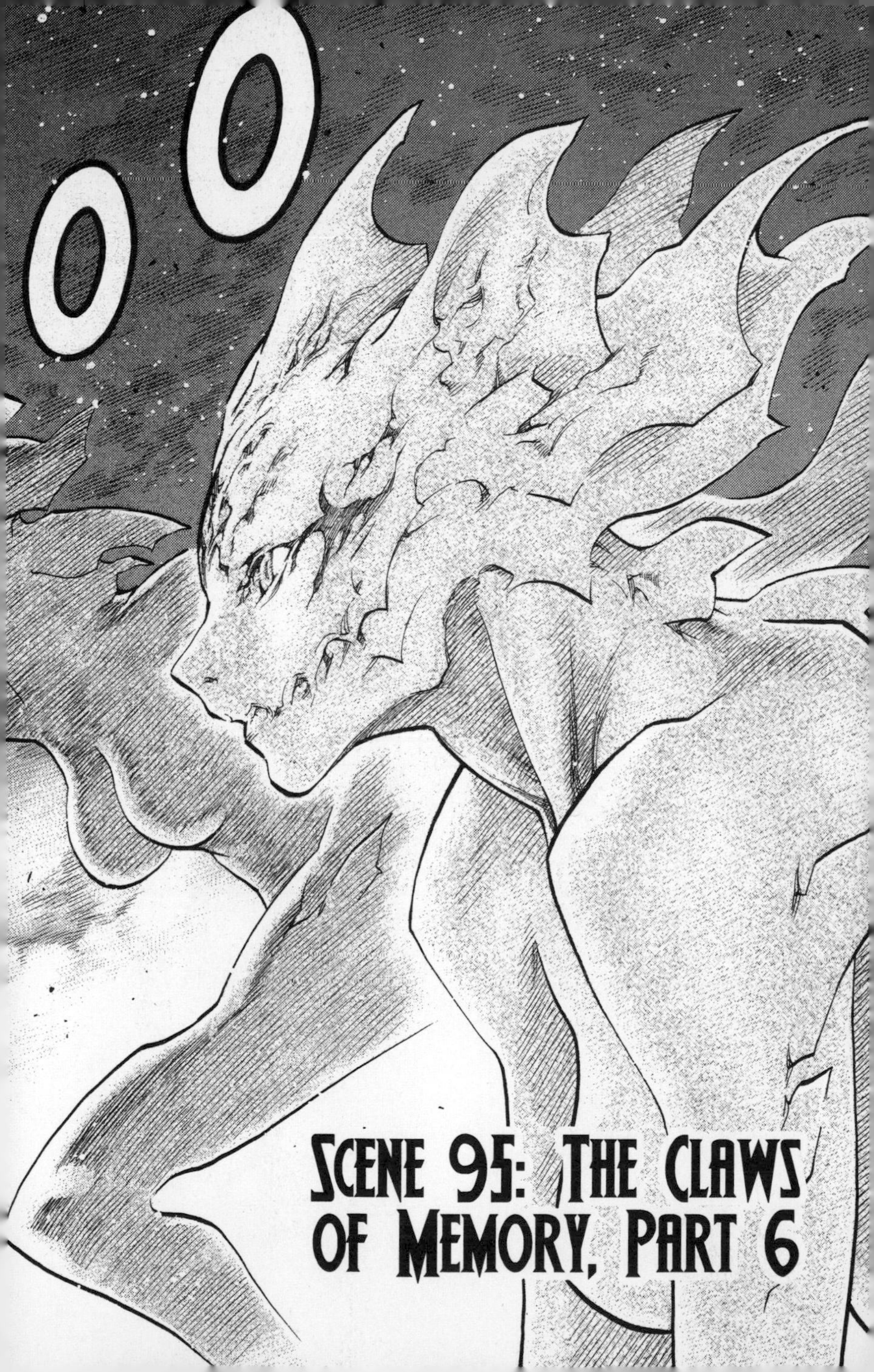
OO
SCENE 95: THE CLAWS OF MEMORY, PART 6

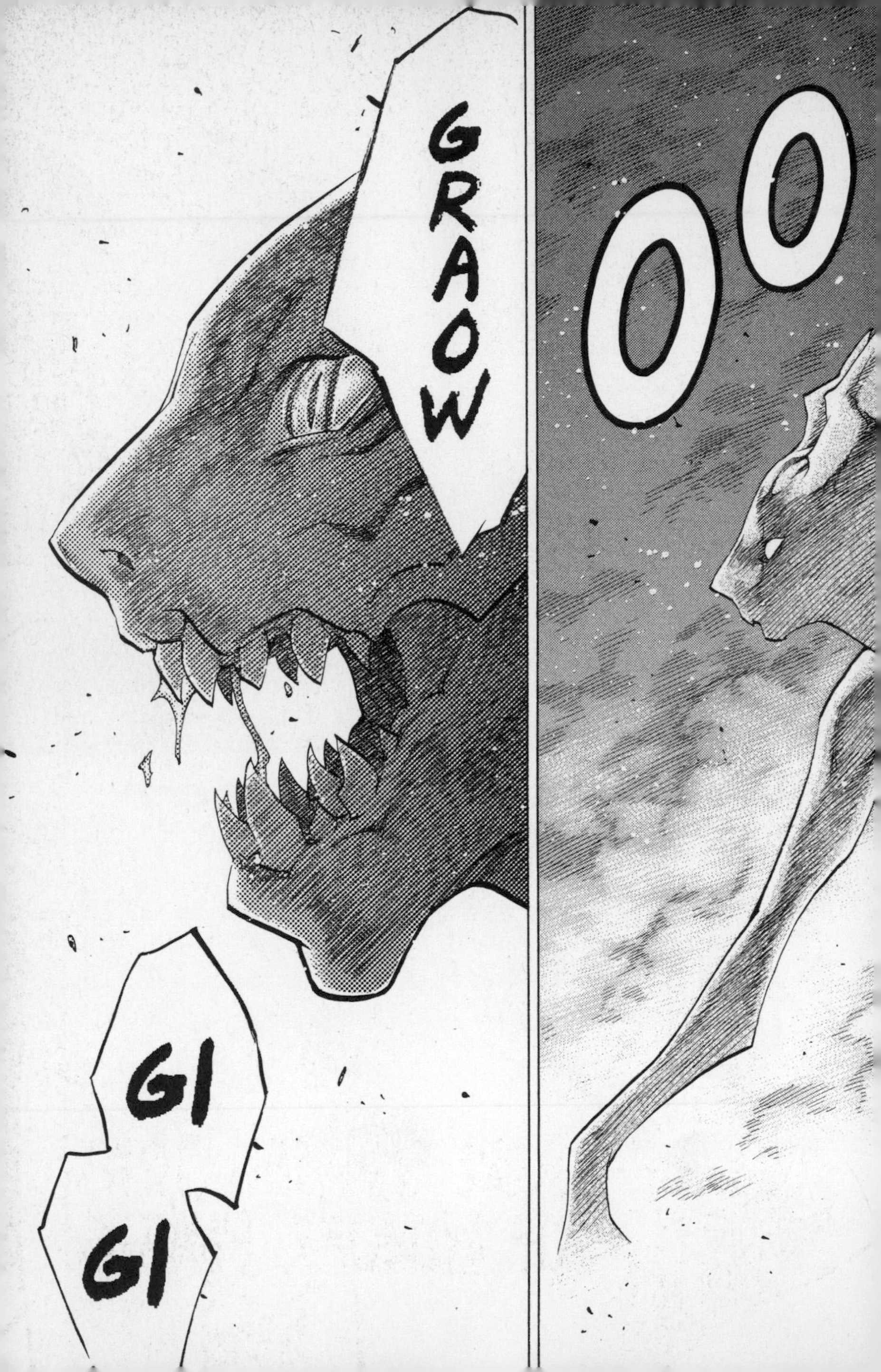
OOO
GRAOW
GI GI

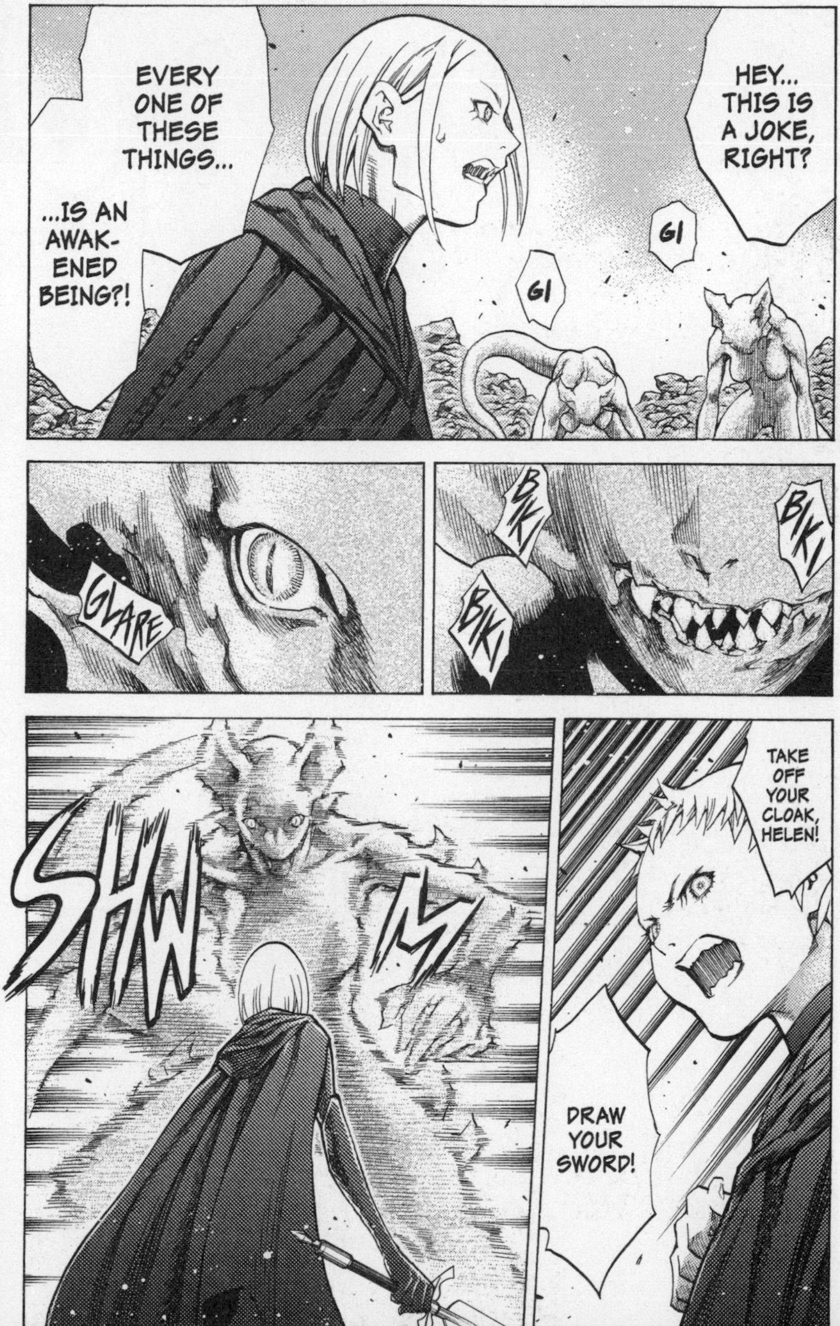
HEY... THIS IS A JOKE, RIGHT?
GI
GI
EVERY ONE OF THESE THINGS...
...IS AN AWAK-ENED BEING?!
BIKI
BIKI
BIKI
GLARE
TAKE OFF YOUR CLOAK, HELEN!
DRAW YOUR SWORD!
SHWM

READ THIS WAY

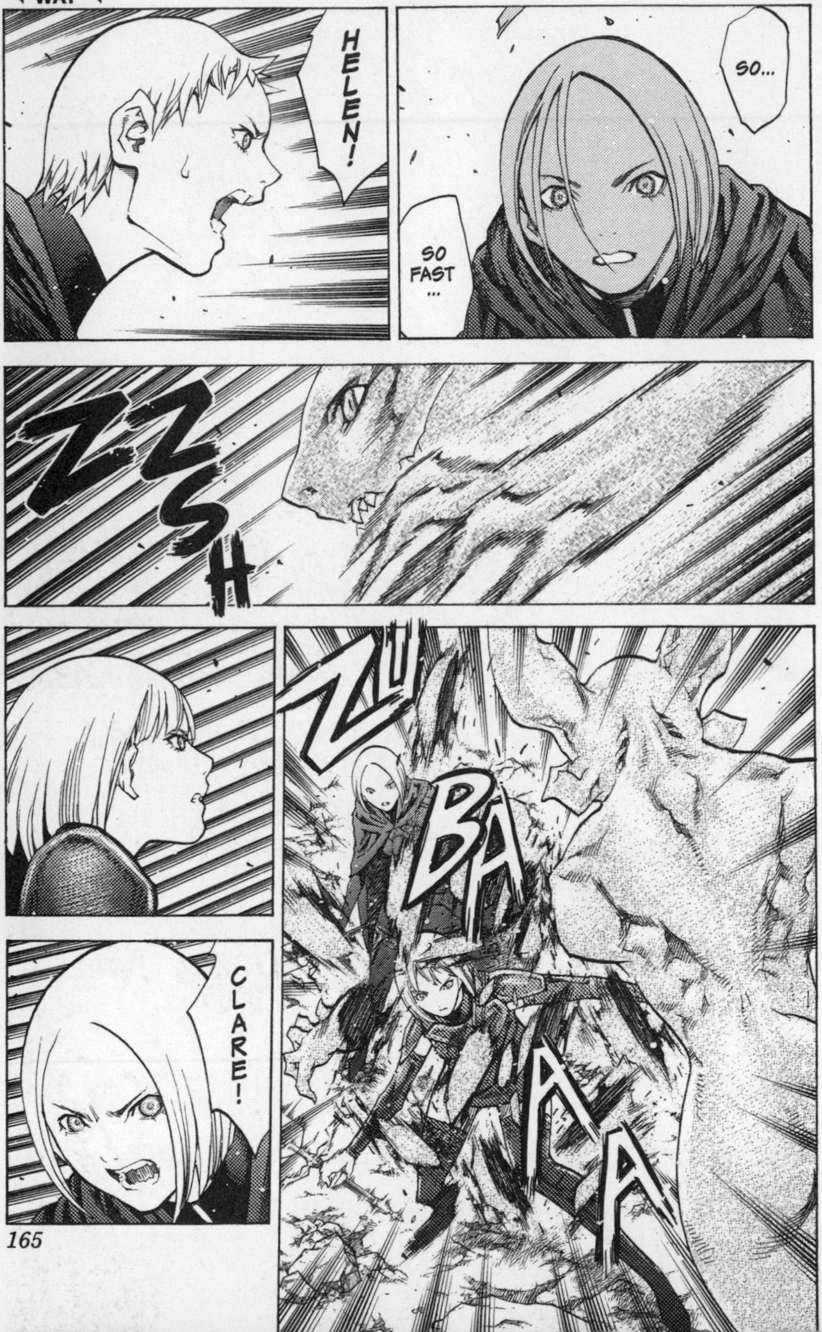
SO...
SO FAST ...
HELEN!
ZZSH
ZUBAAAA
CLARE!

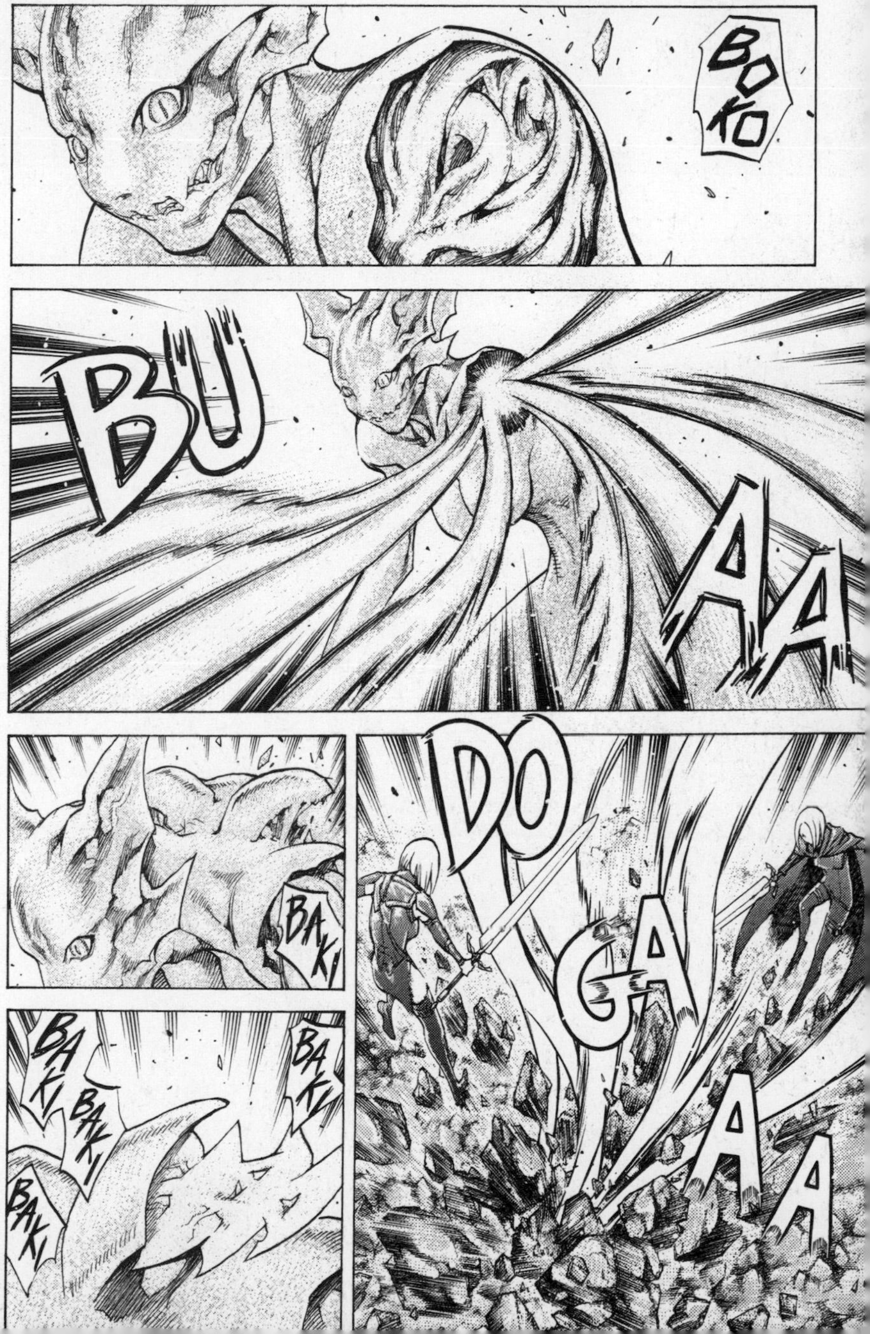
BOKO
BU
AAA
DO
GA
AA
BAKI
BAKI
BAKI
BAKI
BAKI

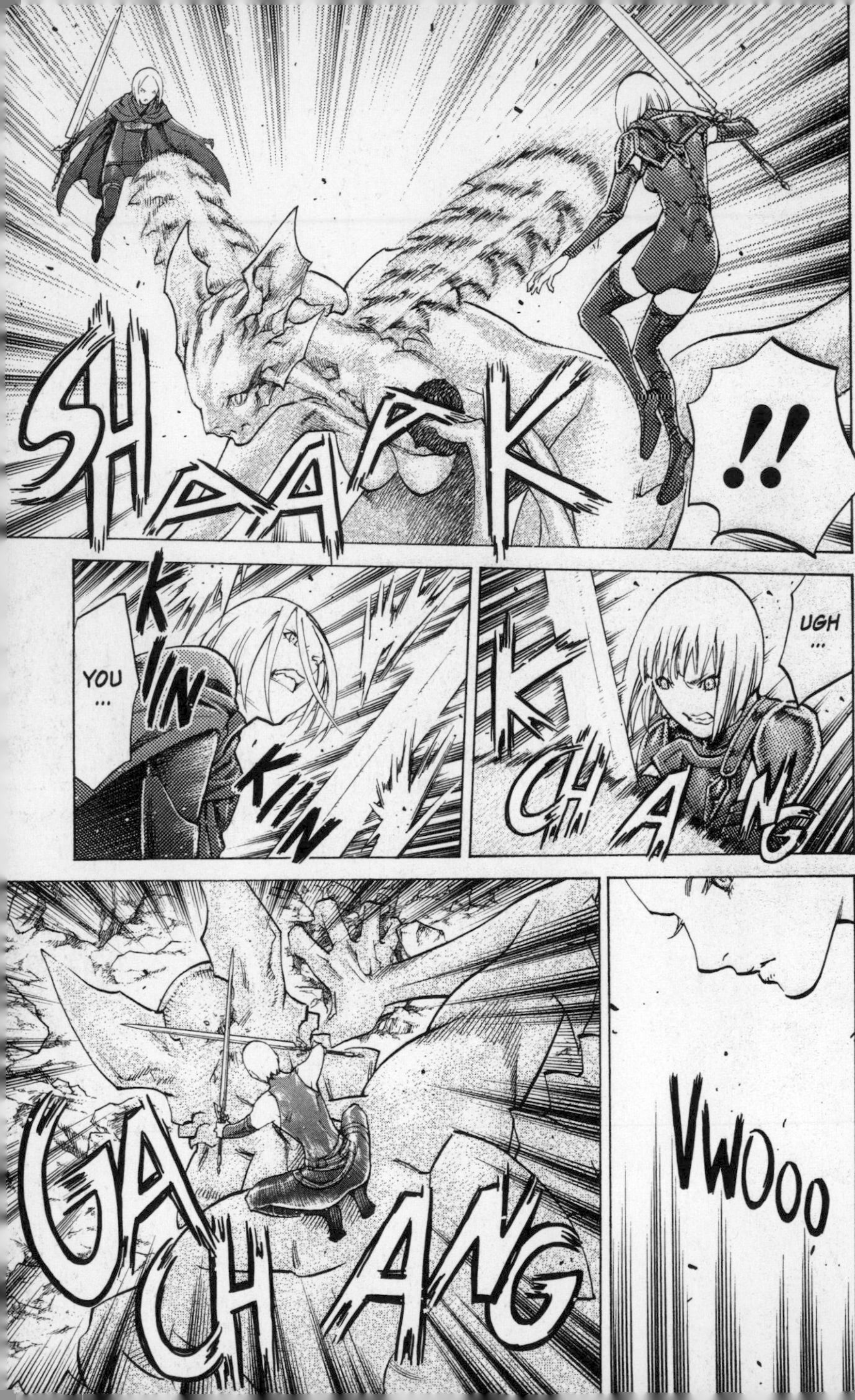
!!
SHAAAK
UGH ...
K CHANG
KIN KIN KIN
YOU ...
VWOOO
GACHANG

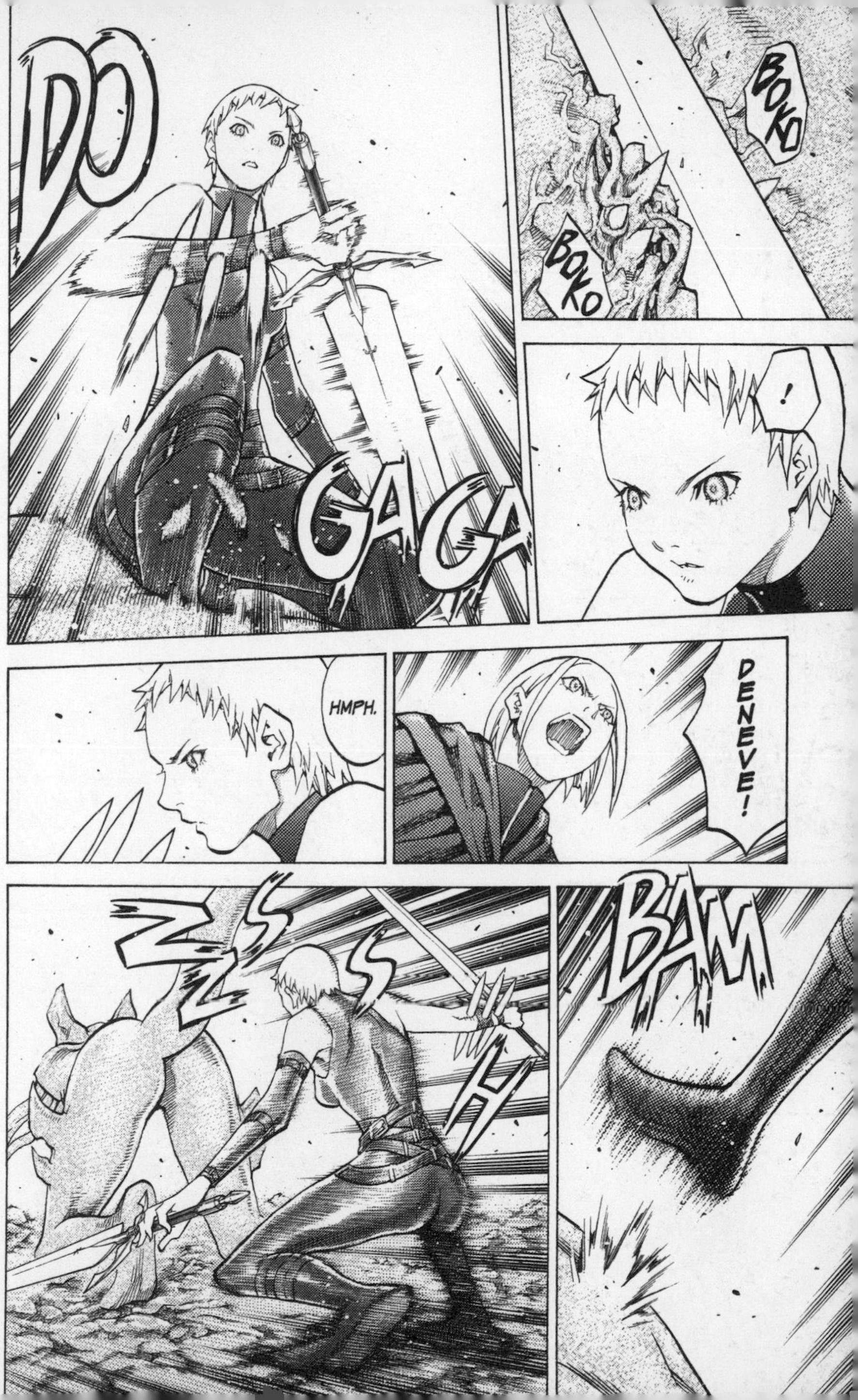
BOKO
BOKO
!
DO
GAGA
DENEVE!
HMPH.
BAM
ZSSH

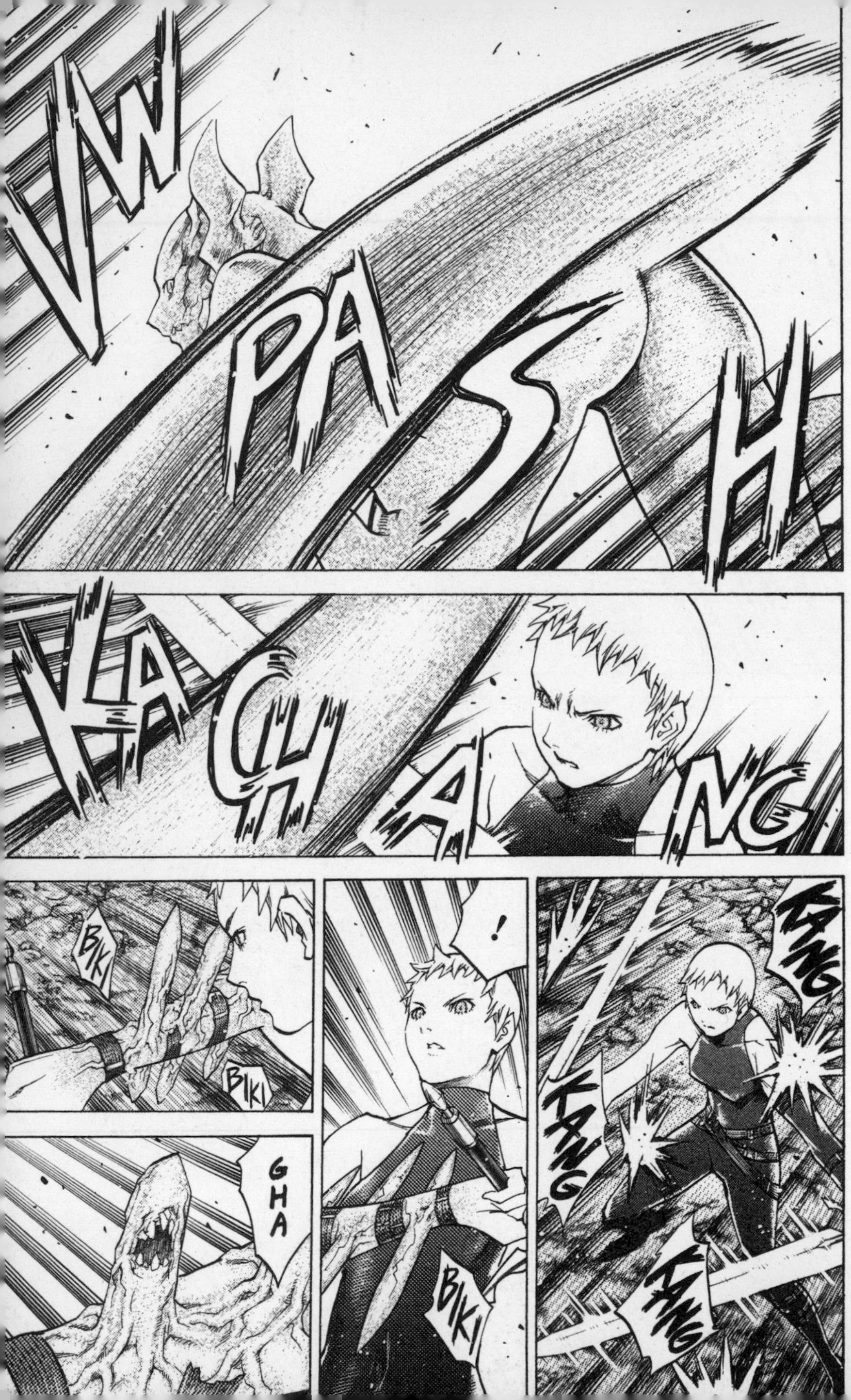
PASH
VVW
KLACHANG
KANG
KANG
KANG
!
BIKI
BIKI
BIKI
GHA

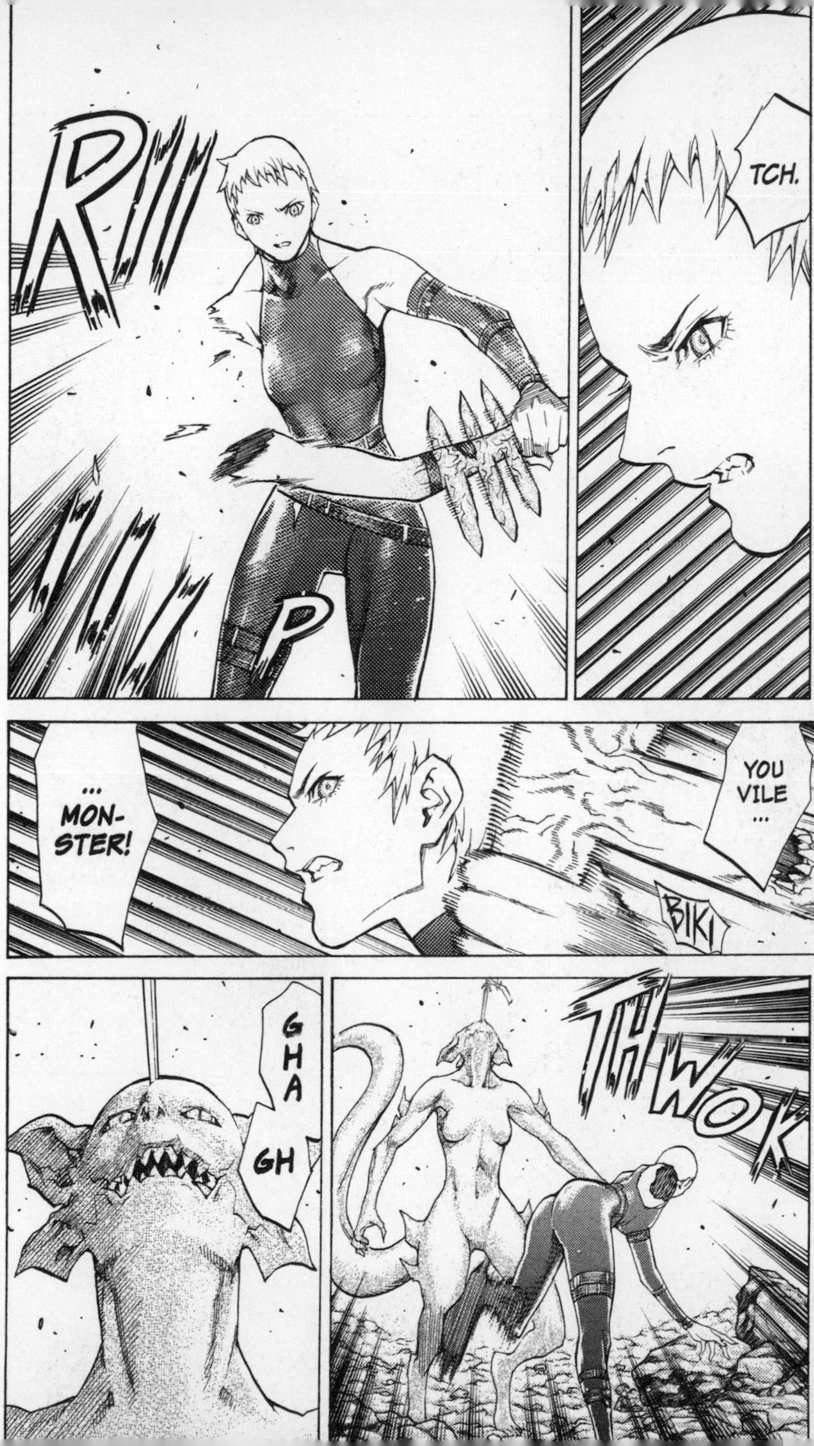
TCH.
RIIIP
YOU VILE ...
BIKI
... MON-STER!
THWOK
GHAGH

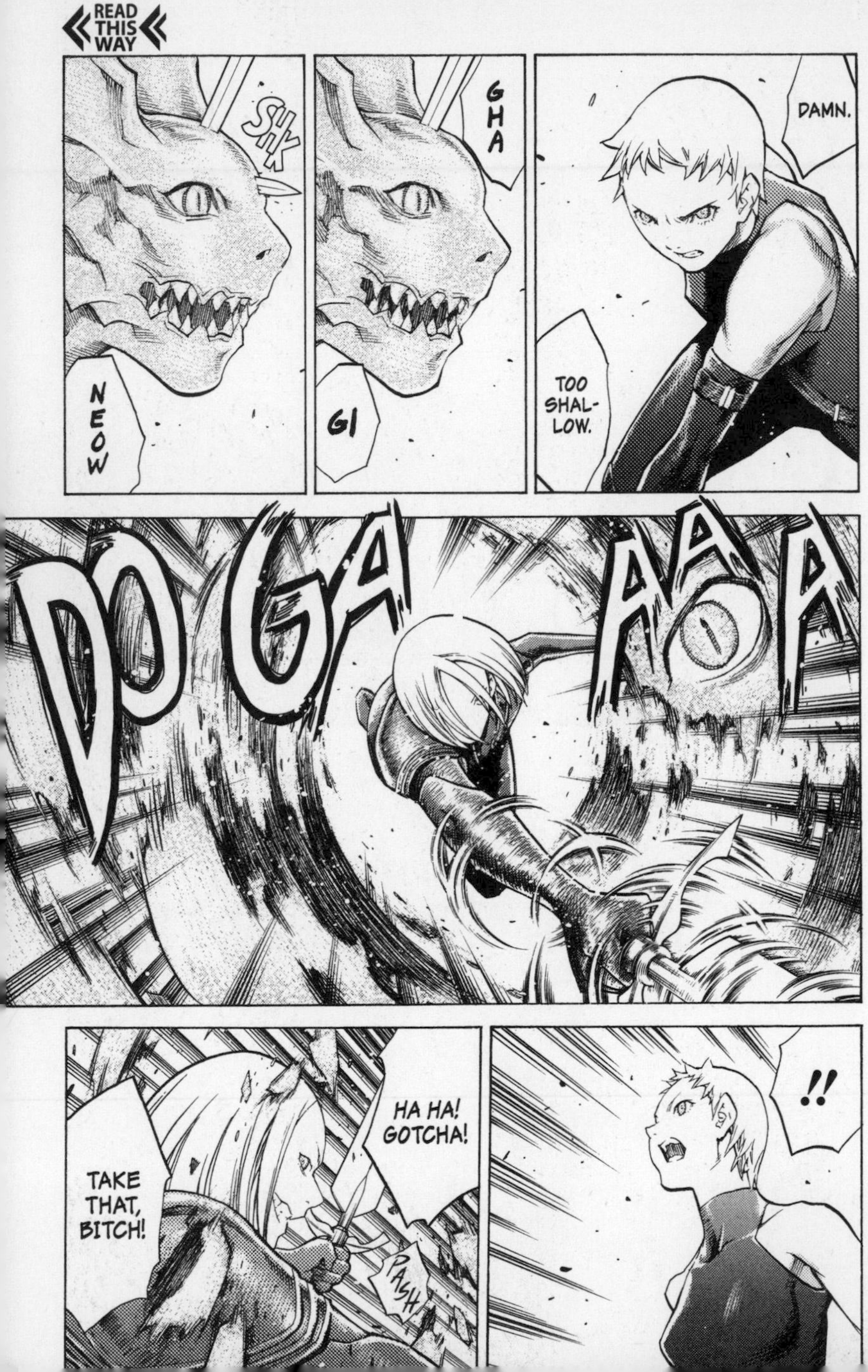
READ THIS WAY
DAMN.
TOO SHAL-LOW.
GHA
GI
SHK
NEOW
DOGAAAA
!!
HA HA! GOTCHA!
TAKE THAT, BITCH!
PASH

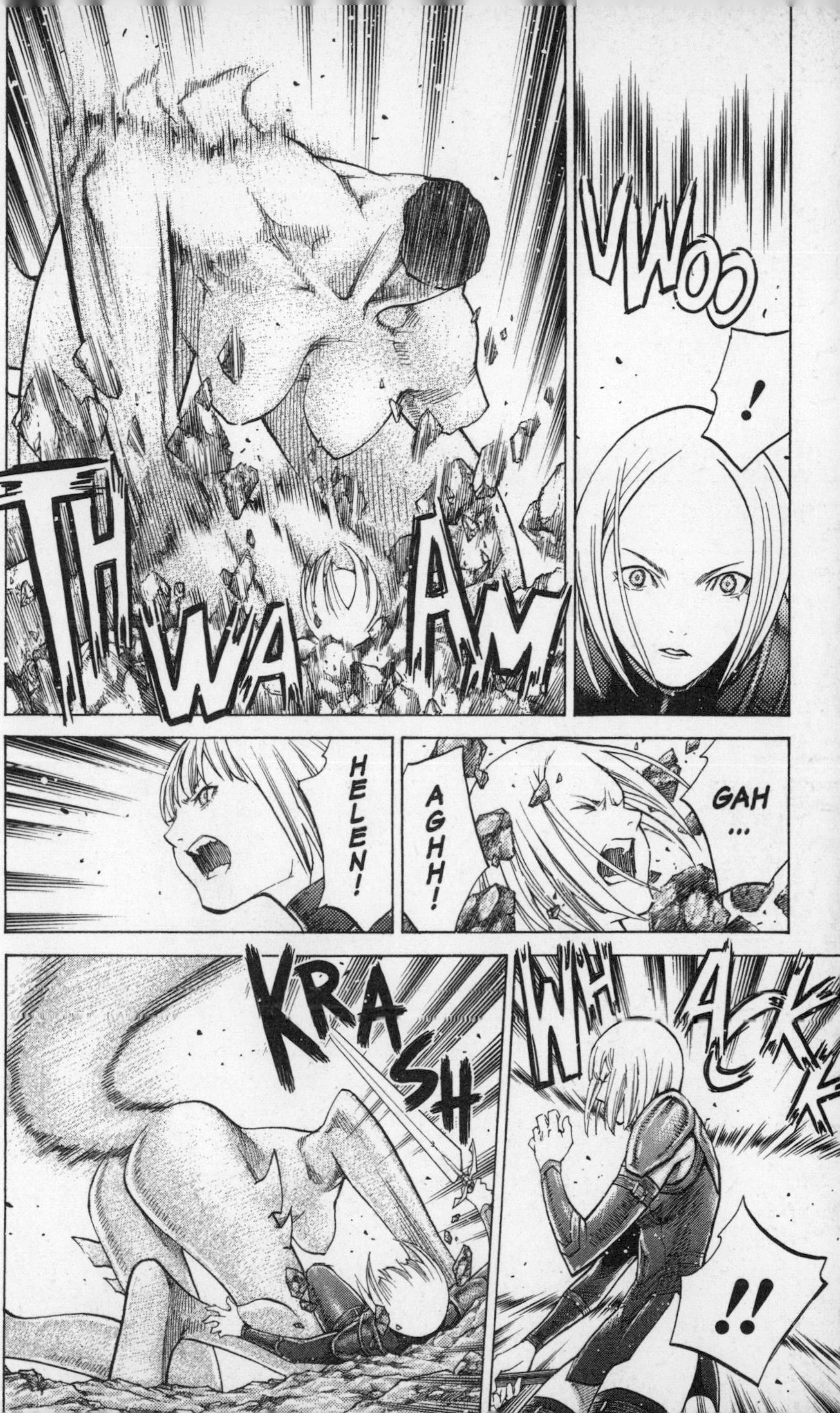
VWOO
!
THWAAM
GAH...
AGHH!
HELEN!
WHACK
!!
KRASH

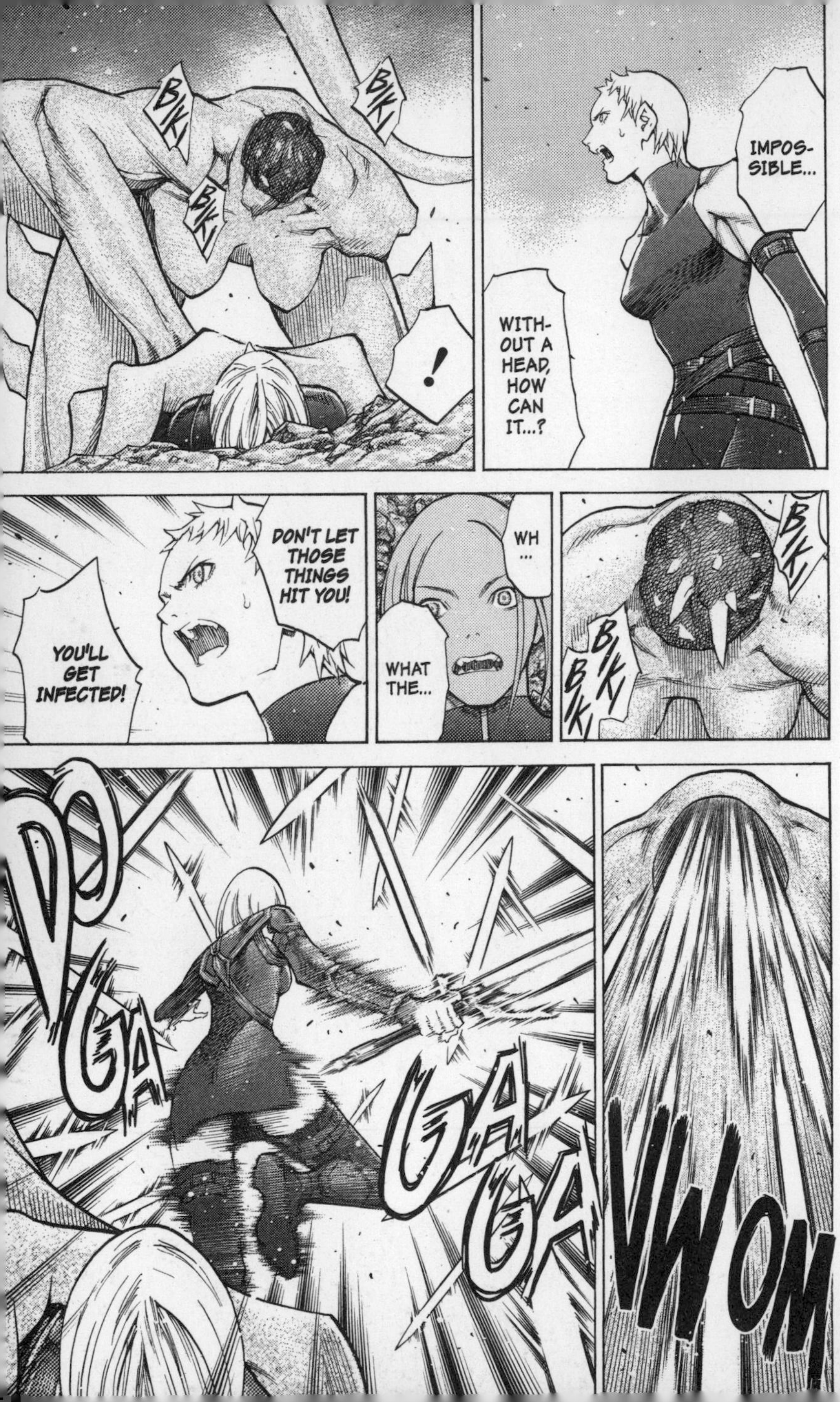
IMPOS-SIBLE...
WITH-OUT A HEAD, HOW CAN IT...?
BIKI
BIKI
!
BIKI BIKI
WH...
WHAT THE...
DON'T LET THOSE THINGS HIT YOU!
YOU'LL GET INFECTED!
VWOM
GA GA
GA
DO

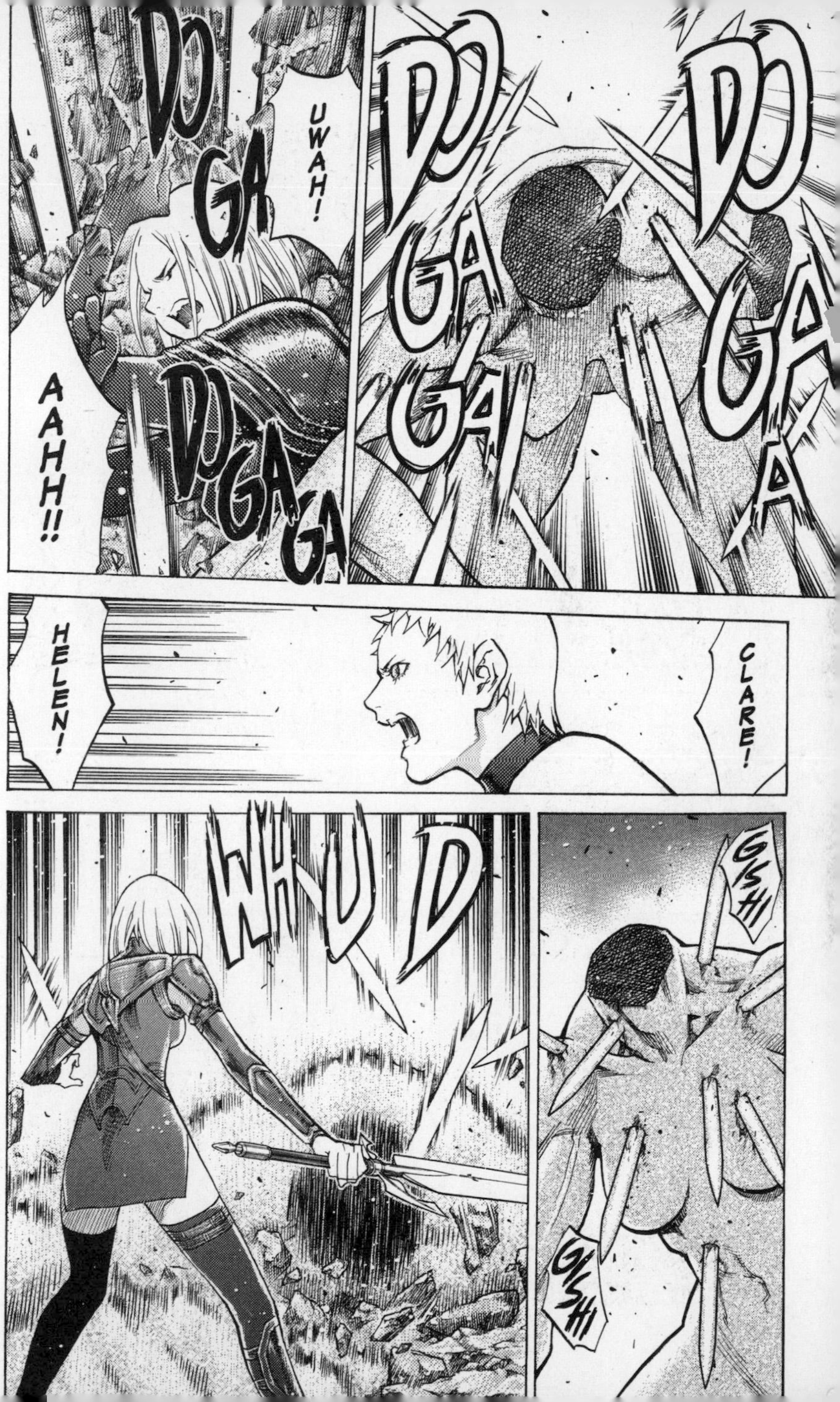
DOGAGA
DOGAGA
UWAH!
DOGA
DOGAGA
AAHH!!
CLARE!
HELEN!
GISHI
GISHI
WHUD

READ THIS WAY

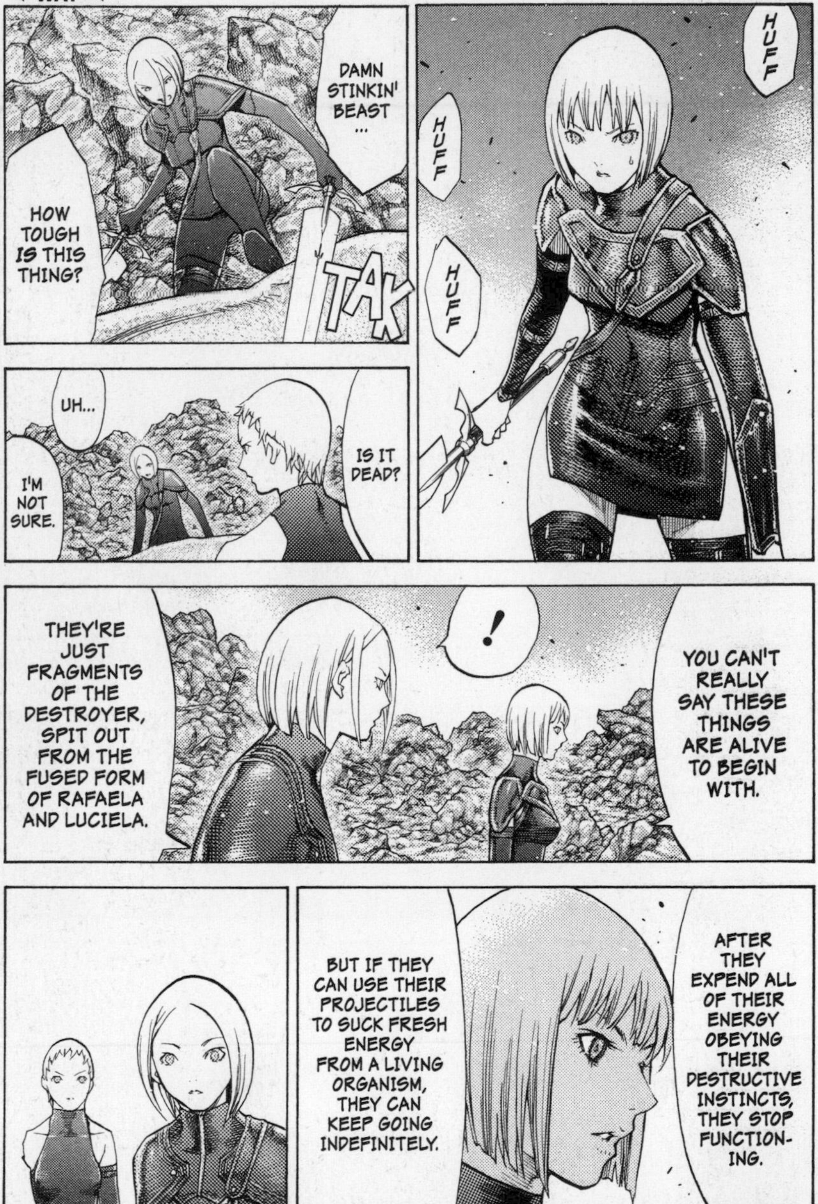
HUFF HUFF
HUFF
HUFF
DAMN STINKIN' BEAST ...
HOW TOUGH IS THIS THING?
TAK
IS IT DEAD?
UH...
I'M NOT SURE.
YOU CAN'T REALLY SAY THESE THINGS ARE ALIVE TO BEGIN WITH.
!
THEY'RE JUST FRAGMENTS OF THE DESTROYER, SPIT OUT FROM THE FUSED FORM OF RAFAELA AND LUCIELA.
AFTER THEY EXPEND ALL OF THEIR ENERGY OBEYING THEIR DESTRUCTIVE INSTINCTS, THEY STOP FUNCTION-ING.
BUT IF THEY CAN USE THEIR PROJECTILES TO SUCK FRESH ENERGY FROM A LIVING ORGANISM, THEY CAN KEEP GOING INDEFINITELY.

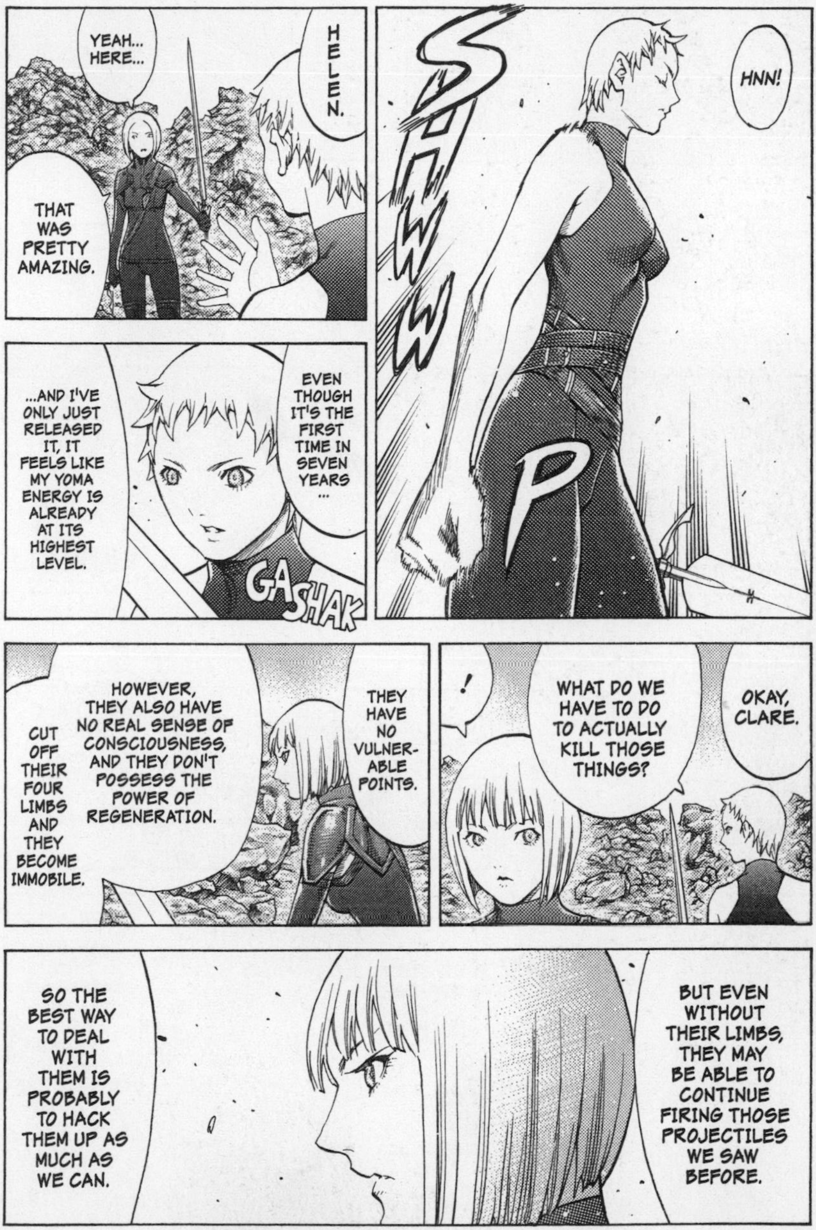
HNN!
SHWWWP
HELEN.
YEAH... HERE...
THAT WAS PRETTY AMAZING.
EVEN THOUGH IT'S THE FIRST TIME IN SEVEN YEARS ...
...AND I'VE ONLY JUST RELEASED IT, IT FEELS LIKE MY YOMA ENERGY IS ALREADY AT ITS HIGHEST LEVEL.
GASHAK
OKAY, CLARE.
WHAT DO WE HAVE TO DO TO ACTUALLY KILL THOSE THINGS?
!
THEY HAVE NO VULNER-ABLE POINTS.
HOWEVER, THEY ALSO HAVE NO REAL SENSE OF CONSCIOUSNESS, AND THEY DON'T POSSESS THE POWER OF REGENERATION.
CUT OFF THEIR FOUR LIMBS AND THEY BECOME IMMOBILE.
BUT EVEN WITHOUT THEIR LIMBS, THEY MAY BE ABLE TO CONTINUE FIRING THOSE PROJECTILES WE SAW BEFORE.
SO THE BEST WAY TO DEAL WITH THEM IS PROBABLY TO HACK THEM UP AS MUCH AS WE CAN.

READ THIS WAY

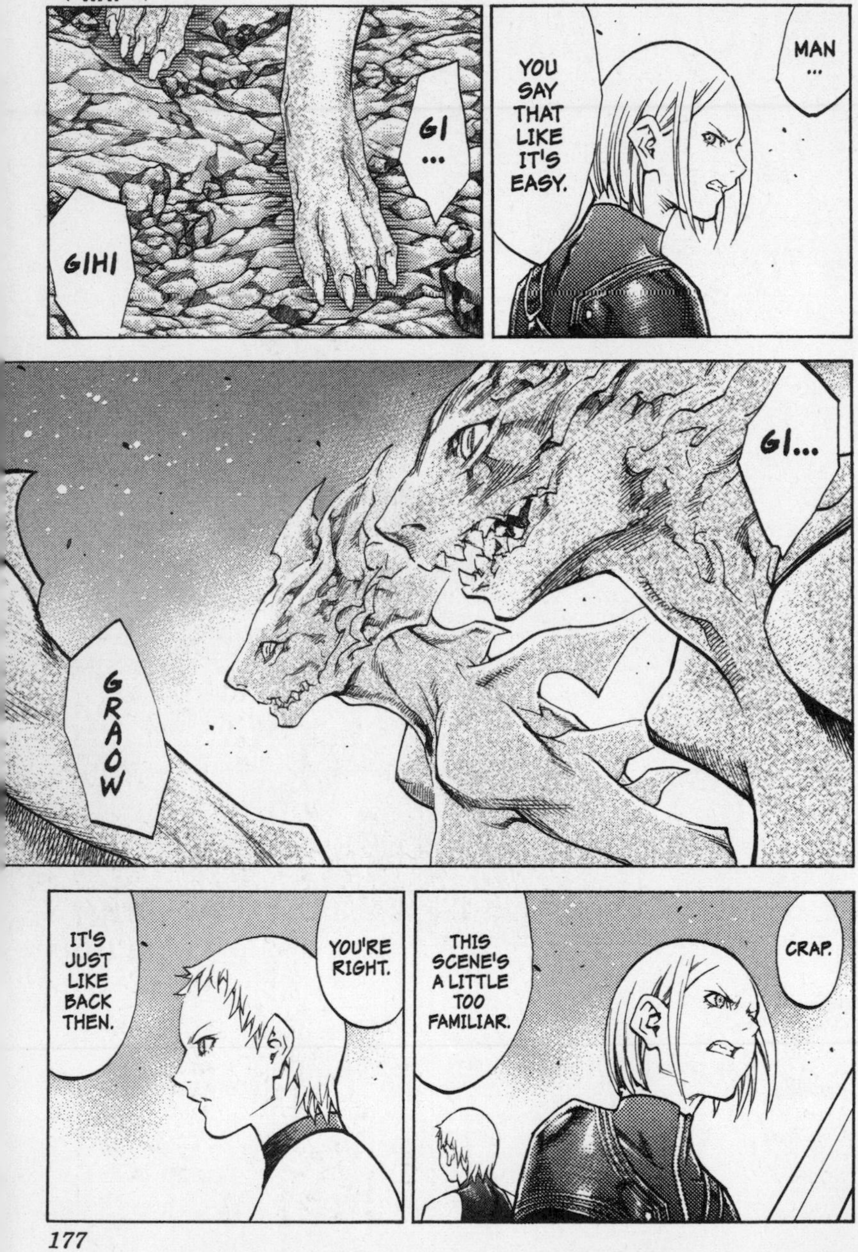
MAN ...
YOU SAY THAT LIKE IT'S EASY.
GI ...
GIHI
GI...
GRAOW
CRAP.
THIS SCENE'S A LITTLE TOO FAMILIAR.
YOU'RE RIGHT.
IT'S JUST LIKE BACK THEN.

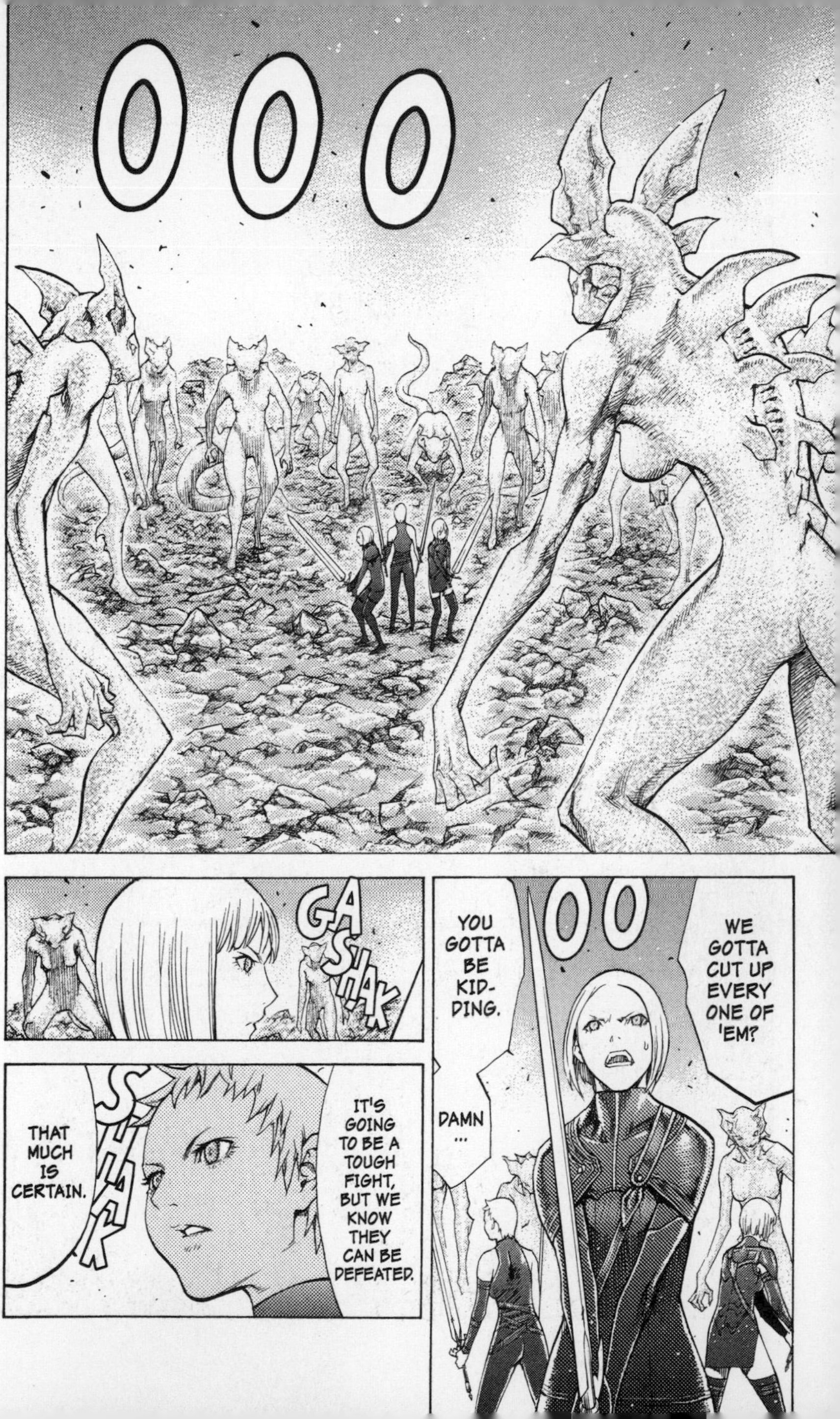
OOO
OO
WE GOTTA CUT UP EVERY ONE OF 'EM?
YOU GOTTA BE KID-DING.
DAMN ...
GASHAK
SHAK
IT'S GOING TO BE A TOUGH FIGHT, BUT WE KNOW THEY CAN BE DEFEATED.
THAT MUCH IS CERTAIN.

READ THIS WAY

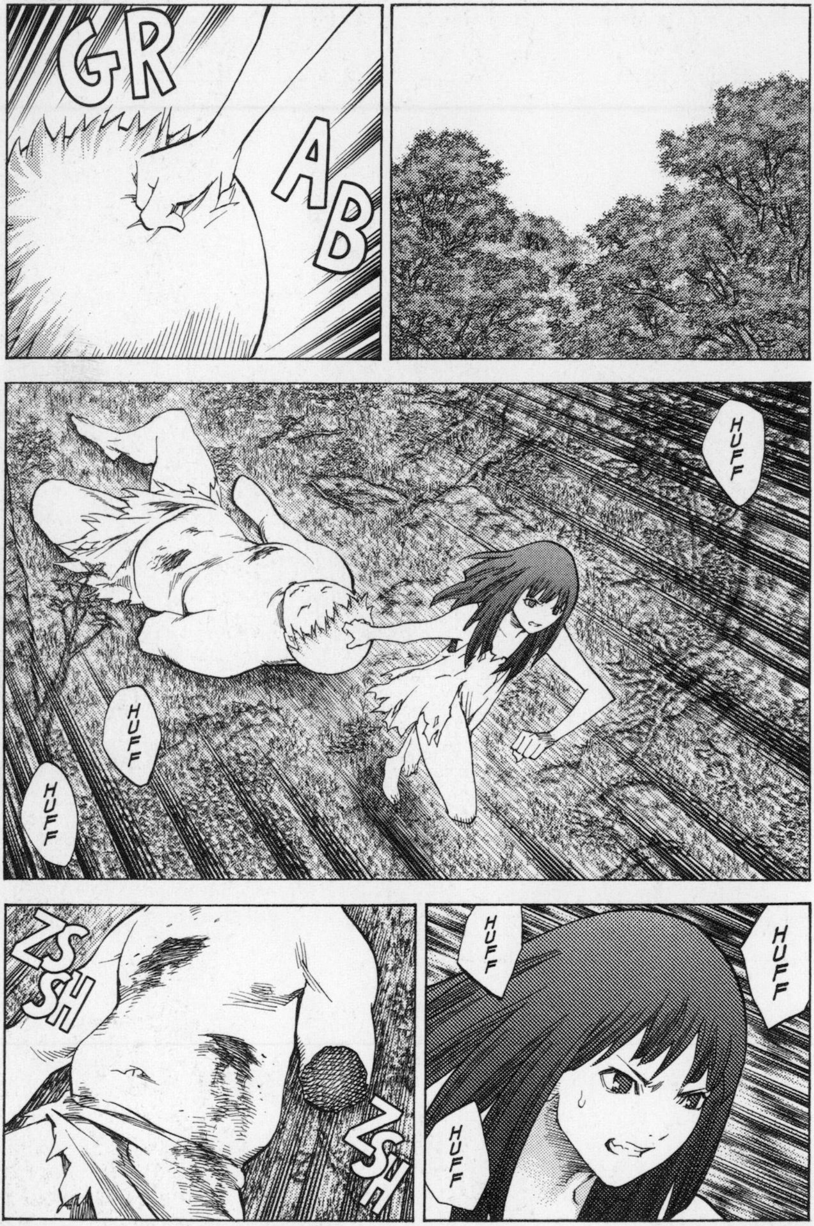
GRAB
HUFF
HUFF
HUFF
HUFF
HUFF
HUFF
ZSSH
ZSH

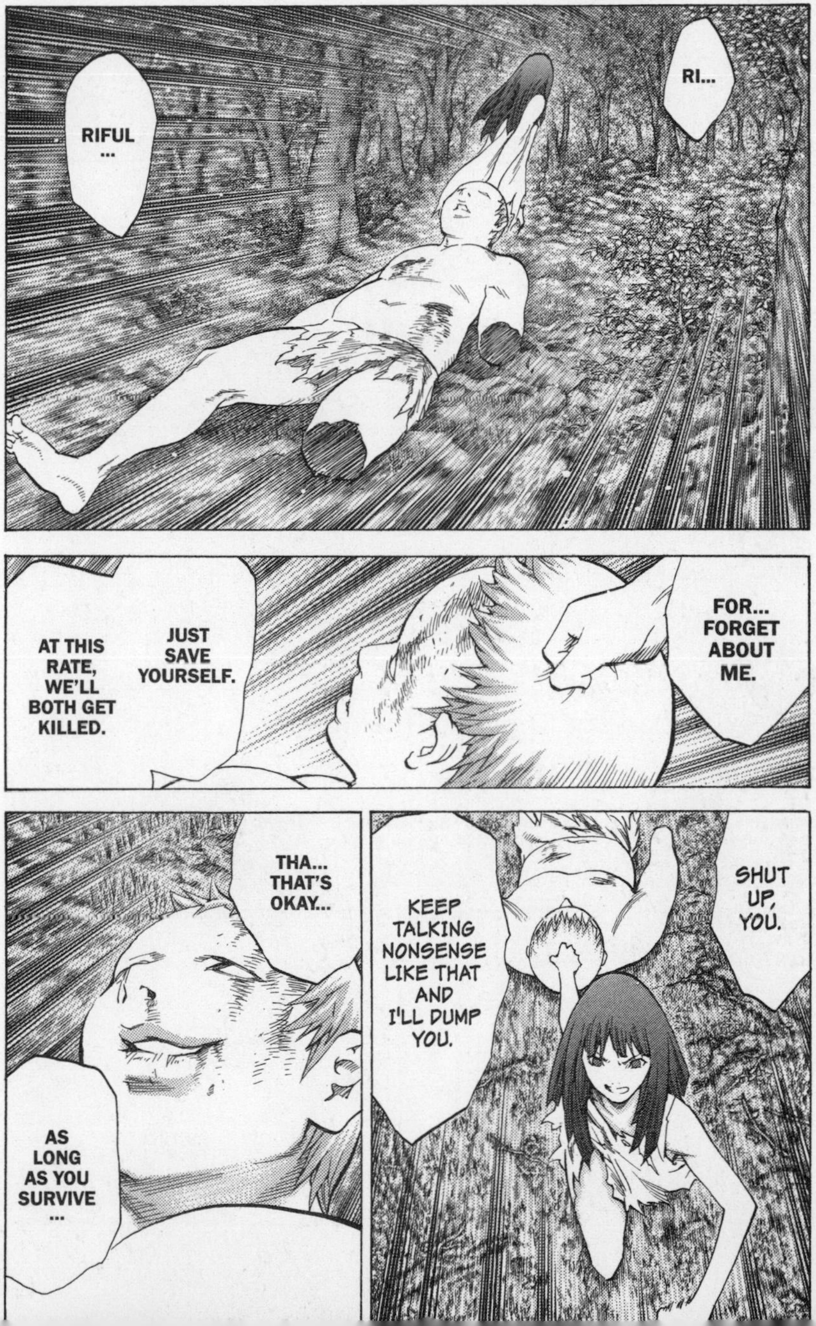
RI...
RIFUL ...
FOR... FORGET ABOUT ME.
JUST SAVE YOURSELF.
AT THIS RATE, WE'LL BOTH GET KILLED.
SHUT UP, YOU.
KEEP TALKING NONSENSE LIKE THAT AND I'LL DUMP YOU.
THA... THAT'S OKAY...
AS LONG AS YOU SURVIVE ...

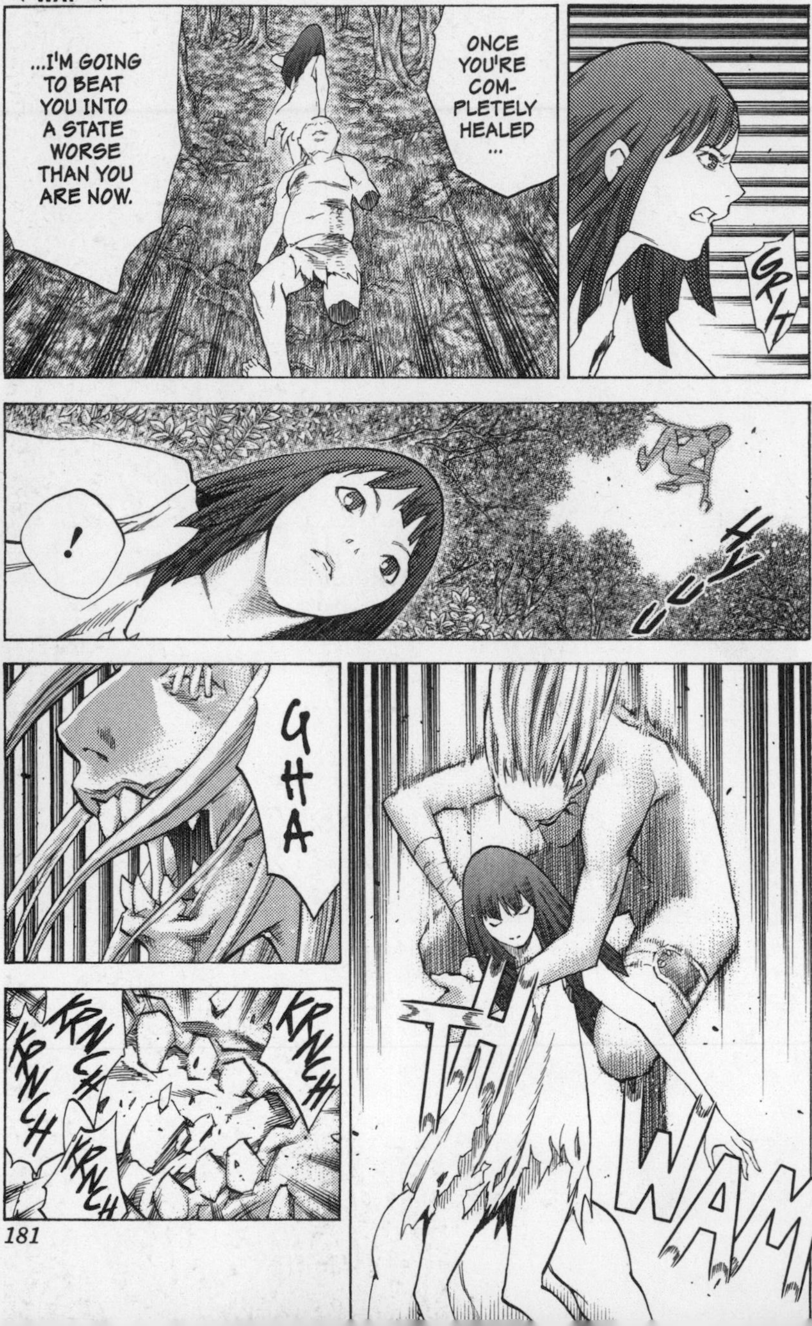
GRIT
ONCE YOU'RE COMPLETELY HEALED ...
...I'M GOING TO BEAT YOU INTO A STATE WORSE THAN YOU ARE NOW.
HYUUU
!
THWAM
GHA
KRNCH
KRNCH
KRNCH
KRNCH
KRNCH

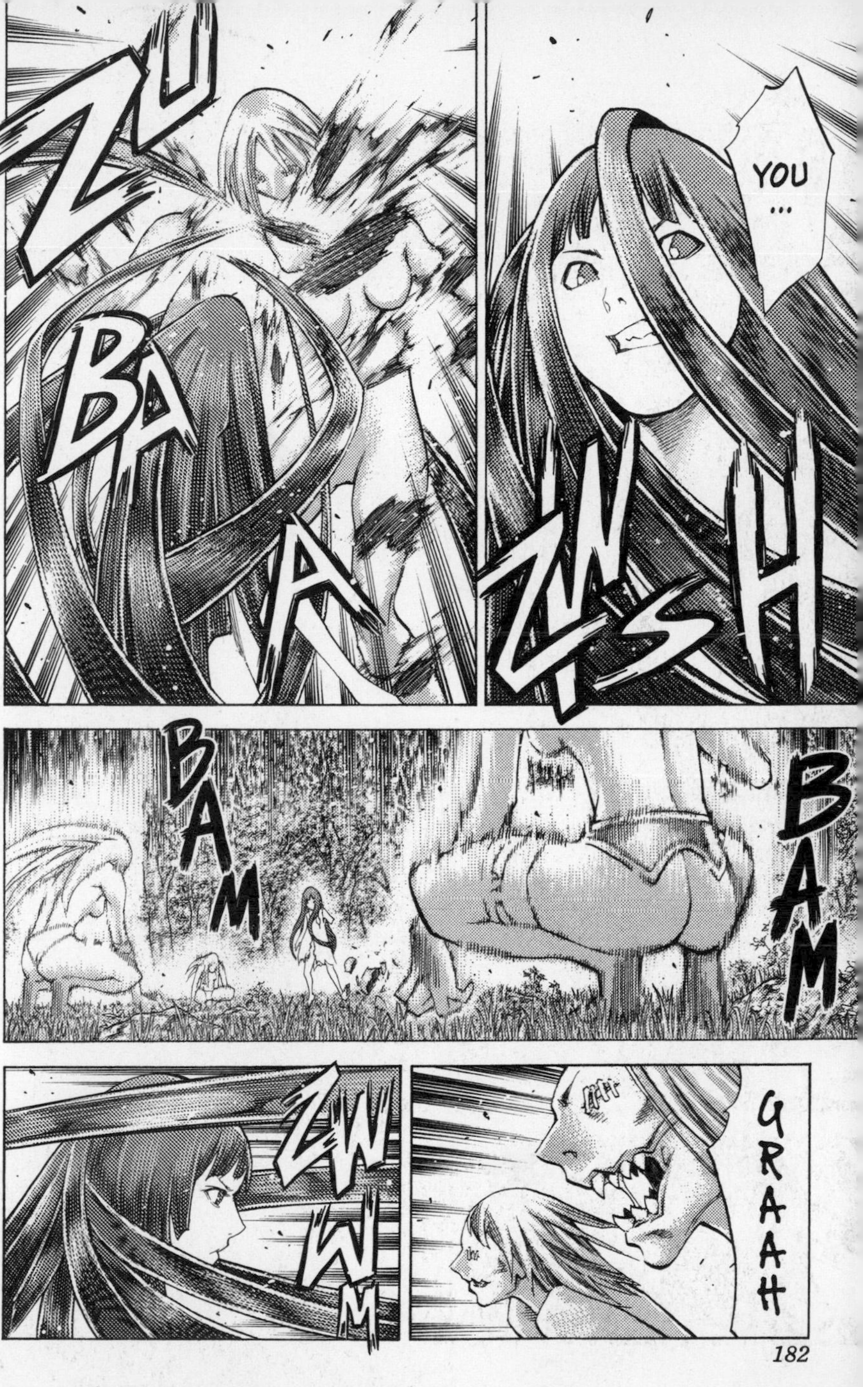
YOU ...
ZWSH
ZU
BA
A
BAM
BAM
GRAAH
ZWWM

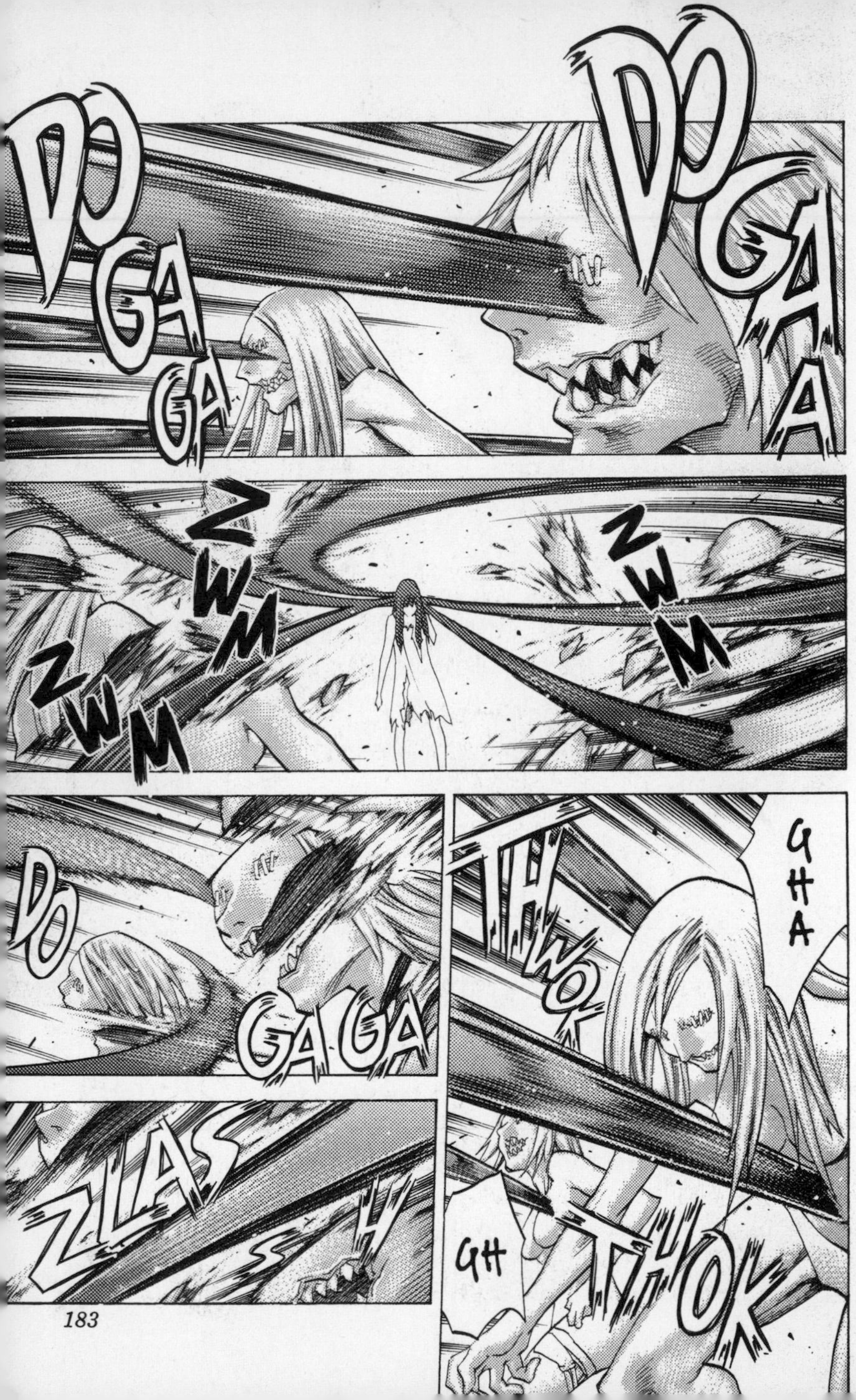
DOGAA
DOGAGA
ZWM
ZWM
ZWM
THWOK
GHA
THOK
GH
DO GAGA
ZZLASSH

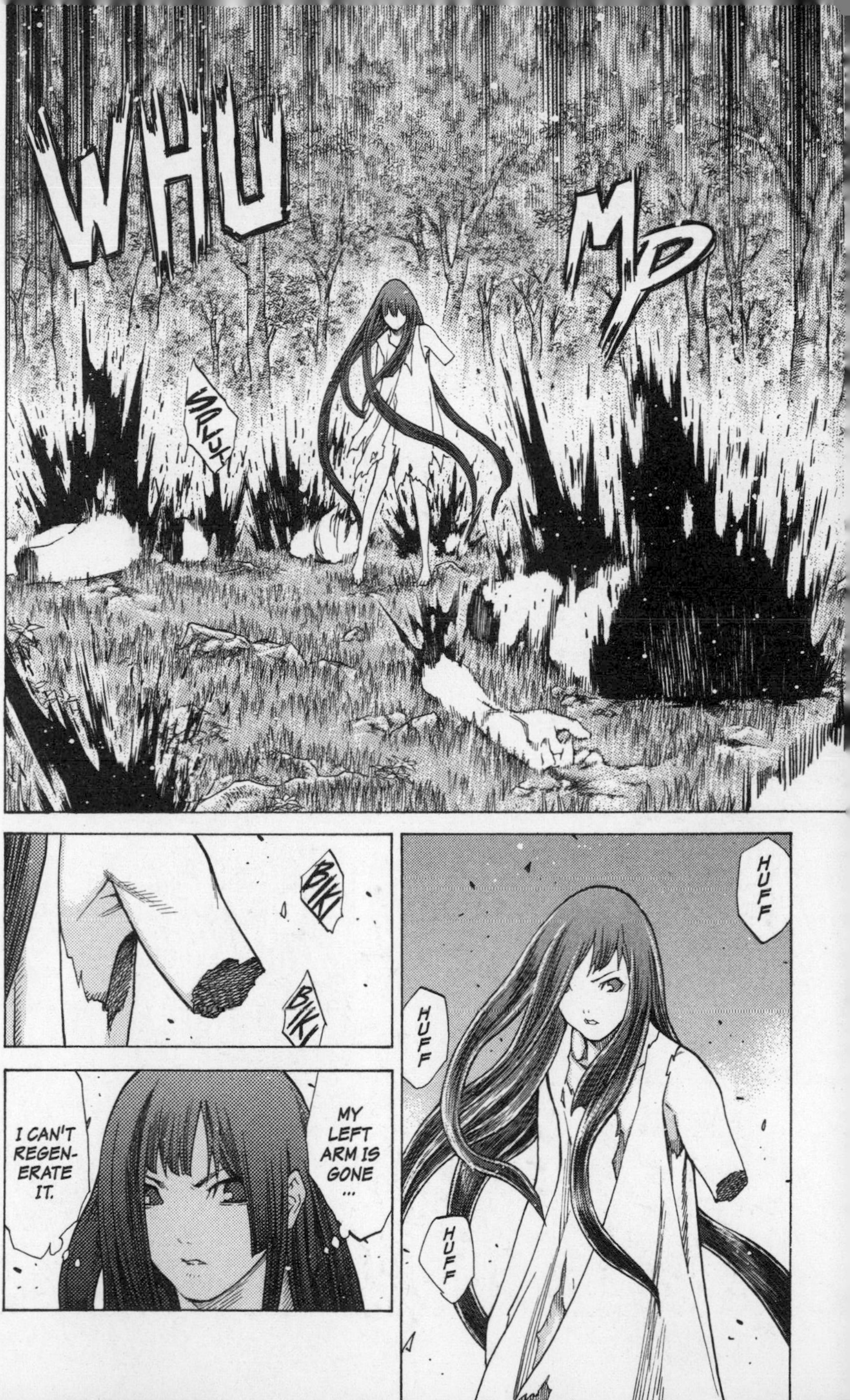
WHU
MD
SPLUT
HUFF
HUFF
HUFF
BIKI
BIKI
MY LEFT ARM IS GONE ...
I CAN'T REGEN-ERATE IT.

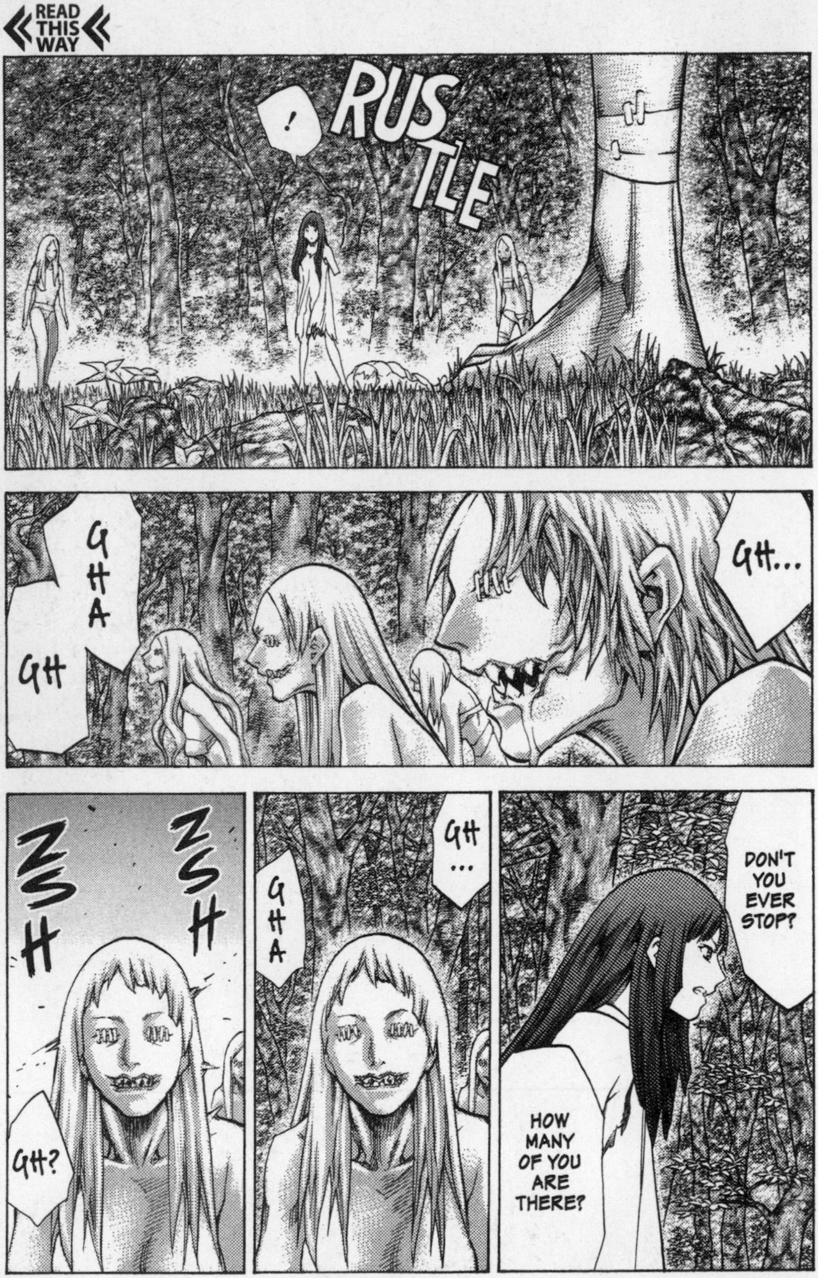
READ THIS WAY
RUSTLE
!
GH...
GHA
GH
DON'T YOU EVER STOP?
HOW MANY OF YOU ARE THERE?
GH...
GHA
ZSH
ZSH
GH?

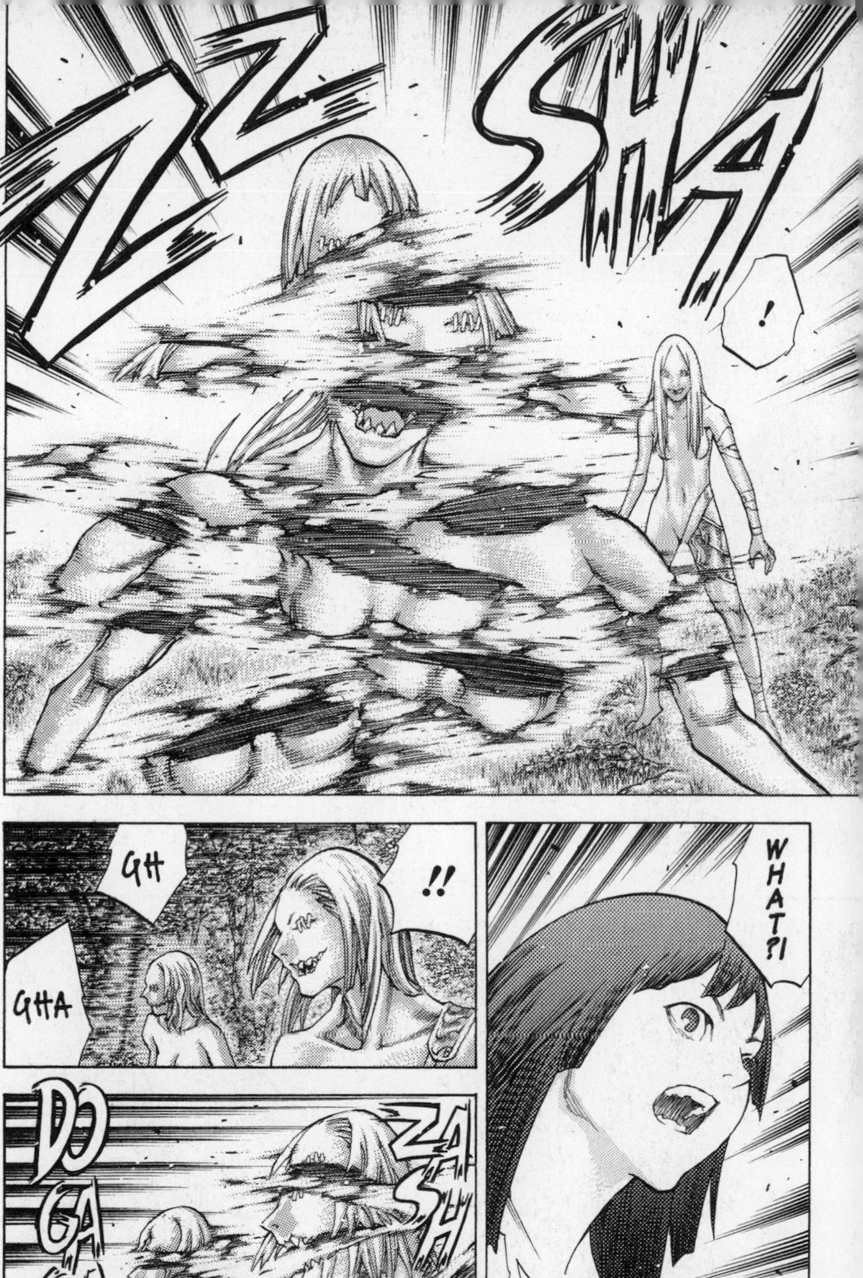
ZZSHA
!?
WHAT?!
!!
GH
GHA
ZASH
DOGAGA

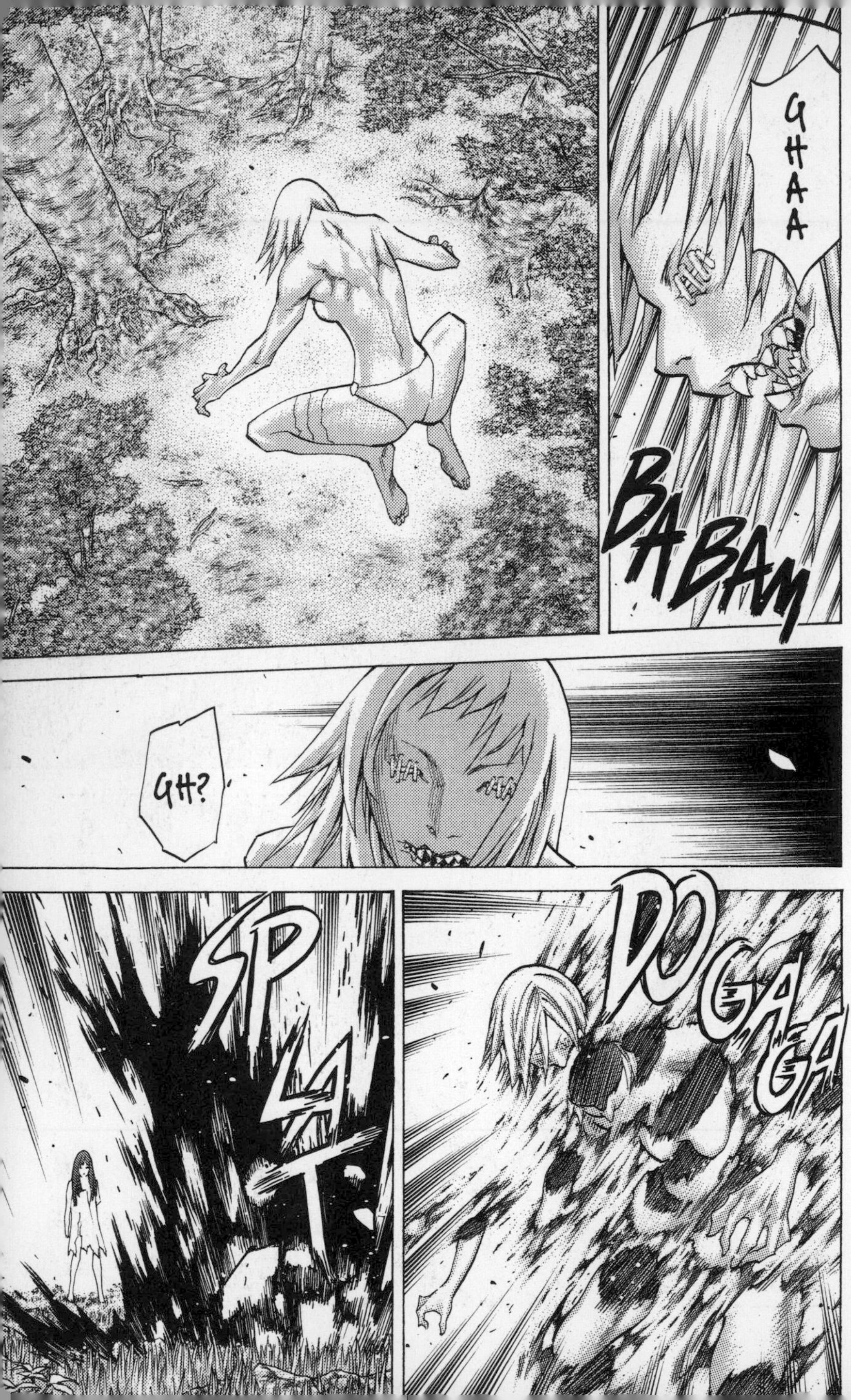
GHAA
BABAM
GH?
DOGAGA
SPLAT

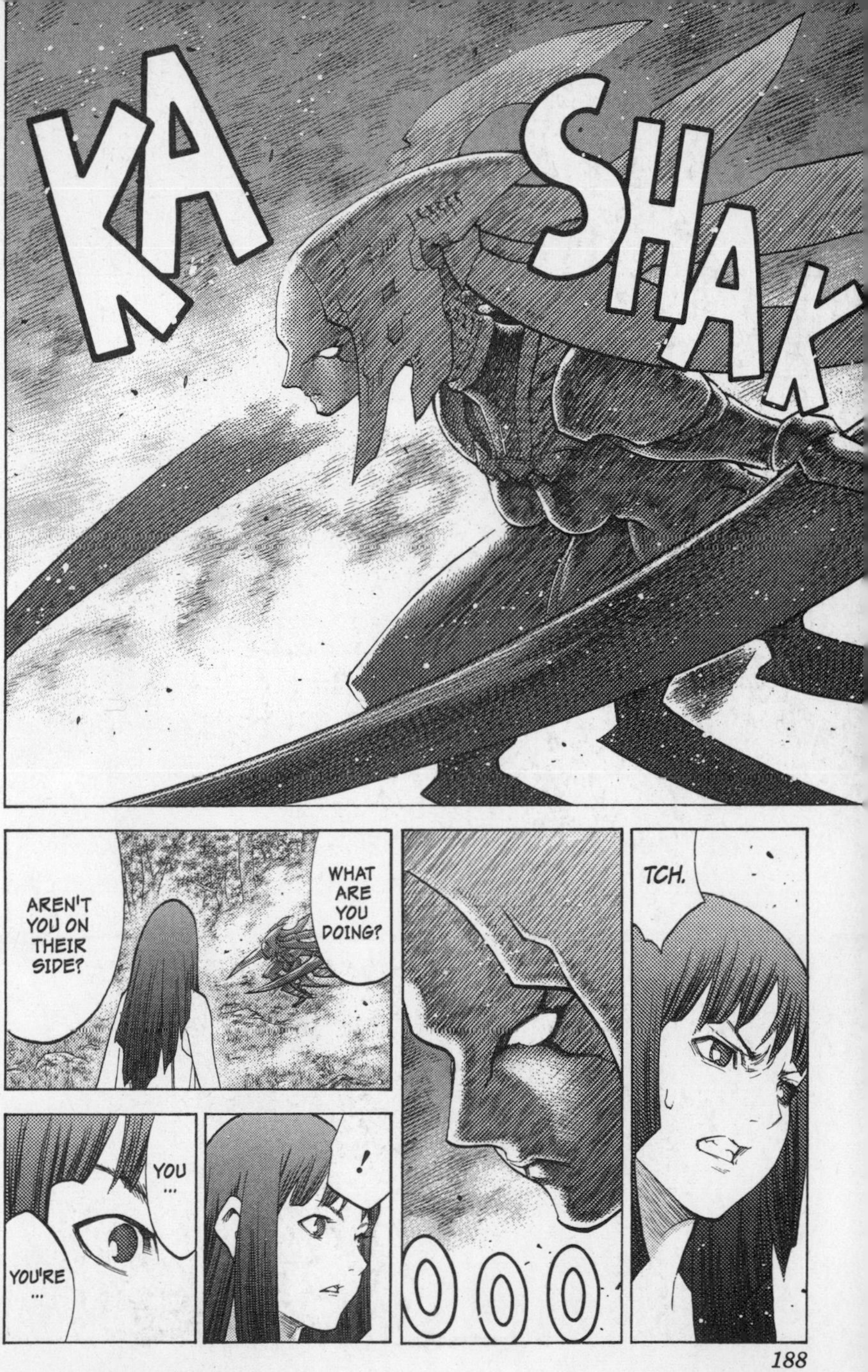
KA
SHAK
TCH.
OOO
WHAT ARE YOU DOING?
AREN'T YOU ON THEIR SIDE?
!
YOU ...
YOU'RE ...

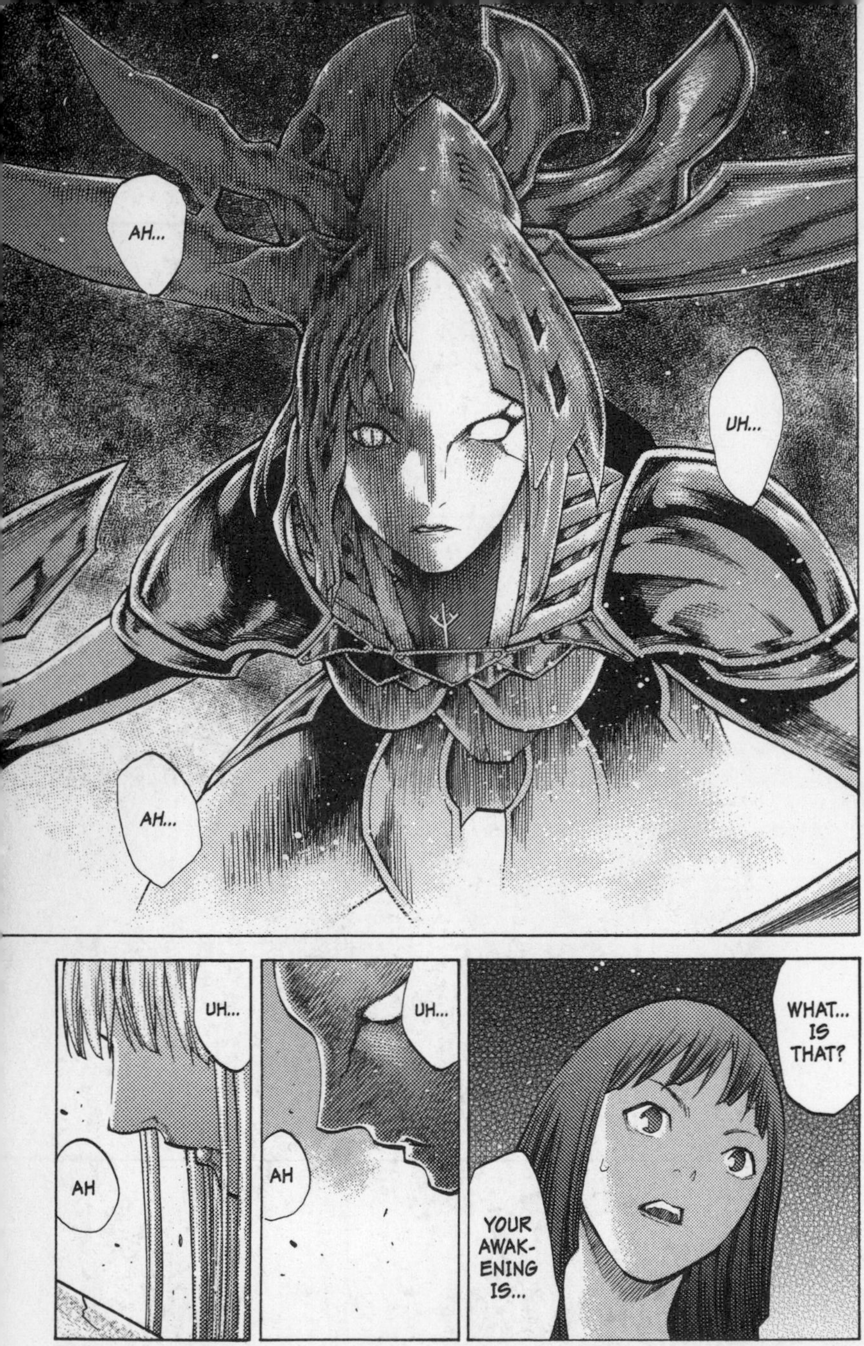
AH...
UH...
AH...
WHAT... IS THAT?
YOUR AWAK-ENING IS...
UH...
AH
UH...
AH

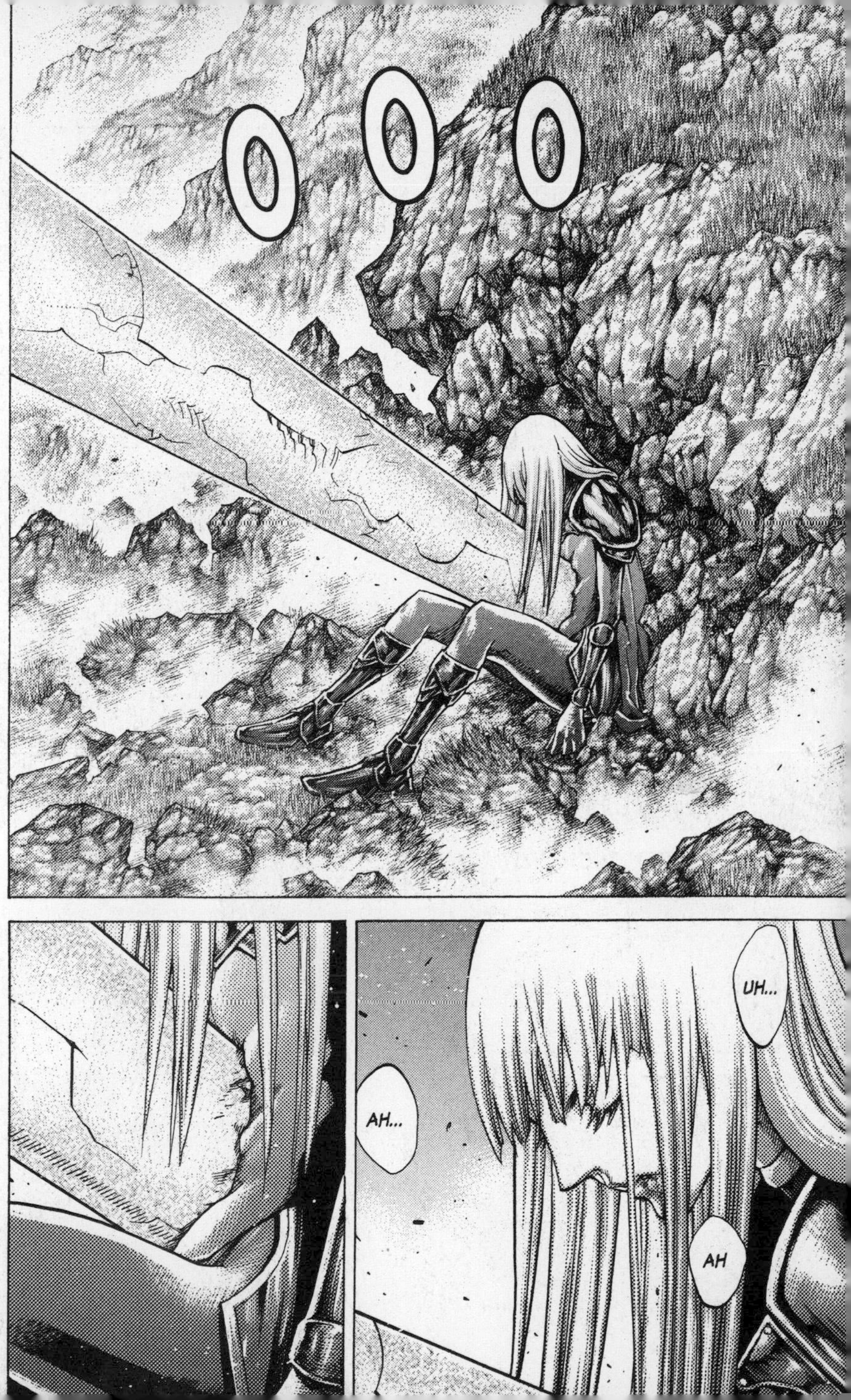
UH...
AH...
AH

READ THIS WAY

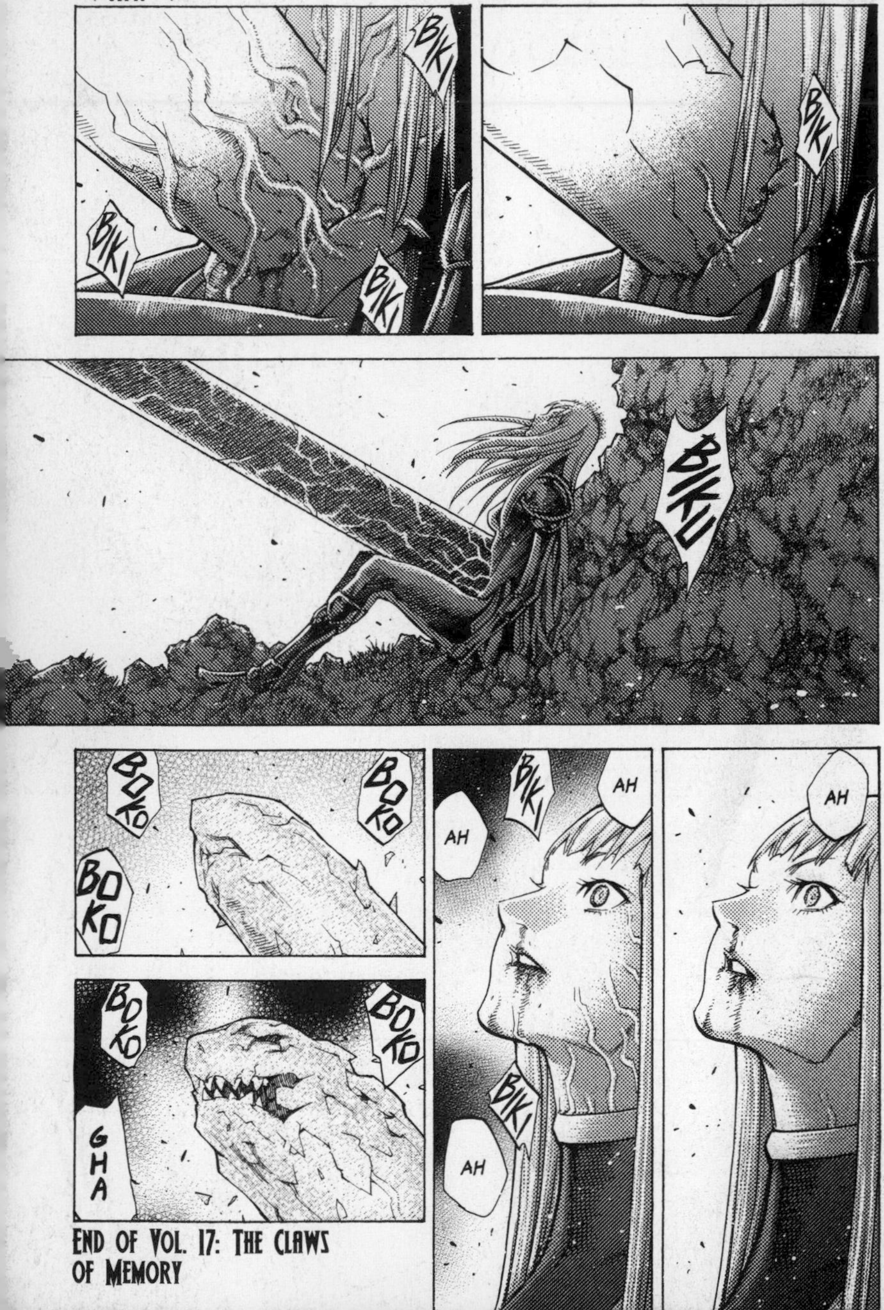
BIKI
BIKI
BIKI
BIKI
BIKU
AH
AH
BIKI
AH
BIKI
AH
BOKO
BOKO
BOKO
BOKO
BOKO
GHA

END OF VOL. 17: THE CLAWS OF MEMORY

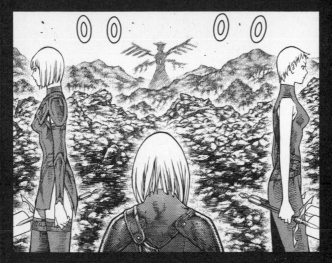

IN THE NEXT VOLUME

After finding herself mysteriously drawn to the lair of Riful of the West, Clare made contact with the fused form of Rafaela and Luciela, which Awakened and transformed into the terrible being known as the Destroyer. Now, the entire land of Lautrec is subject to its dreadful, relentless assault. It seems that nothing, and no one, can halt the devastation. But there may be one force that is greater still...

Available June 2011